COMPLETE ALL COLOUR COOKBOOK

COMPLETE ALL COLOUR COOKBOOK

Barbara Rias-Bucher

Christian Teubner

Annette Wolter

WHSMITH

EXCLUSIVE
·BOOKS·

This edition produced exclusively for W H Smith

Published in 1990 by
The Hamlyn Publishing Group Limited
part of Reed International Books
Michelin House, 81 Fulham Road, London SW3 6RB

Copyright © 1990 Reed International Books Limited

ISBN 0 600 57050 9

The recipes in this book have been previously published by
The Hamlyn Publishing Group Limited
Copyright © 1979, 1982, 1984, 1986, 1987
and Gräfe und Unzer GmbH, München
Copyright © 1978, 1980, 1982, 1985

Printed in Portugal

CONTENTS

Introduction 7

Before You Start 9

Cooking for the
Family 11

Soups 12
Snacks 20
Meat 30
Casseroles 52
Poultry 62
Fish and Seafood 68
Pasta and Rice 78
Vegetables 90
Salads 114
Desserts 130

Healthy Cooking 149

Fish 150
Poultry 160
Meat 166
Salads 172

Vegetables 178
Vegetarian 188
Desserts 212

Cooking for Friends 219

Nibbles and Snacks 220
Sandwiches 244
Buffets 254
Starters 272
Dinners from Around the
World 284

Home Baking 303

Bread 304
Tea Time 318
Tarts 338
Cakes 346
Gâteaux and Cream Cakes 364
Holiday Specialities 378
The Art of Baking 392

Index 394

INTRODUCTION

The Complete All Colour Cookbook is a comprehensive collection of recipes for today's home cooking. Each recipe is illustrated in full colour, so you can see the finished result. When you need a recipe for something satisfying and nutritious, whether classic or just a little unusual, you are sure to find it here.

There are lots of ideas for family meals, from simple salads to hearty stews, casseroles and roasts, favourite vegetables to traditional puddings. All too often the family's demanding activities mean that your family can only rarely sit down to eat together at mealtimes, so there are plenty of delicious snacks and light dishes to choose from that can be eaten whenever they are wanted.

All of us are becoming more health conscious and the specially selected recipes are full of goodness and flavour yet lower in fat. There are abundant choices for those who wish to eat less meat with delicious vegetarian dishes. The focus is on fresh vegetables, whole grains and lean fish, poultry and meat for wholesome family eating. To help in the maintenance of good health, each recipe provides a nutritional analysis in addition to the calorie count.

When you're cooking for friends and you want to be able to enjoy the party yourself, you can count on the excellent recipes all chosen to help make entertaining as simple as possible. A salad buffet with cheese or cold meat is always a winner and can easily be made to look impressive, or make a meal of nibbles and snacks for a change. There are exciting and unusual starters, many quite simple to make. Dinners with a foreign flavour are especially festive and can give an interesting theme to a party. As an added bonus, they can often be prepared in advance.

The chapter on home baking will inspire you to produce cakes and biscuits for family treats. Try baking your own bread now and then – it's rewarding and relaxing. There are also luscious fruit-filled gâteaux and superbly rich chocolate tortes to make for special occasions and many of them are easier to create than you might imagine. The holiday baking ideas will help you make a real celebration with traditional breads, cakes and biscuits to give as presents or enjoy at home.

About the recipes

Each recipe in the main section of this book includes a colour photograph of the finished dish. Where space for the text of the recipe is somewhat limited, instructions have been given as concisely as possible. In some instances, lack of space has not allowed us to include details on serving or decorating the dish, but the photo should serve as a sufficient guide here. It will help you understand the ingredients and methods more fully if you read the following hints before beginning.

Teaspoons and tablespoons: level spoons are meant in every case, unless the recipe specifically indicates heaped spoons. Where an ingredient is described as 1–2 teaspoons or 2–3 tablespoons, the amount can be varied to taste, so always begin with the smaller amount and add more where necessary.

Spices and herbs: you will find a good guide on when and how to use herbs and spices in the table on pages 17 to 22. The recipes list small quantities of seasoning, salt and dried herbs, for only personal taste can determine whether you prefer a certain dish saltier, more spicy, or only mildly seasoned. To increase the seasoning before serving, always add a little more of the herbs listed in the recipe rather than adding a completely new seasoning, since a mixture of too many seasonings can ruin the flavour of a dish. In the case of pepper, the recipes always indicate whether black, white or green is suitable. Bear in mind that pepper will not be full-flavoured unless freshly milled! So always grind pepper into a dish, pepper from a pot will have lost most of its flavour several weeks after grinding.

Other flavourings, such as sugar, syrup, sauces, fruit juices or spirits are also to be regarded as a minimum quantity, but it is a matter of personal taste whether this will be sufficient for you.

Citrus fruits: in many recipes the rinds of citrus fruits are used for flavouring. If you intend paring or grating the rind from oranges, lemons or limes, then it is a good idea to wash and dry the fruit first. This way, any dust or dirt will be removed.

Meat and vegetable stock: meat, chicken, bone or vegetable stocks are frequently needed for soups and sauces. If you have no fresh or frozen home-made stock available, stocks made from cubes are almost as good.

Frozen products: these are usually recommended when the food in question is out of season for most of the year, or is generally available only in frozen form. Where a recipe does not require a whole packet you can keep the remainder in the freezer for as long as indicated on the packet, provided you have not defrosted it. But if you have to defrost a whole packet in order to get the quantity you need, keep the rest in a covered container in the refrigerator and try and use it in some other way for the next meal.

Cream and crème fraîche: cream is the best way of adding a touch of luxury to your cooking. Many recipes call for soured cream or *crème fraîche*, both of which give a slightly different flavour from ordinary cream. *Crème fraîche* has a special culture added in order to give a slight tang, not as pronounced as that of soured cream. An alternative can be prepared by mixing 1 tablespoon buttermilk into 600 ml/1 pint of single or whipping cream, then leaving it in a warm place for 2–3 hours. Our calorie count is based on a 40% fat content.

Butter, oil, lard: if preferred, butter can be replaced by margarine. Both fats melt at 30 c (86 f), are easily digestible and when heated beyond this temperature provide their own individual flavour. But butter or margarine should never be heated for too long, since above 100 c (212 f), they turn brown and can be damaging to health. So for roasting or frying it is better to use oil, lard, coconut or palm oil. For salads oil is usually recommended. It is advisable to keep a small stock of cold-pressed oil for use with salads.

Temperatures and cooking times: all the cooking times given in the recipes in this book are average times based on our experience with several types of cookers. You will have to check whether these baking, roasting and cooking times are right for your own particular oven, since the exact cooking times and temperatures will vary from oven to oven.

Bear in mind that electric ovens take 10–20 minutes to preheat. Gas ovens take only a few minutes. Owners of ovens that work on circulated hot air are advised to follow the manufacturer's instructions. For cooking on the hob, terms such as 'over a very low, low, moderate or high heat' are used. It is very simple to regulate a gas flame accordingly.

While electric hotplates usually have several heat settings, these can vary considerably, not only from oven to oven, but also depending on variations in the power supply. So it is important for everyone to get to know her or his own oven.

COOKING FOR THE FAMILY

Family meals are a great challenge for today's cook, particularly with limited time available for meal preparation. Serving balanced, nutritious meals several times a day is not easy and sometimes you can run out of inspiration. This chapter offers a wide range of ideas for everyday dishes with an extra something to make what might have been monotonous into something exciting. Since some family members may be weight conscious, all the recipes in this chapter are calorie counted.

Home-made soups are a wholesome and economical family favourite, and can make a simple meal in themselves, perhaps served with the snacks that follow. The selection of meats and casseroles offers a wide variety of hearty traditional fare, followed by poultry and fish dishes to satisfy the whole family. Sample the pasta and rice dishes, particularly when time is short and you want to please everybody. Vegetables are an important part of family meals and these recipes offer some unusual combinations. There are lots of tempting salads, some the perfect accompaniment for a substantial main course and others suitable for eating on their own. For a pleasing finish to family meals, there is an array of favourite home-style puddings.

Thick Goulash Soup

350 g/12 oz lean boneless pork
225 g/8 oz brisket of beef
2 onions
100 g/4 oz carrots
1 green pepper
450 g/1 lb tomatoes
2 tablespoons oil
1 litre/1¾ pints hot water
salt and freshly milled black
   pepper
1 tablespoon paprika
pinch each of cayenne and
   garlic powder
4 tablespoons single cream

550 calories per serving

Cut the meat into small, even
cubes. Cut the onions into
rings. Scrape, wash and slice
the carrots. Halve the pepper,
remove the core and seeds,
wash and cut into strips. Peel
and dice the tomatoes, making
sure that you do not lose the
juice.

Heat the oil in a saucepan
and fry the onion rings. Add
the meat and fry for 5 minutes,
stirring occasionally, so that
the meat is completely sealed.
Add the carrots, peppers, tomatoes and juice, fry quickly
and then pour on the hot water.
Season with salt and paprika,
cover the pan and simmer gently over a low heat for 1 hour.

Season to taste with pepper,
cayenne, garlic powder and a
little more salt if necessary. Stir
in the cream just before serving.
Serves 6

Tomato Soup with Rice

2 onions
2 tablespoons olive oil
225 g/8 oz minced steak
150 g/5 oz long grain rice
1 litre/1¾ pints tomato juice
salt and freshly milled black
* pepper*
1 teaspoon caraway seeds
pinch each of sugar and cayenne
2 tablespoons chopped parsley to
* garnish*

300 calories per serving

Finely dice the onions. Heat the oil in a large saucepan and fry the onions until transparent, stirring from time to time. Add the minced beef and rice and fry for a few minutes, stirring occasionally. Add the tomato juice, season with salt and pepper, then bring to the boil.

Cover the pan and reduce the heat, then simmer for 20 minutes. Finally season with caraway seeds, sugar and cayenne and sprinkle with chopped parsley. *Serves 4*

Cook's tip

If you plan to serve the soup as a meal in itself, increase the quantity of minced beef, add a few diced fresh tomatoes and enrich with soured cream.

Potato Soup with Mince Dumplings

1 kg/2 lb potatoes
2 onions
450 g/1 lb leeks
2 tablespoons oil
1 litre/1¾ pints hot meat stock
1 day-old bread roll
1 egg
350 g/12 oz minced beef or pork
1 pinch each of grated nutmeg,
* black pepper and salt*
3 tomatoes
generous pinch each of dried
* marjoram and celery salt*
1 tablespoon chopped parsley to
* garnish*

520 calories per serving

Peel and wash the potatoes and cut them into 2-cm/1-in cubes. Finely dice the onions and keep just under half the quantity to one side. Trim the leeks, wash thoroughly and then slice them. Heat the oil in a large pan and fry the onions and leeks for 5 minutes, stirring from time to time. Add the potatoes and hot stock, cover the pan and simmer for 20 minutes.

Soften the roll in cold water, squeeze out excess moisture and then mix with the egg, minced meat, the remaining onion, the nutmeg, pepper and salt. When thoroughly mixed, shape the mixture into balls about the size of a walnut. Drop the dumplings into the soup and simmer for about 10 minutes, until cooked through.

Cut the tomatoes into wedges and add them to the soup. When the tomatoes are cooked, season the soup with marjoram and celery salt and sprinkle with chopped parsley. *Serves 4*

Pearl Barley Soup

60 g/2½ oz pearl barley
1.5 litres/2¾ pints water
225 g/8 oz leeks
a few celery leaves (optional)
225 g/8 oz celeriac
2 carrots
450 g/1 lb white cabbage
1 tablespoon oil
3 white peppercorns
1 bay leaf
3 cloves
100 g/4 oz rindless streaky
  bacon
350 g/12 oz lean smoked belly
  pork
225 g/8 oz braising steak
225 g/8 oz potatoes
salt

3 tablespoons chopped parsley to
  garnish

550 calories per serving

Wash the barley thoroughly in
cold water. Bring the water to

the boil, add the barley, cover
the pan and simmer over a low
heat for 30 minutes.

Wash, trim and chop all the
vegetables. Heat the oil in a
large pan and fry the vegetables, stirring occasionally.
Crush the peppercorns and add
them to the vegetables with the
bay leaf and cloves. Dice the
bacon, pork and beef and add
them to the vegetables. Add the
barley with its cooking water,
cover the pan and simmer over
a low heat for 1 hour.

Peel, wash and dice the potatoes and add to the soup 15
minutes before the end of the
cooking time. Season the soup
to taste before serving and
sprinkle with parsley. *Serves 6*

Hungarian Bean Soup

225 g/8 oz haricot beans
1.25 litres/2¼ pints water
2 green peppers
2 onions
1 small bunch of herbs, for
  example parsley, chives,
  thyme
2 cloves garlic
2 tablespoons oil
450 g/1 lb beef tomatoes
1 (241-g/8½-oz) smoked pork
  sausage
salt and freshly milled white
  pepper
1 generous pinch of cayenne
1 pinch of sugar
1 tablespoons chopped chives to
  garnish

620 calories per serving

Rinse the beans in cold water
and soak them in the 1.25

litres/2¼ pints of water for 12
hours. Then cook the beans in
the soaking water for 1½–2
hours over a low heat, adding
more boiling water as
necessary.

Halve the peppers, remove
the core and seeds, wash and
cut into strips. Dice the onions.
Wash, trim and chop the herbs.
Finely dice the garlic.

Heat the oil in a large pan and
fry the onion, garlic and herbs.
Add the peppers and beans.
Stir well, cover the pan and
simmer for a further 20 minutes. Peel and chop the tomatoes and add them to the pan.

Slice the sausages and warm
them through in the soup. Finally season to taste with the
salt, pepper, paprika and sugar
and sprinkle with chives.
Serves 4

Cabbage Soup with Beef

1.5 litres/2¾ pints water
350 g/12 oz brisket of beef
½ onion
1 bay leaf
salt and freshly milled white
*   pepper*
4 white peppercorns
50 g/2 oz rindless streaky bacon
1 large pickled beetroot
350 g/12 oz white cabbage
100 g/4 oz leeks
1 tablespoon pork dripping
1 tablespoon concentrated
*   tomato purée*
2–3 tablespoons wine vinegar
sugar
100 ml/4 fl oz soured cream to
*   garnish*

430 calories per serving

Bring the water to the boil.
Add the beef and bring back to
the boil, removing the scum.
Seal the cut side of the unpeeled
onion half on an electric hob,
or skewer it on a fork and hold
it over a gas flame until brown
and add to the meat, together
with the bay leaf, salt and
peppercorns.

Simmer the meat over a low
heat for about 1 hour with the
lid of the pan slightly open.

Dice the bacon. Cut up the
beetroot. Clean the cabbage
and cut it into strips. Clean and
slice the leeks. Heat the dripping in a large saucepan and fry
the bacon. Add the cabbage
and leeks and fry for a few minutes. Stir in the beetroot and its
juice with the tomato purée.

Lift the beef out of the stock
and slice it. Gradually stir the
meat stock into the vegetables.
Add the beef, season to taste
with the vinegar, sugar, salt and
white pepper. When serving,
add a spoon of soured cream to
each portion. *Serves 4*

Cress Soup with Croûtons

2 boxes mustard cress
50 g/2 oz butter
1 onion, finely chopped
1 tablespoon chopped chives
750 ml/1¼ pints hot vegetable or
 chicken stock
salt and freshly milled white
 pepper
pinch of grated nutmeg
3 tablespoons dry white wine
2 egg yolks
150 ml/¼ pint single cream
2 slices bread

300 calories per serving

Snip off the cress with kitchen
scissors, rinse it in a sieve and
drain thoroughly. Keep 2 tablespoons of cress to one side,
together with half the butter.

Melt the remaining butter in
a saucepan and braise the onion and cress for 2 minutes,
stirring from time to time. Add
the chives and stock and bring
to the boil. Season the soup
with salt, pepper and nutmeg.

Beat the white wine with the
egg yolks and cream, then stir
in 4 to 5 tablespoons of the hot
soup. Remove the soup from
the heat and stir in the egg and
cream mixture. Reheat the soup
but do not allow it to boil.

Dice the bread and fry it in
the remaining butter until
golden brown. Serve the soup
garnished with the croûtons
and the remaining cress.
Serves 4

Cream of Mushroom Soup

350 g/12 oz button mushrooms
1 onion
100 g/4 oz butter
3 tablespoons chopped parsley
4 tablespoons flour
750 ml/1¼ pints hot vegetable,
 meat or chicken stock
salt and freshly milled white
 pepper
150 ml/¼ pint single cream

325 calories per serving

Trim, wipe and finely slice the
mushrooms. Finely dice the onion, then melt 50 g/2 oz of the
butter in a heavy based
saucepan and fry the onion and
mushrooms. Add half the parsley, then remove the ingredients
and set them to one side.

Melt the remaining butter in
the pan, sprinkle in the flour
and fry until golden, stirring
from time to time. Gradually
stir in the hot stock, then bring
the soup to the boil and boil for
several minutes, stirring continuously and season to taste.
Add the onion and mushroom
mixture, then stir in the cream.

Heat gently for 1–2 minutes,
without boiling. Sprinkle the
remaining parsley over the
soup. *Serves 4*

Health tip

You can substitute low-
fat natural yogurt for
the cream in the recipe.

Sardinian Celery Soup

1 onion
1 clove garlic
1 medium carrot
350 g/12 oz stewing beef
2 tablespoons olive oil
2 tablespoons concentrated to-
    mato purée
1 head of celery
1 litre/1¾ pints hot water
1 teaspoon salt
generous pinch of cayenne
2 slices bread
1 oz/25 g butter
100 g/4 oz freshly grated Parme-
    san or pecorino cheese to
    serve

470 calories per serving

Finely chop the onion and garlic. Wash, scrape and finely
dice the carrot. Cut the meat
into small cubes. Heat the oil in
a large saucepan and fry the
meat and vegetables for 3 to 4
minutes, stirring from time to
time. Dilute the tomato purée
with a little water, add to the
meat, cover the pan and simmer gently for 20 minutes.

Wash and trim the celery and
cut into 1-cm/½-in slices. Add
the celery to the meat and simmer for a further 5 minutes.
Add the hot water, salt and
cayenne and simmer gently for
a further 30 minutes.

Dice the bread and fry in the
butter until golden brown. Add
the croûtons to the soup and
serve boiling hot. Serve the
grated Parmesan separately.
Serves 4

Sorrel Soup

450 g/1 lb young sorrel leaves
100 g/4 oz butter
1 litre/1¾ pints hot vegetable
    stock
2 egg yolks
pinch of cayenne
150 ml/¼ pint single cream
salt
2 slices bread

320 calories per serving

Wash the sorrel thoroughly
several times, drain well and
cut into fine strips. Keep 2
tablespoons to one side.
Melt 75 g/3 oz of the butter and
braise the sorrel for a few minutes over a low heat. Add the
stock, cover the pan and simmer gently for 15 minutes.

Beat the egg yolks with the
cayenne and cream, then stir in
5–6 tablespoons hot soup. Take
the soup off the heat and stir
the egg mixture into the soup.
with a little parsley.
Strain the soup, adjust the
seasoning and keep hot.

Fry the bread in the remaining butter until golden brown
on both sides, break into pieces
and add to the soup with the
remaining strips of
sorrel. *Serves 4*

Health tip

A number of different
edible hedgerow plants
can be used in this soup,
for example, young net-
tle tops gathered when
about 6 in high, or
young dandelion leaves.
However, do be careful
to gather recognisable
edible species, which are
not polluted by exhaust
fumes or chemical
sprays.

Consommé with Pancake Swirls

150 g/5 oz plain flour
1 egg
150 ml/¼ pint milk
150 ml/¼ pint mineral water
salt and freshly milled white
  pepper
2 tablespoons oil
1 large onion
225 g/8 oz sausagemeat
100 g/4 oz lamb's liver, minced
generous pinch of celery salt
1 litre/1¾ pints prepared con-
  sommé (canned or
  homemade)
1 tablespoon chopped parsley to
  garnish

465 calories per serving

Sift the flour into a bowl, make
a well in the middle, then
gradually beat in the egg, milk,
mineral water and a pinch of

salt. Cover the bowl and leave
to stand for 30 minutes.

Heat a little oil in a frying
pan. Add the batter a little at a
time to make small thin pancakes, keeping the cooked pancakes hot. Heat the consommé.

Finely dice the onion. Mix
the sausage meat with the
minced liver and diced onion
and season with salt, pepper
and celery salt. Fry for a few
minutes in the remaining oil,
stirring from time to time.
Spread the mixture on to the
pancakes, roll up the pancakes
and cut them into 1 cm/½ in
slices.

Place the pancakes in soup
bowls and pour on the hot consommé. Sprinkle each serving
with a little parsley. Serves 4

Liver Dumpling Soup

2 day-old bread rolls
150 ml/¼ pint lukewarm milk
2 eggs, beaten
1 onion
450 g/1 lb ox or lamb's liver,
  minced
1 tablespoon chopped parsley
pinch of dried marjoram
½ teaspoon grated lemon rind
salt and freshly milled black
  pepper
1 tablespoon breadcrumbs
1½ litres/2¾ pints water
750 ml/1¼ pints prepared con-
  sommé (canned or
  homemade)

320 calories per serving

Tear the rolls into small pieces
and soften them in a little cold
water. Squeeze out the excess
moisture, place the pieces in a

basin and pour on the milk and
eggs. Finely chop the onion.
Then add it to the egg mixture
with the liver, parsley, marjoram, lemon rind, seasoning and
breadcrumbs. Work all the ingredients together until
smooth.

Divide the mixture into 12
and form each piece into a walnut-sized ball. Bring the water
to the boil, add a pinch of salt
and the dumplings and simmer
them over a low heat for about
20 minutes until cooked.

While the dumplings are
cooking, heat the consommé.
Lift the dumplings out of the
saucepan with a draining
spoon. Pour the consommé into
soup plates, then add the
dumplings to the hot soup.
Serves 4

Minestrone

100 g/4 oz potatoes, peeled
2 medium carrots
350 g/12 oz white cabbage
100 g/4 oz leeks
1 onion
100 g/4 oz celeriac
1 clove garlic
50 g/2 oz rindless streaky bacon
2 tablespoons oil
1 litre/1¾ pints hot beef stock
100 g/4 oz frozen peas
100 g/4 oz frozen green beans
salt and freshly milled white
  pepper
4 tablespoons chopped parsley
1 tablespoon chopped lovage and
  celery leaves
100 g/4 oz boiled rice

100 g/4 oz Parmesan cheese,
  grated, to serve

345 calories per serving

Wash and trim the vegetables.
Cut the potatoes, carrots and
cabbage into thin strips and
slice the leeks and onion. Finely
dice the celeriac. Finely chop
the garlic.

Dice the bacon. Heat the oil
in a large pan, add and fry the
bacon. Add and quickly fry the
prepared vegetables and garlic,
then pour in the stock. Add the
frozen peas and beans, bring
back to the boil, then cover the
pan and simmer the minestrone
over a low heat for 20 minutes.

Season to taste. Stir in the
herbs and rice, warm through
and serve. Serve the Parmesan
separately with the minestrone.
Serves 4

Dutch Fish Soup

1 onion
1 bunch parsley
675 g/1½lb fish trimmings (tails,
  fins and heads)
1 bay leaf
6 black peppercorns
250 ml/8 fl oz dry white wine
1.25 litres/2¼ pints water
225 g/8 oz celery
50 g/2 oz butter
450 g/1 lb each of prepared eel,
  carp and pike, or 1–1.5 kg/2–
  3 lb firm white fish, for
  example, cod, haddock, hali-
  but or coley
½ teaspoon dried thyme
salt and freshly milled white
  pepper

290 calories per serving

Cut the onion into rings. Wash
and coarsely chop the parsley.
Wash the fish trimmings and
place them in a large saucepan
with the onion rings, parsley,
bay leaf and peppercorns. Add
the wine and water, bring to the
boil and then simmer for 30
minutes over a low heat to
make a fish stock.

Meanwhile, trim and slice the
celery. Melt the butter in a
large saucepan, add the celery,
cover the pan and braise for
about 10 minutes. Strain the
fish stock and add it to the
celery.

Wash the fish, cut it into
bite-sized pieces, then add it to
the stock, season with thyme,
salt and pepper and simmer for
about 10 minutes. Do not
overcook or the fish will break
up. Check the seasoning before
serving. *Serves 6*

Asparagus Omelette with Prawns

450 g / 1 lb asparagus
salt and freshly milled white
  pepper
6 eggs
4 tablespoons cream
75 g / 3 oz butter
200 g / 7 oz frozen peeled prawns,
  thawed

330 calories per serving

Trim the asparagus, tie into a bundle and boil in a saucepan of salted water for 20–30 minutes, depending on thickness.

Beat the eggs with the cream and season to taste. Heat just under a quarter of the butter in a frying pan, pour in a quarter of the egg mixture and tip the pan from side to side. Cook until the mixture has set but the top is still shiny.

Place each omelette on a prewarmed plate and keep warm in a very cool oven (110C, 225F, gas ¼) until all the omelettes are cooked.

Warm the prawns over a low heat in the remaining butter, stirring from time to time. Lift the asparagus out of the pan (reserve the liquid to use for a vegetable soup), drain and arrange on the omelettes. Fold the omelettes over the asparagus and garnish each omelette with prawns. *Serves 4*

Serve with: fresh green salad.

Cook's Tip

If you are unable to get fresh asparagus, use tender mangetout or broccoli instead.

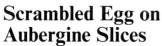

Scrambled Egg on Aubergine Slices

450 g/1 lb aubergines
salt and freshly milled white
* pepper*
100 g/4 oz lean cooked ham
1 onion
50 g/2 oz butter
3 tablespoons oil
100 g/4 oz frozen peas
4 eggs

320 calories per serving

Wash and dry the aubergines, cut them into finger-thick slices, lay out on a plate, then sprinkle the slices with salt and leave for 30 minutes.

Heat the oil in a frying pan. Wipe both sides of the aubergine slices dry and fry for 3 minutes each side in the hot oil. Remove from the pan and keep hot on a warm plate.

Dice the ham and onion. Melt the butter in a frying pan, fry the onion until transparent, add the ham and frozen peas and cook for a few minutes, stirring frequently.

Beat the eggs and season to taste, pour the eggs over the onion, ham and peas and stir with a wooden spoon over a low heat to make scrambled egg. Serve on the aubergine slices. *Serves 4*

Egg and Ham Bake

6 hard-boiled eggs
100 g/4 oz lean cooked ham
225 g/8 oz Emmental cheese
50 g/2 oz butter
2 tablespoons flour
250 ml/8 fl oz milk
150 ml/¼ pint single cream
salt and freshly milled white
* pepper*
pinch of grated nutmeg
pinch of garlic powder
3 tablespoons breadcrumbs

315 calories per serving

Shell and thinly slice the eggs. Cut the ham into narrow strips. Grate the cheese. Grease an ovenproof dish with butter.

Melt half the butter in a saucepan, stir in the flour for a few minutes, then gradually stir in the milk. Bring to the boil, stir in the cream and season with salt and pepper, the nutmeg and garlic powder. Remove the pan from the heat.

Fill the baking dish with alternate layers of egg, ham and grated cheese, covering each layer with a little of the white sauce.

Finally cover with the breadcrumbs and dot with the remaining butter. Bake in a hot oven (220c, 425f, gas 7) for 30 minutes. *Serves 8*

Ham Sandwich with Poached Egg

*4 (50-g/2-oz) slices white bread
butter
4 eggs
2 litres/3 pints water
salt
2 tablespoons vinegar
1 (100-g/4-oz) piece lean,
 cooked ham
4 teaspoons mayonnaise
4 teaspoons tomato ketchup
4 generous pinches of coarsely
 ground white pepper*

420 calories per serving

Toast the bread, leave it to
cool, then butter on one side
only. Crack the eggs one at a
time into a cup. Bring the water
to the boil with a generous
pinch of salt and the vinegar,
reduce the heat, then slide the
eggs one at a time into the gen-

tly simmering water. Remove
the saucepan from the heat
and, using a broad knife, try to
stop the egg white spreading
too much. Return the pan to
the heat. As soon as the water
begins to boil once more, remove the pan from the heat
and leave the poached eggs to
finish cooking in the hot water
for 4 minutes.

Cut the ham into even strips.
Lift the eggs out of the water,
cut off some of the white to
even up the edges and leave the
eggs to cool.

When cool, place each egg in
the centre of a slice of toast,
surround with the ham and top
each egg with a stripe of mayonnaise and a stripe of ketchup.
Sprinkle the egg whites with the
pepper. *Serves 4*

Scrambled Egg and Tomato Sandwich

*4 (40-g/1½-oz) slices white
 bread
50 g/2 oz thin rashers rindless
 streaky bacon
4 tomatoes
1 teaspoon mustard
50 g/2 oz butter
4 eggs
2 tablespoons milk
salt and freshly milled white
 pepper
2 tablespoons chopped chives*

340 calories per serving

Lightly toast the bread without
browning it. Fry the bacon on
both sides until brown and
crisp, remove from the frying
pan and keep hot on a prewarmed covered plate.

Wash and dry the tomatoes
and cut them into 16 equal
slices. Mix the mustard into
half the butter, spread the mixture over the toast and cover
with tomato slices.

Melt the remaining butter
with the bacon fat in the frying
pan. Beat the eggs with the
milk and season to taste. Tip
into the hot fat and stir until
the egg sets.

Divide the scrambled egg
into 4 portions and arrange
over the tomatoes. Garnish
with 2 rashers of bacon and the
chopped chives.
Serves 4

Stuffed Pancakes

200 g/7 oz plain flour
salt and freshly milled black
  pepper
4 eggs
150 ml/¼ pint mineral water
150 ml/¼ pint milk
5 tablespoons oil
50 g/2 oz rindless streaky bacon
1 onion
1 clove garlic
350 g/12 oz Cervelat sausage
1 teaspoon paprika
2 tablespoons concentrated to-
  mato purée
pinch of sugar
pinch of cayenne
4 tablespoons grated Emmental
  cheese

470 calories per serving

To make the pancakes, beat the
flour with a pinch of salt, the
eggs, mineral water and milk
until smooth, cover the bowl
and leave for 30 minutes.

Heat 3 tablespoons of oil a
little at a time in a frying pan
and fry thin pancakes from the
batter.

Finely chop the bacon, onion
and garlic and fry in the remaining oil until transparent.
Chop and add the sausage and
fry for a few minutes.

Dissolve the paprika and tomato purée in a little hot water
and stir into the sausage mixture. Season with salt and pepper, the sugar and cayenne and
spread the mixture over the
pancakes.

Roll up the pancakes and arrange them in a buttered baking dish. Sprinkle with the
cheese and dot with butter.

Brown in a hot oven (220 c,
425 f, gas 7) until the cheese has
melted. *Serves 8*

Herb Pancakes au Gratin

100 g/4 oz plain flour
1 egg plus 2 egg yolks
150 ml/¼ pint single cream
300–400 ml/½–¾ pint milk
salt and freshly milled white
  pepper
50 g/2 oz butter
225 g/8 oz cottage cheese, sieved
2 egg whites
225 g/8 oz lean cooked ham
4 fresh basil leaves, chopped
1 tablespoon chopped parsley
½ teaspoon dried thyme
4 tomatoes
100 g/4 oz Cheddar cheese,
  grated

375 calories per serving

Beat the flour with the egg,
yolks and cream until smooth,
then stir in sufficient milk to
give a thin batter. Season with
salt, cover and leave to stand
for at least 1 hour.

Melt the butter a little at a
time in a frying pan, add and
fry the batter to make thin pancakes about the size of a breakfast plate. Beat the cottage
cheese with the egg whites. Dice
the ham and stir it into the mixture with seasoning to taste and
the herbs. Spread the mixture
over the pancakes, then roll up
the pancakes.

Grease a baking dish with
butter and fill with the pancakes. Peel and chop the tomatoes and spread them over the
pancakes. Sprinkle with the
cheese.

Brown in a hot oven (220 c,
425 f, gas 7) until the cheese has
melted. *Serves 8*

Individual Cheese Soufflés

1 small stick celery
50 g / 2 oz butter
3 tablespoons flour
250 ml / 8 fl oz hot milk
salt and freshly milled black
    pepper
pinch of grated nutmeg
3 egg whites
2 egg yolks
100 g / 4 oz cheese, freshly grated

315 calories per serving

Thinly slice the celery. Melt the butter in a saucepan and quickly fry the celery, sprinkle with the flour and cook for a few minutes. Stir in the milk and simmer until thick, stirring continuously. Season with salt, pepper and nutmeg. Allow the sauce to cool.

Grease four 8-cm/3-in deep individual soufflé dishes. Whisk the egg whites until stiff. Gradually beat the egg yolks and cheese into the cooled sauce. Stir in a little of the egg white, then carefully fold in the remainder, using a metal spoon. Divide the mixture between the prepared soufflé dishes.

Bake the cheese soufflés in a moderate oven (180 C, 350 F, gas 4) for 30 minutes, until golden brown. On no account should the oven door be opened during the first 15 minutes. Serve hot. Serves 4

Health tip

Try replacing some of the ingredients listed with low-fat substitutes, such as vegetable margarine, skimmed milk and low-fat cheese.

Ham Soufflés

225 g / 8 oz lean, boiled ham
50 g / 2 oz butter
3 tablespoons flour
250 ml / 8 fl oz hot milk
salt
1 teaspoon paprika
2 egg yolks
3 egg whites

320 calories per serving

Remove any fat from the ham and cut the ham into small cubes. Purée in a blender, or chop it very finely with a chopping knife.

Melt the butter in a saucepan, sprinkle in the flour and cook, stirring continuously. Gradually stir in the milk and simmer until thick. Season with salt and paprika. Remove from the heat and stir in the egg yolks and ham.

Grease four 8-cm/3-in deep individual ovenproof dishes. Whisk the egg whites until stiff, fold into the soufflé mixture and then spoon the mixture into the dishes.

Bake the soufflés on the second shelf from the bottom of a moderate oven (180 C, 350 F, gas 4) for 30 minutes. On no account should the oven door be opened during the first 15 minutes or the soufflés will not rise. Serve immediately. Serves 4

Cook's tip

If your soufflé dishes are too shallow, you can make them deeper by running a strip of greaseproof paper around the inside edge, held in place by buttering the sides of the dishes.

Mini Quiches

150 g/5 oz plain flour
salt and freshly milled black
* pepper*
2 tablespoons water
75 g/3 oz butter plus 25 g/1 oz
* for topping*
50 g/2 oz rindless streaky
* bacon*
4 eggs
150 ml/¼ pint single cream
4 tablespoons freshly grated
* Emmental cheese*

560 calories per serving

Sift the flour on to a worktop
and make a well in the centre.
Sprinkle the seasoning and
water into the well. Cut up the
75 g/3 oz butter and scatter
around the edge. Mix these ingredients quickly together to
make a dough and cut the
dough into four equal portions.

Roll each piece to fit an individual flan dish, 8–10 cm/3–4 in.
in diameter. Lightly grease
the cases and line them with
pastry.

Finely dice the bacon, fry it
for a few minutes, then sprinkle
over the flan bases. Beat the
eggs with the cream, seasoning
to taste and add the cheese.
Pour the mixture over the bacon. Dot each flan with a little
butter.

Bake the flans on the middle
shelf of a moderately hot oven
(200 C, 400 F, gas 6) for 15–20
minutes. If they begin to brown
too quickly, cover them with
greaseproof paper. *Serves 4*

Individual Broccoli Flans

150 g/5 oz plain flour
salt and freshly milled white
* pepper*
2 tablespoons cold water
75 g/3 oz butter
450 g/1 lb broccoli
pinch each of dried thyme and
* basil*
2 teaspoons powdered gelatine
4 tablespoons vegetable stock, or
* water*
150 ml/¼ pint double cream
2 egg whites
2 tablespoons freshly grated
* Parmesan cheese*

390 calories per serving

Grease four flan cases 8 cm/
3 in. in diameter. Mix together
the flour, seasoning, water and
butter to make a shortcrust
pastry, following the method in
the recipe alongside, and use
the pastry to line the flan cases.

Cover the broccoli with
salted water and boil for 15
minutes. Bake the flan cases
blind on the middle shelf of a
moderately hot oven (200 C,
400 F, gas 6) for 15 minutes.
Drain the broccoli and leave it
to cool, then purée the broccoli
in the blender. Season to taste
and add the thyme and basil.
Dissolve the gelatine in a little
hot water in a bowl over a
saucepan of hot water. Heat the
stock. Add the gelatine to the
stock, then stir the stock into
the puréed broccoli.

Whip the cream until stiff,
fold it into the broccoli mixture
and then fill the flan cases with
the mixture. Whisk the egg
whites until stiff, fold in the
Parmesan and top each flan
with meringue. Bake in a hot
oven (230 C, 450 F, gas 8) for
two minutes, until golden.
Serves 4

Onion Flan

For the pastry:
500 g / 18 oz plain flour
25 g / 1 oz yeast
250 ml / 8 fl oz lukewarm milk
65 g / 2½ oz butter
1 egg
salt

For the topping:
1 kg / 2 lb onions
75 g / 3 oz butter
800 g / 1¾ lb cottage cheese, sieved
1 egg
salt
1 tablespoon flour
100 g / 4 oz cheese, grated

320 calories per serving

Sift the flour into a mixing bowl, make a well in the centre and crumble in the yeast. Stir with a little of the flour and milk, cover the bowl and leave for 20 minutes.

Melt the butter, sprinkle it over the flour in the bowl, add the egg and a pinch of salt. Work all the ingredients in the bowl together with the remaining milk to make a dough and beat until light and airy. Cover the bowl and leave the dough to rise until doubled in volume.

Cut the onions into rings and fry them in half the butter until transparent. Beat the cottage cheese with the egg, the remaining butter, a little salt and the flour and mix with the onion.

Roll out the dough to a thickness of about 1 cm / ½ in. Cut into 15-cm / 6-in rounds and turn up the edges slightly. Cover the rounds with the onion topping and bake for 15 minutes on a greased baking tray in a moderately hot oven (200 c, 400 f, gas 6). Sprinkle with the cheese and return to the oven until golden. *Serves 4*

Artichoke Pizza

For the pastry:
300 g / 11 oz plain flour
20 g / ¾ oz yeast
150 ml / ¼ pint lukewarm water
salt
25 g / 1 oz soft butter

For the topping:
350 g / 12 oz tomatoes
100 g / 4 oz salami, thinly sliced
1 (396-g / 14-oz) can artichoke hearts
10 black olives
200 g / 7 oz Mozzarella cheese, sliced
pinch each of dried basil, dried oregano, dried rosemary
2 tablespoons oil

675 calories per each of 6 servings

Sift the flour into a mixing bowl, crumble the yeast into the centre and stir with a little of the flour and water. Cover the bowl and leave for 15 minutes. Then work the flour in the bowl with the remaining water, a pinch of salt, the butter and yeast mixture to make a smooth dough.

Knead for 10 minutes, cover the bowl and leave the dough to rise for 30 minutes.

Shape the dough into 2 rounds and place the rounds on a baking tray. Peel and dice the tomatoes and spread over the pizza bases with the salami. Cut up the artichoke hearts and spread over the pizzas with the olives and sliced Mozzarella. Sprinkle with the herbs and the oil.

Leave to rise for 15 minutes, then bake in a hot oven (220 c, 425 f, gas 7) for about 25 minutes. *Serves 4*

Mushroom Piroshki

*50 g / 2 oz rindless rashers
    streaky bacon
1 large onion
150 g / 5 oz button mushrooms
1 tablespoon concentrated tom-
    ato purée
½ teaspoon celery salt
generous pinch of white pepper
50 g / 2 oz butter
300 g / 11 oz frozen puff pastry,
    thawed
2 egg yolks*

**170 calories per each of 12
servings**

Dice the bacon and onion and
fry both in a frying pan until
golden brown. Wipe and thinly
slice the mushrooms, then add
them to the onion and bacon
with the tomato purée, celery
salt, pepper and butter. Fry un-

til all the liquid has evaporated,
stirring frequently.

Roll out the pastry on a
floured board to about the
thickness of the blade of a
knife, then cut it into 12
rounds. Spoon the mushroom
mixture into the centre of each
round. Brush the edges with
water, fold the pastry over and
press the edges firmly together,
using a fork.

Rinse a baking tray under
cold water. Beat the egg yolks.
Arrange the piroshki on the wet
baking tray and brush them
with beaten egg. Prick the pastry several times with a fork to
allow steam to escape.

Bake in a moderate oven
(180 C, 350 F, gas 4) for 25 minutes and serve hot. *Serves 4*

Bacon Pasties

*375 g / 13 oz plain flour
20 g / ¾ oz yeast
scant 150 ml / ¼ pint lukewarm
    milk
100 g / 4 oz butter
2 eggs
salt
225 g / 8 oz rindless rashers
    streaky bacon
2 onions
4 tablespoons soured cream
2 tablespoons chopped parsley*

**490 calories per each of 16
pasties**

Sift the flour into a mixing
bowl, crumble the yeast into
the centre and mix with a little
of the flour and lukewarm
milk. Leave to stand for 20
minutes. Dot 75 g / 3 oz of the
butter around the edges of the
bowl and beat 1 of the eggs, the
remaining milk and a pinch of

salt with the flour and the yeast
mixture in the bowl until light
and airy. Cover the bowl and
leave to rise for 1 hour.

Dice the bacon and onions.
Melt the remaining butter in a
frying pan. Add and fry the bacon until transparent and the
onion until golden brown. Stir
in the soured cream. Remove
the pan from the heat and stir
in the parsley.

Roll out the pastry to a
thickness of 1¼ cm / ¾ in and cut
into 16 rounds of 8 cm / 3¾ in. in
diameter. Cover the rounds
with the filling. Beat the remaining egg. Brush the edges of
the rounds with the beaten egg,
fold together and press down
the edges firmly.

Place the pasties on a greased
baking tray, cover and leave to
rise for 20 minutes.

Bake in a moderate oven
(180 C, 350 F, gas 4) for 25 minutes until golden and serve hot.
Serves 4

Potato Omelette

800 g / 1¾ lb potatoes
salt and freshly milled white
  pepper
2 onions
1 clove garlic
3 tablespoons oil
4 eggs
pinch of grated nutmeg
1–2 tablespoons chopped mixed
  herbs to garnish

340 calories per serving

Wash the potatoes, drop them
into a saucepan of boiling
salted water and cook for 25–
30 minutes. Rinse the potatoes
in cold water, then peel and
slice them. Chop the onions
and finely chop the garlic.
  Heat the oil in a large frying
pan and fry the onion and garlic until golden. Add the potato
and fry until crisp and brown,
turning frequently.

Beat the eggs with salt, pepper and the nutmeg, pour over
the potatoes and cook until set.
Serve sprinkled with chopped
herbs.

Serve with: fresh mixed salad.

Cook's tip

For a more filling om-
elette, add leftover meat
or chicken, diced sau-
sage or ham.

Potato Puffs

1 kg / 2 lb large, semi-floury
  potatoes
2 tablespoons flour
2 eggs
salt
1 large onion
100 g / 4 oz lard

445 calories per serving

Peel and wash the potatoes and
grate them into a bowl of cold
water, then squeeze out well in
a tea-towel over a basin. Leave
the water in the basin to stand
until the potato flour settles on
the bottom, then carefully
drain off the water and add the
potato flour to the grated
potato.
  Beat the flour, eggs and a
generous pinch of salt into the
potatoes. Grate the onion into
the mixture. Heat the lard a little at a time in a large frying

pan. Add 2 tablespoons of the
mixture at a time, flatten gently
and fry the puffs one after the
other, until brown and crisp on
either side. Keep hot in a very
cool oven (110 c, 225 f, gas ¼).
Serves 4

Cook's tip

You can use other root
vegetables in this recipe,
substituting an equal
quantity for half the po-
tato. Try parsnips,
celeriac or swedes.

Potato Pan with Shrimps

675 g/1½ lb potatoes
salt
50 g/2 oz rindless streaky bacon
1 large onion
350 g/12 oz frozen peeled
  shrimps or prawns, thawed
75 g/3 oz butter
2 eggs
2 tablespoons soda water
1 teaspoon soy sauce
1 tablespoon chopped dill to
  garnish

430 calories per serving

Wash the potatoes and boil them in a covered saucepan of salted water for 25–30 minutes. Finely chop the bacon, then finely chop the onion. Rinse the cooked potatoes in cold water, peel and cut them into 1-cm/½-in thick slices. Rinse the shrimps or prawns in cold water and pat them dry.

Fry the bacon in a large frying pan until crisp, add the butter and allow it to melt. Fry the onion until golden, add the shrimps or prawns and potato and fry well, stirring frequently.

Beat the eggs with the soda water, a generous sprinkling of salt and the soy sauce, pour the mixture over the shrimps or prawns and potatoes, reduce the heat and cook slowly until the egg has set. Serve sprinkled with dill. *Serves 4*

Serve with: fresh green salad.

Potato Pan with Sausagemeat Balls

800 g/1¾ lb potatoes
salt and freshly milled white
  pepper
50 g/2 oz rindless streaky bacon
2 onions
1 large red pepper
250 ml/8 fl oz meat stock
225 g/8 oz pork sausagemeat
3 tablespoons oil
generous pinch of cayenne
2 tablespoons chopped parsley to
  garnish

520 calories per serving

Wash the potatoes and boil them in a saucepan of salted water for 25–30 minutes, until soft. Meanwhile, dice the bacon and onions. Halve the pepper, remove seeds and core, wash and cut the pepper into strips.

Heat the stock. Shape the sausagemeat into small balls, drop them into the boiling stock and simmer for 10 minutes over a very low heat. Drain, peel and slice the potatoes.

Heat the oil in a frying pan and fry the bacon until crisp. Add the onion and pepper and fry over a high heat. Stir in the potatoes and seasoning and brown the potatoes. Reduce the heat and add the sausagemeat balls. Serve sprinkled with parsley. *Serves 4*

Classic Steaks

4 (175-g/6-oz) fillet or rump
   steaks
4 tablespoons oil
salt and freshly milled white
   pepper

**335 calories per serving without
sauce**

Rinse the steaks in cold water,
pat thoroughly dry and cut off
any skin. Cut notches in the fat
at about 2.5 cm/1-in intervals
to prevent the steaks curling up
during cooking.

Heat an empty frying pan,
add 1 tablespoon oil for each
steak and heat. Then reduce the
heat, add the steaks and cook
for 1 minute each side. Reduce
the heat even further and cook
the steaks for 3 minutes each
side. Season to taste.

For rare steaks fry for only
1–2 minutes per side; for a well
done steak fry for 5 minutes
each side. *Serves 4*

Variations:

Tournedos

(*bottom left of picture*)
These are cut from the narrow
end of the fillet and a 3-cm/1¼-
in thick steak should weigh
only about 125 g/4½ oz. Before
cooking, tie twine round the
tournedos so that they cook
evenly.

Fry the tournedos over a
moderate heat for 5–6 minutes
each side and serve with herb
butter.

Porterhouse Steaks

(*top left of picture*)
A steak on the bone and including the fillet, weighing
about 800 g/1¾ lb. Brush the
steak with oil and fry over a
moderate heat for 9–12 minutes
each side.

Sweet and Sour Beef with Red Wine Sauce

800 g / 1¾ lb silverside of beef
1 carrot
1 celeriac
1 parsley root (optional)
1 bay leaf
4 allspice berries
4 peppercorns
1 sprig fresh thyme
450 ml / ¾ pint red Burgundy wine
150 ml / ¼ pint red wine vinegar
250 ml / 8 fl oz water
salt and freshly milled black
   pepper
50 g / 2 oz fat bacon
4 tablespoons oil
2 tablespoons concentrated to-
   mato purée

680 calories per serving

Wash and dry the beef. Scrape or peel the carrot and celeriac and chop them coarsely. Chop the parsley coarsely. Add the vegetables and parsley to the meat with the bay leaf, allspice and peppercorns, the thyme and red wine.

Bring the vinegar and water to the boil, leave to cool and pour over the meat. Cover the dish and marinate in the refrigerator for 1–2 days, turning the meat from time to time.

Dry the beef and rub in salt and pepper. Strain the marinade. Dice the bacon and fry until crisp in a roasting tin. Add the oil, heat, add and brown the meat. Add the vegetables and seasonings from the marinade, stir in the tomato paste and gradually dilute the mixture with the marinade. Cover the roasting tin and cook on the bottom shelf of a hot oven (220 C, 420 F, gas 7) for 2 hours.

At the end of the cooking time transfer the meat to a warm plate, turn off the oven and leave the meat to stand in the oven for 10 minutes. Strain the sauce, adjust sweet and sour flavouring and serve the sauce with the meat. *Serves 4*

Serve with: potato dumplings made with boiled potatoes, cabbage salad and vegetables.

Beef Stroganoff

800 g/1¾ lb fillet of beef
2 onions
100 g/4 oz gherkins
50 g/2 oz button mushrooms
4 tablespoons bottled beetroot
3 tablespoons oil
salt and freshly milled black
pepper
2 tablespoons capers
1 teaspoon sugar
4 tablespoons soured cream

370 calories per serving

Cut the meat into fingers. Cut
the onions into rings. Peel the
gherkins and cut them into
 Trim and very
finely slice the mushrooms.
Dice the beetroot.

Heat the oil thoroughly in a
frying pan, and fry the onions
until golden brown, stirring frequently. Gradually add the
meat and stir until completely

browned. It is essential to
brown each portion of meat before adding any more.

When all the meat is
browned, season to taste and
add the gherkins, capers,
beetroot, mushrooms and
sugar.

Stir well, cover the pan and
cook over a low heat for a further 10 minutes. Stir in the
soured cream just before
serving. *Serves 4*

Serve with: fresh white bread or
boiled long-grain rice.

North German Pepper Pot

2 onions
675 g/1½ lb braising steak
1 (150-g/5-oz) piece lean boiled
ham
3 tablespoons oil
1 tablespoon paprika
salt and freshly milled black
pepper
1 red chilli
250 ml/8 fl oz red wine
225 g/8 oz potatoes
1–1½ teaspoons sugar

505 calories per serving

Cut the onions into rings. Wash
and dry the braising steak and
cut it into 2.5-cm/1-in cubes
with the ham.

Heat the oil in a pan, add the
onion, ham and beef and fry
over a high heat for 5 minutes,
stirring continuously. Add the

paprika, salt and pepper, the
whole chilli and red wine. Cover the pan and braise over a
moderate heat for 40 minutes.

Meanwhile peel the potatoes
and cut them into 2.5-cm/1-in
cubes. When the 40 minutes are
up, add the potatoes to the pan,
leave off the lid and cook for a
further 20 minutes over a low
heat. Finally season to taste
with sugar. *Serves 4*

Serve with: cucumber or white
cabbage salad.

Rolled Beef with Mushroom Filling

1 large thin slice chuck steak
  (1 kg/2¼ lb)
225 g/8 oz button mushrooms
100 g/4 oz rindless streaky
  bacon
3 tablespoons oil
1 onion
½ teaspoon dried thyme
salt and freshly milled black
  pepper
1 teaspoon mustard
250 ml/8 fl oz hot meat stock
150 ml/¼ pint cream
1 teaspoon cornflour

470 calories per serving

Press the steak to flatten it. Trim and very finely slice the mushrooms. Dice the bacon and fry in 1 teaspoon oil until crisp, add the mushrooms and cook for a further 3 minutes, then keep until required.

Finely chop the onion, mix with the thyme, salt, mustard, pepper and 1 teaspoon oil and spread over the meat. Cover the meat with three-quarters of the mushroom and bacon mixture, roll up the meat and secure it with cooking twine.

Heat the remaining oil in a large saucepan and brown the meat roll all over. Add about half the stock. Cover the pan and simmer for 1–1¼ hours, adding more stock as required and turning the meat from time to time.

Five minutes before the end of the cooking time add the remaining mushrooms and bacon and the cream. Thicken the sauce with the cornflour dissolved in a little water. *Serves 6*

Rolled Beef with Ham

4 medium slices chuck steak
1 onion
1 clove garlic
½ leek
bouquet garni
4 thin slices lean uncooked ham
  (25 g/1 oz each)
¼ teaspoon dried marjoram
¼ teaspoon dried lovage
salt and freshly milled black
  pepper
2 tablespoons oil
450 ml/¾ pint hot meat stock

385 calories per serving

Flatten each slice of steak with the ball of your hand. Finely chop the onion and garlic. Trim, wash and thinly slice the leek. Trim, wash and finely chop the herbs. Place a slice of ham on each slice of steak.

Mix together the onion, garlic, leek, marjoram, lovage, pepper and salt and spread the mixture over the ham. Roll up and secure the steak slices with cooking twine or wooden cocktail sticks.

Heat the oil in a saucepan, quickly fry the chopped herbs and brown the beef rolls. Add half the stock. Cover the pan and braise for 50–60 minutes, gradually adding the remaining stock. *Serves 4*

Veal Rolls

4 (100-g/4-oz) slices veal fillet
1 teaspoon mild mustard
salt and freshly milled white
*   pepper*
225 g/8 oz minced veal
1 egg
1 tablespoon chopped parsley
100 g/4 oz leeks
100 g/4 oz carrots
1 onion
3 tablespoons oil
250 ml/8 fl oz hot meat stock
1 bay leaf
2 cloves
3 peppercorns
1 teaspoon capers
150 ml/¼ pint white wine
50 g/2 oz thin, rindless rashers

*   streaky bacon*

410 calories per serving

Season the veal slices with mustard, salt and pepper. Mix the minced veal with the egg and parsley and spread the mixture on the veal slices. Roll up the slices and secure them with cooking twine. Trim, peel and chop all the vegetables.

Brown the rolls in the oil in a large frying pan, then remove them from the pan. Fry the vegetables before returning the veal rolls to the pan. Add the stock and all the seasoning. Cover the pan and braise the rolls for about 30 minutes, gradually adding the wine.

In a separate pan, fry the bacon until crisp. To serve, strain the braising juices and pour them over the veal rolls. Garnish with the bacon. *Serves 4*

Ossobuco

Braised Shin of Veal

1 onion
1 clove garlic
1 tablespoon flour
salt and freshly milled white
*   pepper*
pinch of dried marjoram
1 large or 2 small shins of veal
*   sawn into 4–8 pieces, 1 kg/2 lb*
*   total weight*
50 g/2 oz butter
4 tablespoons dry white wine
1 small piece orange and lemon
*   peel*
6 tablespoons hot meat stock
pinch of grated nutmeg

400 calories per serving

Cut the onion into rings and finely chop the garlic. Season the flour with salt, pepper and marjoram. Dip the veal in the seasoned flour, melt half the butter in a large frying pan, then fry the veal until golden brown on both sides, together with the onion and garlic. Add the wine and orange and lemon peel.

Cover the pan and braise over a low heat for about 1 hour, adding a few spoons of the hot stock as and when required. Turn the veal once.

When cooked, remove the veal from the pan and keep it hot. Strain the sauce, stir in the remaining butter and season the sauce with the nutmeg and salt to taste. *Serves 4*

Serve with: pasta shapes and mixed salad.

Veal Escalopes in Cream

4 (150-g/5-oz) veal escalopes
50 g/2 oz butter
salt and freshly milled white
    pepper
150 ml/¼ pint hot stock
5 tablespoons crème fraîche
generous pinch of dried lovage
    or sage

330 calories per serving

Wash and dry the escalopes, cut off any skin and flatten each cutlet evenly with the ball of your hand. Heat the butter in a frying pan and fry the escalopes for 3–4 minutes each side, until brown and crisp. After turning, season to taste. Remove the cooked escalopes from the pan and keep them hot on a warm plate.

Dilute the cooking juices in the pan with the hot stock, stir in the cream and boil up once. Crumble the lovage or sage and add to the sauce. Season to taste. *Serves 4*

Cook's Tip

If preferred, the sauce can be made with half cream, half low-fat natural yogurt.

Saltimbocca

Veal escalopes with Sage

8 (65-g/2½-oz) veal escalopes
8 fresh sage leaves
100 g/4 oz Parma ham in 8 thin
    slices
4 tablespoons oil
salt and freshly milled white
    pepper
4 tablespoons dry white wine
50 g/2 oz butter

360 calories per serving

Wash and dry the escalopes, cut off any skin and flatten each cutlet evenly with the ball of your hand. Wash and dry the sage leaves. Cover each escalope with a slice of ham and a sage leaf and secure these in place with a woooden cocktail stick.

Heat the oil in a frying pan and fry the veal for 2–3 minutes each side over a moderate heat. Season the plain side of the escalopes with salt and pepper. Sprinkle about 1 tablespoon of the white wine over the escalopes, remove them from the pan and keep them hot on a warmed plate.

Dilute the juices in the pan with the remaining wine, melt the butter in the wine and pour the sauce over the cutlets. *Serves 4*

Serve with: spaghetti or boiled rice and mixed salad.

Roast Shin of Veal

3 onions
3 litres/5 pints water
salt and freshly milled white
  pepper
bouquet garni
1 bay leaf
3 juniper berries
3 white peppercorns
1 kg/2 lb shin of veal
½ teaspoon cayenne
2 tablespoons oil
225 g/8 oz button mushrooms
450 g/1 lb courgettes
4 tomatoes
50 g/2 oz butter
generous pinch each of dried ba
  sil and thyme
100 ml/4 fl oz crème fraîche

525 calories per serving

Wash and halve 1 onion (without peeling). Bring the water to

the boil in a large saucepan
with a little salt, the bouquet
garni, onion, bay leaf, juniper
berries and peppercorns. Add
the veal and boil it for 30 minutes in an open pan.

Remove the veal from the
saucepan, reserving the stock,
wipe the meat dry and rub with
salt, pepper and the paprika.
Heat the oil in a roasting tin on
the hob and seal the veal, then
transfer the tin to a hot oven
(220 C, 425 F, gas 7) and bake on
the bottom shelf for 45 minutes. Spoon 450 ml/¾ pint of
the stock around the meat.

Chop the remaining onions.
Trim and slice the mushrooms.
Dice the courgettes and cut the
tomatoes into quarters. Braise
the vegetables in the butter,
season to taste and add the basil and thyme. Serve the vegetables with the meat. Strain the
roasting juices and thicken
them with the crème fraîche.
Serves 4

Stuffed Breast of Veal

1 day-old bread roll
250 ml/8 fl oz milk
2 large onions
450 g/1 lb mixed minced meat
2 eggs
salt and pepper
2 tablespoons chopped parsley
1 (1-kg/2-lb) boned breast of
  veal with envelope cut into it
4 tablespoons oil
2 carrots
1 medium celeriac
450 ml/¾ pint hot meat stock
4 tablespoons double cream

555 calories per serving

Soften the roll in the milk. Dice
one of the onions. Mix the
minced meat with the eggs, onion and squeezed roll, and season with salt, pepper and
parsley. Season the breast of

veal with salt and pepper, stuff
it with the minced meat and
sew it up with cooking thread.

Heat the oil in a roasting tin
on the hob, seal the meat, then
transfer the tin to a hot oven
(220 C, 425 F, gas 7) and roast
on the bottom shelf for 1½
hours.

Peel and chop the carrots
and celeriac. Cut the remaining
onion into wedges. After 30
minutes, arrange the vegetables
around the meat, reduce the
heat to 200 C (400 F, gas 6) and
add a little stock if necessary.

When the meat is cooked,
dilute the roasting juices with
the remaining stock, strain,
thicken with cream and serve
with the veal. *Serves 6*

Roast Loin of Veal

1 (1.5-kg/3-lb) loin of veal with
    kidney
salt and freshly milled white
    pepper
2 bouquets garnis
1 onion
1 tomato
4 tablespoons oil
1 bay leaf
450 ml/¾ pint hot meat stock
1 teaspoon paprika
4 tablespoons double cream

490 calories per serving

Wash the meat well in cold
water, wipe it dry and rub in
salt and pepper. Trim and
coarsely chop the herbs. Cut
the onion into wedges. Wash
and quarter the tomato.

Heat the oil in a roasting tin
on the hob and brown the veal
all over, then transfer the tin to
a hot oven (220c, 425f, gas 7)
and roast the meat on the bottom shelf for 1½ hours. After 30
minutes, add the chopped
herbs, vegetables and bay leaf.
Gradually add the hot stock,
reserving a small quantity, and
baste the meat. After 1 hour,
reduce the heat to 200c, (400f,
gas 6). When the meat is
cooked, transfer it to a warm
plate.

Dilute the roasting juices
with the remaining stock,
strain, add the paprika, thicken
with the cream and season to
taste. *Serves 6*

Veal Fillet with Herbs

1 kg/2 lb veal fillet
salt and freshly milled white
    pepper
1 tablespoon each chopped pars-
    ley, burnet and chives
450 ml/¾ pint hot meat stock
1 cauliflower
2 large tomatoes
50 g/2 oz butter
pinch of grated nutmeg
150 ml/¼ pint double cream

540 calories per serving

Rub the veal with salt and pepper. Sprinkle half the herbs
over the meat and press in gently. Roast the meat on the bottom shelf of a moderately hot
oven (200c, 400f, gas 6) for 20
minutes, until golden brown,
adding a little hot stock from
time to time, then cover the
meat with aluminium foil.

Meanwhile, clean the cauliflower, boil until very soft,
drain and crush with a fork.
Wash and halve the tomatoes
and remove the seeds. Season
the cauliflower with salt, butter
and nutmeg and use it to stuff
the tomatoes.

After 50 minutes roasting
time, remove the foil from the
meat, sprinkle the remaining
herbs over the veal and add the
remaining stock. Arrange the
stuffed tomatoes with the meat
on a flat ovenproof dish and
bake for 10 minutes.

Thicken the roasting juices
with the cream and serve separately with the veal.

Serve with: buttered peas and
salad.

Roast Leg of Lamb

1 (1.5-kg/3-lb) leg of lamb
3 cloves garlic
2 tablespoons concentrated to-
   mato purée
1 tablespoon flour
salt
2 tablespoons lemon juice
generous pinch of ground
   caraway
4 black peppercorns, crushed
3 small onions
3 tablespoons oil
250 ml/8 fl oz hot meat stock
150 ml/¼ pint dry white wine
1 teaspoon cornflour

420 calories per serving

Cut a lattice pattern into the skin of the lamb. Cut the garlic into thin sticks and use to spike the lamb. Mix the tomato purée with the flour, salt, lemon juice, caraway and crushed peppercorns. Brush the mixture on to the lamb and leave it to marinate in a cool place for 12 hours.

Quarter the onions. Heat the oil in a roasting tin on the hob, seal the lamb and add the onions and half the stock. Roast the lamb on the bottom shelf of a very hot oven (240 c, 475 f, gas 9) for 15 minutes, then reduce the heat to moderately hot (200 c 400 f, gas 6) and roast the meat for a further 40 minutes, basting frequently with the roasting juices and gradually adding the wine and the remaining stock.

At the end of the cooking time, turn off the oven, transfer the lamb to a plate and leave it to stand in the oven for about 10 minutes. Dilute the roasting juices with a little hot water and thicken with the cornflour dissolved in a little cold water. *Serves 6*

Rolled Shoulder of Lamb

1 (1-kg/2-lb) shoulder of lamb,
   cut ready for rolling
pinch each of dried marjoram,
   oregano and thyme
2 cloves garlic
4 tablespoons olive oil
salt and pepper
150 ml/¼ pint hot meat stock
150 ml/¼ pint dry white wine
4 tablespoons soured cream

485 calories per serving

Wash and thoroughly dry the lamb. Rub the herbs and mix them together in a bowl. Finely chop the garlic and mix it with the herbs and oil. Rub 3 tablespoons of the mixture into the meat and season to taste. Roll up the lamb, secure with cooking twine, then place in a roasting tin and sprinkle with the remaining oil.

Roast the lamb on the second shelf from the bottom of a hot oven (220 c, 425 f, gas 7) for about 40 minutes, gradually adding the stock and basting the meat from time to time. Ten minutes before the end of the cooking time, pour the white wine over the meat.

At the end of the cooking time, transfer the lamb to a plate, turn off the oven and leave the meat to stand in the oven for 10 minutes.

Mix the soured cream into the roasting juices and season to taste. *Serves 6*

Serve with: new potatoes, tomato slices and beans in bundles, wrapped round with a rasher of bacon.

Barbecued Saddle of Lamb with Coconut Pears

1 (1.5-kg/3-lb) saddle of lamb
5 tablespoons honey
1 teaspoon curry powder
2 tablespoons lemon juice
2 tablespoons oil
4 medium pears
50 g/2 oz butter
100 g/4 oz grated coconut
1 teaspoon sugar

450 calories per serving

Wash the lamb well in cold water, and wipe it dry. Cut a 2.5-cm/1-in deep lattice pattern into the side above the ribs. Mix the honey with the curry powder, lemon juice and oil, brush the marinade generously over the lamb and marinate the meat for 4 hours in a covered bowl in the refrigerator.

About 30 minutes before you are ready to start cooking, light the barbecue and get the charcoal glowing hot. Place the grid about 10 cm/4 in above the charcoal and leave it to get hot.

Thinly peel the pears, cut in half and core them. Place the pears side by side in an ovenproof dish. Melt the butter in a pan, fry the coconut until golden brown and sprinkle it over the pears. Sprinkle with sugar and bake the pears on the middle shelf of a moderately hot oven (200 C, 400 F, gas 6) for about 20 minutes, until golden brown, then turn off the oven and keep the pears warm at the bottom of the oven.

Meanwhile, place the lamb on the hot grid and cook for 25–30 minutes, turning frequently. As the lamb cooks, brush it frequently with the marinade, making sure the lattice is covered generously.

Put the lamb on its grid in the warm oven for 15 minutes. This will ensure that the juices are evenly distributed throughout the meat so that it remains juicy after carving. Serve the lamb with the pears. *Serves 8*

Serve with: white bread and grilled tomatoes flavoured with rosemary (optional).

Cook's Tip

If preferred, the lamb can be cooked under an electric grill or in a roasting tin in the oven. To roast, place in a very hot oven (240 C, 475 F, gas 9), cook the lamb for 10 minutes, then reduce the heat to moderately hot (200 C, 400 F, gas 6) and cook for a further 40–60 minutes.

Lamb Chops with Tomato and Peppers

8 (75-g/3-oz) lamb chops
1 clove garlic
3 tablespoons olive oil
¼ teaspoon black pepper
pinch of dried rosemary
pinch of dried sage
450 g/1 lb tomatoes
225 g/8 oz red peppers
1 onion
salt and freshly milled white
    pepper
½ teaspoon dried basil
2 tablespoons concentrated to-
    mato purée
150 ml/¼ pint vegetable stock

530 calories per serving

Cut notches in the fat along the
side of the chops. Halve the
garlic. Season 2 tablespoons of

the oil with the pepper, rosemary and sage. Using a garlic
press, crush half the garlic clove
into the oil. Brush the marinade
over the chops, cover and leave
to marinate for 3 hours.

Peel and dice the tomatoes.
Halve and deseed the peppers,
and cut them into thin strips.
Dice the onion and the remaining garlic and fry in the remaining oil in a large frying pan
until golden brown. Add the
strips of pepper and cook for a
few minutes, then add the tomatoes and season with salt,
pepper and basil.

Dissolve the tomato purée in
the stock in a small saucepan
and stir into the vegetables.
Simmer the vegetables for 25
minutes.

Fry the chops in a very hot
pan for 3–4 minutes each side
then serve with the vegetables.
Serves 4

Lamb Cutlets

4 (150-g/5-oz) lamb cutlets
3 tablespoons oil
salt and freshly milled white
    pepper
½ teaspoon dried rubbed mint

340 calories per serving

Wash and dry the chops. Cut
through the fat at 2.5-cm/1-in
intervals to prevent the chops
curling up during cooking. Season 2 tablespoons of the oil
with salt and pepper and the
mint. Brush generously over
the chops.

Heat the remaining oil in a
large frying pan. Seal the chops
on each side, then reduce the
heat and fry for a further 3
minutes each side.

Have ready a warmed serv-
ing platter or individual plates.
Drain the cutlets on absorbent
kitchen paper and serve

immediately. *Serves 4*

Serve with: a vegetable salad of
boiled cauliflower and green
beans, fried green peppers,
peeled tomatoes and olives.

Cook's Tip

Alternatively, you can
grill the lamb cutlets.
Successful seasonings in-
clude rosemary, mint,
thyme, marjoram, garlic
and sesame seeds, which
can all be added to the
cutlets as they are
cooked.

Shashlik

450 g / 1 lb leg of lamb
4 onions
2 teaspoons dried rosemary
100 g / 4 oz rindless streaky
  bacon
½ teaspon black pepper
1 clove garlic
salt
2 tablespoons oil

525 calories per serving

Cut the lamb into 3-cm/1½-in cubes. Cut the onions into wedges. Crush the rosemary in a mortar and coat the onions in the rosemary. Cut the bacon into fairly large pieces and dip them in the pepper. Finely chop the garlic and crush it with salt.

Divide the lamb, onions and bacon between 4 kebab skewers. Put the oil in a bowl and stir in the garlic salt. Brush the kebabs with the mixture, cover

and leave them to marinate for 3 hours.

Thoroughly heat a cast-iron grill pan. Seal the kebabs under a strong heat, then cook them under a lower heat for 10–15 minutes, turning frequently.
Serves 4

Serve with: curried rice and a salad of red and green peppers.

Lamb Kebabs

1 kg / / 2 lb lean leg of lamb
3 onions
3 peppers
4 green chillies
4 tomatoes
salt and freshly milled white
  pepper
1 tablespoon paprika
3 tablespoons oil

620 calories per serving

Authentic Yugoslav lamb kebabs are cooked over charcoal, but these large kebabs can be cooked under the grill. Wash and dry the lamb and remove any skin. Cut the meat into 6-cm/2½-in cubes.

Thickly slice the onions. Quarter the peppers and chillies, remove core and seeds and cut each piece in half again. Wash the tomatoes and cut them into wedges. Season the lamb with salt, pepper and paprika. Thread all the ingredients alternately on to large skewers and brush well with oil.

Cook the lamb kebabs on a grid over hot charcoal for 25 minutes, turning frequently and brushing with oil. Under a grill the kebabs will take about 15 minutes to cook. Transfer the meat and vegetables from the skewers into a large bowl.
Serves 4

Serve with: chopped onion and green chillies.

Shoulder of Pork with Prunes

6 stoned prunes
150 ml/¼ pint water
1 (1-kg/2-lb) shoulder of pork with rind
salt
1 onion
2 cloves
2 tablespoons oil
450 ml/¾ pint hot water
150 ml/¼ pint cream

680 calories per serving

Soak the prunes in the water in a covered bowl. Cut a lattice pattern in the pork rind and rub the pork with salt. Halve the onion and spike it with the cloves.

Heat the oil in a roasting tin and place the pork in the tin rind side downwards. Add 250 ml/8 fl oz of the hot water and roast the pork on the bottom shelf of a very hot oven (240 C, 475 F, gas 9) for 20 minutes. Then turn the roast over, add the onion with the cloves and roast for 1 hour, gradually adding the remaining hot water and basting the meat from time to time.

Turn off the oven and leave the meat to stand in the oven for 10 minutes.

Dilute the roasting juices with a little hot water, transfer to a saucepan, stir in the cream and simmer for a few minutes. Quarter the prunes and add them to the sauce. *Serves 6*

Stuffed Rolled Pork

225 g/8 oz celery
½ red pepper, deseeded
1 clove garlic
1 kg/2 lb leg of pork, cut ready for rolling
1 teaspoon mustard
salt
½ teaspoon dried thyme
½ teaspoon dried rosemary
½ teaspoon paprika
3 tablespoons oil
250 ml/8 fl oz hot meat stock
150 ml/¼ pint soured cream
1 teaspoon cornflour

380 calories per serving

Trim and slice the celery. Cut the red pepper into strips and chop the garlic. Spread the pork with mustard and sprinkle with salt, the herbs and paprika. Arrange the celery and red pepper on the pork and sprinkle with the garlic. Roll up the meat and secure it with cooking twine.

Heat the oil in a roasting tin and quickly seal the meat. Add half the stock and roast the pork on the bottom shelf of a very hot oven (240 C, 475 F, gas 9) for 60–70 minutes. After the first 20 minutes, reduce the heat to moderately hot (200 C 400 F, gas 6) and add the remaining stock.

When the meat is cooked, transfer it to a plate, turn off the oven and leave the meat to stand in the oven for 10 minutes.

Dilute the roasting juices with a little water and stir in the soured cream. Thicken the sauce with the cornflour dissolved in a little cold water and serve with the pork. *Serves 6*

Flemish-Style Pork Chops

4 (150-g/5-oz) pork chops
1 large cooking apple
75 g/3 oz butter
salt and freshly milled white
  pepper
2 tablespoons freshly chopped
  mint
2 tablespoons crème fraîche

650 calories per serving

Wash and dry the chops and cut notches right through the fat at 2.5-cm/1-in intervals, to prevent the chops curling up during cooking. Using a sharp knife loosen the meat slightly along the bone. Peel, quarter and core the apple and thinly slice each quarter lengthways.

Heat 50 g/2 oz of the butter in a large frying pan and fry the chops until deep brown on both sides, seasoning with salt and pepper after turning.   Transfer the chops to an ovenproof dish. Quickly fry the apple slices on both sides in the frying pan, then arrange them on top of the chops. Dot the apple with the remaining butter and roast the chops on the middle shelf of a moderately hot oven (200 C, 400 F, gas 6) for 15 minutes.

Stir the mint into the crème fraîche and use to garnish the chops. *Serves 4*

Serve with: bread and a salad.

Pork Chops aux fines herbes

Chops Stuffed with Herbs

4 (150-g/5-oz) pork chops
1 onion
2 cloves garlic
4 sprigs fresh rosemary leaves
2 tablespoons Roquefort cheese
1 tablespoon chopped parsley
1 tablespoon chopped lovage
  or parsley
1 tablespoon chopped chives
2 tablespoons oil
salt

610 calories per serving

Wash and dry the chops and cut through the fat at 2.5-cm/1-in intervals. Using a sharp knife, loosen the meat at the bone so that the chops will cook evenly.

Finely chop the onion and garlic. Chop the rosemary. Mash the Roquefort cheese with a fork and mix in the onion, garlic and herbs. Cut an envelope in the thickest part of each chop, fill it with the herb mixture and secure with a cocktail stick.

Heat the oil in a large frying pan and fry the chops until brown on each side, seasoning with salt after turning. Reduce the heat and fry for a further 6 minutes each side. *Serves 4*

Serve with: grilled or baked tomatoes and buttered new potatoes.

Pork Fillet in Yogurt Sauce

2 (approx 400-g/14-oz) pork
* fillets or pieces of leg*
salt
1 teaspoon paprika
100 g/4 oz Emmental cheese or
* fairly stale Gouda cheese*
1 tablespoon flour
1 onion
50 g/2 oz butter
300 ml/½ pint natural yogurt
2 tablespoons chopped parsley

595 calories per serving

Wash the pork in cold water,
pat dry, cut off any fat and remove the skin with a sharp
knife. Rub salt and the paprika
into the pork. Cut the cheese
into 4-cm/2-in lengths. With a
knife cut small holes in the
pork and insert the cheese,
leaving about a quarter of the

length showing. Then dip the
fillets in the flour. Dice the
onion.
  Melt the butter in a large casserole and fry the pork until
golden brown all over. The
cheese will melt during the
frying. Add the onion and fry
for a few minutes, then pour on
the yogurt. Cover the casserole
and braise the pork over a low
heat for 40 minutes.
  Before serving, stir the parsley into the yogurt sauce.
Serves 4

Serve with: parsley potatoes
and Brussels sprouts.

Sweet and Sour Pork

675 g/1½ lb pork fillet
3 tablespoons soy sauce
salt and freshly milled black
* pepper*
3 teaspoons cornflour
oil for deep frying plus 2
* tablespoons*
5 tablespoons wine vinegar
2 tablespoons sugar
4 tablespoons pineapple juice
4 slices pineapple

500 calories per serving

Cut any skin and fat off the
pork and cut the meat into 2.5-
cm/1-in cubes. Season 2 tablespoons of the soy sauce with
salt and pepper. Dip the pork
first in the soy sauce, then into
2 teaspoons of the cornflour.
  Heat the 2 tablespoons of oil
in a saucepan. Stir in the vin-

egar, sugar, the remaining soy
sauce and the pineapple juice.
Cut up the pineapple and add it
to the sauce. Simmer for 1
minute. Dissolve the remaining
cornflour in a little cold water
and add it to the sauce to
thicken it.
  Heat the remaining oil to
180 c (350 f) in a deep fryer. Fry
a few pieces of meat at a time,
for 6 minutes per batch, until
brown and crisp, drain and
keep hot. Stir the meat into the
sauce and serve immediately.
Serves 4

Serve with: rice.

Cook's Tip

Instead of pork fillet,
you could use leg of
pork or chicken equally
successfully for this
recipe.

Bohemian Schnitzel

4 (150-g/5-oz) boned slices
    neck of pork
2 teaspoons mustard
1 tablespoon flour
1 tablespoon paprika
50 g/2 oz rindless streaky bacon
2 onions
1 tablespoon oil

685 calories per serving

Wash and dry the pork and
flatten each slice evenly with
the ball of your hand. Cut off
any skin or fat. Thinly spread
the pork with mustard. Season
the flour with paprika. Dip the
pork in the flour and place on a
wire rack to dry slightly. Finely
dice the bacon. Dice the
onions.

Heat the oil in a frying pan
and fry the bacon and onion,
then remove them from the pan
and keep to one side. Fry the
pork in the fat in the pan for 2–
3 minutes each side, until well
browned, then reduce the heat
and fry the slices for a further 4
minutes each side.

Return the bacon and onion
to the pan and warm through.

Serve with: red cabbage and
fried potatoes.

Stuffed Pork Fillets

4 (175-g/6-oz) thick slices pork
    fillet
2 slices bread
2 cloves garlic
1 tablespoon chopped parsley
1 tablespoon chopped chervil
1 tablespoon chopped chives
1 tablespoon single cream
salt and freshly milled white
    pepper
3 tablespoons oil

470 calories per serving

Cut horizontally across the
pork fillets, stopping just short
of the edge. Break up the bread
and soften it in cold water.
Finely dice the garlic.

Squeeze excess moisture
from the bread and mix it with
the garlic, chopped herbs,
cream, salt and pepper. Spread
each fillet with some of the mixture and press the meat firmly
together.

Brush a grill pan with oil and
grill the pork fillets under a
moderate heat for 20 minutes,
turning them frequently and
brushing with oil each time you
turn them. *Serves 4*

Cook's Tip

This recipe is just as
good using entrecôte
steaks or lamb fillets.

Spanish-Style Hamburgers

1 day-old bread roll
1 onion
10 stuffed green olives
2 eggs
450 g / 1 lb mixed minced meat
salt and freshly milled white
    pepper
generous pinch of garlic salt
2 tablespoons oil
1 tomato
4 caper-stuffed anchovy fillets
250 ml / 8 fl oz dry red wine
2 tablespoons concentrated to-
    mato purée
1 tablespoon curry paste
½ teaspoon dried oregano

300 calories per serving

Tear up the roll and soften it
for about 15 minutes in cold
water. Chop the onion and olives. Squeeze out the roll and
mix it in a bowl with the onion,
olives, eggs, minced meat and
seasonings.

Heat the oil in a large frying
pan. Shape the meat mixture
into 4 equal-sized hamburgers
and brown them on each side.
Reduce the heat and fry for a
further 15 minutes, until
cooked, then remove the hamburgers from the pan and keep
them warm on a hot plate.

Wash and dry the tomato
and cut into four thick slices.
Fry the tomato slices on each
side, place one on each ham-
burger and top with an
anchovy.

Dilute the cooking fat in the
pan with the red wine. Stir the
tomato purée in a bowl with
the curry paste and oregano,
stir the mixture into the red
wine sauce, bring to the boil
once and season to taste. Pour
the sauce over the hamburgers.
Serves 4

Mince Ring in Cabbage

about 675 / 1½ lb Savoy cabbage
2 onions
1 day-old bread roll
2 eggs
675 g / 1½ lb mixed minced meat
salt and freshly milled white
  pepper
½ teaspoon ground caraway
1 tablespoon oil

500 calories per serving

Remove the stalk and any damaged leaves from the cabbage, then boil the cabbage for 10 minutes in salted water. Leave it to cool, separate the leaves, cut out the thick stalks from the outer leaves and finely chop the inner leaves.

Dice the onions. Soften the roll in cold water. Mix the chopped cabbage, eggs and  onion into the minced meat and season with salt, pepper and caraway. Squeeze excess moisture from the roll and work the roll into the mixture until smooth.

Brush a ring mould with oil and line it with large cabbage leaves. Fill the mould with the meat mixture and cover with the remaining cabbage leaves. Wrap the mould tightly in aluminium foil and stand it in a pan of boiling water. Simmer for 1½ hours, then turn out the mince ring onto a hot plate. *Serves 4*

Serve with: tomato sauce and potatoes with parsley.

Viennese Meat Loaf

1 day-old bread roll
2 onions
2 cloves garlic
450 g / 1 lb mixed minced meat
100 g / 4 oz pig's liver, chopped
2 eggs
salt and freshly milled black
  pepper
1 teaspoon paprika
1 teaspoon medium-hot mustard
100 g / 4 oz thin rindless rashers
  streaky bacon
250 ml / 8 fl oz hot meat stock
1 teaspoon cornflour
150 ml / ¼ pint soured cream

625 calories per serving

Soften the roll in cold water. Finely chop the onions and garlic. Squeeze excess moisture from the roll and mix into the minced meat with the onion, garlic, liver and eggs and season with salt, pepper, paprika and mustard.

Shape the mixture into a loaf. Line a roasting tin with half the bacon rashers, place the meat loaf in the tin and cover with the remaining bacon.

Roast the meat loaf on the second shelf from the bottom of a hot oven (220 C, 425 F, gas 7) for 45 minutes, basting from time to time with the stock, then remove the meat loaf from the tin and keep it warm.

Dilute the cooking juices with the remaining stock and a little hot water and heat in a saucepan. Stir the cornflour into the soured cream and use to thicken the sauce. *Serves 4*

Puff Pastry Mince Roll

1 (368-g/3-oz) packet frozen
  puff pastry
2 onions
1 small leek
350 g/12 oz white cabbage
100 g/4 oz mushrooms
450 g/1 lb mixed minced meat
1 tablespoon butter
2 egg yolks
salt and freshly milled white
  pepper
1 teaspoon soy sauce
100 g/4 oz Gouda cheese
1 egg, separated

435 calories per serving

Defrost the pastry. Dice the onions. Trim, wash and cut the leek into rings and the cabbage into fine strips. Trim, wash and finely slice the mushrooms.

Fry the onion and minced meat in the butter in a large frying pan. Add the vegetables and braise for 10 minutes, stirring frequently. Remove the minced meat and vegetables from the heat and work in the egg yolks, salt and pepper and the soy sauce. Finely dice the cheese.

Roll out the pastry into a large rectangle and spread it with the meat mixture, leaving 2.5-cm/1 in pastry around the edges. Sprinkle with the cheese. Brush the pastry edges with beaten egg white and roll up the pastry, pressing the edges lightly together.

Place the roll on a moist baking sheet and brush with egg yolk. Bake for 35 minutes in a moderately hot oven (200 C, 400 F, gas 6) and serve hot. *Serves 6*

Meat Loaf with Egg

1 day-old bread roll
1 onion
225 g/8 oz minced pork
225 g/8 oz minced veal
225 g/8 oz minced beef
salt and freshly milled white
  pepper
$\frac{1}{4}$ teaspoon dried thyme
$\frac{1}{4}$ teaspoon dried oregano
2 tablespoons chopped parsley
2–3 tablespoons milk
2 hard-boiled eggs
1 tablespoon flour
1 bouquet garni
450 ml/$\frac{3}{4}$ pint hot meat stock
100 g/4 oz mushrooms
2 tablespoons soured cream
1 teaspoon mustard
2 tablespoons tomato ketchup

610 calories per serving

Soften the roll in cold water. Dice the onion. Squeeze excess moisture from the roll and mix it into the minced meat with the onion. Season to taste, add the herbs and stir in the milk. Shape the mixture into a loaf around the hard-boiled eggs. Sprinkle the meat loaf with flour.

Roast the meat loaf on the bottom shelf of a hot oven (220 C, 425 F, gas 7) for 1 hour. Trim, wash and coarsely chop the bouquet garni and add after the first 5 minutes of cooking time. Gradually add the stock. Trim and slice the mushrooms.

Transfer the meat loaf to a plate and keep it hot. Pour the cooking juices into a small pan, add the mushrooms and simmer for 5 minutes, then stir the soured cream, mustard and ketchup into the sauce and serve it with the loaf. *Serves 4*

Pickled Tongue in Madeira Sauce

1 (1.5-kg/3-lb) pickled ox
  tongue
1 onion
1 small leek
2 bouquets garnis
3 litres/5 pints water
450 g/1 lb celery
50 g/2 oz butter
2 teaspoons sugar
2 tablespoons flour
1 bay leaf
1 clove
4 tablespoons cream
150 ml/¼ pint Madeira wine
1–2 teaspoons lemon juice
salt and black pepper
cayenne

640 calories per serving

Wash the tongue under cold running water, scrubbing the top thoroughly. Soak the tongue in cold water for 8–12 hours.

Quarter the onion. Trim, wash and slice the white of the leek. Bring the bouquets garnis and prepared vegetables to the boil in the water in a large, heavy-based saucepan. Lower the tongue into the pan and boil it vigorously for 20 minutes, scooping off any scum that forms. Then cover the pan, leaving the lid a fraction open, reduce the heat and simmer the tongue gently for a further 3 hours.

Trim and wash the celery, cut into 5-cm/2-in lengths and add to the pan 30 minutes before the end of the cooking time. The tongue is cooked when a fork goes easily into the tip. When cooked, lift the tongue from the pan, rinse it in cold water and remove the skin, together with the gristle at the base. Lift the celery from the pan and keep it warm. Strain the stock into a bowl, measure off 450 ml/¾ pint and set it to one side. Keep the tongue warm in the stock remaining in the bowl.

Melt the butter in a saucepan, sprinkle in the sugar and flour and cook until golden, stirring continuously. Do not allow the flour to colour too much. Gradually add the reserved stock. Add the bay leaf and clove, cover the pan and simmer gently for 20 minutes. Remove the pan from the heat and stir in the cream and madeira. Season well with lemon juice, salt, pepper and cayenne.

Lift the tongue from the bowl and carve into thin slices. Arrange the slices on a warm plate with the celery and cover in sauce. Serve the remaining sauce separately. *Serves 8*

Cook's Tip

Since the pickled tongue is very salty, you do not need to add salt when cooking it. If, however, you are boiling a fresh tongue add 2 teaspoons salt to the cooking water.

Milan-Style Calf's Liver

2.5 litres/4¼ pints water
salt and freshly milled white
  pepper
225 g/8 oz macaroni
50 g/2 oz butter
50 g/2 oz grated Parmesan
  cheese
4 (150-g/5-oz) slices calf's liver
250 ml/8 fl oz milk
2 tablespoons flour
pinch of dried marjoram
3 tablespoons oil

640 calories per serving

Bring the water to the boil with
a generous pinch of salt, tip in
the macaroni and cook for
about 20 minutes, until tender.
Drain the macaroni through a
sieve, transfer to a warmed
plate and keep it hot. Melt the
butter, and mix it into the hot

macaroni with the Parmesan.
  Wash the liver in cold water,
wipe it dry and remove the skin
and any sinews. Dip both sides
of the liver slices in milk and allow the excess to drip off. Season the flour with salt, pepper
and rubbed marjoram and dip
the liver in the flour, shaking
off any excess. Place the liver
on a wire grill tray to dry for a
few minutes.
  Heat the oil in a frying pan
and fry the liver for 3 minutes
each side. Arrange the cooked
liver over the macaroni.
Serves 4

Berlin-Style Calf's Liver

4 (150-g/5-oz) slices calf's liver
2 onions
2 apples
2 tablespoons flour
50 g/2 oz butter
salt and freshly milled white
  pepper

395 calories per serving

Wash and dry the liver and remove any skin and sinews. Cut
the onions into rings. Peel the
apples, core with an apple-corer
and cut across into eight equal
rings. Dip the liver in the flour,
shake off any excess and leave
to dry slightly.
  Melt half the butter in a
frying pan and fry the apple
slices until golden on both
sides, then remove the slices
from the pan and keep them
warm. Fry the onion rings in

the butter in the pan until
brown and crisp, then remove
and keep them warm with the
apple.
  In a separate pan, melt the
remaining butter and fry the
liver for 3–4 minutes each side.
Season to taste, arrange the
liver on a hot plate and garnish
with the onion and apple.
Serves 4

Normandy-Style Calf's Kidney

675 g/1½ lb small calf's or pig's
kidneys without fat
salt and freshly milled black
pepper
1 cooking apple
1 onion
3 tablespoons oil
25 g/1 oz butter
1½ tablespoons Calvados
5 tablespoons cream
½ teaspoon sugar
parsley to garnish (optional)

385 calories per serving

Wash, dry and thickly slice the
kidneys. Rub the kidneys with
salt, cover and leave to stand
for 30 minutes. Peel the apple,
core using an apple-corer and
cut the apple into thick rings.
Dice the onion. Wash the kidneys and pat them dry.

Heat the oil in a large frying
pan, fry the onion until transparent, add the kidneys, then
the butter and Calvados. Flame
the Calvados using a match
and leave it to burn out.

Season the cream with salt
and pepper and add it to the
kidneys. Sprinkle the apple
slices with sugar and add them
to the pan. Simmer over a low
heat for 5 minutes and season
to taste. Sprinkle with chopped
parsley if liked. *Serves 4*

Flambéed Kidneys

675 g/1½ lb calf's kidneys, with-
out fat
salt and pepper
1 onion
1 clove garlic
3 tablespoons oil
1 tablespoon flour
3 tablespoons Cognac
4 tablespoons double cream
25 g/1 oz butter
1 teaspoon sugar
2 teaspoons hot mustard

440 calories per serving

Wash, dry and halve the kidneys, cut out the white sinew
and slice. Rub the kidneys with
salt and leave them to stand for
30 minutes. Wash the kidneys
in lukewarm water and pat
them dry. Finely dice the onion
and garlic.

Heat the oil in a frying pan
and fry the onion and garlic until transparent. Season the kidneys with pepper, dip in flour,
shake off any excess and fry the
kidneys for 5 minutes, turning
frequently. Pour the Cognac
over the kidneys, flame and
leave to burn out.

Season the cream with salt
and stir it into the kidneys. Stir
the butter, sugar and mustard
into the sauce and heat for 8
minutes, without allowing the
sauce to boil. *Serves 4*

Serve with: braised courgettes,
French bread and Waldorf
salad.

Beef Stew with Sweetcorn

100 g/4 oz shin of beef
675 g/1½lb neck of beef
3 onions
1 clove garlic
1 green pepper
1 red pepper
3 tablespoons oil
salt and freshly milled black
  pepper
1 bay leaf
pinch of cayenne
150 ml/¼ pint hot meat stock
1 (198-g/7-oz) can sweetcorn
200 g/7 oz gherkins
150 ml/¼ pint cream

535 calories per serving

Wash and dry the beef and cut it into 3-cm/1½-in cubes. Dice the onion and garlic. Halve and deseed the peppers, wash, dry and cut into strips.

Heat the oil in a casserole and fry the onion and garlic until transparent. Add and brown the meat. Stir in the red and green pepper, salt, the bay leaf, pepper and cayenne and finally the stock. Cover the casserole and simmer over a low heat for 70–80 minutes, adding a little hot water as and when necessary.

Drain the sweetcorn and dice the gherkins and add them to the stew 10 minutes before the end of the cooking time. Just before serving, thicken with the cream and adjust seasoning. *Serves 4*

Serve with: rice.

Oxtail Stew

1 kg/2 lb oxtail, chopped into 5-
  cm/2-in lengths
1 onion
1 clove garlic
50 g/2 oz rindless fat bacon
2 tablespoons olive oil
salt
250 ml/8 fl oz dry white wine
salt
150 ml/¼ pint–450 ml/¾ pint hot
  meat stock
2 sticks celery
4 tomatoes, peeled and halved
1 tablespoon chopped parsley to
  garnish

500 calories per serving

Wash and dry the pieces of oxtail. Finely chop the onion and garlic. Chop the bacon.

Heat the oil in a casserole with the bacon, add and fry the onion and garlic until transparent. Add the oxtail and brown all over. Pour in the white wine, season with salt, cover the pan and braise the oxtail over a low heat for 2 hours, shaking the pan from time to time and adding a little hot stock as and when required.

Wash and trim the celery and cut it into 3-cm/1½-in lengths. Add the celery to the stew 30 minutes before the end of the cooking time, and the tomatoes 10 minutes before the end of the cooking time. Before serving sprinkle the stew with parsley. *Serves 4*

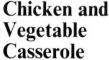

Chicken and Vegetable Casserole

2 litres/3½ pints water
salt
1 (1-kg/2-lb) boiling chicken
4 peppercorns
1 onion
1 bouquet garni
450 g/1 lb cauliflower
100 g/4 oz leeks
225 g/8 oz carrots
225 g/8 oz Brussels sprouts
100 g/4 oz vermicelli
few drops of soy sauce
2 tablespoons chopped parsley to
    garnish

460 calories per serving

Bring the water and a generous
sprinkling of salt to the boil in
a large, heavy-based saucepan.
Place the chicken in the water,
add the peppercorns and boil in
an open pan for about 20 minutes, scooping off the scum as it
forms. Quarter the onion. Trim
and wash the bouquet garni, if
necessary, and add it to the
chicken with the onion. Cover
the pan and simmer gently for
1½ hours.

Trim and wash the cauli-
flower and separate it into
florets. Halve the leeks lengthways, wash and slice. Scrape
and slice the carrots. Clean the
sprouts and cut larger ones in
half.

Lift the chicken out of the
pan and strain the stock into a
large saucepan. Add the vegetables to the stock and cook in
a covered pan for 25 minutes.

Boil the vermicelli in salted
water for 8 minutes, then drain.
Dice the chicken and add it to
the cooked vegetables with the
vermicelli. Season to taste with
soy sauce and sprinkle with
parsley. *Serves 6*

Lamb and Vegetable Hotpot

675 g/1½ lb leg of lamb
2 onions
2 cloves garlic
2 tablespoons oil
1 teaspoon curry powder
450 ml/¾ pint meat stock
salt and freshly milled black
    pepper
good pinch of ground caraway
    seeds
pinch of cayenne
450 g/1 lb green beans
1 green pepper
1 red pepper
225 g/8 oz aubergine
1–2 sprigs savory (optional)
450 g/1 lb tomatoes
2 tablespoons chopped parsley to
    garnish

400 calories per serving

Wash the meat and cut it into
fairly large cubes. Finely chop
the onions and garlic.

Heat the oil in a heavy-based
saucepan or casserole, add and
seal the meat with the onion
and garlic. Add the curry powder, then pour in the stock a little at a time. Season with salt
and pepper, the ground caraway seeds and cayenne, cover
the pan and simmer for 30
minutes.

Trim and wash the beans and
break them into pieces. Wash
and deseed the peppers and cut
them into strips. Wash and slice
the aubergine. Add the vegetables and savory to the meat
and simmer for a further 30
minutes.

Peel the tomatoes, cut them
into wedges and add to the pan
10 minutes before the end of
the cooking time. Serve the hotpot sprinkled with parsley.
Serves 6

53

Paella

1 (1-kg/2-lb) chicken
1 onion
2 cloves garlic
1 green pepper
3 tomatoes
generous pinch of saffron
salt and freshly milled white
  pepper
4 tablespoons olive oil
225 g/8 oz long-grain rice
750 ml/1¼ pints hot chicken
  stock
225 g/8 oz cod or haddock fillet
225 g/8 oz frozen scampi,
  thawed
100 g/4 oz frozen peas
150 ml/¼ pint dry white wine
10 stuffed green olives to garnish

430 calories per serving

Cut the chicken into 8 equal
pieces. Finely chop the onion
and garlic. Halve, wash and
deseed the green pepper and cut

it into strips. Peel the tomatoes
and cut them into wedges. Soak
the saffron in a little water.
Season the chicken with salt
and pepper.

Heat the oil in a large heavy-
based saucepan or paella pan,
then add and seal the chicken
pieces. Add the onion, garlic
and rice and fry until transparent. Add the tomato, peppers,
chicken stock and saffron,
cover the pan and simmer for
15 minutes.

Dice the fish, season with salt
and add it to the pan with the
scampi, peas and wine. Cover
the pan and simmer very gently
for 10 minutes. Garnish the
paella with the olives. *Serves 8*

Polish Stew

100 g/4 oz rindless rashers
  streaky bacon
450 g/1 lb leg of pork
450 g/1 lb braising beef
2 onions
450 g/1 lb white cabbage
350 g/12 oz chanterelles or other
  mixed mushrooms
1 bay leaf
1 teaspoon caraway seeds
1 pinch dried thyme
3 tablespoons concentrated
  tomato purée
250 ml/8 fl oz dry white wine
2 cloves garlic
salt and freshly milled white
  pepper
sugar

460 calories per serving

Cut the bacon and meat into
small cubes. Finely chop the
onions. Trim and wash the cabbage and tear it into fairly large

pieces. Trim and wash the
mushrooms and cut larger ones
in half.

Fry the bacon until crisp in a
large, heavy-based saucepan or
fireproof casserole, add the
meat and onion and fry over a
moderate heat, stirring continuously. Add the cabbage, mushrooms, bay leaf, caraway seeds,
thyme, tomato purée and wine.
Squeeze the garlic into the stew
through a garlic press. Add
enough water to cover.

Cover the pan and simmer
for about 1 hour 10 minutes,
then adjust the seasoning.

Serve with: boiled potatoes or
wholemeal bread. *Serves 8*

Hungarian Pepper Stew

450 g / 1 lb yellow, green and red
  peppers
100 g / 4 oz rindless rashers
  streaky bacon
1 large onion
450 g / 1 lb tomatoes
1 tablespoon pork dripping
1 tablespoon paprika
4 Hungarian sausages
salt and freshly milled white
  pepper

585 calories per serving

Halve and deseed the peppers,
wash, dry and cut them into
strips. Dice the bacon and onion. Peel the tomatoes and cut
them into wedges.

Melt the dripping in a large
frying pan, then add and fry the
bacon until crisp. Add the onion and fry until golden. Add

the peppers and cook over a
low heat for 10 minutes. Then
stir in the tomatoes and paprika and place the sausages
over the vegetables.

Cover the pan and cook over
a very low heat for a further 15
minutes. Finally season to
taste. *Serves 4*

Serve with: boiled rice or
French bread.

Health tip

To reduce the fat and
calorie intake omit the
streaky bacon and sub-
stitute a little sunflower
oil for the pork
dripping.

Italian Mixed Stew

1 bouquet garni
1 onion
1 clove garlic
3 litres / 5 pints water
1 bay leaf
2 allspice corns
salt
450 g / 1 lb beef brisket
350 g / 12 oz pig's tongue
450 g / 1 lb chicken legs
225 g / 8 oz carrots
100 g / 4 oz leeks

405 calories per serving

Trim, wash and chop the bouquet garni. Coarsely chop the
onion and garlic. Bring the
water to the boil in a large,
heavy-based saucepan, add the
bouquet garni, onion, garlic,
bay leaf, allspice and a generous sprinkling of salt.

Wash the brisket, drop it into
the boiling water and remove
any scum that forms during the
first 15 minutes. Simmer the
meat over a low heat for 2
hours. After the first hour, add
the tongue and after 1½ hours
add the chicken legs.

Trim and wash the carrots
and leeks. Quarter the carrots
lengthways, cut the white of the
leeks and the inner leaves into
pieces and add to the stew 25
minutes before the end of the
cooking time.

Lift the meat out of the pan.
Skin the tongue and cut it into
slices. Slice the beef. Arrange
on a serving dish with the
chicken legs and vegetables and
keep hot while you serve the
stock as a clear soup. *Serves 6*

Sausage with Potato and Apple Mash

1 kg/2 lb floury potatoes
1 teaspoon salt
450 g/1 lb cooking apples
250 ml/8 fl oz water
2 tablespoons sugar
100 g/4 oz rindless streaky
*   bacon*
2 large onions
salt and freshly milled white
*   pepper*
350 g/12 oz black pudding or 4
*   pork sausages*

620 calories per serving

Peel the potatoes and boil them in a covered saucepan of salted water over a low heat for 20–25 minutes. Peel, quarter, core and thinly slice the apples. Add the apple to the water and sugar in a saucepan, cover the pan and boil gently for 15 minutes, until the apples are just tender.

Drain the potatoes, evaporate the moisture and mash them. Whisk the apple and its juice into the potatoes. Dice and fry the bacon until crisp. Cut the onions into rings and brown them in the bacon fat. Stir the bacon and onion mixture into the potato and apple mixture and season to taste.

Cut the black pudding into 8 thick slices. Fry the black pudding or pork sausages in the bacon fat until brown and crisp and arrange over the potato mixture.

Potato Stew

800 g/1¾ lb potatoes
100 g/4 oz rindless streaky
*   bacon*
225 g/8 oz onions
1 tablespoon paprika
salt
generous pinch of cayenne
300 ml/½ pint meat stock
2 teaspoons caraway seeds
150 ml/¼ pint soured cream

490 calories per serving

Peel, wash and cube the potatoes. Finely chop the bacon and fry it in a large frying pan until crisp. Chop the onions and fry them in the bacon fat until golden. Add the potato, season with paprika, salt and cayenne and fry for a few minutes, stirring continuously.

Heat the stock and add it to the potatoes with the caraway seeds. Cook over a low heat for 20–25 minutes. Stir in the soured cream and season liberally to taste. *Serves 4*

Serve with: white cabbage salad.

Cook's tip

New potatoes can be substituted for the old ones in this recipe. Select small, even-sized potatoes and scrub or scrape them before cooking whole, as above.

Polish Cabbage Casserole

450 g/1 lb lean, boneless pork
2 tablespoons pork dripping
750 ml/1¼ pints meat stock
675 g/1½ lb white cabbage
100 g/4 oz carrots
100 g/4 oz leeks
225 g/8 oz onions
50 g/2 oz celeriac
1 small piece parsley root
  (optional)
salt and freshly milled white
  pepper
½ teaspoon cayenne
1 teaspoon caraway seeds
225 g/8 oz Polish or other garlic
  sausage

600 calories per serving

Wash and dry the pork and cut it into fairly large cubes. Heat the dripping in a large, heavy-based saucepan or casserole and brown the pork. Meanwhile heat 250 ml/8 fl oz of the stock, pour it over the meat, cover the pan and braise the meat over a low heat for 20 minutes.

Quarter the cabbage, cut out the stalk and cut into fairly thick strips. Scrape, wash and slice the carrots. Halve the leeks lengthways, wash thoroughly and slice. Cut the onions into rings. Peel, wash and dice the celeriac. Wash the parsley root and cut it into pieces.

Heat the remaining stock. Add all the vegetables to the pork, season with salt, pepper, the cayenne and caraway seeds, stir in the heated stock, cover the pan and cook over a moderate heat for a further 40 minutes.

During the cooking time keep an eye on the amount of liquid in the pan and add more stock or water as necessary.

Wash the sausage in cold water, dry and cut into fairly thick slices. Add the sausage to the pan 10 minutes before the end of the cooking time to warm through. *Serves 6*

Cook's tip

A casserole like this is excellent when you have a lot of guests to feed. All ingredients should then be doubled or increased according to the number to be served. An alternative cooking method is to brown the meat in a large casserole, preferably cast-iron, mix all the remaining ingredients and the stock into the meat, then cook in a moderate oven (160 C, 325 F, gas 3) for 2–3 hours, depending on quantity. This slow method of cooking brings out the various flavours very well.

Brussels Sprouts with Smoked Sausages

1 kg/2 lb Brussels sprouts
900 ml/1½ pints water
salt
225 g/8 oz small smoked
  sausages
50 g/2 oz butter
1 tablespoon flour
150 ml/¼ pint milk
pinch of sugar
pinch of grated nutmeg
1 egg
1 tablespoon chopped parsley
50 g/2 oz Emmental cheese,
  freshly grated

550 calories per serving

Remove damaged outer leaves from the sprouts, cut off the stalks, cut a cross in the base of the sprouts and wash them.

Bring the water and a little salt to the boil in a large saucepan, tip in the sprouts, cover the pan and simmer gently for 15 minutes.

Slice the sausages. Drain the sprouts, reserving 150 ml/¼ pint of the cooking water. Heat half the butter in a saucepan, sprinkle in the flour and cook until golden stirring continuously. Gradually stir in the hot sprout water, add the milk and simmer for 5 minutes, stirring continuously. Remove the sauce from the heat and stir in the sugar, nutmeg, salt to taste and egg.

Arrange the sprouts and sausage in a buttered ovenproof dish and cover them with the sauce. Sprinkle with the parsley and cheese and dot with the remaining butter.

Brown in a hot oven (220 C, 425 F, gas 7) for about 15 minutes. *Serves 4*

Pepper and Ham Rolls

1 kg/2 lb green peppers
2 tablespoons oil
½ teaspoon dried thyme
½ teaspoon dried oregano
½ teaspoon dried basil
salt and freshly milled white
  pepper
350 g/12 oz lean cooked ham,
  sliced
250 ml/8 fl oz hot water
2 slices processed cheese
1 tablespoon chopped chives to
  garnish

300 calories per serving

Halve and deseed the peppers, dry and cut them into 2-cm/1-in wide strips. Season the oil with the herbs and salt and pepper, sprinkle over the peppers, cover and leave them to marinate for 1 hour.

Cut the ham into 5-cm/2-in wide strips. Grease an ovenproof dish with a little of the seasoned oil. Wrap a few strips of pepper at a time in a strip of ham, arrange the rolls in the dish and sprinkle with the remaining seasoned oil. Pour the hot water around the rolls and cover the dish with aluminium foil.

Bake on the second shelf from the bottom of a hot oven (220 C, 425 F, gas 7) for 30 minutes. Five minutes before the end of the cooking time cut the cheese into strips, arrange the strips in a criss-cross pattern over the rolls and return the rolls to the oven until the cheese melts. Sprinkle with the chives. *Serves 4*

Serve with: potatoes baked in foil, topped with soured cream.

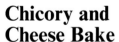

Chicory and Cheese Bake

450 g/1 lb chicory
275 g/10 oz lean cooked ham
1 tablespoon oil
salt and freshly milled white
  pepper
65 g/2½ oz butter
2 tablespoons flour
250 ml/8 fl oz milk
150 ml/¼ pint dry white wine
100 g/4 oz soft cheese
2 egg yolks, beaten
2 tablespoons breadcrumbs
1 tablespoon chopped parsley

540 calories per serving

Wash and dry the chicory and cut off the stalks. Cut the chicory into strips about 1 cm/½ in wide and the ham into 5-mm/¼-in wide strips.

Heat the oil in a frying pan, add and fry the chicory and ham, season with salt and pepper and keep to one side.

Melt 50 g/2 oz of the butter in a saucepan, add and cook the flour until golden. Stir in the milk a little at a time and simmer for 5 minutes, stirring continuously. Stir in the wine. Add the cheese in small pieces and stir until melted. Remove the sauce from the heat and stir in the beaten egg yolks.

Grease an ovenproof dish with butter and fill with the ham and chicory mixture. Cover with the cheese sauce, sprinkle with the breadcrumbs and parsley and dot with the butter.

Bake in a moderately hot oven (200 c, 400 f, gas 6) for 25 minutes. *Serves 4*

Moussaka

1 kg/2 lb aubergines
salt and freshly milled black
  pepper
4 tablespoons oil
2 onions
575 g/1¼ lb minced lamb
5 tablespoons dry vermouth
6 tablespoons water
1 teaspoon sugar
1 teaspoon oregano
5 tablespoons breadcrumbs
450 g/1 lb tomatoes, sliced
100 g/4 oz Gouda cheese, grated
For the sauce:
50 g/2 oz butter
2 tablespoons flour
250 ml/8 fl oz milk
3 eggs, beaten
salt and freshly milled white
  pepper

610 calories per serving

Peel and thickly slice the aubergines, sprinkle with salt and leave to stand for 1 hour. Then rinse, wipe dry and fry the aubergine slices in 2 tablespoons of the oil

Grate the onions and fry in the remaining oil with the minced lamb. Stir in the vermouth, water, sugar, oregano, salt, pepper and breadcrumbs.

Cover the base of an ovenproof dish with aubergines, sprinkle with cheese, cover with the meat sauce and repeat until you have used up all the ingredients. Cover the top meat layer with tomatoes.

Melt the butter, sprinkle in the flour and stir over a low heat until golden. Stir in the milk a little at a time and simmer for 5 minutes, stirring continuously. Remove from the heat and stir in the beaten eggs. Season to taste. Pour the sauce over the moussaka.

Bake for 1 hour in a moderately hot oven (200 c, 400 f, gas 6). *Serves 6*

Cassoulet

450 g / 1 lb small haricot beans
100 g / 4 oz leeks
3 onions plus 3 tablespoons diced
  onion
2 litres / 3½ pints chicken stock
225 g / 8 oz rindless streaky
  bacon
100 g / 4 oz garlic sausage
1 leg of goose
salt and freshly milled black
  pepper
½ teaspoon garlic salt
½ teaspoon dried thyme
2 sprigs parsley
1 bay leaf
450 g / 1 lb tomatoes
3 tablespoons diced celery
2 tablespoons oil
150 ml / ¼ pint dry white wine

640 calories per serving

Soak the beans for 12 hours.
  Trim and finely chop the
leeks. Finely chop the onions.
Bring the stock to the boil with

the beans, bacon, sausage and
goose leg, add the onions and
leeks and all the seasonings and
simmer for 1¼ hours.
  Peel and dice the tomatoes.
After the first 45 minutes remove the sausage, bacon and
goose from the pan and cut
them into slices or cubes. Reserve the stock. Drain the
beans.
  Fry the diced onion, celery
and tomatoes in the oil, stir in
the wine and then stir the mixture into the beans. Fill an
ovenproof dish with alternate
layers of beans, goose, sausage
and bacon, pour on the stock
and bake in a hot oven (220 C,
425 F, gas 7) for 1¼ hours.
Serves 8

Hunter's Casserole

450 g / 1 lb game
50 g / 2 oz rindless streaky bacon
225 g / 8 oz onions
450 g / 1 lb chanterelles
450 g / 1 lb potatoes
225 g / 8 oz carrots
25 g / 1 oz butter
salt and freshly milled white
  pepper
250 ml / 8 fl oz meat stock

420 calories per serving

Remove all skin and gristle
from the meat and cut the meat
into fairly large cubes. Finely
chop the bacon and onion.
Trim and wash the chanterelles,
cut larger ones in half and leave
smaller ones whole. Peel and
slice the potatoes and carrots.
  Melt the butter in a fireproof
casserole, add and fry the ba-

con until crisp. Add the meat
and onion and brown, stirring
frequently. Season to taste,
then add the chanterelles, potatoes, carrots and stock. Cover
and cook for 1 hour.

Serve with: cranberry sauce.

Cook's tip

If chanterelles are out of
season or too expen-
sive, replace them with
flat mushrooms or
mixed wild mushrooms.

Lentil Casserole with Dumplings

450 g / 1 lb lentils
1 bouquet garni
1 onion
2 cloves
4 soup bones, washed
salt

For the dumplings:
150 g / 5 oz semolina
375 ml / 13 fl oz milk
salt
pinch of grated nutmeg
2 eggs

To complete the casserole:
2 tablespoons concentrated to-
* mato purée*
salt and pepper
½ teaspoon marjoram
½ teaspoon thyme
225 g / 8 oz smoked pork sausage

555 calories per serving

Soak the lentils in water for 12 hours. Wash and coarsely chop the bouquet garni. Spike the onion with the cloves.

Simmer the lentils in the soaking water with the bouquet garni, onion, bones and a generous pinch of salt for 1 hour in a covered casserole.

Simmer the semolina in the milk with a pinch each of salt and nutmeg, stirring continuously until the mixture comes away from the base of the pan. Remove the pan from the heat and beat in the eggs. Spread the dough on a wet board, cut into 5-mm / ¼-in wide strips and scrape into boiling water. Dip the knife into cold water after each cut. The dumplings are cooked when they rise to the top of the pan. Lift out.

Remove the onion and bones from the lentils. Stir in the tomato purée and seasonings. Slice the sausage and warm through in the casserole. *Serves 6*

Rice and Pork Casserole

450 g / 1 lb lean, boneless pork
1 onion
750 ml / 1¼ pints meat stock
150 g / 5 oz long-grain rice
2 tablespoons oil
1 tablespoon flour
salt and freshly milled black
* pepper*
2 cooking apples
350 g / 12 oz frozen peas
3 tablespoons chopped chives to
* garnish*

600 calories per serving

Cut the pork into fairly large cubes. Finely chop the onion. Heat the stock. Wash and drain the rice.

Heat the oil in a large, heavy based saucepan. Dip the pork in the flour, then brown the meat in the oil, add the onion and fry for a few minutes. Season to taste, add the rice and hot stock, cover the pan and simmer gently for 20 minutes.

Peel, quarter and dice the apples and stir into the casserole with the peas. Re-cover the pan and simmer for a further 10 minutes. Sprinkle with the chives. *Serves 6*

Cook's tip

If preferred, the apple and peas can be replaced with peeled, diced tomatoes and diced peppers.

Spit-Grilled Herby Chicken

1 (1.25-kg/2½-lb) oven-ready chicken
salt
a few sprigs each chives, parsley, thyme and lovage
1 stem fresh basil
1 stem fresh rosemary
1 teaspoon paprika
4 tablespoons soured cream
1 tablespoon flour
1 tablespoon oil

535 calories per serving

Rub the inside of the chicken with salt. Wash and shake dry the herbs and tie them into a bunch. Place the herbs inside the chicken and seal the opening with a wooden skewer.

Stir together the paprika, salt to taste, the soured cream, flour and oil until thoroughly mixed, then spread the purée all over the chicken. Tie the legs and wings into place with cooking thread. Skewer the chicken on the spit of the grill and secure it firmly in place.

Grill for 1 hour, turning continuously. If the chicken browns too quickly, either reduce the heat or move the chicken further away from the grill. *Serves 4*

Stuffed Chicken

1 (1.25-kg/2½-lb) oven-ready chicken
salt and freshly milled white pepper
½ teaspoon paprika
100 g/4 oz mushrooms
225 g/8 oz goose liver pâté
50 g/2 oz pistachios
½ teaspoon dried thyme
1 egg
3 tablespoons breadcrumbs
2 tablespoons melted butter

750 calories per serving

Rub the inside of the chicken with a mixture of salt, pepper and paprika. Trim and wipe the mushrooms and chop them with the pâté and pistachios. Mix these ingredients in a bowl with the thyme, egg and breadcrumbs.

Stuff the chicken with the mixture and sew up the opening with kitchen thread. Tie the legs and wings securely to the body of the chicken. Brush all over with melted butter and place the chicken breast downwards in a roasting tin.

Roast on the second shelf from the bottom of a hot oven (220 C, 425 F, gas 7) for 50 minutes. After 20 minutes turn the chicken over and brush again with butter. *Serves 4*

Chicken in Red Wine

1 (1.25-kg/2½-lb) oven-ready
  chicken
salt
½ teaspoon paprika
generous pinch of cayenne
½ clove garlic
1 tablespoon butter
3 tablespoons oil
150 ml/¼ pint hot vegetable stock
250 ml/8 fl oz dry red wine
3 tomatoes
½ teaspoon dried thyme
100 ml/4 fl oz crème fraîche

680 calories per serving

Wipe the chicken and cut it into
eight pieces, removing all visi-
ble fat. Rub in the salt, paprika
and cayenne.

Rub a large frying pan well
with the garlic, then heat the
butter and oil. Brown the
chicken pieces and then transfer
them to a large casserole.
Sprinkle on the frying juices,
add the hot stock and half the
wine, cover the casserole and
cook gently for 35 minutes.

Peel and quarter the tomatoes and remove the seeds. Ten
minutes before the end of the
cooking time add the tomatoes,
thyme and the remaining wine.

Keep 1 tablespoon of crème
fraîche to one side and stir the
rest into the sauce. Serve the
chicken garnished with the remaining crème fraîche. *Serves 4*

Serve with: mixed salad and
white bread.

Chicken with Almonds

1 (1.25-kg/2½-lb) oven-ready
  chicken
salt
1 apple
1 onion
generous pinch of ground cloves
generous pinch of ground ginger
1 tablespoon honey
50 g/2 oz butter, softened
250 ml/8 fl oz chicken stock
  1 tablespoon flaked almonds

585 calories per serving

Rub the inside of the chicken
with salt. Cut the apple into
wedges and remove the core.
Cut the onion into wedges.
Stuff the chicken with the apple
and onion and secure the opening with wooden skewers.

Work the ground cloves, ginger and honey into the soft
butter and spread the mixture
over the chicken.

Roast in a roasting tin on the
bottom shelf of a moderately
hot oven (200 C, 400 F, gas 6) for
1 hour. After 30 minutes add a
little hot stock, if necessary,
and baste the chicken with the
roasting juices. Ten minutes before the end of the cooking
time sprinkle with the almonds.

When the chicken is cooked,
turn off the oven and leave the
chicken to stand for 10 minutes
before removing it from the
oven and cutting into portions.
Serves 4

Serve with: boiled rice mixed
with 1 tablespoon of chopped,
preserved ginger and 1 tablespoon of the cooking juices.

Roast Turkey Roll

225 g/8 oz prunes
1 kg/2 lb turkey breast in one
  piece ready for rolling
salt and freshly milled white
  pepper
1 teaspoon mustard
few dashes cider vinegar
2 onions
1 clove garlic
1 tablespoon chopped lemon
  balm
4 tablespoons breadcrumbs
1 egg
3 tablespoons oil
450 ml/¾ pint boiling water
150 ml/¼ pint dry red wine
150 ml/¼ pint crème fraîche

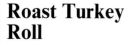

510 calories per serving

Cover the prunes with warm
water and soak them for about
4 hours. Rub one side of the
turkey breast with salt and pepper, spread with the mustard
and sprinkle with a little vinegar. Drain, stone and dice the
prunes. Finely dice the onions
and garlic and mix with the
prunes, lemon balm,
breadcrumbs and egg. Spread
the stuffing over the turkey.
Roll up the meat and secure
with cooking twine.

Heat the oil in a roasting tin
on the hob and seal the meat
roll, then transfer it to a hot
oven (220 c, 425 f, gas 7) and
roast for 30 minutes. After 10
minutes of cooking time, pour
the boiling water into the tin
and baste the meat repeatedly
with the roasting juices.

When the meat is cooked,
turn off the oven, transfer the
meat to a plate and leave in the
warm oven for 10 minutes. Stir
the wine and cream into the
roasting juices and serve with
the turkey roll. *Serves 6*

Turkey Schnitzel with Almonds

4 (175-g/6-oz) slices turkey
freshly milled white pepper
2 tablespoons flour
salt
1 teaspoon paprika
50 g/2 oz butter
100 g/4 oz flaked almonds
2 canned peach halves

570 calories per serving

Remove any skin from the turkey. Rub each slice with pepper. Season the flour with salt
and paprika and coat the turkey slices with the mixture,
shaking off any excess flour.

Heat half the butter in a
large frying pan and fry the turkey for 1 minute each side. Remove the meat from the pan
and dip in the almonds, pressing the almonds on firmly.

Add the remaining butter to
the pan, return the turkey to
the pan and fry each side for a
further 3–4 minutes, then transfer the meat to a warm plate
and keep it hot.

Drain and slice the peaches,
warm them through in the pan
and serve with the turkey.

Serve with: French bread and a
green salad.

Roast Pheasant

225 g/8 oz carrots
100 g/4 oz leeks
2 (800-g/1¾-lb) oven-ready
   pheasants
salt and freshly milled white
   pepper
juice of 1 lemon
8 thin, rindless rashers streaky
   bacon
150 ml/¼ pint game stock
150 ml/¼ pint soured cream
150 ml/¼ pint dry white wine
5 tablespoons cranberry sauce

530 calories per serving

Trim or peel and wash the carrots and leeks and cut them into thin slices. Rub the pheasant inside with salt and pepper and sprinkle outside with lemon juice. To truss the pheasant: thread a trussing needle with cooking thread and take it through both wings, then through the legs and tie firmly so that the legs and wings lie close to the breast. Cover the back, breast and legs of each pheasant with 1 rasher of bacon each and secure in place with thread.

Place the pheasant on their sides in a roasting tin. Wash the livers and keep them to one side. Roast the pheasant on the second shelf from the bottom of a hot oven (220 C, 425 F, gas 7) for 40–50 minutes.

Heat the stock and add it to the tin with the vegetables after the first 10 minutes of the cooking time. Baste the pheasant every 10 minutes, adding a little hot water each time, and turning on to the other side each time, before finally turning the pheasant breast uppermost.

About 10 minutes before the end of the cooking time, remove the bacon and return the pheasant to the tin. Coat the pheasant in soured cream (keeping 1 tablespoon in reserve) and brown well.

After 40 minutes, test to see if the pheasant are cooked: if the meat springs back into shape when pressed with your finger it is cooked but still pink and juicy inside.

Transfer the pheasant to a warm plate, turn off the oven and leave the meat to stand in the oven for 15 minutes with the door slightly ajar. Add the bacon to the plate with the pheasant. Remove the trussing thread.

Dilute the roasting juices with little hot water, strain into a saucepan, reserving the vegetables to serve with the pheasant, and stir in the wine. If you have the pheasant livers, chop them into small pieces, crush with a fork and stir into the sauce, cook for a few minutes, then stir in the remaining soured cream. Season the sauce liberally with salt and pepper and serve separately with the pheasant. Serve with cranberry sauce. *Serves 4*

Duck with Red Cabbage

1 (2-kg/4½-lb) young duck
salt and freshly milled white
*   pepper*
2 large apples
100 g/4 oz fresh figs
1 teaspoon curry powder
1 tablespoon finely chopped
*   butter*
3 tablespoons oil
250 ml/8 fl oz hot water

690 calories per serving

Rub the inside of the duck with
a mixture of salt and pepper.
Wash the apples and figs thoroughly and wipe them dry.
Peel, quarter, core and thickly
slice the apples. Cut the stalks
off the figs and dice. Season the
apple and figs with the curry
powder and salt and pepper
and use the mixture to stuff the
duck, together with the butter.
Using cooking thread, sew up
the opening and secure the legs
and wings to the body of the
duck.

Heat the oil in a large roasting tin on the hob and brown
the duck all over; this should
take about 15 minutes. Then,
with the duck standing breast
downwards, transfer the tin to
the oven and roast in a moderately hot oven (200 c, 400 f, gas
6) for about 40 minutes. Then
turn the duck over, pour the
hot water into the tin and roast
the duck for a further 1 hour,
until cooked.

Baste the duck repeatedly
throughout the roasting time,
adding more hot water as and
when necessary. *Serves 8*

Serve with: braised red cabbage, boiled potatoes, and apple sauce, flavoured with a little
white wine and lemon juice.

Roast Wild Duck

2 cooking apples
2 onions
1 (1.5-kg/3-lb) oven-ready wild
    duck
salt and freshly milled white
    pepper
3 tablespoons oil
100 g/4 oz thin, rindless rashers
    streaky bacon
4 juniper berries, crushed
250 ml/8 fl oz hot meat or game
    stock
250 ml/¼ pint dry red wine
1 teaspoon cornflour
2 tablespoons single cream

525 calories per serving

Peel the apples, cut them into
wedges, core and cut each
wedge in half again. Cut the
onions into wedges. Rub the inside of the duck with salt and
pepper.
    Heat the oil in a roasting tin

on the hob, brown the duck
and cover it with bacon. Add
the apple, onion and juniper
berries and 150 ml/¼ pint of the
stock. Roast the duck on the
bottom shelf of a hot oven
(220 C, 425 F, gas 7) for 1 hour,
basting repeatedly and adding
more hot stock as and when
required.
    When cooked, turn off the
oven, transfer the duck to a
plate and leave it to stand in
the oven. Dilute the juices in
the tin with a little hot water,
strain into a saucepan and stir
in the wine. Stir the cornflour
into the cream and use to thick-
en the sauce.
Serves 6

Stuffed Partridge

50 g/2 oz raisins
2 day-old bread rolls
2 onions
2 (450-g/1-lb) oven-ready
    partridge
salt and freshly milled white
    pepper
8 thin, rindless rashers fat bacon
150 ml/¼ pint game stock

630 calories per serving

Rinse the raisins in hot water,
then soak them in fresh hot
water. Soften the rolls in cold
water. Dice the onions. Rub the
insides of the partridge with
salt and pepper. Squeeze excess
moisture from the rolls and mix
them in a bowl with the onion
and drained raisins.
    Use the mixture to stuff the
partridge, sew up the opening
and truss. Lay 1 rasher of bacon on the back, breast and

each leg of the two partridge
and tie into place.
    Roast the partridge in a
roasting tin in a hot oven
(230 C, 450 F, gas 8) for 30–35
minutes (after 30 minutes the
meat will still be pink inside,
after 35 minutes it will be well
done). After 15 minutes of the
cooking time, turn the partridge over and add the stock.
    When cooked, remove the
bacon, transfer the partridge to
a plate, turn off the oven and
leave the partridge to stand in
the oven. Dilute the roasting
juices with a little hot water.
Serves 4

Serve with: sauerkraut mixed
with braised pears and bacon
cubes

Herby Mackerel with Apple Sauce

2 tablespoons chopped, mixed
herbs, eg parsley, chives,
thyme, rosemary, sage
25 g/1 oz soft butter
salt and freshly milled white
pepper
4 small tomatoes
2 (225-g/8-oz) smoked mackerel
1–2 teaspoons lemon juice
1 heaped tablespoon freshly
grated horseradish
150 ml/¼ pint crème fraîche
1 large apple

495 calories per serving

Wash the herbs, shake dry and
chop them coarsely. Work 1
teaspoon herbs into the butter
and season to taste. Wash the
tomatoes and wipe them dry.
Cut a deep cross at the stalk
end of each tomato and fill

with the herb butter.
    Place the mackerel on a large
piece of aluminium foil and
sprinkle them with the remaining herbs. Arrange the tomatoes alongside the fish, wrap
loosely in the foil and bake in a
moderately hot oven (200 c,
400 f, gas 6) for 15–20 minutes.
    To make the sauce, stir the
lemon juice and horseradish
into the crème fraîche. Peel the
apple and grate it into the
cream. Mix well. *Serves 2*

Serve with: French bread.

Pike Cooked in Stock

(1-kg/2-lb) prepared pike
3 litres/5 pints water
5 tablespoons wine vinegar
1 onion
1 stick celery
small sprig dill
1 bay leaf
1 teaspoon mustard seeds
½ teaspoon white peppercorns
salt
100 g/4 oz butter
1 teaspoon lime juice
2 tablespoons chopped parsley
Garnish
small sprig parsley
½ lemon, sliced

420 calories per serving

Wash the fish well in cold
water. Bring the water to the
boil with the vinegar in a large
saucepan. Quarter the onion.

Chop the celery and add it to
the boiling water with the dill,
onion, bay leaf, mustard seeds,
peppercorns and salt. Cover the
pan and simmer for 15 minutes.
    Place the whole pike in the
boiling stock and cook for 40–
45 minutes without allowing
the stock to boil.
    Melt the butter in a small
pan and stir in the lime juice
and chopped parsley. Lift the
fish from the saucepan and
transfer it to a warm plate.
Sprinkle a few drops of hot
butter over the pike and serve
the remaining butter separately.
Garnish the pike with the sprig
of parsley and lemon slices.
Serves 4

Trout with Bacon

4 (225-g/8-oz) prepared trout
juice of 1 lemon
salt
1 clove garlic
4 teaspoons chopped dill
4 teaspoons chopped parsley
65 g/2½ oz cream cheese
2 tablespoons milk
100 g/4 oz thin rashers streaky
  bacon
2 shallots
25 g/1 oz butter
150 ml/¼ pint chicken stock
  3 rosemary needles, chopped

Garnish
Wedges of lemon
rosemary sprigs

490 calories per serving

Wash the trout under cold running water. Season the lemon
juice with salt and rub into
both sides of the fish. Cover the

fish and leave it to stand in the
refrigerator.

Chop the garlic very finely.
Stir together the garlic, dill,
parsley, cream cheese and milk
and spoon the mixture into the
stomach cavities of the fish.
Wrap each trout in 3 rashers of
bacon. Arrange the fish side by
side in a large oven-proof dish
and bake on the middle shelf of
a hot oven (220 C, 425 F, gas 7)
for about 30 minutes, until
cooked.

Peel and finely chop the
shallots and fry them in the
butter until transparent. Add
the chicken stock and chopped
rosemary. Simmer gently for 5
minutes. Ten minutes before
the end of the cooking time
pour the stock over the fish.

Garnish with wedges of
lemon and sprigs of rosemary.
Serves 4

Serve with: potatoes cooked in
stock and a fresh salad.

Foil-Baked Cod

800 g/1¾ lb tailpiece of cod
juice of 1 lemon
salt and freshly milled white
  pepper
1 teaspoon medium-hot mustard
100 g/4 oz spring onions
100 g/4 oz leeks
100 g/4 oz carrots
1 stem parsley
50 g/2 oz butter
50 g/2 oz thin, rindless rashers
  streaky bacon

335 calories per serving

Wash the fish in cold water, pat
dry and sprinkle inside and out
with the lemon juice. Rub in
seasoning to taste. Spread the
outside of the fish with
mustard.

Slice the onions, trim and
wash the leeks and cut them
into rings. Scrape the carrots
and cut into thin sticks. Wash,

shake dry and coarsely chop
the parsley.

Grease a large piece of aluminium foil with a little fat and
lay the fish in the centre. Spoon
half the vegetables into the
stomach cavity and sprinkle the
remainder over the fish with the
parsley. Dot the vegetables
with butter and top with the
bacon.

Fold the foil loosely over the
fish, place in an ovenproof dish
and bake in a hot oven (220 C,
425 F, gas 7) for 40 minutes, until the fish is cooked. *Serves 4*

Serve with: parsley potatoes
and a fresh salad.

Oven-Baked Haddock

1 (1-kg/2¼-lb) tail piece of
*   haddock*
1 tablespoon lemon juice
salt and freshly milled white
*   pepper*
1 large sprig dill
100 g/4 oz streaky bacon
1 green pepper
675 g/1½ lb small potatoes
½ teaspoon paprika
150 ml/¼ pint dry white wine
4 medium tomatoes
25 g/1 oz butter

650 calories per serving

pat dry and sprinkle with the
lemon juice. Sprinkle the fish
inside and out with salt and
place the dill in the stomach
cavity.
Dice the bacon and fry until

crisp in the tin in which the fish
is to be cooked. Halve the pepper, remove core and seeds,
wash and cut into strips. Peel
the potatoes. Lay the fish along
one side of the tin and fill the
other side with the potatoes
and strips of pepper. Season the
vegetables with salt, paprika
and pepper.
Add the wine and bake on
the second shelf from the bottom of a moderately hot oven
(200 C, 400 F, gas 6) for about 45
minutes. Wash the tomatoes,
cut a cross in the top, season
with salt, dot with butter and
cook with the fish for the last
10 minutes. *Serves 4*

Plaice with Bacon

4 (225-g/8-oz) prepared plaice
4 teaspoons lemon juice
50 g/2 oz streaky bacon
4 small onions
100 g/4 oz button mushrooms
2 tablespoons chopped parsley
salt and freshly milled white
*   pepper*
4 tablespoons plain flour
100 g/4 oz butter

570 calories per serving

Wash the plaice thoroughly
under cold running water, pat
dry and sprinkle with lemon
juice. Finely dice the bacon.
Dice the onions. Trim, wash,
drain and chop the
mushrooms.
Fry the bacon until crisp in a
small frying pan, add the onion
and fry until golden brown. Stir
in the mushrooms and parsley,
season with pepper and keep

hot on a low heat.
Season the plaice with salt,
dip in flour and shake off any
excess. Melt 25 g/1 oz butter in
a large pan for each plaice and
fry each one in turn for 4–5
minutes either side. As each
plaice is cooked transfer it to a
warm plate, top with some of
the bacon mixture and keep
warm in a very cool oven
(110 C, 225 F, gas ¼). *Serves 4*

Serve with: potato salad made
with cucumber, sweetcorn,
diced onion and dill.

Haddock with Mushrooms

800 g/1¾ lb haddock fillets
juice of 1 lemon
salt and freshly milled white
*   pepper*
50 g/2 oz rindless streaky bacon
225 g/8 oz button mushrooms
150 ml/¼ pint white wine
100 g/4 oz crème fraîche
½ teaspoon onion salt
1 tablespoon soy sauce
Garnish
1 lemon
1 tomato
sprig of parsley
1 tablespoon chopped chives

425 calories per serving

Butter an ovenproof dish.
Wash the fish, pat dry, sprinkle
with lemon juice and salt and
arrange in the dish.

Dice the bacon and fry until
crisp. Trim and wash the mushrooms, quarter or halve larger
mushrooms and spoon them
over the fish. Add the bacon
and wine.

Bake the fish on the middle
shelf of a hot oven (220 C, 425 F,
gas 7) for 15–20 minutes, then
remove from the dish and keep
the fish hot on a warm plate.
Stir the crème fraîche into the
cooking juices, season with onion salt, pepper and soy sauce
and pour the sauce over the
fish.

Garnish with lemon wedges,
sliced tomato and sprigs of
parsley and sprinkle with
chives. *Serves 4*

Serve with: parsley potatoes
and lettuce.

Hake Cutlets with Mixed Vegetables

4 hake cutlets (225-g/8-oz)
juice of 1 lemon plus ½ lemon
1 onion
600 ml/1 pint water
150 ml/¼ pint wine vinegar
salt
1 bay leaf
3 peppercorns
1 tomato
450 g/1 lb canned or frozen
*   mixed vegetables*
1 tablespoon cornflour
4 tablespoons single cream
1 tablespoon dill sprigs
1 tablespoon chopped parsley
¼ teaspoon sugar

475 calories per serving

Wash the fish and sprinkle with
lemon juice. Cut the onion into
rings and slice the ½ lemon.

Bring the water to the boil in
a saucepan, together with the
vinegar, salt, the onion rings,
lemon slices, bay leaf and
peppercorns and boil for 10
minutes. Add the fish cutlets
and cook them for about 10
minutes, reducing the heat to
prevent the stock boiling.

Peel, deseed and dice the tomato. Heat or cook the mixed
vegetables and arrange them in
a warm bowl. Lift the cutlets
out of the pan, place them on
top of the vegetables and keep
the bowl warm in a low oven.

Dissolve the cornflour in a
little water. Strain 250 ml/8 fl oz
of the fish stock into a small
saucepan, then stir in the dissolved cornflour. Bring to the
boil once. Stir in the diced tomato, cream and herbs to make
the sauce and season to taste
with a little sugar and salt.
Serves 4

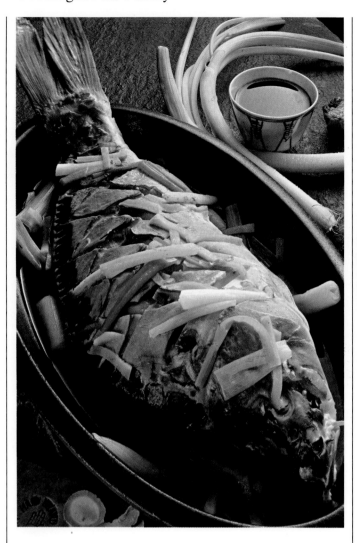

Chinese-Style Carp

1 (1-kg/2-lb) prepared golden carp or grey mullet
salt
1 tablespoon soy sauce
2 tablespoons dry sherry
2 tablespoons oil
1 teaspoon sugar
1 tablespoon fresh shredded ginger
2 spring onions with leaves

450 calories per serving

Wash the fish well inside and out in cold water and remove any large scales. Wipe the fish dry and with a sharp knife cut 5-mm/¼-in deep slits at 1-cm/½-in intervals along both sides. Season with salt inside and out and arrange the carp in an ovenproof dish.

Stir together the soy sauce,

sherry, oil and sugar and sprinkle over the fish together with the ginger. Trim and wash the onions, cut into 5-cm/2-in lengths and arrange them over the fish.

Fill a fish kettle up to the level of the perforations with water and bring it to the boil. Place the fish in the ovenproof dish on the perforated plate of the kettle, then cover and steam the fish for 15–20 minutes. Add more water if necessary.
Serves 4

Serve with: noodles and a fresh salad.

Blue Trout

4 (225-g/8-oz) trout
1 onion
1 leek
1 stick celery
2 sprigs dill and parsley
150 ml/¼ pint dry white wine
4 tablespoons wine vinegar
100 g/4 oz butter
Garnish
1 lime
½ bunch parsley

445 calories per serving

Wash the trout inside and out with cold water, taking care not to damage the outermost layer, as it is this that gives the fish its blue colour.

Cut the onion into rings. Cut the green leaves off the leek, then wash, trim and slice the white part. Trim and slice the celery. Wash the herbs in cold water and simmer them for 10

minutes in salted water with the vegetables. Add the white wine and vinegar. Place the trout in the boiling stock and reduce the heat immediately. Cook for 12 minutes.

Melt the butter and brown slightly, then keep it warm in a sauce boat to serve with the trout. Wash the lime in warm water, wipe dry and slice. Wash the parsley, pat dry and separate it into sprigs.

Drain the trout, arrange on a warm plate and garnish them with the lime slices and parsley.
Serves 4

Pickled Herrings

4 prepared fresh herrings
juice of 1–1½ lemons
salt
4 tablespoons flour for coating
6 tablespoons oil
450 ml/¾ pint mild wine vinegar
450 ml/¾ pint water
3 bay leaves
8 peppercorns
2 allspice berries
225 g/8 oz onions

315 calories per serving

Wash the herrings well inside and out in cold water and wipe dry. Sprinkle the stomach cavity with lemon juice and sprinkle the fish with salt inside and out. Leave the herrings to dry slightly, then dip them in flour.

Heat the oil and fry the herrings one after the other for 3 minutes each side, turning carefully as the herrings will break easily. Transfer them to a large shallow dish and leave to cool.

Bring the vinegar and water to the boil with the bay leaves, peppercorns and allspice. Cut the onions into rings, add to the pan and boil for 5 minutes. Leave the liquid to cool before pouring it over the herrings.

Cover the dish and leave to marinate for 24 hours in the refrigerator. *Serves 4*

Serve with: roast potatoes.

Cook's Tip

Cut into chunks or slices pickled herrings can be combined with fresh salad ingredients, gherkins and creamy dressings to make a delicious starter.

Dutch-Style Fried Herrings

4 prepared young fresh herrings
salt and freshly milled white
  pepper
4 tablespoons flour
4 tablespoons oil

280 calories per serving

Wash the herrings thoroughly inside and out in cold water and pat dry. Mix the seasoning and rub it into the herrings inside and out. Tip the flour onto a plate, dip the herrings in the flour and shake off any excess.

Heat the oil in a large frying pan and fry the herrings for 6 minutes each side until brown and crisp.

Serve with: early new potatoes with freshly chopped parsley, cauliflower with toasted breadcrumbs and a salad of young lettuce. *Serves 4*

Cod in Scallop Shells

2 litres/3½ pints water
salt and freshly milled white
  pepper
3 cloves
2 onions
575 g/1¼ lb cod fillets
2 tomatoes
100 g/4 oz button mushrooms
2 tablespoons butter
150 ml/¼ pint white wine
4 tablespoons single cream
1 tablespoon chopped fresh dill
4 tablespoons grated Parmesan
  cheese
Garnish
4 green olives
4 small sprigs fresh dill

290 calories per serving

Bring the water and a generous
pinch of salt to the boil in a
large saucepan. Stick the cloves
into one of the onions and add
it to the saucepan, together
with the fish fillets. Simmer for
10 minutes, then remove the
fish from the saucepan and set
it to one side.

Peel and dice the tomatoes.
Trim, wash and drain the
mushrooms. Finely chop the
second onion and fry it in the
butter until transparent. Add
the tomatoes and mushrooms
and fry gently for a few minutes. Flake the cod fillets into
small pieces, removing the skin
and any bones. Add to the onion, tomatoes and mushrooms.
Season to taste, then add the
wine. Cook for a few minutes,
turning occasionally until most
of the liquid has evaporated.
Stir in the cream and dill.

Spoon the mixture into four
scallop shells, sprinkle with
Parmesan and brown in a hot
oven (220 C, 425 F, gas 7). Serve
garnished with olives and sprigs
of dill. *Serves 4*

Mussels au Gratin

1 onion
1 clove garlic
2 tablespoons oil
150 ml/¼ pint white wine
2 tablespoons concentrated
  tomato purée
salt and freshly milled white
  pepper
generous pinch of cayenne
pinch of dried thyme
generous pinch of sugar
400 g/14 oz frozen mussels,
  thawed
1 tablespoon chopped parsley
4 tablespoons freshly grated
  Cheddar cheese
25 g/1 oz butter

220 calories per serving

Finely chop the onion and garlic. Heat the oil. Fry the onion
and garlic in the oil until transparent. Stir in the wine and tomato purée, season with salt,
pepper, cayenne and thyme,
and cook over a low heat for 10
minutes, stirring from time to
time. Stir in the sugar.

Spoon the tomato sauce into
four ovenproof dishes and top
with the mussels. Sprinkle the
chopped parsley and grated
Cheddar over the mussels and
dot with butter. Bake in a moderately hot oven (200 C, 400 F,
gas 6) until the cheese begins to
melt. *Serves 4*

Serve with: white bread.

Chinese-style Scampi

675 g / 1 lb 8 oz scampi
250 ml / 8 fl oz water
salt
350 g / 12 oz frozen peas
100 g / 4 oz leeks
4 tablespoons oil
generous pinch of cayenne
1 teaspoon celery salt
½ teaspoon ground ginger
1 teaspoon sugar

290 calories per serving

Cover the scampi and leave to defrost at room temperature if necessary. Then rinse the scampi under cold water and pat dry.

Bring the water to the boil with a little salt, tip in the peas, cover the pan and simmer for 6 minutes; then drain. Halve the leeks lengthways, trim, wash thoroughly, wipe dry and slice thinly.

Heat the oil in a large frying pan and fry the leek until transparent. Add the scampi and fry until golden brown all over. Stir in the peas and heat through. When well heated, season with the cayenne, celery salt, ginger and sugar and serve immediately. *Serves 4*

Serve with: French bread or cooked noodles.

Prawn Fritters

2 slices bread
4 tablespoons cold chicken stock
6 canned water chestnuts
2 eggs
450 g / 1 lb frozen peeled prawns, thawed
salt
¼ teaspoon finely chopped ginger root
2 tablespoons flour
oil for deep frying

270 calories per serving

Cut the crusts off the bread, break the bread into small pieces and moisten with the chicken stock. Finely chop the water chestnuts. Separate the eggs.

Squeeze any excess moisture from the bread and mix it with the prawns, water chestnuts, salt, ginger, flour and egg yolks. Whisk the egg whites until stiff, fold them into the prawn mixture and shape into small balls.

Heat the oil to 180 c, 350 f in a deep frying pan. Fry 6 fritters at a time, making sure that they do not touch each other. Turn occasionally for 4–5 minutes until the fritters are golden brown. Drain them on absorbent paper and keep hot until all the fritters are cooked. *Serves 4*

Prawns with Scrambled Egg

50 g/2 oz streaky bacon
1 onion
225 g/8 oz boiled potatoes
2 tablespoons oil
450 g/1 lb frozen peeled prawns,
   thawed
3 eggs
3 tablespoons cream
salt and freshly milled white
   pepper
2 tablespoons chopped dill
2 slices bread
25 g/1 oz butter

445 calories per serving

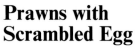
Finely dice the bacon. Dice the onion. Peel and dice the potatoes.

Heat the oil in a large frying pan, fry the bacon until crisp, add the onions and fry until transparent, then stir in the po-tato and prawns. Continue cooking, stirring frequently. Whisk the eggs with the cream, seasoning and dill.

Dice the bread and fry in the butter in a small pan until golden brown. Pour the eggs over the prawn mixture and stir gently until the egg has set. Before serving sprinkle with the croutons. *Serves 4*

Serve with: fresh green salad.

Provençal-style Scampi

675 g/1 lb 8 oz scampi
1 litre/1¾ pints water
salt and pepper
1 stem parsley
juice of ½ lemon
1½ tablespoons cognac
few dashes Worcestershire sauce
1 large onion
4 cloves garlic
1 red pepper
2 tablespoons chopped mixed
   herbs, eg. parsley, chervil,
   lovage
1 tablespoon oil
50 g/2 oz butter

200 calories per serving

Tip the scampi into a bowl, cover and leave to defrost. Bring the water to the boil with a little salt and the parsley, add the scampi and simmer for 1 minute. Lift out the scampi with a skimmer, drain, then season with the lemon juice, cognac, Worcestershire sauce and pepper. Cover and leave to marinate for 30 minutes.

Finely chop the onion and garlic. Wash and dry the pepper, cut in half, remove core and seeds and chop finely. Mix the chopped onion, pepper and garlic with the herbs and fry in the oil for 2 minutes. Stirring continuously. Salt to taste.

Heat the butter, pat the scampi dry and fry in the butter until golden brown. Serve the scampi topped with the herb mixture.

Rice with Seafood

450 g/1 lb mussels
1 litre/1¾ pints boiling water
1 onion
1 clove garlic
100 g/4 oz leeks
100 g/4 oz carrots
2 tablespoons oil
salt
225 g/8 oz rice
generous pinch of saffron
   threads
600 ml/1 pint meat stock
150 ml/¼ pint white wine
1 bay leaf
350 g/12 oz frozen scampi
100 g/4 oz canned squid
1 sprig thyme

400 calories per serving

Soak a clay casserole in cold
water for 20 minutes. Scrub the
mussels under cold running
water and discard the beards.
Tip them into the boiling water
and boil until the shells open,
then remove the mussels from
the pan. Discard any mussels
which do not open.

Finely chop the onion and
garlic. Wash and trim the leeks
and cut them into rings. Scrape
the carrots and cut them into
sticks. Braise the vegetables in
the oil for 4 minutes, then
transfer them to the clay casserole with the rice and season
with salt.

Soften the saffron in a little
cold water and add it to the
casserole with the stock and
wine. Add the bay leaf. Cover
the casserole and place it on the
bottom shelf of a cold oven.
Heat the oven to 200°C, (400F,
gas 6) and bake for 50 minutes,
until the rice is cooked. Then
arrange the scampi, pieces of
squid, the thyme and the mussels over the rice and cook for a
further 20 minutes. Stir all the
ingredients together before
serving. *Serves 4*

Prawn Fricassée

350 g/12 oz carrots
1 small onion
25 g/1 oz butter
1 teaspoon sugar
1 tablespoon flour
150 ml/¼ pint hot vegetable stock
salt and freshly milled white
   pepper
3 medium tomatoes
1 stem dill
150 ml/¼ pint cream
675 g/1½ lb frozen peeled
   prawns, thawed

400 calories per serving

Scrape and wash the carrots
and cut them into thin sticks.
Finely dice the onion.

Melt the butter in a
saucepan, stir in the sugar and
allow to caramelise. Toss the
carrot and onion in the
caramelised butter for a few
minutes, sprinkle on the flour
and cook until golden. Gradually stir in the hot stock, then
season to taste. Cover the pan
and simmer for 20 minutes.

Peel and dice the tomatoes,
removing the seeds. Add the
diced tomato with any juice to
the pan.

Wash the dill, shake dry and
chop it. Stir the cream into the
vegetables, add the prawns and
cook gently for 10 minutes
without allowing the fricassée
to boil. Stir in the dill. *Serves 4*

Ham and Pasta Bake

400 g/14 oz flour
3 eggs
salt and freshly milled white
  pepper
3 litres/5 pints water
75 g/3 oz butter
225 g/8 oz lean cooked ham
2 eggs
150 ml/¼ pint soured cream
2 tablespoons breadcrumbs

575 calories per serving

Work the flour, eggs and a pinch of salt with a little water to make a smooth, firm dough

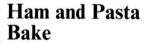

Roll out the dough very thinly. Leave the dough to dry slightly, then cut it into 1½-cm/¾-in squares.

Bring the water and a little salt to the boil in a large

saucepan, add and cook the pasta squares for about 5 minutes until still fairly firm. Rinse the pasta in cold water and drain.

Melt 50 g/2 oz butter in a large frying pan and coat the pasta in butter. Dice the ham. Separate the eggs, then beat the yolks with the soured cream and season with salt and pepper. Stir the diced ham into the mixture. Whisk the whites until stiff and fold them into the yolk mixture. Fold the mixture into the pasta.

Grease an ovenproof dish with butter, fill with the pasta mixture, then cover with the breadcrumbs and dot with the remaining butter.

Bake in a moderately hot oven (200c, 400f, gas 6) for 30 minutes. *Serves 6*

Macaroni Bake

225 g/8 oz macaroni
450 g/1 lb pork fillet
1 onion
1 clove garlic
3 tablespoons oil
250 ml/8 fl oz hot meat stock
1 tablespoon chopped mixed
  herbs
salt
4 tomatoes
225 g/8 oz courgettes
generous pinch of dried thyme
100 g/4 oz Emmental cheese,
  grated
1 tablespoon chopped parsley to
  garnish

440 calories per serving

Cook the macaroni according to the manufacturer's instructions, then rinse in cold water and drain.

Finely chop the pork, onion and garlic. Heat 2 tablespoons

of the oil in a large frying pan, add and fry the onion and garlic until transparent, then add and brown the pork. Pour in the stock and simmer for 6 minutes. Add the herbs and salt to taste.

Peel and dice the tomatoes. Wash and slice the courgettes. Heat the remaining oil in a frying pan and fry the courgettes lightly on each side. Season with a pinch of salt and the thyme.

Drain the oil from the courgettes into an ovenproof dish and fill with alternate layers of macaroni, meat, tomato and courgette, finishing with a layer of macaroni. Sprinkle with the cheese.

Bake in a moderately hot oven (200c, 400f, gas 6) for 20 minutes and serve sprinkled with parsley. *Serves 6*

Pastizio

225 g/8 oz macaroni
50 g/2 oz butter
1 egg white
4 tablespoons grated Parmesan
  cheese
2 heaped tablespoons
  breadcrumbs
1 small onion
225 g/8 oz minced pork
225 g/8 oz minced beef
salt and white pepper
1 (2.5-cm/1-in) piece cinnamon
  stick
150 ml/¼ pint dry white wine
2 tablespoons concentrated
  tomato purée
150 ml/¼ pint meat stock

For the sauce:
50 g/2 oz butter
3 tablespoons flour
450 ml/¾ pint milk
salt and white pepper
3 tablespoons grated Parmesan
  cheese

1 egg yolk
1 tablespoon single cream

For the topping:
2 tablespoons breadcrumbs
2 tablespoons grated Parmesan
  cheese
25 g/1 oz butter

600 calories per serving

Cook the macaroni according
to the manufacturer's instructions, then rinse in cold water
and drain in a sieve.

Melt half the butter in a
saucepan and coat the macaroni. Whisk the egg white until
stiff, fold in half the cheese,
then stir the mixture into the
macaroni. Grease a large baking dish with butter and sprinkle with half the breadcrumbs.
Tip half the macaroni into the
dish.

Chop the onion and fry it in
the remaining butter in a large
frying pan until golden brown.

Add and fry the meat, separating it with a fork. Add salt and
pepper, the cinnamon, wine, tomato purée and stock and simmer in an open pan until you
have a thick sauce. Remove the
cinnamon. Stir the remaining
breadcrumbs and cheese into
the minced meat mixture and
spread the mixture over the
macaroni in the dish. Cover
with the remaining macaroni.

To make the sauce, melt the
butter in a saucepan, sprinkle
in the flour and stir over a low
heat until golden. Gradually
stir in the milk, season to taste
and simmer for 5 minutes, stirring continuously. Stir the
cheese into the sauce. Beat the
egg yolk with the cream, stir 2
tablespoons of hot sauce into
the egg and cream, remove the
sauce from the heat and stir the
egg and cream mixture into the
sauce. From this point on the
sauce should not be allowed to
reach boiling point.

Pour the cheese sauce over
the macaroni in the dish. Mix
the breadcrumbs with the
grated cheese, sprinkle the mixture over the sauce and dot
with the butter.

Bake on the middle shelf of a
moderately hot oven (200 C,
400 F, gas 6) for 40 minutes.
Serves 6

Serve with: tomato salad.

Lasagne

3.5 litres/6 pints water
salt and freshly milled white
  pepper
225 g/8 oz lasagne
2 onions
300 g/11 oz minced beef
300 g/11 oz minced pork
2 tablespoons olive oil
½ teaspoon dried oregano
1 teaspoon paprika
50 g/2 oz butter
2 tablespoons flour
450 ml/¾ pint milk
250 ml/8 fl oz dry white wine
100 g/4 oz grated Emmental
  cheese
50 g/2 oz Parmesan cheese,
  grated

640 calories per serving

Bring the water and a generous
pinch of salt to the boil in a
large saucepan, add the

lasagne, reduce the heat and
simmer the lasagne until
cooked, then rinse it in cold
water. Finely chop the onions.

Fry the onions in the oil with
the minced meat until the meat
turns pale brown. Season with
the oregano, paprika and a little salt.

Melt the butter in a saucepan, sprinkle in the flour and
cook until golden. Gradually
dilute with the milk and white
wine and simmer for 5 minutes,
stirring frequently. Season to
taste.

Coat the inside of an
ovenproof dish with a thin
layer of the white sauce and fill
with alternate layers of pasta
and meat, spooning a little
sauce over each layer of meat.
Pour the remaining sauce over
the top and sprinkle with the
cheese. Top with the cream.

Bake the lasagne in a moderately hot oven (200 c, 400 f, gas
6) for 40 minutes. *Serves 6*

Cannelloni

3.5 litres/6 pints water
salt and pepper
225 g/8 oz cannelloni
100 g/4 oz uncooked ham
100 g/4 oz mushrooms
1 onion
1 tablespoon olive oil
450 g/1 lb minced neck of veal
1 (397-g/14-oz) can tomatoes
2 cloves garlic
150 ml/¼ pint single cream
½ teaspoon dried basil
100 g/4 oz Emmental cheese,
  grated
50 g/2 oz butter

520 calories per serving

Bring the water and a generous
pinch of salt to the boil in a
large saucepan, add the
cannelloni and simmer vigorously for about 12 minutes,
then tip the cannelloni into a
sieve and leave it to drain.

Chop the ham, mushrooms and
onion.

Heat the oil in a large frying
pan, add and fry the minced
veal with the ham, mushrooms
and onion, stirring frequently.
Add salt to taste.

Purée the tomatoes with their
juice. Finely chop the garlic
and mix it with the tomatoes,
cream and basil. Season to
taste.

Fill the cannelloni with the
meat mixture. Coat the inside
of an ovenproof dish with the
tomato sauce, arrange the
cannelloni in the dish and cover
it with the remaining tomato
sauce. Sprinkle with the cheese
and dot with the butter.

Bake in a hot oven (220 c,
425 f, gas 7) for 30 minutes.
Serves 6

Pasta Bake with Spinach

450 g / 1 lb spinach
225 g / 8 oz tagliatelle
3.5 litres / 6 pints water
salt and freshly milled black
  pepper
generous pinch of garlic powder
100 g / 4 oz rindless rashers
  streaky bacon
2 eggs
150 ml / ¼ pint single cream
pinch of grated nutmeg
50 g / 2 oz Emmental cheese,
  grated

635 calories per serving

Sort and wash the spinach. Place the wet spinach in a pan and cook until it becomes limp. Remove the pan from the heat.

Bring the water and a generous pinch of salt to the boil in a large saucepan, add the tagliatelle and cook for about 10 minutes. Rinse the pasta under cold water and leave it to drain.

Coarsely chop the spinach and season it with the garlic powder. Dice the bacon and fry until crisp in a frying pan. Beat the eggs with the cream and season with salt, pepper and the nutmeg.

Grease an ovenproof dish with the bacon fat from the pan, cover the base with a thin layer of pasta, add the spinach and fried bacon, then cover with the remaining noodles. Pour on the egg and cream mixture.

Bake on the middle shelf of a moderately hot oven (200 C, 400 F, gas 6) for 20 minutes. Then sprinkle with the cheese and bake for a further 10 minutes, until the cheese begins to melt. *Serves 4*

Cook's tip

If preferred, you can replace the bacon with diced sausage or ham and grease the dish with butter or margarine.

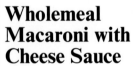

Wholemeal Macaroni with Cheese Sauce

3.5 litres/6 pints water
salt and freshly milled white
    pepper
3 tablespoons oil
350 g/12 oz short wholemeal
    macaroni
225 g/8 oz leeks
225 g/8 oz curd cheese
100 g/4 oz Parmesan or pecorino
    cheese
150 ml/¼ pint crème fraîche
generous pinch of ground ginger
1 tablespoon finely chopped
    fresh sage or 1 tablespoon
    chopped parsley to garnish

630 calories per serving

Bring the water to the boil with
a generous sprinkling of salt
and 2 drops of oil. Tip the mac-

aroni into the boiling water,
cook for 15 minutes and drain
in a sieve.

Use only the white of the
leeks. Halve the leeks lengthways, wash well and slice them.
Braise the leeks in 1 tablespoon
of the oil and sufficient water
to cover for 10 minutes.

Spoon the curd cheese into a
small saucepan, grate in the
hard cheese and stir in the
crème fraîche. Season with the
ginger and with salt and pepper. Warm the sauce through
over a low heat and stir it into
the leeks.

Heat the drained macaroni in
the remaining oil in a large
frying pan, stirring frequently.
Transfer the macaroni to a hot
serving dish and top with the
cheese and leek sauce.

Sprinkle the sage or parsley
over the sauce. *Serves 4*

Serve with: fresh mixed salad.

Wholemeal Macaroni with Tomato Sauce

3.5 litres/6 pints water plus
    250 ml/8 fl oz
salt and freshly milled white
    pepper
350 g/12 oz wholemeal macaroni
1 kg/2 lb tomatoes
2 onions
1 clove garlic
2 tablespoons oil
few drops maple syrup
4 tablespoons single cream
1 tablespoon chopped fresh basil
    to garnish

490 calories per serving

Bring the 3.5 litres/6 pints
water to the boil with a generous sprinkling of salt, tip in the
macaroni, boil for 15 minutes
and drain in a sieve. Wash and

chop the tomatoes and braise
them in the 250 ml/8 fl oz water
in a covered pan for about 10
minutes. Chop the onions and
garlic very finely.

Heat the oil in a large
saucepan and fry the onion and
garlic until transparent, stirring
continuously. Tip the tomatoes
and their juice into a sieve over
the pan and strain them into
the onion and garlic mixture.

Season the sauce with salt
and pepper and boil for a few
minutes, stirring continuously.
Season to taste with maple syrup and add a little more salt if
required. Stir in the cream.

Stir the drained macaroni
into the sauce and warm
through over a very low heat.
Before serving, sprinkle with
the chopped basil. *Serves 4*

Macaroni with Basil Sauce

1 tablespoon pine kernels
1 clove garlic
1 large bunch fresh basil
salt
100 g/4 oz Pecorino cheese
generous pinch of cayenne
6 tablespoons olive oil
3.5 litres/6 pints water
350 g/12 oz macaroni
4 tablespoons meat stock

480 calories per serving

Finely chop the pine kernels and garlic. Wash, shake dry and finely chop the basil. Then pound the basil in a mortar (or purée in a blender) with a generous pinch of salt, the garlic, pine kernels, cheese, cayenne and olive oil.

Bring the water to the boil with a generous sprinkling of salt, add the macaroni and boil for about 16 minutes, until 'al dente' (firm when bitten). Drain, rinse and tip the macaroni into a warmed bowl.

Heat the stock, stir it into the basil sauce and pour over the macaroni. *Serves 4*

Serve with: cabbage lettuce or cos lettuce salad and thin slices of Parma ham (optional).

Italian Tomato and Garlic Sauce

2 onions
2 cloves garlic
575 g/1¼ lb canned peeled tomatoes
3 tablespoons olive oil
1 (142-g/5-oz) can concentrated tomato purée
1 teaspoon dried oregano
1 tablespoon chopped fresh basil
1 bay leaf
2 teaspoons sugar
salt and freshly milled black pepper

135 calories per serving

Finely chop the onions and garlic. Drain and chop the tomatoes, keeping the juice in reserve.

Heat the oil in a large frying pan or saucepan and fry the onion until transparent, stirring continuously. Then add the garlic and fry for 2 minutes. Stir in the tomatoes with their juice and the remaining ingredients.

Bring the sauce to the boil and simmer for 1 hour in an open pan, stirring frequently. The sauce should then resemble a thick purée. Remove the bay leaf. Season to taste. *Serves 4*

Serve with: any Italian pasta.

Cook's tip

The sauce will keep in the freezer for about a month.

Spaghetti with Vegetable Sauce

100 g/4 oz spring onions
1 clove garlic
225 g/8 oz carrots
2 tablespoons olive oil
250 ml/8 fl oz meat stock
3.5 litres/6 pints water
salt and freshly milled white
  pepper
225 g/8 oz spaghetti
350 g/12 oz mushrooms
4 tomatoes
2 tablespoons chopped parsley to
  garnish

355 calories per serving

Trim, wash and chop the spring onions. Finely chop the garlic. Scrape, wash and chop the carrots. Heat the oil in a large frying pan and fry the spring onion and garlic. Add the carrots and fry for a few minutes, then add the stock. Cover the pan and simmer gently for 10 minutes.

Bring the water to the boil with a generous sprinkling of salt, add the spaghetti, stir and boil for 12–13 minutes in an open pan. Drain the spaghetti.

Wipe and slice the mushrooms. Peel the tomatoes, remove the seeds, then chop. Add the mushrooms and tomatoes to the vegetable sauce and cook for 5 minutes. Season to taste.

To serve, pour the sauce over the spaghetti and sprinkle with parsley. *Serves 4*

Fusilli with Bolognese Sauce

3.5 litres/6 pints water
salt and freshly milled white
  pepper
225 g/8 oz fusilli
1 large onion
2 cloves garlic
2 tablespoons oil
450 g/1 lb minced beef
1 (397-g/14-oz) can peeled
  tomatoes
2 tablespoons concentrated
  tomato purée
2 bay leaves, crumbled
4 dried rosemary leaves
½ teaspoon dried basil
½ teaspoon dried oregano
½ teaspoon dried thyme
50 g/2 oz Parmesan, grated
50 g/2 oz butter
1 tablespoon chopped parsley to
  garnish

595 calories per serving

Bring the water to the boil with a generous sprinkling of salt, add the pasta and boil for 12–16 minutes, then drain. Finely chop the onion and garlic.

Heat the oil in a large frying pan and fry the onion and garlic until transparent. Add the minced meat to the pan and brown it lightly, stirring continuously.

Drain the tomatoes and add them to the pan with the tomato purée, crumbled bay leaves and the herbs. Season to taste. Cover the pan and simmer the sauce for 15 minutes.

Arrange the fusilli and sauce in alternate layers in an ovenproof dish, keeping a generous layer of sauce for the top. Sprinkle with the grated cheese. Cut the butter into pieces and dot over the dish.

Heat in a hot oven (220 C, 425 F, gas 7) until the cheese begins to melt and serve sprinkled with parsley. *Serves 4*

Spinach Triangles

For the dough:
400 g / 14 oz plain flour
salt
150 ml / ¼ pint lukewarm
  water
1 tablespoon wine vinegar
5 tablespoons oil

For the filling:
450 g / 1 lb spinach
1 onion
1½ day-old bread rolls
225 g / 8 oz minced meat
225 g / 8 oz sausage meat
1 tablespoon chopped parsley
2 eggs
salt and freshly milled white
  pepper

For cooking:
1.5 litres / 2¾ pints meat stock
1 tablespoon chopped chives to
  garnish

680 calories per serving

Mix the flour with a pinch of salt, the water, vinegar and oil to make a smooth, glossy dough and leave to stand under a warm bowl for 20 minutes.

Meanwhile, sort the spinach, then wash and blanch it for 3 minutes in a little salted water. Finely chop the onion. Soften the rolls in cold water. Drain and finely chop the spinach.

Squeeze excess moisture from the rolls and mix them with the minced meat and sausage meat, the onion, parsley, spinach and eggs, then season the mixture with salt and pepper.

Roll out the dough on a lightly floured work surface to a thickness of about 3 mm / ⅛ in and cut into 15-cm/6-in squares. Place 1 tablespoon of filling on each square, fold over into a triangle and press the edges together using a fork.

Bring the stock to the boil in a large saucepan and cook the triangles in the open pan for about 10 minutes, until they rise to the surface. Serve in stock, sprinkled with the chives. *Serves 6*

Cook's tip

The triangles can be served with plenty of onion rings, fried until golden brown, and without the stock. To serve them in this way, drain off the stock, dip in beaten egg and fry them in oil until golden brown. Sprinkle with chopped chives and serve with a fresh salad.

Dutch Rice Speciality

350 g/12 oz lean, boneless pork
50 g/2 oz celeriac
1 leek
100 g/4 oz white cabbage
4 tablespoons olive oil
300 ml/½ pint meat stock
225 g/8 oz long-grain rice
salt
1 tablespoon cornflour
½ tablespoon castor sugar
½ teaspoon ground ginger
dash of wine vinegar
50 g/2 oz flaked almonds

685 calories per serving

Dice the meat. Peel and dice the celeriac. Trim and halve the leek and wash it thoroughly under cold running water, then cut into slices. Shred the cabbage.

Heat the oil in a large saucepan, brown the pork, then add the vegetables and stock, cover the pan and simmer gently for 30 minutes.

Meanwhile, wash the rice and boil it in a covered saucepan of salted water for 20–25 minutes until fluffy.

Dissolve the cornflour, sugar, ginger and a generous pinch of salt in the wine vinegar and a little water. Use the mixture to thicken the stock and bring to the boil. Stir in the almonds.

Transfer the rice to a serving dish and top with the meat sauce. *Serves 4*

Cook's tip

If liked, add peeled, diced tomatoes to the sauce 10 minutes before the end of the cooking time.

Wild Rice with Chicken

225 g/8 oz wild rice
salt and freshly milled white
    pepper
575 g/1¼ lb boned, skinned
    chicken, cooked
1 small fennel bulb
2 tablespoons oil
350 g/12 oz frozen peas
150 ml/¼ pint chicken stock
1 tablespoon chopped dill to
    garnish

530 calories per serving

Wash the rice thoroughly and
boil it in a covered saucepan of
salted water for 40 minutes.
Cut the chicken into small,
equal pieces. Peel and chop the
fennel. Chop the leaves and
keep them to one side. Rinse
the cooked rice with cold water
and drain.

Heat the oil in a large
saucepan and fry the chicken
and chopped fennel in it, stirring from time to time. Add the
peas and stock and bring to the
boil. Stir in the rice and season
to taste, cover the pan and simmer gently for 10 minutes.
    Garnish with dill and fennel
leaves. *Serves 4*

Cook's tip

Instead of chicken you
can use any leftover
roast meat.

Tomato Rice with Garlic

225 g/8 oz wild rice
salt
2 onions
2 cloves garlic
1 small leek
4 beef tomatoes
2 tablespoons oil
1 (150-g/5-oz) can concentrated
    tomato purée
150 ml/¼ pint vegetable stock
1 teaspoon paprika
2 tablespoons chopped parsley to
    garnish

290 calories per serving

Wash the rice and boil in a
covered pan of salted water for
40 minutes. Rinse in cold water
and leave the rice to drain.
    Finely chop the onions and
garlic. Trim, wash and slice the
leek. Peel and halve the tomatoes, remove cores and seeds,
then dice the tomatoes.
    Heat the oil in a large
saucepan and fry the onion and
garlic, stirring frequently, add
the leek, fry for a few minutes,
then stir in the tomato purée.
Add the stock and tomato. Stir
in the rice and season with salt
and the paprika.
    Cover the pan and simmer
gently for 10 minutes. Before
serving sprinkle with chopped
parsley. *Serves 4*

Serve with: green salad or endive salad.

Pepper Risotto

350 g / 12 oz rice
1 onion
1 red pepper
1 green pepper
2 tablespoons olive oil
450 ml / ¾ pint dry white wine
450 ml / ¾ pint vegetable stock
salt and freshly milled white
   pepper
pinch of grated nutmeg
100 g / 4 oz Emmental cheese,
   grated

525 calories per serving

Wash the rice in a sieve under
cold running water until the
water runs clear. Drain the rice
and pat it dry in a tea towel.
Finely chop the onion. Halve
and deseed the peppers, wash,
dry and cut into squares.

   Heat the oil in a large
saucepan and fry the onion and
rice until transparent, stirring

continuously. Add the peppers
and fry for a few minutes, then
stir in the wine and stock and
season with salt, pepper and the
nutmeg. Cover the pan and
simmer gently for 20–25
minutes.

   Stir in the grated cheese before serving, reserving a little to
sprinkle on top. *Serves 4*

Mushroom Rice

275 g / 10 oz long-grain rice
450 g / 1 lb button mushrooms
50 g / 2 oz butter
1 teaspoon lemon juice
½ teaspoon grated lemon rind
salt and freshly milled white
   pepper
900 ml / 1½ pints water
4 tablespoons grated Emmental
   cheese
2 tablespoons chopped parsley to
   garnish

410 calories per serving

Wash the rice in a sieve under
cold water until the water runs
clear, then drain and pat dry in
a tea-towel. Wipe and cut the
mushrooms into very thin
slices.

   Melt the butter in a large
saucepan and fry the mushrooms. Add the lemon juice
and rind, seasoning to taste and

the rice and cook for a few minutes. Add the water, bring to
the boil, cover and simmer for
20–25 minutes.

   Stir the cheese into the
cooked rice and sprinkle with
parsley. *Serves 4*

Serve with: fresh mixed salad.

Cook's tip

In summer you may pre-
fer to replace the button
mushrooms with fresh,
mixed wild mushrooms.

Vegetable Rice with Ham

1 kg/2 lb leeks
175 g/6 oz rice
25 g/1 oz butter
450 ml/¾ pint meat stock
salt and freshly milled white
  pepper
pinch of dried thyme
225 g/8 oz lean cooked ham
225 g/8 oz tomatoes
2 tablespoons chopped parsley to
  garnish

440 calories per serving

Cut off the roots from the leeks and remove any damaged outer leaves and the dark green leaves. Halve thick leeks lengthways, then wash the leeks thoroughly, drain and cut them into slices. Wash the rice in a sieve under cold running water until the water runs clear, then pat

dry in a tea-towel.

Heat the butter in a large saucepan and fry the rice until transparent, stirring continuously. Add the leek and fry for a few minutes, then pour in the stock. Season with salt and pepper and the thyme, bring to the boil and simmer gently for 20–25 minutes, adding a little hot water as and when necessary.

Dice the ham. Peel, chop and deseed the tomatoes. Ten minutes before the end of the cooking time, lightly fold the ham and tomato into the rice. Sprinkle with chopped parsley before serving. *Serves 4*

Curried Rice with Bananas in Ham

225 g/8 oz long-grain rice
300 ml/½ pint vegetable stock
1–2 tablespoons curry powder
50 g/2 oz raisins
6 tablespoons orange juice
2 bananas
25 g/1 oz butter
225 g/8 oz lean boiled ham cut
  into 4 slices
salt and freshly milled white
  pepper
1 tablespoon chopped parsley to
  garnish

430 calories per serving

Wash the rice in a sieve under cold running water until the water runs clear. Bring the stock to the boil in a saucepan. Tip the rice into the stock with 1 tablespoon of the curry powder, bring to the boil, cover,

then simmer gently for 20–25 minutes. Wash the raisins in hot water, drain and soak them in the orange juice. Halve the bananas, lengthways.

Melt the butter in a frying pan. Brown the bananas on each side then roll each half in a slice of ham and secure with a cocktail stick. Return the banana rolls to the pan and fry gently for 5 minutes, turning frequently. Stir the raisins and orange juice into the curried rice.

Season the rice with curry powder, salt and pepper, serve with the banana rolls on top and garnish with the chopped parsley. *Serves 4*

Serve with: chicory salad.

Creamed French Beans

800 g/1¾ lb French beans
salt and freshly milled white
    pepper
bean leaves, if available
1 large onion
25 g/1 oz butter
150 ml/¼ pint crème fraîche
Garnish
2 tablespoons chopped fresh dill
2 tablespoons chopped parsley

180 calories per serving

Top and tail the beans and remove any stringy threads.
Wash the beans in cold water,
drain and halve larger beans.
    Bring sufficient water to cov-
er the beans to the boil with a
little salt. Tip the beans and
leaves into the boiling water,
cover the saucepan and simmer
for 10–15 minutes.

Finely dice the onion. Melt
the butter in a large frying pan
and cook the onion until transparent. Drain the beans in a
sieve and add them to the onion. Stir in the crème fraîche,
reheat over a low heat and season to taste. Serve sprinkled
with chopped dill and parsley.
Serves 4

Cauliflower in Herb Sauce

1 (about 800-g/1¾-lb)
    cauliflower
salt
1 litre/1¾ pints water
juice of 1 lemon
1 vegetable stock cube
50 g/2 oz butter
2 tablespoons flour
4 tablespoons single cream
4 tablespoons chopped parsley
1 tablespoon chopped basil
1 teaspoon chopped borage
1 teaspoon chopped lemon balm

200 calories per serving

Remove the thick stalk and
outer leaves from the cauliflower. Soak the cauliflower
upside down in cold salted
water for 30 minutes to make
sure you get rid of any insects.
    Bring the water to the boil

with the lemon juice and boil
the cauliflower for 10 minutes.
Lift the cauliflower out of the
water and keep it hot. Measure
off 450 ml/¾ pint of the cooking
water and dissolve the stock
cube in it.
    Melt the butter in a pan,
sprinkle in the flour, stir until
golden and then gradually
dilute with the hot stock. Stir in
the cream and season with salt.
Stir in the herbs and pour the
sauce over the cauliflower.
Serves 4

Serve with: grilled chicken or
bacon, or to accompany a vegetarian main dish.

Cauliflower with Cheese Sauce

1 (800-g/1¾-lb) cauliflower
2 litres/3½ pints water
1 tablespoon lemon juice
100 g/4 oz Cheddar cheese
50 g/2 oz butter
1 tablespoon flour
150 ml/¼ pint vegetable stock
150 ml/¼ pint milk
salt
generous pinch of grated nutmeg
1 egg yolk
2 tablespoons breadcrumbs
1 tablespoon chopped parsley

290 calories per serving

Separate the cauliflower into florets and wash thoroughly. Bring the water to the boil with the lemon juice, tip in the cauliflower, cover the pan and boil for about 15 minutes. Drain the cauliflower through a sieve and keep it warm over the boiling water. Grate the cheese.

Melt half the butter in a saucepan, sprinkle in the flour and stir until golden. Gradually stir in the stock and bring to the boil. Whisk in the milk, add the salt, nutmeg and cheese and simmer for 8 minutes, stirring frequently.

Whisk the egg yolk in a bowl and stir in 2–3 tablespoons of the hot sauce, then stir the mixture back into the sauce.

Melt the remaining butter in a small frying pan and fry the breadcrumbs until golden brown. Sprinkle the cauliflower with the breadcrumbs and parsley and serve with the cheese sauce. *Serves 4*

Ratatouille

1 red pepper
1 green pepper
1 yellow pepper
1 courgette
2 onions
3 cloves garlic
450 lb/1 lb aubergines
6 tablespoons olive oil
salt
½ teaspoon dried rosemary
1 bunch herbs (fresh thyme and basil)
150 ml/¼ pint water
2 beef tomatoes or 450 g/1 lb small tomatoes
1 tablespoon chopped parsley

260 calories per serving

Halve and deseed the peppers, wash and cut into strips. Slice the washed courgette and the onions. Finely chop the garlic. Wash, dry and dice the aubergines.

Heat the oil in a large casserole and fry the onion until transparent. Add the peppers and fry them for a few minutes, then stir in the aubergines and sprinkle with salt. Top with the courgette slices, sprinkle with salt and the garlic. Add the rosemary, the bunch of herbs and the water. Braise the vegetables for 25 minutes.

Meanwhile scald the tomatoes, peel, cut into wedges, deseed and add them to the pan 10 minutes before the end of the cooking time. Before serving, sprinkle the ratatouille with the parsley. *Serves 4*

Serve with: sautéed chicken breasts and wholemeal bread.

White Cabbage au Gratin

1 kg / 2¼ lb white cabbage
2 litres / 3 pints water
salt
25 g / 1 oz lard or clarified butter
2 teaspoons caraway seeds
4 tablespoons vegetable or meat
*   stock*
5 tablespoons soured cream
50 g / 2 oz breadcrumbs
1 tablespoon butter

165 calories per serving

Remove the outer damaged
leaves from the cabbage, cut off
the stalk and cut the cabbage
 **Bring the**
water to the boil with a little
salt in a large saucepan, add the
cabbage, cover and boil for 15
minutes. Rinse the cabbage in
cold water and drain it
thoroughly.

Melt the lard in a casserole,
add and fry the cabbage all
over. Sprinkle the caraway
seeds, a pinch of salt and the
stock over the cabbage, cover
and braise over a low heat for
15 minutes.

Pour the soured cream over
the cabbage, sprinkle with the
breadcrumbs, dot with butter
and brown in a hot oven (220 C,
425 F, gas 7) for 5–8 minutes.
Serves 4

Serve with: pork chops or
boiled beef and parsley
potatoes.

Mixed Spring Vegetables

450 g / 1 lb young green peas
350 g / 12 oz baby carrots
450 g / 1 lb asparagus
100 g / 4 oz morels
salt
50 g / 2 oz butter
2–3 tablespoons water
½ teaspoon sugar
1 egg yolk
2 tablespoons single cream
1 tablespoon chopped parsley to
*   garnish*

140 calories per serving

Shell the peas. Scrub or scrape
the carrots, then wash and dice
them. Peel the asparagus and
cut off the woody ends. Cut the
ends off the morel stalks and
wash the morels well under
cold running water. Cut large
morels in halves or quarters.

Boil the asparagus in salted
water for 25–30 minutes. Melt
the butter in a large saucepan
or frying pan and fry the peas
and carrots for a few minutes.
Add the water with a little salt
and the sugar, cover the pan
and braise over a low heat for
20 minutes. After 5 minutes
add the morels.

Drain and halve the asparagus. Cover the asparagus tips
and keep them to one side.
(You can use the lower ends in
some other dish.)

Beat the egg yolk with the
cream and stir the mixture into
the vegetables with the asparagus tips. Warm through but do
not boil from now on. Serve
sprinkled with parsley. *Serves 4*

Mixed Peppers

800 g/1¾ lb yellow, green and red
peppers
2 onions
1 clove garlic
2 tablespoons oil
150 ml/¼ pint vegetable stock
salt
1 tablespoon paprika
2 tablespoons chopped parsley to
garnish

120 calories per serving

Place the peppers on a baking
tray and bake them in a very
hot oven (240c, 475f, gas 9) for
8–10 minutes.
When the skin begins to
darken take the peppers out of
the oven and wrap them in a
damp cloth for 5 minutes. Then
peel off the fine skin and cut off
the stalks. Halve the peppers
lengthways and remove the
seeds and cores. Rinse in cold
water and wipe them dry, then
cut across the peppers in thick
strips. Dice the onions. Chop
the garlic very finely.
Heat the oil in a large frying
pan or saucepan and fry the onion and garlic until transparent.
Add the peppers and fry for a
few minutes, stirring continuously. Pour in the stock, season
with salt, cover the pan and
braise the vegetables over a low
heat for 5–10 minutes. Season
to taste, stir in the paprika and
sprinkle with parsley. *Serves 4*

Kohlrabi in Herb and Cream Sauce

1 kg/2¼ lb kohlrabi
2 litres/3½ pints water
1 tablespoon lemon juice
50 g/2 oz butter
salt
generous pinch of sugar
scant 150 ml/¼ pint vegetable
stock
5 tablespoons crème fraîche
1 teaspoon chopped parsley
1 teaspoon chopped burnet
1 teaspoon chopped lovage

170 calories per serving

Wash the kohlrabi under lukewarm running water. Cut off
the tender inner leaves and
keep them to one side. Peel the
kohlrabi, remove any woody
parts, cut into quarters and
then into fairly thick sticks.
Bring the water to the boil
with the lemon juice. Place the
kohlrabi in a sieve and suspend
it in the boiling water. Blanch
the kohlrabi for 5 minutes,
rinse in cold water and drain it
thoroughly.
Melt the butter in a large
saucepan and braise the kohlrabi, stirring frequently. Add
salt to taste, the sugar and
stock and simmer for 15–20
minutes. Chop the kohlrabi
leaves and mix them into the
herbs. Stir the crème fraîche
and herbs into the kohlrabi.
Serves 4

Serve with: hamburgers and
boiled potatoes.

Spinach with Pistachios

2 tablespoons raisins
4 tablespoons apple liqueur or natural apple juice
1 kg/2¼ lb spinach
3 litres/5 pints water
salt and freshly milled white pepper
1 small onion
65 g/½ oz butter
pinch of grated nutmeg
2 tablespoons pistachios or flaked almonds

190 calories per serving

Wash the raisins thoroughly in lukewarm water, drain and soak in the apple liqueur or juice in a small basin.

Sort the spinach and wash it several times in lukewarm water. Bring the water to the boil with a pinch of salt, in the spinach. Boil for 3 minutes, drain well in a sieve and press out excess water. Finely dice the onion.

Melt 50g/2 oz of the butter in a large frying pan, fry the onions until transparent, stirring frequently, then add the spinach, loosening it with 2 forks. Add the raisins and the soaking liquid. Stir well and season with salt, pepper and nutmeg. Steam the spinach for 5 minutes.

Coarsely chop the pistachios. Heat the remaining butter, stir in the pistachios or almonds, then sprinkle them over the spinach. *Serves 4*

Serve with: pork chops or poached fish fillets and steamed potatoes.

Spinach with Garlic Cream

1 kg/2¼ lb spinach
3 litres/5 pints water
salt and freshly milled white pepper
1 onion
2 tablespoons oil
40 g/1½ oz butter
pinch of garlic powder
150 ml/¼ crème fraîche
3 cloves garlic
1 tablespoon slivered almonds

310 calories per serving

Sort the spinach and wash it several times in lukewarm water. Bring the water and a pinch of salt to the boil in a large saucepan, then tip in the spinach. Blanch the spinach for about 3 minutes, drain thoroughly in a sieve and press out excess moisture. Transfer the spinach to a board and coarsely chop it. Finely chop the onion.

Heat the oil and 25 g/1 oz of the butter in a large frying pan, stir in and fry the onion until golden. Add the spinach, cover the pan and cook over the lowest possible heat for 10 minutes. Season with salt, pepper and garlic powder.

Whip the crème fraîche in a bowl. Press the garlic cloves through a garlic press into the crème fraîche.

Melt the remaining butter in a small pan and fry the almonds, until golden brown. Pour the garlic cream on to the spinach and sprinkle with the almonds. *Serves 4*

Serve with: fish or meat dishes, or with cooked brown rice.

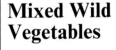

Mixed Wild Vegetables

*450 g/1 lb mixed wild green
vegetables including nettle
leaves, dandelion leaves, daisy
leaves, daisy buds, white
chard leaves, burnet, creeping
bugle, coltsfoot leaves, shep-
herd's purse, sorrel and
ribwort*
*1 handful mixed strawberry and
raspberry leaves*
250 ml/8 fl oz water
salt and pepper
5 shallots
50 g/2 oz butter
1 tablespoon flour
*250 ml/8 fl oz strong, hot vegeta-
ble stock*
150 ml/¼ pint single cream
2 egg yolks

260 calories per serving

Wash all the leaves thoroughly in cold water and remove any withered leaves. Bring the water to the boil with a little salt, add the leaves, then cover the saucepan and simmer gently for 3 minutes. Drain and coarsely chop the leaves. Peel and dice the shallots.

Melt the butter in a pan, fry the shallots until transparent, sprinkle on the flour and gradually stir in the stock. Simmer for 5 minutes.

Beat the cream in a bowl with the egg yolks and 2 table-spoons of the sauce. Remove the sauce from the heat and thicken it with the egg yolks and cream. Stir the vegetables into the sauce and season to taste. *Serves 4*

Swiss Chard with Breadcrumbs

2 litres/3½ pints water
*salt and freshly milled white
    pepper*
1 kg/2¼ lb Swiss chard
50 g/2 oz butter
100 ml/4 fl oz crème fraîche
4 tablespoons breadcrumbs

360 calories per serving

Bring the water to the boil with a little salt in a large saucepan. Wash the chard thoroughly and then drain it. Strip the leaves from the stalks and pull off the threads from the stalks from top to bottom (in the same way as peeling rhubarb). Cut the chard leaves and stalks into 4-cm/1½-in pieces, tip into the boiling salted water, cover the pan and boil for 20 minutes, then drain the chard in a sieve.

Melt half the butter, stir in the chard, season to taste and stir in the crème fraîche. Keep the chard hot in an open pan over a low heat.

Melt the remaining butter in a small saucepan, brown the breadcrumbs and sprinkle over the chard before serving.
Serves 4

Broccoli with Hazelnut Butter

1 kg/2¼ lb broccoli
1 litre/1¾ pints water
salt
2 tablespoons lemon juice
50 g/2 oz whole hazelnuts, shelled
50 g/2 oz butter

265 calories per serving

Cut the ends off the broccoli stalks and peel as far as the leaves. Cut a cross into each stalk. Wash the broccoli several times in cold water. Bring the water to the boil with a little 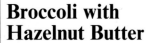 and the lemon juice and broccoli to the boiling water, cover the pan and boil for 15 minutes.

Thinly slice the hazelnuts. Slightly brown the butter in a pan, add and fry the hazelnuts until golden, then keep them to one side.

Drain the broccoli, arrange it on a hot plate and sprinkle with the hazelnut butter. *Serves 4*

Serve with: tender roasts, quick-fried meat and boiled potatoes, or as part of a vegetarian meal with a light potato soufflé.

Variation

Broccoli with Almond Sauce: beat 6 tablespoons of milk into 150 g/5 oz cream cheese. Stir in 65 g/2½ oz ground almonds, 1 egg yolk, a pinch each of salt and pepper and 150 ml/¼ pint double cream, whipped until semi-stiff. Cook the broccoli as above and serve with the almond sauce.

Fennel au Gratin

800 g/1¾ lb small fennel bulbs
50 g/2 oz butter
1 tablespoon sugar
salt
150 ml/¼ pint dry white wine
1 teaspoon lemon juice
65 g/2½ oz Cheddar cheese, diced

270 calories per serving

Cut the feathery leaves off the fennel. Wash, dry and chop the leaves and keep them to one side in a covered bowl. Trim, wash and halve the fennel bulbs.

Melt the butter in a large frying pan or saucepan and caramelise the sugar in it, stirring continuously. Add the fennel, sprinkle with salt and stir until completely covered in the caramelised sugar, then lightly brown the fennel over a moderate heat. Add the wine, reduce the heat and braise in a covered pan for 25 minutes, until tender.

Drain the fennel, reserving the cooking liquid. Stir the lemon juice and diced cheese into the cooking liquid. Arrange the fennel in an ovenproof dish, pour on the cheese sauce and brown in a hot oven (220 C, 425 F, gas 7) for 10 minutes.

Before serving, sprinkle the fennel with the chopped leaves. *Serves 4*

Beetroot

800 g/1¾ lb beetroot
1 medium onion
3 tablespoons oil
250 ml/8 fl oz meat stock
salt
3 cloves
1 teaspoon sugar
½ teaspoon cornflour
1 tablespoon wine vinegar
4 tablespoons dry red wine
3 small pickled cucumbers

190 calories per serving

Scrub the beetroot well under cold running water, then dry and peel it. Cut the beetroot into 5-mm/¼-in slices and then into 1-cm/½-in wide sticks. Chop the onion.

Heat the oil in a casserole and fry the onions until golden, stirring frequently. Add the beetroot and cook for about 10 minutes, stirring continuously.

Meanwhile, heat the stock. Pour it over the beetroot and season with salt to taste, cloves and sugar. Boil gently over a low heat for 25–30 minutes.

Stir the cornflour in a bowl with the vinegar and wine and use the mixture to thicken the vegetables. Cut the pickled cucumbers into thin strips and stir into the beetroot. Cook over the lowest possible heat for a further 3 minutes.

Before serving, adjust the sweet-sour flavour to taste.
Serves 4

Stuffed Kohlrabi

4 medium kohlrabi
salt and freshly milled white
*   pepper*
1 day-old bread roll
1 onion
350 g/12 oz minced beef
½ teaspoon paprika
1 tablespoon chopped parsley
1 egg
75 g/3 oz thin, rindless rashers
*   streaky bacon*

455 calories per serving

Peel the kohlrabi. Wash and
chop the feathery leaves and
keep them to one side in a
covered dish. Boil the kohlrabi
in salted water for 30 minutes,
then drain, reserving about 6 tablespoons of the cooking water,
and leave them to cool. Cut a
lid in the top of each kohlrabi
and spoon out the inside. Finely dice the insides.

Soften the roll in cold
water. Finely chop the onion.
Squeeze excess moisture from
the roll. Mix the minced meat
with the chopped kohlrabi, the
onion and the roll and season
with salt, pepper and paprika.
Work in the chopped kohlrabi
leaves, the parsley and the egg.

Arrange the kohlrabi in a
buttered ovenproof dish, fill
each one with the minced meat
mixture and cover the kohlrabi
with the lids. Top each kohlrabi
with 2 rashers of bacon. Pour
the reserved stock into the dish
and bake in a moderately hot
oven (200 c, 400 f, gas 6) for 25
minutes. *Serves 4*

Chicory with Ham

4 heads chicory
2 litres/3½ pints water
salt and freshly milled white
*   pepper*
50 g/2 oz butter
4 (100-g/4-oz) slices lean
*   cooked ham*
1 tablespoon flour
150 ml/¼ pint dry white wine
150 ml/¼ pint single cream
2 tablespoons breadcrumbs
1 tablespoon chopped parsley to
*   garnish*

420 calories per serving

Remove any limp outer leaves
from the chicory and cut off
some of the stalk. Bring the
water and a generous pinch of
salt to the boil in a large
saucepan, add the chicory and
simmer for 10 minutes. Drain

the chicory and leave it to one
side until cold.

Grease an ovenproof dish
with half the butter. Wrap
each chicory head in a slice of
ham and arrange in the dish.

Melt the remaining butter in
a small pan, add and cook the
flour until golden, then dilute
with the white wine and bring
to the boil, stirring continuously. Stir the cream into the
sauce, season with salt and pepper and pour the sauce over the
chicory.

Sprinkle with the bread-
crumbs and brown on the middle shelf of a moderately hot
oven (200 c, 400 f, gas 6) for
about 15 minutes. Before serving sprinkle with the chopped
parsley. *Serves 4*

Serve with: French or
wholemeal bread or parsley
potatoes.

Celery au Gratin

450 g / 1 lb celery
salt and freshly milled black
   pepper
675 g / 1½ lb marrow bones
   (optional)
1 tablespoon flour
150 ml / ¼ pint Madeira wine
6 tablespoons milk
3 tablespoons freshly grated
   cheese
50 g / 2 oz butter

345 calories per serving

Separate the celery sticks, cut
off the ends and the leaves.
Wash, dry and finely chop the
leaves and keep them to one
side in a covered dish. Wash the
celery and peel off the thick
threads (as for rhubarb). Arrange the celery sticks in a
buttered ovenproof dish, then
season to taste.

   Cover the marrow bones

with boiling water. Press the
marrow out of the bones, using
the handle of a wooden spoon
and cut it into 1-cm / ½-in slices.
Arrange the slices over the
celery.
   Stir the flour with the Madeira and milk and pour the mixture over the celery. Sprinkle
with the celery leaves and
cheese and dot with the butter.
   Bake the celery on the middle
shelf of a moderately hot oven
(200 C, 400 F, gas 6) for 40 minutes. *Serves 4*

Serve with: rye bread and
smoked ham.

Leeks au Gratin

1 kg / 2 lb leeks
2 litres / 3½ pints water
salt and freshly milled white
   pepper
generous pinch of grated nutmeg
50 g / 2 oz butter plus butter for
   greasing
50 g / 2 oz flour
250 ml / 8 fl oz milk
2 tablespoons single cream
1 tablespoon chopped parsley
100 g / 4 oz Emmental cheese,
   grated

390 calories per serving

Use only the white of the leeks
(about 575 g / 1¼ lb). You can
keep the green leaves to go in a
soup. Cut off the roots and
halve thicker leeks lengthways,
then wash the leeks thoroughly.
   Bring the water with a little
salt and the nutmeg to the boil
in a large saucepan, then add

and boil the leeks for 20 minutes. Butter an ovenproof dish.
Drain the leeks and arrange
them in the dish.
   To make the sauce, melt the
butter, sprinkle in the flour
and, stirring continuously,
cook until golden. Gradually
stir in the milk and boil up several times, stirring continuously. Finally stir in the cream
and season with salt and pepper. Pour the sauce over the
leeks, sprinkle with parsley and
cheese.
   Cook in a hot oven (220 C,
425 F, gas 7) until the cheese begins to brown. *Serves 4*

Serve with: meat loaf and parsley potatoes.

Stuffed Onions

2 large Spanish onions (675 g/
  1½ lb)
1.4 litres/2½ pints water
salt and freshly milled white
  pepper
100 g/4 oz long-grain rice
1 tablespoon butter
250 ml/8 fl oz hot meat stock
3 medium tomatoes
100 g/4 oz lean boiled ham
1 tablespoon oil
1 tablespoon chopped parsley
2 generous pinches of paprika
100 g/4 oz Cheddar cheese,
  grated
3 tablespoons milk
150 ml/¼ pint soured cream
1 tablespoon mixed fresh
  chopped herbs

480 calories per serving

Cut off the onion tops almost
one-third of the way down,
then remove the centre from
each onion. Bring the water
and a little salt to the boil in a
large saucepan, add the onion
outsides and boil them for 20
minutes.

   Wash and drain the rice, pat
dry and cook for a few minutes
in the butter. Add the stock
and simmer for 20 minutes.
Chop the onion lids and insides. Peel the tomatoes and cut
them into strips. Dice the ham.
Heat the oil in a frying pan,
add and fry the chopped onion
until transparent. Add the ham,
tomato and rice and season
with the parsley, salt, pepper
and paprika.

   Stuff the onions with the
mixture and arrange them in a
buttered ovenproof dish. Stir
the cheese with the milk and
soured cream. Season the sauce
with paprika and herbs and
pour it over the onions.

   Bake in a hot oven (220 C,
425 F, gas 7) for 15 minutes.
Serves 2

Tomatoes Stuffed with Pecorino Cheese

1 kg/2 lb medium tomatoes
salt and freshly milled white
  pepper
2 cloves garlic
450 g/1 lb pecorino cheese
6 tablespoons breadcrumbs
1 tablespoon chopped parsley
1 tablespoon chopped basil
1 tablespoon olive oil

495 calories per serving

Wash and dry the tomatoes
and cut a lid from each one.
Remove and discard the tomato centres using a teaspoon
and sprinkle inside with salt
and pepper. Finely chop the tomato lids. Finely chop the
garlic.

   Crumble the cheese in a
basin, mix with the garlic,
breadcrumbs, chopped tomato
and herbs. Fill the tomatoes
with this mixture and sprinkle
with oil.

   Grease an ovenproof dish
with butter. Arrange the tomatoes in the dish and bake them
on the middle shelf of a moderately hot oven (200 C, 400 F, gas
6) for 20 minutes. *Serves 4*

Serve with: wholemeal toast
and fresh green salad.

Lyons-Style Aubergines

4 medium aubergines
salt
3 tablespoons olive oil
2 teaspoons hot mustard
3 onions
2 cloves garlic
8 tablespoons breadcrumbs
50 g / 2 oz butter
1 stem fresh rosemary

260 calories per serving

Wash the aubergines, halve lengthways, sprinkle generously with salt and leave them to sweat for 15 minutes.

Heat 2 tablespoons of the olive oil in an ovenproof dish. Rub the salt off the aubergines and cut out two-thirds of the flesh. Fry the aubergines all over in the oil, then leave them to cool. Coat with the mustard.

Finely chop the onions, garlic and the flesh from the aubergines. Fry these ingredients in the remaining oil, season with salt and spoon the mixture into the aubergines.

Sprinkle each aubergine half with 1 tablespoon of breadcrumbs, dot with butter and sprinkle with a few rosemary leaves. Place the remaining rosemary between the aubergine halves in the dish.

Crisp up the aubergines on the middle shelf of a moderately hot oven (200 C, 400 F, gas 6) for 15 minutes. *Serves 4*

Cook's tip

As it stands, this is an excellent, flavoursome dish for those on a low fat diet, but if you prefer a main course to contain meat you can include 350 g / 12 oz of minced meat in the filling.

Stuffed Artichokes

4 artichokes
2 litres/3½ pints water
salt
2 onions
1 clove garlic
50 g/2 oz butter
350 g/12 oz frozen peeled
  prawns, thawed
4 tablespoons breadcrumbs
1 tablespoon chopped dill
5 tablespoons crème fraîche
2 tablespoons grated Parmesan
  cheese
1 tablespoon oil
150 ml/¼ pint dry white wine

Cut the stalks and about one third of the leaf tips off the artichokes. Bring the water and a little salt to the boil in a large saucepan, drop in the arti-chokes, cover and boil them for 20 minutes before draining. Push open the leaves, remove and discard the choke from the centre.

Finely chop the onions and garlic. Heat the butter in a large frying pan, add the onion and garlic and fry them until transparent. Add the prawns, breadcrumbs, salt and the dill and fry gently, stirring continu-ously. Stir the crème fraîche and Parmesan into the prawn mixture, then spoon the mix-ture into the artichokes. Grease an ovenproof dish.

Arrange the artichokes in the dish, sprinkle with the oil, pour on the white wine and bake the stuffed artichokes in a moder-ately hot oven (200C, 400F, gas 6) for 20 minutes. *Serves 4*

Corn-on-the-cob with Bacon

4 fresh corn cobs
3.5 litres/6 pints water
salt
100 g/4 oz butter
100 g/4 oz thin, rindless rashers
  streaky bacon

360 calories per serving

Strip the outer green leaves from the cobs, pull off the silky threads and shorten the stalks if necessary.

Bring the water and a little salt to the boil in a large saucepan. Add the corn cobs, cover the pan and boil for 15–20 minutes, depending on thickness. Then drain the cobs.

Melt the butter in a large frying pan and fry the cobs, turning them frequently and sprinkling with salt.

In a second frying pan, fry the bacon until crisp and golden brown, and serve it with the corn cobs. *Serves 4*

Serve with: bread.

Cook's tip

Young corn cobs do not need boiling, but can be sautéed in oil over a low heat for about 10 min-utes, until brown all over. (Simply reduce the quantity of butter and omit the bacon if on a low-fat diet. The corn cobs will still be tasty!)

Crispy Corn with Creamed Carrots

1 egg
salt
generous pinch of cayenne
8 tablespoons maize meal
1 (340-g/12-oz) can sweet corn
800 g/1¾ lb baby carrots
50 g/2 oz butter
2 teaspoons sugar
150 ml/¼ pint hot vegetable stock
150 ml/¼ pint single cream
450 ml/¾ pint oil
1 tablespoon chopped parsley
  (optional)

445 calories per serving

Beat the egg with a generous pinch of salt and the cayenne. Mix in the maize meal and leave to soak for 30 minutes. Drain the sweetcorn.

Scrape the carrots, halve thick carrots lengthways and leave thinner ones whole. Melt the butter in a saucepan and caramelise the sugar, stirring continuously. Coat the carrots in the sugar.

Add the hot stock and braise the carrots for 25 minutes. Season with salt, stir in the cream and keep the carrots hot in the covered pan.

Mix the sweet corn into the soaked maize meal. Heat the oil in a large frying pan. Drop the corn mixture 1 tablespoon at a time into the hot oil and fry for 4–5 minutes each side.

Drain on absorbent paper and keep hot.

Sprinkle the carrots with parsley and serve with the crispy corn. *Serves 4*

Braised Mushrooms

800 g / 1¾ lb small field
  mushrooms
2 medium onions
100 g / 4 oz rindless streaky
  bacon
5 tablespoons vegetable stock
salt and pepper
generous pinch of garlic powder
2 beef tomatoes
1 teaspoon flour
50 g / 2 oz butter
150 ml / ¼ pint single cream
2 teaspoons chopped thyme

390 calories per serving

Cut off any damaged parts
from the mushrooms, scrape
the caps if necessary and cut off
the stalk ends. Wash the mushrooms several times in lukewarm water and drain them.
Quarter larger mushrooms and
leave small ones whole. Finely
chop the onions and bacon.

Fry the bacon until crisp in a
large frying pan, then fry the
onions in the bacon fat until
transparent. Add the mushrooms, cook for a few minutes,
stirring continuously, then add
the stock. Season with salt,
pepper and garlic powder,
cover the pan and simmer over
a low heat for 8 minutes. Peel,
deseed and dice the tomatoes,
add them to the mushrooms
and cook for a further 5
minutes.

Work the flour into the
butter, dissolve in the mushroom mixture and simmer for a
few minutes. Stir in the cream.
Sprinkle the mushrooms with
thyme. Serves 4

Mushroom Risotto

450 g / 1 lb chanterelles, cup or
  other mushrooms
150 ml / ¼ pint vegetable stock
225 g / 8 oz round-grain rice
1 large onion
1 tablespoon oil
500 g / 17 fl oz water
4 tablespoons freshly grated
  Gruyère cheese

305 calories per serving

Remove any damaged parts
and large gills from the mushrooms. Scrape the caps and
stalks and cut off the stalk
ends. Wash the mushrooms
several times in lukewarm
water, drain and thinly slice
them.

Bring the stock to the boil in
a large saucepan. Add the
mushrooms, cover the pan and
simmer over a low heat for 10
minutes. Wash the rice well in
cold water and drain. Dice the
onion.

Heat the oil in a second large
saucepan, add and fry the onion until golden. Fry the rice
with the onions for 5 minutes,
stirring continuously, then add
the water and a generous pinch
of salt, cover the pan and cook
the rice for 20–25 minutes over
a low heat.

Drain the rice and mix it
with the mushrooms and their
cooking liquid. Serve sprinkled
with the grated Gruyère.
Serves 4

Serve with: fresh lettuce salad
and tomato wedges, or steamed
lightly seasoned courgette
slices.

Deep-Fried Oyster Mushrooms

8 oyster mushrooms
100 g/4 oz plain flour
2 eggs
2 tablespoons double cream
salt and freshly milled white
  pepper
225 g/8 oz breadcrumbs
2 tablespoons grated stale
  Gouda cheese
oil for deep frying

380 calories per serving

Cut off the tough mushroom stalks just below the cap. Remove any broken edges and dirt from the mushrooms but do not wash them.

Season with salt and dip the mushrooms into the flour. Beat the eggs with the cream and season with salt and pepper. Coat the mushrooms with the mixture.

Mix the breadcrumbs with the grated cheese and tip on to a plate. Dip the mushrooms in the breadcrumbs and press the crumbs gently on to the mushrooms.

Heat the oil to 180 C (350 F) in a large saucepan or deep-fryer. Fry the mushrooms one after the other for 2–3 minutes each side, until brown and crisp, drain on absorbent paper and keep the mushrooms hot.
Serves 4

Serve with: potato salad.

Cook's tip

When picking or buying oyster mushrooms make sure you get young mushrooms with shiny white, dry gills.

Mushrooms with Braised Onions and Tomatoes

*800 g/1¾ lb cup or button
   mushrooms*
2 large onions
4 beef tomatoes
10 black olives
3 tablespoons olive oil
*salt and freshly milled white
   pepper*
1 teaspoon chopped rosemary
*1 tablespoon chopped mixed
   herbs (parsley, chervil and
   tarragon)*

290 calories per serving

Cut any damaged parts from
the mushrooms, scrape the caps
and stems if necessary and cut
off the stalk ends. Wash in
lukewarm water and drain
thoroughly, then halve the
mushrooms or cut them into
thick slices. Cut the onions into
wedges. Peel the tomatoes and
cut them into wedges. Rinse the
olives in lukewarm water and
drain.

   Heat the oil in a large frying
pan and fry the onion until
transparent. Add the mushrooms and fry both sides, then
add the olives and tomato
wedges and season to taste.
Cover the pan and braise over a
low heat for about 10 minutes.

   Transfer the mushroom mixture to a hot plate and sprinkle
with the herbs. *Serves 4*

Serve with: boiled rice or fresh
Granary bread.

Mushroom and Potato Dish

450 g/1 lb button mushrooms
50 g/2 oz butter
salt
juice of 1 lemon
*1 quantity home-made Potato
   Purée*
pinch of grated nutmeg
*4 tablespoons freshly grated
   Emmental cheese*
150 ml/¼ pint soured cream
2 tablespoons breadcrumbs

450 calories per serving

Trim the mushrooms, cut off
the stalk ends, wash thoroughly
and drain. Melt half the butter
in a frying pan, add and lightly
fry the mushrooms. Season the
mushrooms with salt and sprinkle them with the lemon juice.
Butter an ovenproof dish.

   Season the potato purée with
a generous pinch of salt and the
nutmeg and fill the dish with
two-thirds of the potato. Arrange the mushrooms in the
centre of the dish. Pipe the remaining potato purée in whirls
around the mushrooms.

   Beat the cheese into the
soured cream and pour the
mixture over the mushrooms.
Sprinkle with breadcrumbs and
dot with the remaining butter.

   Brown in a hot oven (220 c,
425 F, gas 7) for about 20 minutes. *Serves 4*

Health tip

Substitute sunflower or
corn oil for the butter
and natural yogurt for
the cream. For a sub-
stantial, interesting
meal, add mashed car-
rots, parsnips and
celeriac to the potatoes.

Viennese Potatoes

*675 g/1½ lb leftover boiled
  potatoes*
100 g/4 oz leeks
225 g/8 oz veal escalope
50 g/2 oz butter
*salt and freshly milled white
  pepper*
1 teaspoon dried marjoram
150 ml/¼ pint hot milk
150 ml/¼ pint hot meat stock

310 calories per serving

Dice the potatoes. Trim and
wash the leeks and cut them
into fine strips. Wash and dry
the veal. Heat half the butter in
a frying pan and brown the
veal, then remove it from the
pan, leave to cool slightly and
cut into small cubes.

Melt the remaining butter in
a fireproof casserole, add and
fry the leek, stirring frequently.
Mix the potatoes with the veal,

season to taste and add to the
leek. Sprinkle with the marjoram. Pour the milk and stock
over the potatoes.

Bake on the second shelf
from the bottom of a hot oven
(220 C, 425 F, gas 7) for 15 minutes. *Serves 4*

Serve with: buttered seasonal
vegetables.

Potato Cake with Soured Cream

1 kg/2 lb floury potatoes
5 eggs
salt
175 g/6 oz flour
150 ml/¼ pint soured cream
1 piece bacon rind

525 calories per serving

Peel and wash the potatoes and
grate them into a bowl of
water. Transfer to a sieve and
drain out excess moisture over
a bowl. Leave the water that
collects in the bowl to stand until the potato flour settles on
the bottom. Pour off the water
and add the potato flour to the
potatoes.

Beat the eggs with salt to
taste and pour over the potatoes with the flour and the
soured cream. Work all the in-

gredients together into a
smooth dough.

Rub a large, heavy frying
pan with the bacon rind and
heat through. Fill the pan with
the potato dough, flatten into a
cake and fry until the underside
is brown and crisp. Using a pan
lid to help you, turn the potato
cake and fry it until the second
side is brown and crisp. Cut
like a cake to serve. *Serves 4*

Serve with: mixed salad or
vegetables.

107

Potato Cake

675 g/1½ lb leftover boiled
*   potatoes*
1 onion
salt and freshly milled white
*   pepper*
75 g/3 oz butter

325 calories per serving

Coarsely grate the potatoes
into a bowl. Wash, drain and
dry the potatoes on a clean tea-
towel. Grate the onion and stir
it gently into the potato with
seasoning to taste.

Melt half the butter in a
frying pan, tip the potatoes into
the pan and flatten them firmly
into a cake. Cook the potatoes
fairly gently until the underside
is brown and crisp.

Using a plate or pan lid to
help you, carefully turn the potato cake, adding and heating
the remaining butter before

sliding the cake back into the
pan. Continue cooking the potato cake until the second side
is brown and crisp and the potatoes are cooked through.
Serve cut into wedges. *Serves 4*

Cook's tip

For a filling main
course, add crisp-fried
bacon to the potato cake
and serve with a fresh
mixed salad.

Dauphinoise
Potatoes

450 g/1 lb floury potatoes
salt
generous pinch of grated nutmeg
2 tablespoons butter
choux pastry:
250 ml/8 fl oz water
50 g/2 oz butter
salt
150 g/5 oz flour
4 eggs
oil for deep frying

635 calories per serving

Peel and wash the potatoes and
boil them in a saucepan of
salted water for 30 minutes until nice and soft. Evaporate excess moisture, mash the
potatoes and mix in salt, the
nutmeg and butter.

To make the pastry, bring
the water to the boil in a

saucepan, dissolve the butter
and a pinch of salt in the water
and remove the pan from the
heat. Tip all the flour into the
boiling water at one go and
beat to give a smooth dough.
Return the pan to the heat and
stir until the mixture forms a
ball. Remove the pan from the
heat and beat in the eggs, one
after the other.

Mix the potato into the
choux pastry and with floured
hands shape the mixture into
walnut-sized balls.

Heat the oil in a large
saucepan or deep-fryer to 180 C
(350 F) and fry the potato balls
in batches until golden brown.
Serves 6

Serve with: roast meat or game
birds.

Béchamel Potatoes

800 g/1¾ lb potatoes
salt and freshly milled white
* pepper*
50 g/2 oz butter
1 tablespoon flour
450 g/¾ pint hot milk
150 ml/¼ pint cream
pinch of grated nutmeg
1 teaspoon lemon juice
pinch of sugar
2 tablespoons chopped parsley to
* garnish*

385 calories per serving

Wash the potatoes, drop them
into a saucepan of boiling
salted water and cook for 25–
30 minutes.

Melt the butter in a large
saucepan, sprinkle in the flour
and cook until golden brown,
stirring continuously. Gradually stir in the hot milk and simmer for 10 minutes, stirring
frequently. Then turn the heat
right down, but keep the sauce
warm.

Drain the potatoes, rinse
them in cold water, peel and cut
them into fairly thick slices.
Season the sauce with the
cream, salt and pepper, the nutmeg, lemon juice and sugar.

Stir in the potato and warm
through without allowing the
sauce to boil. Sprinkle with
parsley before serving.
Serves 4

Serve with: fried sausages or
pork chops.

Soured Potatoes

800 g/1¾ lb potatoes
salt and freshly milled black
* pepper*
100 g/4 oz rindless streaky
* bacon*
2 onions
225 g/8 oz pickled cucumbers
1 tablespoon flour
450 ml/¾ pint hot meat stock
1 tablespoon small capers
scant 1 teaspoon grated lemon
* rind*
¼ teaspoon dried marjoram
¼ teaspoon dried thyme
1 bay leaf
1 tablespoon wine vinegar
3 tablespoons chopped parsley to
* garnish*

375 calories per serving

Wash the potatoes and boil
them in a saucepan of salted
water for 25–30 minutes. Rinse
the potatoes in cold water, peel
and cut them into fairly thick
slices. Finely chop the bacon,
onion and cucumber.

Fry the bacon in a deep
frying pan until crisp, add the
onions and fry until golden
brown. Sprinkle with the flour
and cook, stirring continuously. Gradually stir in the
stock and boil for a few minutes, stirring continuously. Add
the capers, lemon rind, herbs,
bay leaf, salt and pepper and
the vinegar.

Warm the cucumber and po-
tato through in the sauce. Serve
sprinkled with chopped parsley.
Serves 4

Potato Bake

1 kg/2 lb potatoes
salt and freshly milled black
  pepper
225 g/8 oz lean ham
150 ml/¼ pint milk
100 g/4 oz Parmesan cheese,
  grated
pinch of grated nutmeg
150 ml/¼ pint soured cream
2 eggs
4 tablespoons chopped fresh
  mixed herbs
1 tablespoon breadcrumbs
25 g/1 oz butter

620 calories per serving

Scrub the potatoes, drop them
into a large saucepan of salted
boiling water and boil for
about 30 minutes, until cooked.

Meanwhile, cut the ham into
equal cubes. Drain the cooked
potatoes, evaporate some of the
moisture, peel and mash. Mix
the mashed potato with the
milk, ham and Parmesan and
season with salt, pepper and
nutmeg.

Grease an ovenproof dish
with butter and fill with the potato mixture. Beat the soured
cream with the eggs and
chopped herbs and pour over
the potato. Sprinkle with the
breadcrumbs and dot with the
butter.

Bake on the middle shelf of a
hot oven (220 C, 425 F, gas 7) for
about 20 minutes. *Serves 4*

Serve with: fresh mixed salad of
radicchio and lamb's lettuce.

Cook's tip

For a chunkier dish slice
the cooked potatoes in-
stead of mashing them.

Potato and Tomato Bake

*675 g/1½ lb potatoes boiled in
 their skins*
2 onions
450 g/1 lb tomatoes
450 g/1 lb steak fillet
1–2 tablespoons oil
*salt and freshly milled black
 pepper*
butter for greasing
½ teaspoon dried thyme
*50 g/2 oz Cheddar cheese,
 grated*
150 ml/¼ pint soured cream

400 calories per serving

Peel and slice the potatoes.
Slice the onions. Wash and slice
the tomatoes. Cut the meat into
5–6 thin slices.

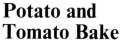

Heat half the oil in a frying
pan, add and brown the meat
for about 2 minutes each side,
then remove the meat from the
pan and season it with salt and
pepper.

Grease an ovenproof dish
with butter and cover the base
with a layer of sliced potato.
Arrange the meat over the potato, sprinkle it with the remaining oil and cover with
alternate layers of potato, tomato and onion. Sprinkle with
salt and pepper and the thyme.

Stir the cheese into the
soured cream and pour the
mixture into the dish.

Bake in a moderately hot
oven (200 C, 400 F, gas 6) for 15
minutes. *Serves 4*

Serve with: fresh green salad.

Sauerkraut Bake

800 g/1¾ lb sauerkraut
150 ml/¼ pint meat stock
150 ml/¼ pint natural apple juice
2 cloves
2 juniper berries
1 large red pepper
*100 g/4 oz rindless streaky
 bacon*
450 g/1 lb potatoes
150 ml/¼ pint white wine
2 tablespoons chopped parsley
2 tablespoons crème fraîche
25 g/1 oz butter

420 calories per serving

Place the sauerkraut in a
saucepan with the stock, apple
juice, cloves and juniper berries. Cover and braise over a
low heat for about 40 minutes.

Halve and deseed the pepper,
wash, dry and cut into strips.
Dice the bacon and fry in a
frying pan until brown and
crisp. Then add the peppers to
the pan and fry for a few minutes, stirring frequently.

Peel, wash and very thinly
slice the potatoes. Mix the sauerkraut with the bacon and
pepper mixture, stir in the wine
and transfer the mixture to an
ovenproof dish. Top with the
sliced potato and sprinkle with
parsley. Spread the crème
fraîche over the top and dot
with the butter.

Bake on the middle shelf of a
hot oven (220 C, 425 F, gas 7) for
20 minutes. *Serves 4*

Foil-Baked Potatoes with Tasty Sauces

8 (100-g/4-oz) potatoes
1 tablespoon oil
salt
2 tablespoons caraway seeds

175 calories per serving

Scrub the potatoes thoroughly under running water, wipe them dry and cut a cross into one side of each potato. Brush 8 large pieces of aluminium foil with the oil. Mix a generous pinch of salt with the caraway seeds and sprinkle on the foil. Wrap the potatoes tightly in the foil.

Bake the potatoes on the middle shelf of a hot oven (220 c, 425 f, gas 7) for 50 minutes. *Serves 4*

Serve with: flaked butter, soured cream or one of the following sauces.

Dip à la Russe

Stir 150 ml/¼ pint soured cream with 6 tablespoons of diced, bottled beetroot, 4 tablespoons diced pickled cucumber, 1 grated onion, 1 finely chopped clove of garlic and 1–2 tablespoons of grated horseradish.

Herb Cream

Stir 150 ml/¼ pint whipped cream with 100 g/4 oz of finely chopped cooked ham, 1 tablespoon of mild mustard, 1 teaspoon of lemon juice, a dash of Worcestershire sauce and plenty of chopped herbs, including parsley, chives, lemon balm and cress.

Anchovy and Curd Cheese

Stir 225 g/8 oz curd cheese with a little white wine until smooth, then work in 10 chopped anchovy fillets, a handful of chopped capers, 1 chopped onion, 1 chopped pickled cucumber, 2 tablespoons of chopped chives and seasoning to taste.

Stuffed Jacket Potatoes

3 tablespoons oil
8 medium potatoes
100 g/4 oz pig's liver
1 onion
1 clove garlic
225 g/8 oz minced pork
4 tablespoons chopped chives
salt and freshly milled white
    pepper
4 tablespoons grated cheese
25 g/1 oz butter

540 calories per serving

Brush 8 pieces of aluminium foil with 1 tablespoon of the oil. Wash and dry the potatoes. Cut off one third of the potatoes lengthways and remove as much of the potato flesh as possible. Finely chop the potato you have removed as well as the peeled lids.

Wash, dry and finely chop the liver. Very finely chop the onion and garlic. Heat the remaining oil in a frying pan and fry the onion and garlic until transparent. Add the liver, chopped potato, minced pork and chives and fry, stirring continuously, then season to taste. Fill the potatoes with this mixture.

Place each potato on a piece of oiled foil, sprinkle with cheese and dot with butter, then loosely seal the foil. Bake the potatoes in a hot oven (220 c, 425 f, gas 7) for 50–60 minutes. *Serves 8*

Serve with: fresh mixed salad.

Potatoes with Blue-Vein Cheese

8 medium potatoes
salt and freshly milled white
    pepper
225 g/8 oz curd cheese
225 g/8 oz Roquefort cheese
2 tablespoons chopped chives
50 g/2 oz soft butter
2 teaspoons coarse salt
1 teaspoon paprika

480 calories per serving

Scrub the potatoes well under cold running water and boil them in their skins in a covered pan of salted water for 20 minutes.

Drain and cut away one third of the potatoes lengthways to form a lid. Remove the flesh from the inside of the potatoes, using a pointed spoon, and work this into the curd cheese, Roquefort cheese, chives, a little pepper and the butter, until smooth. Fill the potatoes with this mixture and replace the lids.

Butter an ovenproof dish or baking tray. Place the potatoes close together in the dish or on the baking tray standing on their lids. Sprinkle with coarse salt and paprika and warm the potatoes through in the oven for about 10 minutes. Serve hot or cold. *Serves 4*

Serve with: tomato salad with onion rings.

Mixed Iceberg Salad

350 g/12 oz iceberg lettuce
½ cucumber
4 medium tomatoes
1 clove garlic
2 tablespoons tarragon vinegar
salt and freshly milled white
  pepper
4 tablespoons soured cream
2 tablespoons chopped mixed
  herbs (parsley, dill, chives,
  burnet)
2 tablespoons sunflower oil

115 calories per serving

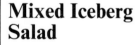
Drain the leaves thoroughly,
then tear them into small
pieces. Wash the cucumber and
tomatoes and wipe them dry.
Cut the cucumber into very
thin slices and the tomatoes

into wedges. Halve the garlic
and rub it round the inside of a
salad bowl.
  Beat the vinegar with pepper
and salt, the soured cream and
mixed herbs. Arrange the lettuce, cucumber and tomatoes in
the salad bowl and toss them in
the oil. Pour the dressing into
the centre and toss the salad at
the table. *Serves 4*

Radiccio Salad with Orange

350 g/12 oz radiccio (red
  chicory)
100 g/4 oz curly endive
1 orange
100 ml/4 fl oz crème fraîche
salt and freshly milled white
  pepper
generous pinch of sugar
15 g/½ oz butter
1 tablespoon flaked almonds

200 calories per serving

Separate the radiccio and endive leaves, wash thoroughly
under cold running water and
shake dry. Tear large radiccio
leaves into pieces and cut the
endive into strips about 3 cm/
1½ in wide. Peel the orange and
remove the skin from each segment. Halve the segments and
remove the pips.

Season the cream with salt,
pepper and the sugar. Melt the
butter and cook the almonds
until golden brown. Mix the
cream into the radiccio, endive
and orange salad and sprinkle
with the toasted almonds.
Serves 4

Cook's tip

To bring out the slightly
bitter flavour of the
radiccio, finely chop
some of the stalk and
mix it into the salad.

Crudités

Carrot Salad with Oranges

450 g / 1 lb carrots
2 medium oranges
juice of 1–1½ lemons
1 tablespoon icing sugar
pinch of ground cinnamon
1 tablespoon oil

140 calories per serving

Scrape and wash the carrots, then cut them into very thin sticks. Peel the oranges, remove the skin from each segment and mix the segments with the carrot.

Beat the lemon juice with the icing sugar, cinnamon and oil and pour the dressing over the salad. *Serves 4*

Fennel Salad

450 g / 1 lb fennel
1 bunch radishes
½ cucumber
3 tablespoons oil
1 tablespoon lemon juice
salt and freshly milled white
*   pepper*
2 tablespoons freshly chopped
*   mixed herbs (chives, parsley,*
*   mint and fennel leaves) to*
*   garnish*

125 calories per serving

Remove the outer fennel leaves, then slice the fennel very thinly. Wash and slice the radishes. Peel and finely slice the cucumber. Mix the salad ingredients together.

Beat the oil with the lemon juice and seasoning, fold the dressing into the salad and sprinkle the herbs over the salad. *Serves 4*

Chicory Salad with Mandarins

4 small heads chicory
juice of 1 lemon
3 seedless mandarins or 1 (312-g / 11-oz) can mandarins
1 teaspoon white wine vinegar
juice of 1 mandarin
salt and freshly milled white pepper
2 tablespoons nut oil
Garnish
rind of ½ orange
1 teaspoon bottled green peppercorns

230 calories per serving

cut 5 mm/¼ in from each stalk. With a sharp knife cut and discard a small wedge from the stalk end. Cut the chicory into 1-cm/½-in wide strips. Place the chicory in a bowl and sprinkle

with the lemon juice.

Peel the mandarins and remove all the pith, separate into segments and cut each segment in half lengthways. Or drain canned mandarins, if used. Sprinkle the mandarins over the chicory.

Beat together the vinegar and mandarin juice and season to taste. Beat in the oil and stir the dressing into the salad.

Wash the ½ orange in hot water and thinly peel off the rind. Cut into very thin strips. Coarsely chop the peppercorns and sprinkle over the salad with the orange rind. *Serves 4*

Serve with: steak, veal escalopes or roast loin of pork.

Dandelion Salad

150 g / 5 oz small, tender dande-lion leaves
1 lettuce heart
1 tablespoon white wine vinegar
salt and freshly milled black pepper
1 teaspoon maple syrup
2 tablespoons walnut oil
150 ml/¼ pint low-fat natural yogurt
2 tablespoons chopped parsley or cress
50 g / 2 oz shelled walnuts to garnish

180 calories per serving

Thoroughly wash the dandelion leaves several times in luke-warm water, then rinse them in cold water and drain well. Separate the lettuce leaves, wash thoroughly and drain. Beat the wine vinegar with a little salt and the maple syrup until the

salt dissolves.

Cut the dry lettuce and dan-delion leaves into strips about 3 cm/1½ in wide, place them in a serving dish and fold in the vin-egar mixture. Sprinkle the oil over the salad. Season the yo-gurt with pepper and parsley or cress and fold the mixture into the salad. Garnish with nuts. *Serves 4*

Cook's tip

Instead of walnuts, you can sprinkle the salad with slices of radish, in which case season the yogurt with chopped sorrel or wild burnet rather than parsley.

Lamb's Lettuce with Bacon

150–200 g/5–7 oz lamb's lettuce
2 small onions (white onions are best)
50 g/2 oz rindless streaky bacon
2 hard-boiled eggs
1 clove garlic
2 tablespoons wine vinegar
2 tablespoons oil
1 tablespoon orange juice
salt and pepper
pinch of sugar

190 calories per serving

Thoroughly trim and wash the lamb's lettuce and shake dry. Cut the onions into thin rings. Finely dice the bacon and fry until crisp and golden. Reserve the fat. Cut the eggs into wedges. Finely chop the garlic.

Beat the vinegar with the oil, bacon fat and orange juice and season with salt, pepper and sugar. Stir in the garlic. Mix the dressing into the lamb's lettuce, onion rings and bacon and garnish with the egg. *Serves 4*

Cook's tip

If you prefer lamb's lettuce without the bacon and egg, try a dressing made from 4 tablespoons curd cheese, 2 tablespoons oil, juice of 1 lemon, 2 tablespoons milk, 1 pinch salt and ½ teaspoon sugar. Beat the curd dressing thoroughly, then grate 1 small onion into it.

Cucumber Salad with Yogurt Dressing

1 medium cucumber
1 onion
1 stem dill
1 tablespoon chopped borage
½ teaspoon salt and freshly milled white pepper
1 tablespoon lemon juice
1 teaspoon maple syrup
150 ml/¼ pint full-milk natural yogurt

60 calories per serving

Wash and dry the cucumber, halve it lengthways and then cut it into sticks about 1 cm/½ in thick. Cut the onion into thin rings and cut each ring into four. Wash the dill, shake dry and chop.

Beat the dill and the other seasonings into the yogurt and fold the dressing into the cucumber and onion. Leave the salad to stand for 10 minutes before serving. *Serves 4*

Cook's tip

To make a cucumber and prawn salad: sprinkle 400 g/14 oz frozen prawns with orange juice and leave to thaw. Make a dressing from the juice of 1 lemon, ½ teaspoon salt, a generous pinch each of white pepper and garlic salt, 1 teaspoon sugar and 3 tablespoons oil. Mix the dressing into the cucumber strips and prawns and sprinkle with chopped dill.

Tomato Salad

4 large tomatoes
salt and freshly milled black
    pepper
1 onion
½ clove garlic
3 tablespoons olive oil
2 tablespoons vinegar
2 tablespoons chopped chives to
    garnish (optional)

95 calories per serving

Wash the tomatoes, or make an
incision in the tomato skins,
pour boiling water over the
tomatoes and leave for 3 minutes, then peel them. Cut the
tomatoes into slices and arrange on a plate. Season to taste.
Finely chop the onion and
garlic and sprinkle over the tomatoes. Beat together the oil
and vinegar and pour over the
tomatoes, then garnish with
chives if liked. *Serves 4*

Cauliflower Salad

1 medium cauliflower
1 hard-boiled egg
1 egg yolk
salt and freshly milled white
    pepper
½ teaspoon mustard
pinch of sugar
2 tablespoons tarragon vinegar
1 tablespoon oil
2 tablespoons single cream
2 tablespoons chopped chives

130 calories per serving

Place the cauliflower in a
saucepan with water to cover,
bring to the boil, simmer for 10
minutes, until soft. Drain and
separate the cauliflower into
florets, then leave to cool.
Chop the hard-boiled egg,
then beat with the remaining
ingredients. Pour the dressing
over the cauliflower and sprinkle with chives. *Serves 4*

Bean Salad

800 g/1¾ lb French beans
salt
sprig of savory (optional)
1 onion
50 g/2 oz rindless streaky bacon
2 tablespoons wine vinegar
generous pinch of cayenne

155 calories per serving

Trim and wash the beans. Place
them in a saucepan with water
to cover, add a little salt and
the savory, then cover the pan,
bring to the boil and simmer
for about 5 minutes, until the
beans are tender. Drain and
leave to cool. Cut larger beans
into halves or quarters.
    Cut the onion into rings.
Dice and fry the bacon until
crisp, then mix it with the vinegar, salt and the cayenne. Mix
the dressing into the beans with
the onion rings. *Serves 4*

Iceberg Salad

1 small iceberg lettuce
2 small mandarins
4 tablespoons orange juice
salt
generous pinch of sugar
1 teaspoon orange rind, cut into
    thin strips
150 ml/¼ pint double cream
50 g/2 oz chopped hazelnuts

225 calories per serving

Separate the lettuce leaves,
wash and cut them into strips.
Peel the mandarins and remove
all the pith, divide them into
segments and cut each segment
in half lengthways.
    Mix the orange juice with
salt, the sugar and orange rind.
Whip the cream until semi-stiff
and fold it into the dressing.
Stir the dressing into the lettuce, together with the nuts and
mandarins. *Serves 4*

Stuffed Chicory

2 heads chicory
3 tablespoons lemon juice
2 large beef tomatoes
1 large seedless mandarin
5 stuffed green olives
salt and freshly milled black
   pepper
1 teaspoon maple syrup
3 tablespoons oil

120 calories per serving

Wash the chicory and wipe it
dry. Remove any damaged
outer leaves and trim the root
end. Using a sharp knife, cut a
small wedge out of the bitter
root end and discard. Halve the
chicory heads lengthways and
sprinkle them with a little lemon juice.

Peel and quarter the tomatoes. Remove the seeds, then
dice the flesh. Carefully peel the
mandarin and divide it into segments. Slice the olives. Beat the
remaining lemon juice with the
seasoning, maple syrup and oil,
then mix these ingredients with
the diced tomato, mandarin
segments and sliced olives.

Cover the bowl and leave to
stand for 10 minutes before
transferring the sauce to the
chicory halves and serving.
Serves 4

Serve with: white toast and
chilled butter.

Stuffed Tomatoes

4 medium tomatoes
1 (283-g/10-oz) can sweetcorn
1 (99-g/3½-oz) can tuna
1 small clove garlic
1 tablespoon chopped parsley
salt and freshly milled white
   pepper
½ teaspoon paprika
1 tablespoon wine vinegar
1 tablespoon mixed herbs to
   garnish

185 calories per serving

Wash the tomatoes, wipe dry
and cut a small lid from the top
of each. Carefully remove the
centres with a small pointed
spoon. Throw away the seeds
but dice the flesh. Drain the
sweetcorn. Drain and flake the
tuna, reserving 1 tablespoon of
the oil.

Chop the garlic very finely,
then beat with the oil, parsley,
salt, pepper, paprika and vinegar. Mix the sauce with the
tuna, sweetcorn and diced tomato. Fill the tomatoes with
the mixture and sprinkle with
the chopped herbs. *Serves 4*

Cook's tip

If preferred, the tuna can
be replaced with cooked
chicken, beef, or pickled
tongue and 1–2 table-
spoons cream may be
added to the mixture.

Marinated Vegetables

4 artichokes
4 tomatoes
1 small courgette
10 tablespoons oil
8 small shallots
1 green pepper
1 red pepper
1 clove garlic
2 chillies
2 bay leaves
250 ml/8 fl oz wine vinegar
2 tablespoons sugar
salt
sprig of thyme

175 calories per serving

Boil the artichokes in salted water for about 40 minutes. Remove the leaves, which are not needed for this recipe, then halve the artichoke hearts and leave them to cool.

Peel and halve the tomatoes and remove the seeds. Thinly slice the courgette, fry lightly on both sides in a little oil in a frying pan and leave to cool. Peel the shallots.

Halve the green and red peppers, remove the core and seeds, blanch the halves in boiling water for 7 minutes and then drain. Slice the garlic. Halve the chillies, remove the seeds and then finely chop.

Arrange the vegetables in a large shallow dish with the bay leaves. Beat the remaining oil with the vinegar, sugar and salt and pour over the vegetables. Top with the sprig of thyme.

Cover the dish and leave the vegetables to marinate in the refrigerator for 12–24 hours. Serve the vegetables in the marinade. *Serves 8*

Serve with: fresh French bread or toasted wholemeal bread.

Stuffed Celery

8 sticks celery
1 ripe avocado
2 tablespoons lime or lemon
   juice
225 g/8 oz cream cheese
1 tablespoon brandy
salt and freshly milled white
   pepper

210 calories per serving

Separate the celery sticks and
cut off the leaves. Wash, dry
and trim the celery and cut it
into 10-cm/4-in lengths. Cut
the avocado in half, remove the
stone, then remove the flesh
from the skin with a pointed
spoon. Beat the avocado flesh
with the lime or lemon juice,
cream cheese and brandy until
smooth. Season to taste.

Pipe the avocado cream into
the celery using a piping bag
and fluted nozzle, or spoon the

cream onto the celery and press
down with the spoon handle.
Arrange the celery on a plate
and keep in the refrigerator until ready to serve. *Serves 4*

Serve with: thinly sliced brown
toast.

Artichokes Vinaigrette

4 medium artichokes
3 litres/5 pints salted water
2 tablespoons wine vinegar
4 tablespoons dry white wine
1 teaspoon sugar
salt and freshly milled black
   pepper
1 teaspoon English mustard
yolks of 3 hard-boiled eggs
4 tablespoons olive oil
1 small onion
½ clove garlic
1 tablespoon chopped fresh
   tarragon
2 teaspoons dried chervil

225 calories per serving

Cut off the stalks and the top
2 cm/1 in of leaves from the artichokes. Boil the artichokes in
the salted water in a covered
pan for 40 minutes. Beat

together the vinegar, wine, sugar, seasoning and mustard.
Mash the egg yolks with a fork
and stir them into the oil, then
beat the mixture into the vinegar and wine marinade. Finely
chop the onion. Crush the garlic and stir it into the sauce with
the onion and herbs.

Drain the artichokes and
serve them on warm plates with
the vinaigrette sauce. To eat,
pluck off the artichoke leaves
one at a time, dip in the sauce
and squeeze the tender artichoke out of the leaves between
your teeth. Very small leaves
and the choke in the centre
should be removed. Finally, eat
the artichoke heart covered
with sauce. *Serves 4*

Italian Salad

575 g/1¼ lb new potatoes, boiled
1 small cauliflower
100 g/4 oz beans
100 g/4 oz carrots
100 g/4 oz frozen peas
salt and freshly milled white
  pepper
100 g/4 oz mushrooms
10 anchovy fillets
2 tablespoons wine vinegar
3 tablespoons oil
2 hard-boiled eggs
2 tablespoons chopped parsley to
  garnish

345 calories per serving

Peel and slice the potatoes
when cool. Separate the cauliflower into florets and boil for
5–10 minutes in unsalted water.
Trim and wash the beans and
carrots. Cut the beans into
4-cm/2-in lengths and dice the
carrots. Boil the beans and carrots in a little salted water for
15 minutes, then drain. Boil the
peas in 2–3 tablespoons salted
water for 3 minutes, then drain.

Trim and wash the mush-
rooms and cut larger ones into
halves or quarters. Cut
the anchovy fillets into strips.
Beat seasoning to taste into the
vinegar.

In a large bowl mix together
the sliced potato, drained vegetables, mushrooms, anchovies
and vinegar. Check the seasoning and fold in the oil. Cut the
eggs into wedges, arrange on
the salad and garnish with
parsley. *Serves 4*

Pasta Salad with Salami

3 litres/5 pints water
salt
200 g/7 oz macaroni
200 g/7 oz thinly sliced salami
100 g/4 oz Emmental cheese
1 red pepper
1 green pepper
100 g/4 oz pickled cucumber
3 tablespoons mayonnaise
4 tablespoons single cream
1 teaspoon lemon juice
generous pinch of sugar
½ teaspoon cayenne
2–3 tablespoons milk

710 calories per serving

Bring the water to the boil with
a generous pinch of salt, sprinkle in the macaroni and boil for
about 12 minutes until cooked,
but still quite firm. Rinse in cold
water and drain.

Cut the salami into 1-cm/½-in
wide strips. Dice the cheese.
Halve the peppers, remove core
and seeds, wash, dry and dice.
Dice the cucumber.

Beat the mayonnaise with the
cream. Season the lemon juice
with salt and pepper, the sugar
and cayenne and stir into the
mayonnaise. For a thinner
dressing stir in a little milk.

Mix all the salad ingredients
in a bowl with the dressing.
Leave the salad to stand for
about 20 minutes at room temperature before serving. *Serves 4*

Sweetcorn and Sausage Salad

225 g/8 oz ham sausage
100 g/4 oz Gouda cheese
2 small onions
½ red pepper
½ green pepper
4 medium tomatoes
100 g/4 oz gherkins
1 (326-g/11½-oz) can sweetcorn
2 tablespoons wine vinegar
3 tablespoons oil
½ teaspoon mustard
½ teaspoon paprika
salt and freshly milled black
  pepper
pinch of sugar
pinch of cayenne

470 calories per serving

Skin the sausage and cut it into narrow strips. Cut the cheese into strips. Cut the onions into rings. Deseed the peppers, wash, dry and cut them into strips. Wash, dry and slice the tomatoes. Slice the gherkins. Drain the sweetcorn. Mix all the salad ingredients together in a bowl.

Beat the vinegar with the oil, mustard, paprika, salt and pepper, the sugar and cayenne. Fold the dressing into the salad and leave the salad to stand for 20 minutes at room temperature. *Serves 4*

Serve with: rye bread.

Spaghetti Salad

3 litres/5 pints water
salt
225 g/8 oz spaghetti
350 g/12 oz cooked turkey
  breast
100 g/4 oz Emmental cheese
2 green peppers
2 bunches radishes
4 tomatoes
2 hard-boiled eggs
4 tablespoons crème fraîche
150 ml/¼ pint low fat natural
  yogurt
3 tablespoons tomato ketchup
dash of Tabasco sauce
1 tablespoon wine vinegar
½ teaspoon paprika
2 tablespoons chopped chives to
  garnish

610 calories per serving

Bring the water to the boil with a little salt in a large saucepan. Break the spaghetti into halves or thirds, sprinkle it into the boiling salted water and boil for 10–12 minutes.

Drain the spaghetti in a sieve, rinse it under cold water and leave to drain.

Cut the turkey into even strips and the cheese into small cubes. Halve the peppers and remove the cores and seeds. Wash and cut the peppers into strips. Wash, dry and slice the radishes. Wash and dry the tomatoes and cut them into wedges. Slice the eggs. Mix all the salad ingredients together in a bowl.

Beat the cream with the yogurt, tomato ketchup, Tabasco and vinegar and season with salt and paprika. Stir the dressing into the salad and sprinkle with chives. *Serves 4*

Scampi Salad

400 g/14 oz scampi
450 g/1 lb asparagus tips
200 g/7 oz bottled mussels
5 tablespoons single cream
2 tablespoons mayonnaise
few drops lemon juice
salt and freshly milled white
    pepper
pinch sugar
1 teaspoon paprika
lettuce leaves
2 teaspoons dill to garnish

255 calories per serving

Defrost the scampi if necessary.
Cover the asparagus with salted
water and boil for 10–15 minutes. Rinse in cold water and
drain the asparagus. Drain the
mussels through a sieve, reserving 2 tablespoons of the liquid
for the dressing. Mix the
scampi, asparagus and mussels
together in a bowl.

Beat the cream with the mayonnaise, mussel liquid, lemon
juice, salt and pepper, the sugar
and paprika. Pour the dressing
over the scampi, asparagus and
mussels and mix well. Arrange
the lettuce on individual plates,
add the salad and serve
sprinkled with dill. *Serves 4*

Windsor Salad

350 g/12 oz fresh celeriac
225 g/8 oz button mushrooms
450 g/1 lb cooked chicken breast
100 g/4 oz pickled cucumber
4 tablespoons mayonnaise
1 teaspoon lemon juice
2 teaspoons freshly grated
    horseradish
salt
generous pinch of sugar
few drops of Worcestershire
    sauce
50 g/2 oz lamb's lettuce

310 calories per serving

Peel the celeriac, cut it into very
thin slices and then into thin
sticks. Wash, drain and slice
the mushrooms. Cut the
chicken and cucumber into
strips.
    To make the dressing, beat
together the mayonnaise,
lemon juice, horseradish, salt,
sugar and Worcestershire
sauce. Stir the dressing into the
salad ingredients, cover the
bowl and leave the salad to
stand for 20 minutes.
    Wash the lamb's lettuce thor-
oughly, drain and arrange it
around the rim of a salad bowl.
Spoon the Windsor salad into
the centre. *Serves 4*

Normandy Rice Salad

1 fairly sour apple
1 stick celery
150 ml/¼ pint single cream
salt and freshly milled white
    pepper
1 tablespoon lemon juice
225 g/8 oz cooked long-grain
    rice

300 calories per serving

Wash the apple, cut it into
wedges, remove the core, then
cut the apple and celery into
thin slices. Finely chop the celery leaves and reserve them to
garnish the salad.
    Beat the cream with the sea-
soning and lemon juice. Mix
the apple, celery and rice
together in a bowl, add the
dressing and sprinkle the celery
leaves over the salad. *Serves 4*

Cheese and Sausage Salad

225 g/8 oz Emmental cheese
350 g/12 oz garlic sausage
1 apple
200 g/7 oz gherkins
1 (198-g/7-oz) can sweet corn
1 onion
1 clove garlic
2 tablespoons wine vinegar
salt and freshly milled white
  pepper
1 teaspoon mild mustard
generous pinch of cayenne
3 tablespoons oil
chives to garnish

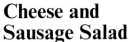

Cut the cheese into very fine strips. Skin and thinly slice the sausage. Wash, dry and quarter the apple and remove the core. Finely dice the apple. Dice the gherkins. Drain the sweetcorn,

then finely dice the onion. Finely chop the garlic and mix it with the diced onion, wine vinegar, salt and pepper, the mustard, paprika and oil.

Mix all the salad ingredients carefully into the dressing. Wash, dry and chop the chives and sprinkle them over the salad before serving. *Serves 4*

Serve with: fresh farmhouse bread or soda bread.

Chicken Salad with Avocado

800 g/1¾ lb boned and skinned
  chicken
1 ripe avocado
225 g/8 oz black grapes
2 seedless mandarins
lettuce leaves
2 tablespoons mayonnaise
3 tablespoons crème fraîche
1 tablespoon dry sherry
3 tablespoons orange juice
salt
50 g/2 oz walnuts, chopped, to
  garnish

615 calories per serving

Cut the meat into equal slices. Halve the avocado, remove the stone, peel each half and slice crossways. Halve the grapes, peel them if preferred and remove the pips. Peel the mandarins and remove the skin from

each segment. Wash and dry the lettuce. Line a salad bowl with lettuce and fill the bowl with a mixture of the chicken, avocado, grapes and mandarins.

Beat the mayonnaise with the crème fraîche, sherry, orange juice and a pinch of salt, pour the dressing over the salad and sprinkle with the chopped nuts. *Serves 4*

Serve with: white toast.

125

Special Sausage Salad

1 cos lettuce
½ cucumber
1 bunch radishes
2 tomatoes
10 cocktail onions
8 small bottled corn cobs or 1
(425-g/15-oz) can baby
sweetcorn
225 g/8 oz ham sausage, sliced
100 ml/4 fl oz soured cream
1 tablespoon lemon juice
1 teaspoon soy sauce
½ teaspoon celery salt
pinch of sugar
1 teaspoon green peppercorns

345 calories per serving

Separate, wash and dry the lettuce. Wash, dry and thinly slice the cucumber and radishes. Cut the tomatoes into wedges. Cover a salad dish with lettuce and top with the cucumber, radishes, tomatoes, onions and corncobs. Skin the sliced sausage, cut to the centre of each slice, roll into a cone and arrange the sausage on the salad.

Beat the soured cream with the remaining ingredients and pour the dressing over the salad.

Variation
To make the sausage salad at the top of the photograph, slice Frankfurter sausages and gherkins and place them in a bowl. Cut cheese and red pepper into strips, add them to the salad and mix the ingredients together.

To make the dressing, beat together 4 tablespoons oil, 1–2 tablespoon winevinegar, mustard, chopped onion and seasoning to taste. Pour the dressing over the salad and garnish with a hard-boiled egg cut into wedges. *Serves 4*

Egg Salad

salt
4 tablespoons water
150 g/5 oz frozen peas
4 hard-boiled eggs
4 tomatoes
225 g/8 oz lean boiled ham
225 g/8 oz grapes
2 tablespoons mayonnaise
150 ml/¼ pint low-fat natural
yogurt
2 tablespoons tomato ketchup
2 tablespoons wine vinegar
4 tablespoons cold vegetable
stock
1 teaspoon paprika
1 bunch parsley to garnish

410 calories per serving

Salt and boil the water, add the peas, cover the pan and cook over a low heat for 6 minutes. Drain the peas in a sieve and leave them to cool.

Cut the eggs into wedges. Wash and dry the tomatoes and cut them into wedges. Cut the ham into strips. Halve the grapes and remove the seeds. Mix all these ingredients together in a bowl.

To make the salad dressing, beat the mayonnaise with the yogurt, ketchup, vinegar and stock and season with salt and paprika. Fold the dressing into the salad ingredients. Cover the bowl and leave to stand in the refrigerator for a few minutes.

Wash, dry and chop the parsley. Before serving, sprinkle the egg salad with parsley.
Serves 4

Serve with: bread or toast

Tuna Salad

2 (198-g/7-oz) cans tuna
½ grapefruit, peeled
1 banana, peeled
1 teaspoon lemon juice
3 hard-boiled eggs
3 tablespoons mayonnaise
1 (150-g/5.29-oz) carton low
  fat natural yogurt
generous pinch salt
1 teaspoon paprika
lettuce leaves

430 calories per serving

Drain the tuna fish and break it into equal pieces. Carefully remove the skin from each grapefruit segment, then cut the segments in half. Slice the banana and sprinkle with the lemon juice. Chop two of the eggs and cut the third into wedges.

Beat the mayonaise with the yogurt and season with salt and

half the paprika. Wash and dry the lettuce and use it to line a salad bowl. Mix the tuna with the banana, grapefruit and chopped egg and fold in the dressing.

Arrange the tuna salad over the lettuce, garnish with the egg wedges and sprinkle with the remaining paprika. *Serves 4*

Cook's tip

To make the tuna salad go further, add a few tablespoons of boiled rice.

Mushroom Salad

350 g/12 oz small button
  mushrooms
2 teaspoons lemon juice
200 g/7 oz lean boiled ham
2 tablespoons mayonnaise
4 tablespoons single cream
1 tablespoon wine vinegar
salt
generous pinch of sugar
endive or lettuce leaves
generous pinch of cayenne to
  garnish

225 calories per serving

Trim and wipe the mushrooms and pat them dry with kitchen towel. Quarter or halve larger mushrooms and leave smaller ones whole. Place the mushrooms in a bowl and sprinkle them with the lemon juice. Dice the ham and stir it into the mushrooms.

Beat the mayonnaise with the

cream and wine vinegar and season well with salt and sugar. Fold the dressing into the salad.

Wash the lettuce or endive, shake the leaves dry in a tea-towel and arrange them in individual bowls. Add the mushroom salad and sprinkle cayenne over the top. *Serves 4*

Cook's Tip

For a more filling meal, add 2–3 chopped hard-boiled eggs to the salad.

Fish Salad with Peas

*600 ml/1 pint cold water plus 6
 tablespoons*
2 tablespoons wine vinegar
salt
2 sprigs parsley
450 g/1 lb cod fillet
350 g/12 oz frozen peas
½ red pepper
2 hard-boiled eggs
lettuce leaves
4 tablespoons mayonnaise
*150 ml/¼ pint low-fat natural
 yogurt*
1–2 teaspoons curry powder
2 shallots
1 clove garlic
1 teaspoon paprika

445 calories per serving

Bring the 600 ml/1 pint water to
the boil with the wine vinegar,
salt and the parsley. Wash the

fish and simmer it gently in the
water for 10 minutes. Cook the
peas in the 6 tablespoons salted
water for 6 minutes. Drain the
peas and leave until cold.

Remove the pith and seeds
from the pepper. Wash and
slice the pepper and the eggs.
Wash and dry the lettuce and
use the leaves to line a salad
bowl.

When the fish is cold, cut it
into 2.5-cm/1½-in cubes.
Arrange alternate layers of egg,
fish, pepper and peas over the
lettuce.

Beat the mayonnaise, yogurt
and curry powder together in a
bowl. Peel and grate the
shallots. Dice the garlic and
crush with a little salt. Mix the
garlic and salt into the dressing,
together with the paprika and
grated shallots. Pour the dressing over the salad. *Serves 4*

Chicken Salad with Grapes

1 small roasting chicken
2 litres/3½ pints cold water
*salt and freshly milled white
 pepper*
bouquet garni
½ cucumber
4 small tomatoes
1 onion
225 g/8 oz black grapes
225 g/8 oz iceberg lettuce
3 tablespoons wine vinegar
2 tablespoons pure grape juice
few drops maple syrup
3 tablespoons oil
*1 tablespoon chopped dill to
 garnish*

415 calories per serving

Wash the chicken thoroughly
inside and out with cold water.
Bring the water to the boil with
a generous pinch of salt. Trim

and wash the herbs and add
them to the pan, then place the
chicken in the pan and remove
any scum as it forms. Boil the
chicken for 40–60 minutes with
the lid a fraction open.

Wash and thinly slice the cucumber. Wash the tomatoes
and cut them into wedges. Cut
the onion into rings. Peel and
halve the grapes and remove
the pips. Wash and dry the lettuce and tear it into small
pieces.

Remove the skin and bones
from the cooked chicken and
cut the meat into 3-cm/1½-in
cubes. Mix all the foregoing ingredients together in a bowl.

Beat together the vinegar,
grape juice, syrup, seasoning to
taste and oil and fold the dressing into the salad. Serve the
salad sprinkled with dill.
Serves 4

Chicken Salad with Green Beans

800 g/1¾ lb cooked chicken
450 g/1 lb frozen green beans
250 ml/8 fl oz water
salt
1 large onion
4 tomatoes
10 stuffed olives
6 tablespoons single cream
3 tablespoons wine vinegar
1 teaspoon English mustard
½ teaspoon sugar

395 calories per serving

Remove any skin and bones from the chicken and dice the meat. Bring the water and a little salt to the boil in a saucepan, tip in the beans, cover the pan and cook over a low heat for 12 minutes. Drain the beans through a sieve and leave them to cool. Cut the

onion into rings. Wash and dry the tomatoes and cut them into wedges. Slice the olives.

Beat together the cream and vinegar and season with mustard and sugar and, if necessary, a little salt. Mix together the chicken, beans, onion, tomatoes and olives. Fold in the dressing and leave the salad to stand for 1 hour before serving. *Serves 4*

Cook's tip

For a more filling dish add cooked diced potato to the salad.

Spicy Beef Salad

1.5 litres/2¾ pints water
salt and pepper
bouquet garni
2 onions
800 g/1¾ lbs brisket of beef
350 g/12 oz gherkins
1 red pepper
100 g/4 oz mushrooms
1 apple
2 tablespoons vinegar from the
  gherkins
2 tablespoons wine vinegar
few dashes Worcestershire sauce
2 tablespoons oil

440 calories per serving

Bring the water to the boil with a little salt and add the bouquet garni. Wash and dry one unpeeled onion, cut it in half and brown both cut edges on an electric plate or in a frying pan.

Add the onion and beef to

the boiling water. Skim the surface several times. Cover the saucepan and boil the beef for 1 hour, then lift out the beef, drain and leave to one side to cool, reserving the cooking liquid.

Peel the second onion and cut it into rings. Slice the gherkins. Halve and deseed the pepper and cut it into strips. Cut the cooled beef into strips. Trim and quarter the mushrooms. Peel and quarter the apple, remove the core and cut the apple into slices. Mix all the foregoing ingredients together. Boil the meat stock in an open saucepan to reduce it.

Beat 4 tablespoons of stock with the remaining ingredients, season to taste, and pour the dressing over the salad. Leave the salad to stand for 20 minutes. *Serves 4*

Vanilla Ice Cream with Candied Fruit

200 g/7 oz mixed candied fruit
1½ tablespoons rum
150 ml/¼ pint double cream
2 tablespoons shelled pistachios
500 ml/17 fl oz vanilla ice cream

440 calories per serving

Cut up the candied fruit. Bring
1 tablespoon of water to the
boil, stir with the rum and pour
over the candied fruit. Cover
and leave to soak for 30
minutes.

Whip the cream until stiff.
Chop the pistachios. Scoop the
vanilla ice cream into balls and
arrange in 4 individual glasses.
Top with the candied fruit in its
juice.

Spoon the cream into a piping bag with a fluted nozzle and
pipe whirls of cream on to the
ice cream. Sprinkle with the
pistachios. *Serves 4*

Cook's tip

To serve vanilla
ice cream with hot rasp-
berries, warm washed
and drained raspberries
in 1–2 tablespoons of
butter over a low heat,
sweeten with icing sugar
and serve hot over the
icecream. Alternatively,
serve vanilla ice cream
with 4 teaspoons of
chopped, crystallised
ginger and a hot sauce
made by melting 100 g/
4 oz of plain chocolate
with 1 tablespoon butter.

Pears Hélène

2 ripe Williams pears
250 ml/8 fl oz Mosel wine
1 tablespoon sugar
1 (25-g/1-oz) sachet vanilla sugar
1 (2.5-cm/1-in) piece cinnamon stick
100 g/4 oz plain chocolate
150 ml/¼ pint single cream
500 ml/17 fl oz vanilla ice cream
12 glacé cherries

390 calories per serving

Peel, halve and carefully core the pears. Poach the pears in a saucepan with the wine, sugar, vanilla sugar and cinnamon over a low heat for 10 minutes. Leave the pears to cool in the liquid.

Chill 4 individual glasses in the refrigerator, or preferably in the freezer.

Break the chocolate into a small saucepan and melt over a low heat. Stir in the cream and keep the sauce hot. Drain the pears.

Cut the ice cream into equal cubes, arrange in the chilled glasses, top with a pear half and cover with the hot chocolate sauce. Garnish each portion with 3 glacé cherries and serve immediately. *Serves 4*

Peach Melba

1 vanilla pod
350 g/12 oz raspberries
6 tablespoons water
100 g/4 oz icing sugar
juice of ½ lemon
1½ tablespoons raspberry brandy
2 fresh ripe peaches or 4 canned peach halves
250 ml/8 fl oz vanilla ice cream
150 ml/¼ pint double cream
1 (25-g/1-oz) sachet vanilla sugar
few chocolate leaves (ready-bought)

350 calories per serving

Slit the vanilla pod lengthways using a sharp knife and scrape out the pith. Sort and wash the raspberries and purée them in a blender with the water, icing sugar, lemon juice, vanilla pith and raspberry brandy. Strain the purée through a sieve and reserve the sauce.

Prick the peaches several times with a fork, scald and peel them. Cut the peaches in half and remove the stones, or drain canned peaches.

Arrange the ice cream in 4 individual glasses, top with the peach halves and cover one side with the raspberry sauce.

Whip the cream with the vanilla sugar until stiff, transfer to a piping bag with a fluted nozzle and pipe cream whirls around the peaches. Decorate with chocolate leaves if liked. *Serves 4*

Fruit Salad with Cream

2 fairly sour apples
2 large oranges
225 g/8 oz black grapes
25 g/1 oz shelled walnuts
150 ml/¼ pint double cream
1 tablespoon vanilla sugar
2 tablespoons orange juice
1½ tablespoons Cointreau (orange liqueur)

275 calories per serving

Wash, dry, quarter, core and slice the apples. Peel the oranges and remove all the pith, cut across the oranges to form round slices and then quarter each slice. Wash and dry the grapes and, if preferred, cut them in half and remove the pips. Coarsely chop the walnuts.

   Mix all the salad ingredients

in a bowl. Whip the cream with the vanilla sugar until stiff, stir in the orange juice and liqueur and spoon the mixture over the fruit salad. *Serves 4*

> **Cook's Tip**
>
> It is not essential to stick rigidly to the ingredients listed. Any seasonal fruit can be included and appropriate liqueur can be used to flavour the cream.

Exotic Fruit Salad

350 g/12 oz fresh pineapple
1 mango
1 kiwi fruit
450 g/1 lb melon
1½ tablespoons grenadine syrup
1½ tablespoons Cointreau (orange liqueur)
juice of ½ lemon
½ vanilla pod
150 ml/¼ pint double cream
½ tablespoon icing sugar

240 calories per serving

Peel the pineapple and remove the woody core. Cut the pineapple into equal chunks. Peel, halve and core the mango and cut it into slices. Peel and thinly slice the kiwi fruit. Halve the melon, remove the seeds and cut out the flesh with a ball cutter.

   Arrange the fruit salad in a glass dish. Mix the grenadine syrup with the liqueur and lemon juice and fold into the fruit.
   Leave the fruit salad to stand in the refrigerator for about 30 minutes. Slit the vanilla pod with a sharp knife and scrape out the pith. Whip the cream with the vanilla until semi-stiff, sweeten with the icing sugar and whip for a few minutes more. Top the fruit salad with the cream and vanilla mixture. *Serves 4*

Gourmet Fruit Desserts

Plums in Red Wine
(Top left of photo)

450 g / 1 lb plums
150 ml / ¼ pint red wine
100 g / 4 oz sugar
1 (2.5-cm / 1-in) piece cinnamon
  stick
2 cloves
150 ml / ¼ pint double cream
2 teaspoons sugar
1 tablespoon toasted almonds

330 calories per serving

Wash, dry, halve and stone the plums. Bring the wine to the boil with the sugar, cinnamon and cloves, add the plums and simmer for 10 minutes. When cool, decorate with sweetened whipped cream and flaked almonds. *Serves 4*

Morello Cherry Dessert
(Bottom left of photo)

450 g / 1 lb morello cherries
150 ml / ¼ pint white wine
150 ml / ¼ pint water
100 g / 4 oz sugar
1 teaspoon cornflour
1½ tablespoons cherry brandy
150 ml / ¼ pint double cream
2 teaspoons sugar
1 tablespoon chopped pistachios

350 calories per serving

Wash and stone the cherries and simmer them gently for 8 minutes in the white wine, water and sugar. Drain the cherries and return the juice to the pan. Thicken the juice with the cornflour dissolved in a little water. Stir the cherry brandy into the cherries and pour the thickened juice over the top.

Serve chilled, decorated with sweetened whipped cream and pistachios. *Serves 4*

Peaches in White Wine
(front right of photo)

2 large white peaches
150 ml / ¼ pint white wine
150 ml / ¼ pint water
2 teaspoons lemon juice
grated rind of ½ lemon
½ teaspoon finely chopped ginger
  root
50 g / 2 oz sugar
1 (2.5-cm / 1-in) piece cinnamon
  stick
1 teaspoon cornflour
2 tablespoons chocolate shavings

260 calories per serving

Blanch, peel, halve and stone the peaches. Bring the wine to the boil with the water, lemon juice, lemon rind, ginger, sugar and cinnamon. Add and poach the peach halves for 10 minutes, then remove from the saucepan and leave them to cool.

Thicken the juice with the cornflour, dissolved in a little cold water, pour it over the peaches and leave to cool. Sprinkle the peach halves with chocolate shavings before serving. *Serves 4*

Stewed Cherries with Wine Sauce
(top right of photo)

450 g / 1 lb stewed cherries
1 egg plus 2 egg yolks
1 tablespoon sugar
2 tablespoons mint liqueur
5 tablespoons Marsala wine

190 calories per serving

Chill the cherries in 4 bowls. Whisk the remaining ingredients together in a bowl over a saucepan of hot water until creamy.

Transfer the bowl to ice-cold water and stir until cold. Pour the sauce over the cherries. *Serves 4*

Apples in Red Wine

4 apples
250 ml/8 fl oz red wine
1 piece lemon rind
1 (2.5-cm/1-in) cinnamon stick
4 tablespoons redcurrant jelly
2 tablespoons sugar
2 teaspoons powdered gelatine
1 teaspoon custard powder
150 ml/¼ pint milk
150 l/¼ pint double cream
1 tablespoon chopped pistachios

390 calories per serving

Peel the apples and remove the cores with an apple corer. Bring 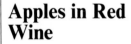 the wine to the boil with the lemon rind and cinnamon, add the apples, cover the saucepan and poach the apples over a low heat for 10 minutes. Remove the apples and leave them to cool. Fill the centre of the apples with the redcurrant jelly.

Remove the lemon rind and cinnamon from the wine. Dissolve the gelatine in a little hot water in a bowl over a saucepan of hot water. Dissolve half the sugar in the hot wine, add the gelatine and pour the mixture over the apples. Leave to set in the refrigerator.

Stir the custard powder with 2 tablespoons of the milk. Bring the remaining milk to the boil with the remaining sugar, stirring frequently. Stir in the dissolved custard powder, boil up once and remove from the heat. Whisk the cream until stiff and fold it into the custard.

Serve the apples topped with the cream custard and sprinkled with pistachios.
Serves 4

Honey Bananas with Chocolate Cream

2 bananas
2 teaspoons lemon juice
1 tablespoons orange juice
2 tablespoons honey
1 tablespoon raisins
1 tablespoon rum
25 g/1 oz plain chocolate
150 ml/¼ pint double cream
1 tablespoon chopped walnuts

265 calories per serving

Peel the bananas and cut them into oblique slices. Stir the lemon and orange juice into the honey. Arrange the banana on individual plates and sprinkle with the honey sauce.

Wash the raisins repeatedly in hot water, drain and soak them in the rum. Grate the chocolate. Whip the cream until stiff and fold in the grated chocolate.

Sprinkle the rum-soaked raisins and the walnuts over the bananas and top each serving with a quarter of the cream.
Serves 4

Cook's tip

For a fresher tasting dessert, mix sliced orange in with the bananas and add up to 1 extra tablespoon of honey to the sauce, depending on the sweetness of the oranges.

Stewed Rhubarb

1 kg/2 lb rhubarb
450 ml/¾ pint white wine
150 g/5 oz sugar
juice and rind of 1 lemon
1 (2.5-cm/1-in) piece cinnamon
* stick*
2 tablespoons cornflour
3 tablespoons bottled raspberry
* syrup*

300 calories per serving

Cut the ends off the rhubarb stalks and peel off the thin outer skin. Wash and dry the rhubarb and cut the sticks into 2.5-cm/1-in lengths.

Bring the white wine to the boil with the sugar, lemon juice, the lemon rind cut in a thin spiral, and the cinnamon. Add the rhubarb and poach over a very low heat for 10 minutes.

Remove the rhubarb from the saucepan with a skimmer, then remove the cinnamon and lemon rind.

Dissolve the cornflour in the raspberry syrup, stir into the juice and bring to the boil. Return the rhubarb to the pan.

Transfer the stewed rhubarb to individual dishes and chill in the refrigerator. *Serves 4*

Serve with: lightly sweetened whipped cream.

Cook's tip

You can use this recipe to stew berries, cherries or apricots, increasing or decreasing the amount of sugar depending on the sweetness of the fruit used.

Bilberry Cream

450 g/1 lb bilberries
250 ml/8 fl oz water
175 g/6 oz sugar
juice of 1 lemon
1½ teaspoons powdered gelatine
150 ml/¼ pint double cream

355 calories per serving

Sort the bilberries, tip them into a bowl of water and skim off any leaves or stalks that rise to the surface. Transfer the bilberries to a sieve, rinse under cold water, then tip them into the water in a saucepan with the sugar and lemon juice. Cover the pan and cook over a  the bilberries are soft.

Keep 12–16 cooked bilberries in reserve for the garnish. Tip the remaining bilberries with the juice into a sieve over a bowl. Press the bilberries

through the sieve and stir with the juice.

Dissolve the gelatine in a little hot water in a bowl over a saucepan of hot water, stir it into the warm bilberries and leave until cold. Whip the cream until stiff, keep 4 tablespoons in reserve and fold the rest into the cold bilberries.

Fill 4 individual glasses with the bilberry cream and chill in the refrigerator until set. Before serving, garnish each bilberry cream with a piped whirl of cream and a few bilberries.
Serves 4

Passion Fruit Cream with Raspberries

1 (25-g/1-oz) sachet custard
  powder
600 ml/1 pint milk
2 tablespoons sugar
4 passion fruits
350 g/12 oz raspberries
150 ml/¼ pint double cream
25 g/1 oz butter
2 tablespoons flaked almonds

295 calories per serving

Stir the custard powder with 4 tablespoons of the milk. Bring the remaining milk to the boil with the sugar stirring frequently. Stir in the custard powder and boil for a few minutes, stirring continuously. Remove the custard from the heat and leave it to cool, stirring

from time to time.

Halve the passion fruits, scoop out the flesh and seeds using a spoon and stir into the custard. Wash and thoroughly drain the raspberries. Whip the cream until stiff, then fold it into the cool custard. Spoon the custard into 4 individual glass dishes and chill in the refrigerator.

Melt the butter in a frying pan, fry the almonds until golden brown, remove from the pan and leave to cool. Before serving, garnish the passion fruit creams with the raspberries and sprinkle with the flaked almonds. *Serves 4*

Fig Dessert

450 g/1 lb dried figs
450 ml/¾ pint dry white wine
4 tablespoons sugar
juice of 2 lemons
3 tablespoons Cognac
4 teaspoons powdered gelatine
300 ml/½ pint double cream
2 tablespoon chocolate shavings
  (optional)

460 calories per serving

Cover the figs in cold water and soak them for 12 hours. Then boil the figs in the soaking water for about 40 minutes, until really soft. Leave the figs to cool, then dice them.

Heat the wine with the sugar, lemon juice and Cognac, stirring frequently until the sugar has completely dissolved. Dissolve the gelatine in a little hot water in a bowl over a saucepan of hot water and stir

it into the hot wine mixture. Leave until cold.

Stir the diced figs into the mixture. Whip the cream until stiff, keep half the quantity to one side and whisk the rest into the fig mixture just before it sets fully. Pour the fig dessert into 6 stemmed glasses and chill in the refrigerator.

Pipe the reserved cream in whirls on the top of the desserts and garnish with chocolate shavings if liked. *Serves 6*

Vanilla Cream with Cherries

450 g/1 lb cherries
150 ml/¼ pint red wine
150 ml/¼ pint milk
1 vanilla pod
3 eggs
100 g/4 oz sugar plus 1
  tablespoon
4 teaspoons powdered gelatine
150 ml/¼ pint double cream
1 tablespoon chocolate shavings

360 calories per serving

Remove the stems from the cherries, wash and stone, then poach the cherries in the red wine and the 1 tablespoon of sugar for about 4 minutes. Leave to cool and then drain.

Bring the milk to the boil. Slit the vanilla pod lengthways and scrape the pith into the milk. Separate the eggs. Whisk

the yolks with the 100 g/4 oz of sugar until frothy.

When the vanilla milk has cooled slightly stir it into the egg yolks. Dissolve the gelatine in a little hot water in a bowl over a saucepan of hot water and stir it into the egg and milk mixture. Leave to cool.

Whisk the egg whites until stiff. Whip the cream until stiff and keep 4 tablespoons to one side. Fold the egg whites and whipped cream into the vanilla cream. Arrange in layers with the cherries in 4 glasses (reserving 4 cherries for decoration), finishing with a layer of vanilla cream.

Leave to set in the refrigerator. Before serving, decorate each vanilla cream with a piped whirl of cream, chocolate shavings and a cherry. *Serves 4*

137

Strawberry Charlotte

To fill 1 rounded loaf tin:
8 egg yolks
150 g/5 oz sugar
3 egg whites
65 g/2½ oz plain flour
150 g/5 oz strawberry jam
225 g/8 oz strawberries
1½ tablespoons Cognac
3 teaspoons gelatine
250 ml/8 fl oz milk
½ vanilla pod
250 ml/8 fl oz double cream
1 tablespoon icing sugar

375 calories per each of 8 slices

Cover a baking tray with baking parchment. Beat 4 of the egg yolks with 3 tablespoons of the sugar until frothy. Whisk the egg whites with 1 tablespoon of the sugar until stiff and fold with the flour into the yolks. Spread the mixture on the baking tray and bake in a very hot oven (240 C, 475 F, gas 9) for 5–7 minutes, until golden brown. Turn out of the tin on to a tea towel, peel off the paper and while still warm spread with the jam. Roll up, wrap in aluminium foil and leave to stand for 12 hours.

Quarter the strawberries and sprinkle with 1 tablespoon of the sugar and the Cognac. Marinate for 2 hours.

Whisk the remaining egg yolks with the remaining sugar until frothy. Bring the milk to the boil with the slit vanilla pod, remove the vanilla and stir the milk into the egg yolks. Dissolve the gelatine in a little hot water in a bowl over a saucepan of hot water. Add the gelatine to the warm milk and strain through a sieve. Whisk the cream with the icing sugar until stiff and fold into the custard when it begins to set.

Line a rounded loaf tin with cling film. Cut the jam roll into 16 slices and line the tin using half the sponge. Fill with two thirds of the cream mixture. Mix the strawberries into the remaining cream and fill up the tin. Top with the remaining slices of sponge.

Leave the strawberry charlotte to set and turn out of the tin just before serving.

Lemon Cream Dessert

6 eggs, separated
200 g/7 oz sugar
1½ tablespoons Cognac
250 ml/8 fl oz single cream
grated rind of 2 lemons
250 ml/8 fl oz fresh lemon juice
4 teaspoons powdered gelatine
150 ml/¼ pint double cream
50 g/2 oz grated coconut
25 g/1 oz butter

380 calories per serving

Whisk the egg yolks with the sugar until frothy. Stir in the Cognac, single cream and lemon rind and whisk over a pan of gently simmering water until the mixture begins to thicken.

Warm the lemon juice. Dissolve the gelatine in a little hot water in a bowl over a saucepan of hot water and add it to the lemon juice. Stir the lemon juice into the egg yolk and cream mixture. Whisk the egg whites until stiff and fold them into the mixture.

Rinse a blancmange mould with cold water, fill with the lemon cream and leave to set in the refrigerator.

Whip the double cream until stiff and spoon it into a piping bag with a fluted nozzle. Fry the coconut in the butter until golden brown and allow to cool.

Turn out the lemon cream onto a plate, decorate the top with whirls of cream and sprinkle the cream with the browned coconut. *Serves 8*

Orange and Wine Cream

4 egg yolks
100 g/4 oz sugar
250 ml/8 fl oz dry white wine
juice of 1 lemon and 1 orange
grated rind of ½ orange plus 1
*   tablespoon orange rind in fine*
*   strips*
4 teaspoons powdered gelatine
2 egg whites
250 ml/8 fl oz double cream
50 g/2 oz candied fruit

465 calories per serving

In a saucepan whisk the egg yolks with the sugar until frothy. Beat in the wine, lemon and orange juice and the grated orange rind. Place the pan in a larger pan of gently simmering water and whip until the mixture is creamy. Remove the pan from the water.

Dissolve the gelatine in a little hot water in a bowl over a saucepan of hot water and add it to the mixture. Leave the cream to set in the refrigerator. Whisk the egg whites until stiff. As soon as the orange wine cream begins to set, fold in the egg whites and finally the cream.

Transfer the orange and wine cream to individual dishes and leave to stand in the refrigerator until fully set.

Before serving, garnish with the fine strips of orange rind and the candied fruit. *Serves 4*

Serve with: butter biscuits.

Crème Caramel

2 eggs
150 g/5 oz sugar plus 4 cubes
1 lemon
1 orange
300 ml/½ pint whipping cream
1 teaspoon icing sugar
2 tablespoons chocolate shavings

415 calories per serving

Beat the eggs with 50 g/2 oz of the sugar until frothy. Grate the rind off the lemon and orange with the sugar cubes and stir the sugar and rind into the egg mixture. Stir 150 ml/¼ pint of the cream into the mixture.

Caramelize the remaining sugar in a small saucepan. Coat the inside of a mould (with lid) with the caramel. Fill the mould with the cream mixture, cover with the lid and stand the mould in boiling water to come two-thirds of the way up the sides. Simmer gently for 1¼ hours, adding more hot water as and when necessary.

Leave the crème caramel until cold, then turn it out on to a plate. Whisk the remaining cream with the icing sugar until stiff and transfer to a piping bag.

Pipe whirls of cream around the top and bottom of the crème caramel and decorate with the chocolate shavings.
Serves 6

Lemon Wine Jelly

2 very ripe lemons
200 g/7 oz sugar
50 g/2 oz butter
250 ml/8 fl oz warm water
250 ml/8 fl oz white wine
rind of 1 lemon
4 teaspoons powdered gelatine

325 calories per serving

Peel the lemons to remove all the pith, and thinly slice. Cover a baking tray with aluminium foil, cover with the lemon slices, sprinkle the slices generously with sugar and dot with butter.

Candy the lemon on the middle shelf of a moderate oven (180c, 350f, gas 4) for 40 minutes. Remove the candied lemon from the baking tray and arrange in 4 stemmed glasses.

Dilute the sugar and lemon juice left on the foil with the water, pour into a saucepan, stir in the wine, the lemon rind cut in a spiral and the remaining sugar and heat. Dissolve the gelatine in a little hot water in a bowl over a saucepan of hot water and stir it into the hot wine mixture. Remove the lemon rind.

When the jelly has cooled to lukewarm, pour into the glasses over the lemon slices and leave in the refrigerator to set.
Serves 4

Serve with: custard mixed with whipped cream.

Chocolate Mousse

100 g/4 oz plain chocolate
25 g/1 oz butter
2 eggs
1 tablespoon sugar
pinch of salt
250 ml/8 fl oz double cream
1 tablespoon icing sugar
1 tablespoon chopped pistachios
4 coffee beans

435 calories per serving

Break the chocolate into a small saucepan with the butter and melt over a very low heat or melt in a bowl over a saucepan of hot water.

Separate the eggs. Whisk the yolks with the sugar until frothy. Whisk the whites with the salt until stiff. Whip the cream with the icing sugar until very stiff.

Remove the melted chocolate from the heat, mix it into the egg yolks and fold in 2 tablespoons of the whites. Leave the mixture to cool slightly, then fold in the remaining egg whites and half the whipped cream.

Rinse 4 individual glasses in cold water, fill them with the mixture and set in the refrigerator. Spoon the remaining cream into a piping bag with a plain nozzle.

Before serving, decorate each chocolate mousse with small balls of cream. Sprinkle the cream with chopped pistachios and top with 1 coffee bean.
Serves 4

Crème Russe

4 egg yolks
4 tablespoons sugar
3 tablespoons arrak or rum
250 ml/8 fl oz double cream
1 tablespoon icing sugar
4 grapes

460 calories per serving

Whisk the egg yolks with the sugar until pale and frothy. Gradually stir in the arrak or rum. Whisk the cream until stiff, keep 4 tablespoons in reserve and fold the rest into the egg yolk mixture. Spoon the mixture into 4 individual glasses.

Transfer the reserved cream to a piping bag with a fluted nozzle and pipe a whirl of cream on to each portion. Decorate with grapes dipped in icing sugar. *Serves 4*

Cook's tip

There are many recipes for Crème Russe, each slightly different and each claiming authenticity. Often the whipped cream is served over the egg yolk mixture and stirred together at the table. Another variation is to garnish with small macaroons soaked in half the rum.

Plum Mould

450 g / 1 lb ripe plums
250 ml / 8 fl oz water
175 g / 6 oz sugar
juice and rind of 2 lemons
4 teaspoons powdered gelatine
4 tablespoons plum brandy
generous pinch of ground
*   cinnamon*
2 (25-g/1-oz) sachets vanilla
*   sugar*
100 g / 4 oz almonds, chopped
150 ml / ¼ pint double cream

290 calories per serving

Wash, halve and stone the
plums and simmer them gently
in the water for 20 minutes.

Purée the plums and return
the purée to the pan. Stir in the
sugar, lemon juice and rind.
Slowly warm the plum purée,
stirring frequently and then stir
in the plum brandy, cinnamon
and vanilla sugar.

Dissolve the gelatine in a little hot water in a bowl over a
saucepan of hot water and add
it to the plum purée.

Rinse a blancmange mould
in cold water, stir the plum
mixture well, pour it into the
mould and leave to cool. Leave
the pudding to stand in the refrigerator for about 4 hours until set.

To serve, turn out the plum
mould and sprinkle with the
chopped almonds. Whip the
cream until stiff and pipe it in
whirls around the mould.
Serves 8

Chocolate Sponge
with Cream

50 g / 2 oz soft butter
100 g / 4 oz sugar
3 eggs
100 g / 4 oz plain chocolate
50 g / 2 oz ground almonds
100 g / 4 oz self-raising flour

**415 calories per serving (without
cream)**

Cream the butter and sugar
together until fluffy. Separate
the eggs. Beat the yolks into the
sugar and butter to give a
smooth, creamy mixture.

Break the chocolate into
pieces and put the pieces in a
bowl over a saucepan of hot
water. Melt the chocolate over
a low heat. Stir the melted
chocolate, sifted flour and
ground almonds into the
creamy mixture to give a drop-
ping consistency.

Whisk the egg whites until
stiff, then fold them slowly into
the mixture. Grease a 1.75-
litre 3-pint pudding basin with
butter and fill with the mixture.

Cover and stand the basin in
gently boiling water to come
two-thirds of the way up the
basin. Boil for 2¼ hours.
Alternatively, cook the sponge
in a steamer.

Turn the chocolate sponge
out on to a plate and serve it
hot. *Serves 6*

Serve with: semi-whipped
cream generously flavoured
with vanilla.

Plum Dumpling

450 ml/¾ pint milk
150 g/5 oz semolina
3 day-old bread rolls
25 g/1 oz butter
2 eggs
pinch of salt
3 tablespoons sugar
1 teaspoon cinnamon
1 (25-g/1-oz) sachet vanilla
    sugar
1 teaspoon grated lemon rind
450 ml/1 lb plums
4 tablespoons breadcrumbs

390 calories per serving

Heat the milk in a saucepan,
stir in the semolina, cook gently
to allow the semolina to swell

and then leave it to cool.

Grate the crusts off the rolls.
Dice the remaining bread and
fry it in the butter, then transfer
the bread to a bowl. Beat the
eggs with the salt, sugar, cinnamon, vanilla sugar and lemon
rind and pour the mixture over
the bread.

Wash, stone and dice the
plums and stir them into the
bread with the cool semolina.
Stir in sufficient breadcrumbs
for the mixture to form a ball.
Bring plenty of salted water to
the boil in a large saucepan.

Shape the plum mixture into
a dumpling, place on a tea-towel and knot the corners over the
dumpling. Suspend the dumpling from the handle of a wood-
en spoon in the water, making
sure that it is above the base of
the pan. Boil gently for 40 minutes. *Serves 6*

Serve with: custard.

Dutch Rice Cake

1 (410-g/14½-oz) can apricot
    halves
1 litre/1¾ pints milk
1 vanilla pod, slit
1 teaspoon grated lemon rind
200 g/7 oz pudding rice
100 g/4 oz butter
4 egg yolks
100 g/4 oz sugar
50 g/2 oz plain flour
50 g/2 oz ground almonds
3 egg whites
pinch of salt
2 tablespoons icing sugar
4 tablespoons whipped double
    cream

330 calories per serving

Drain the apricots. Cut 6 halves
in half again and keep to one
side. Dice the remaining apricots. Bring the milk to the boil
with the slit vanilla pod, lemon
rind and rice, cook over a low
heat for 20 minutes, then leave
to cool.

Beat the butter with the egg
yolks, sugar, flour and almonds
until fluffy. Whisk the egg
whites with the salt until stiff.
Stir the diced apricots and the
butter and egg yolk mixture
into the rice, then fold in the
egg whites. Grease a 24-cm/9½-
in cake tin with butter and
sprinkle with flour.

Fill with the rice mixture and
bake in a moderately hot oven
(200 c, 400 f, gas 6) for 1 hour.
Leave the cake to cool in the tin
for 10 minutes before turning it
out onto a cake plate.

When cold, dust the cake
with icing sugar and decorate
with the whipped cream and
apricot wedges. *Serves 12*

Morello Cherry Pudding

450 g / 1 lb morello cherries
1 litre / 1¾ pints water
7 tablespoons sugar
5 tablespoons raisins
450 g / 1 lb cottage cheese, sieved
2 egg yolks
1 (25-g/1-oz) sachet vanilla
  sugar
1 tablespoon cornflour
6 tablespoons milk
4 egg whites
salt

450 calories per serving

Wash and stone the cherries.
Bring the water to the boil with
1 tablespoon of the sugar, tip
in the cherries, boil for 5 minutes and then drain. Wash the
raisins well in hot water, then
drain them.

Beat the cottage cheese with
the egg yolks, remaining sugar
and the vanilla sugar. Dissolve
the cornflour in the milk and
stir into the pudding mixture.
Whisk the egg whites with a
pinch of salt until stiff and fold
into the pudding mixture with
the raisins.

Fill an ovenproof dish with
the mixture, fold in the cherries
and bake in a moderate oven
(180 C, 350 F, gas 4) for 45 minutes. *Serves 4*

Cook's tip

Alternatively, this pud-
ding can be made with
sweet cherries, raspber-
ries, blackberries or
blackcurrants. Adjust
the amount of sugar
used according to the
sweetness of the fruit.

Rum and Raisin Pancake Pudding

200 g / 7 oz plain flour
3 eggs
pinch of salt
375 ml / 13 fl oz mineral water
50 g / 2 oz butter
3 tablespoons sugar
400 g / 14 oz cottage cheese,
  sieved
50 g / 2 oz raisins
½ vanilla pod
1 egg yolk
1 tablespoon rum
4 tablespoons soured cream
50 g / 2 oz toasted flaked almonds

375 calories per serving

Sift the flour into a bowl and
beat in the eggs, salt and mineral water to make a smooth
batter. Cover and leave to
stand for 20–30 minutes.
Grease an ovenproof dish.

Heat the butter a little at a
time in a large frying pan and
fry the batter to make 4 large
pancakes, keeping each pancake warm as it is cooked.

Beat the sugar into the
cottage cheese until smooth.
Wash the raisins in hot water,
pat dry and fold into the mixture with the pith from the vanilla pod, the egg yolk and
rum. Cover the pancakes with
the filling, roll up the pancakes
and arrange them in the baking
dish.

Pour the soured cream over
the pancakes and bake on the
middle shelf of a moderately
hot oven (200 C, 400 F, gas 6) for
20 minutes. Sprinkle with the
almonds before serving.
Serves 4

Apple and Rice Pudding

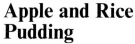

750 ml/1¼ pints milk
pinch of salt
150 g/5 oz pudding rice
butter for greasing
1 vanilla pod
2 eggs
2 tablespoons sugar
450 g/1 lb apples
1 tablespoon lemon juice
2 tablespoons icing sugar

445 calories per serving

Bring the milk to the boil with the salt, sprinkle in the rice and cook over a low heat for about 30 minutes. Leave to cool. Grease a baking dish with butter.

Slit the vanilla pod lengthways with a sharp knife and scrape out the pith. Separate the eggs. Beat the yolks with the sugar and vanilla and stir the mixture into the boiled rice. Whisk the whites until stiff and fold into the rice.

Thinly peel the apples, cut out the cores with an apple corer and cut the apples into equal rings. Fill the baking dish with alternate layers of rice and apple, finishing with a layer of apple. Sprinkle the apple with lemon juice and dust with icing sugar.

Bake on the middle shelf of a moderately hot oven (200 C, 400 F, gas 6) for about 20 minutes until the pudding is golden brown. *Serves 4*

Cherry Bread Pudding

1 kg/2 lb cherries
6 day-old bread rolls
750 ml/1¼ pints lukewarm milk
4 eggs
100 g/4 oz sugar
1 teaspoon cinnamon
50 g/2 oz chopped almonds
pinch of salt
50 g/2 oz butter
2 tablespoons icing sugar

400 calories per serving

Wash, dry, destalk and stone the cherries. Cut the rolls into cubes and soften them thoroughly in the milk. Grease a baking dish with butter.

Separate the eggs. Beat the yolks with the sugar and cinnamon and stir the mixture into the bread, together with the cherries and almonds. Whisk the egg whites with the salt until stiff, fold into the mixture and transfer to the baking dish.

Dot with butter and bake on the second shelf from the bottom of a moderately hot oven (200 C, 400 F, gas 6) for 40–50 minutes. Dust the pudding with icing sugar before serving. *Serves 8*

Cream Strudel

250 g/9 oz plain flour
pinch of salt
1 egg
2 teaspoons oil
few drops of wine vinegar
5–6 tablespoons water

For the filling:
4 day-old bread rolls
250 ml/8 fl oz cold milk
100 g/4 oz butter
200 g/7 oz sugar
grated rind of 1 lemon
3 eggs
150 ml/¼ pint single cream
75 g/3 oz raisins

For baking:
50 g/2 oz butter, melted
150 ml/¼ pint milk
2 tablespoons sugar
½ vanilla pod

750 calories per each of 6 servings

Work the flour with the salt, egg, 1 teaspoon of the oil, the vinegar and water to make a firm, glossy dough. Brush with the remaining oil, place the dough under a warm bowl and leave it for 30 minutes.

Dice the rolls and soak them in the milk. Cream the butter with half the sugar and the lemon rind until fluffy. Separate the eggs. Gradually beat the yolks into the butter mixture. Squeeze excess moisture from the bread, strain through a fine wire sieve and beat into the butter mixture with the cream. Whisk the egg whites until stiff, sprinkling in the remaining sugar as you whisk.

Dust a large tea-towel with flour and roll out the pastry on it to a large 70 × 80-cm/28 × 32-in rectangle. Stretch the pastry until paper thin and leave to rest on the tea-towel. Cut off the thick edges and use to repair any tears.

Fold the egg whites into the filling and then spread the mixture evenly over the pastry to within 5–7 cm/2–3 in of the edge. Wash the raisins in hot water, drain and sprinkle them over the filling. Roll the strudel up lengthways.

Grease a roasting tin or cast-iron casserole with melted butter. Arrange the strudel in the tin and sprinkle with the butter. Bake in a moderately hot oven (200 c, 400 f, gas 6) for 1 hour. Sweeten the milk with the sugar and bring to the boil with the slit vanilla pod. As soon as the strudel begins to brown, pour some of the milk over the strudel.

Just before the end of the cooking time, pour the remaining milk over the strudel. Serve hot. *Serves 6–8*

Cook's tip

You can use the same pastry to make Apple Strudel. Finely chop 1 kg/2 lb peeled cooking apples and sprinkle with a mixture of cinnamon and sugar, 5 tablespoons of breadcrumbs fried in butter, 75 g/3 oz raisins and 75 g/3 oz chopped hazelnuts. Sprinkle with 150 ml/¼ pint soured cream.

Apricot Crêpes

50 g/2 oz plain flour
150 ml/¼ pint mineral water
pinch of salt
pinch of sugar plus 100 g/4 oz
2 eggs
50 g/2 oz butter
450 g/1 lb fresh apricots
juice of ½ lemon
250 ml/8 fl oz water
1 tablespoon apricot or almond
*   liqueur*
icing sugar to sprinkle
*   (optional)*

310 calories per serving

Sift the flour into a bowl and whisk in the mineral water, salt, pinch of sugar and eggs to make a smooth batter. Cover and leave to stand for 30 minutes. Melt the butter in a small saucepan.

Blanch the apricots in boiling water, then peel, halve and stone them. Boil the 100 g/4 oz sugar in the lemon juice and water for about 3 minutes. Thinly slice the apricot halves and braise them gently in the hot syrup for 10 minutes. Stir in the liqueur and leave to cool.

Stir the batter thoroughly. Pour a little of the melted butter into a small frying pan, coat the inside of the pan and pour any excess back into the butter saucepan.

Using a small ladle, pour a little batter into the frying pan, tip the pan to spread the batter and cook to make a very thin pancake, golden brown on each side. Keep the cooked pancakes hot between two plates in the oven.

Drain the apricots. Fold the crêpes into small cones and fill with the apricots. Dust with icing sugar to serve.

Serve with: hot chocolate sauce.

HEALTHY COOKING

We are all becoming increasingly health conscious and the following recipes should give you some ideas for wholesome, yet interesting and attractive looking family food. They use primarily fresh ingredients with an emphasis on fresh vegetables and fruit, fish and lighter poultry and meat dishes.

While many of the recipes are low in calories, they are not boring 'diet' recipes, but are helpful in encouraging healthy eating and each has a comprehensive nutritional analysis. They usually contain only moderate amounts of cream and butter, and favour whole grain products.

You can explore the versatility of fish with the varied selection of fish and seafood recipes or experiment with naturally lean poultry and game, now much more readily available, and other healthy meats. Refreshing salads are a good way to begin a meal – or to end one – and a substantial salad can provide a meal in itself. Investigate the innovative ways with vegetables that follow, either as an accompaniment or a main course, or try the exciting vegetarian creations. Finish your meal with one of the luscious fruit desserts, as beautiful as they are delicious.

Pickled Fillets of Trout

3 cleaned fresh trout, about
   350 g/12 oz each
3 tablespoons lemon juice
3 tablespoons tarragon vinegar
375 ml/13 fl oz water
1 bay leaf
3 juniper berries
2 coriander seeds
1 teaspoon mustard seeds
1 teaspoon white peppercorns
100 g/4 oz fresh basil
2 tablespoons salt
1 tablespoon caster sugar

Rinse the trout inside and out in cold water and wipe thoroughly dry. Cut off the heads, fins and tails. Cut the fish open right along the stomach side, carefully open out and remove the backbone. It is best to use a knife with a thin, flexible blade. Start by loosening the large bones that lie flat in the fish. Then open up the fish as far as it will go and run the knife in short strokes along the left and right of the backbone. Once the bone is completely free of the flesh you can peel it back towards the tail. Remove all the small bones with tweezers, making sure you do not miss any. Separate the fish into fillets but do not skin.

Mix the lemon juice with the tarragon vinegar and water. Place the trout fillets in the liquid, cover the bowl and marinate for 8 hours in a cool place.

Remove the trout fillets from the marinade and wipe dry on absorbent kitchen paper.

Crumble the bay leaf between your fingers. In a mortar, coarsely crush the juniper berries, coriander, mustard seeds and peppercorns.

Rinse the basil in cold water, strip off the leaves, pat dry and finely chop.

Mix the seasonings in the mortar with the bay leaf, basil, salt and sugar.

Sprinkle the flesh side of half the fillets with this mixture and sandwich together in pairs with the skin to the outside. Press each pair of fillets together and wrap in foil. Place the packets between two trays or chopping boards and weight down.

Leave the trout fillets to press for 12 hours in a cool place.

Unwrap the fillets and scrape off the seasoning.

Next skin the fillets. To do this, place each fillet, skin side down, on the worktop and cut about 1 cm/½ in skin loose at the tail end. Hold this piece of skin and run the knife flat between the fillet and the skin.

Serve the pickled trout on individual plates, garnished to taste with lemon slices and fresh herbs.

Delicious with brown bread, horseradish cream and salad.

The quantities given will also make a light main course for 3.

Serves 6

Per Portion
about 115 calories
4 g carbohydrate
17 g protein · 2 g fat

Cook's Tip

Fresh salmon is also delicious pickled in this way. Marinate a tailpiece in the same way as the trout and skin after marinating. If you can't get fresh basil use dill. Eat both the trout and salmon as soon as possible after pickling for they lose their flavour if kept.

Salmon Carpaccio with Chervil

300 g / 11 oz fresh salmon (tail piece)
handful of fresh chervil
5 white peppercorns
1 tablespoon white wine vinegar
2 tablespoons lemon juice
3 tablespoons dry white wine
salt
pinch of caster sugar
1 tablespoon capers
4 tablespoons cold-pressed olive oil

To cut the salmon into really thin slices you will need a special salmon knife with a long, flexible, very sharp blade. The best idea is to ask your fishmonger to fillet, skin and slice the salmon. If you prefer to fillet and skin the fish yourself, proceed as in the trout fillets recipe on the opposite page. Any slices that are too thick can be placed between pieces of cling film and gently flattened with the ball of your hand. Arrange the salmon slices on four plates.

Pick over and wash the chervil, pat thoroughly dry and chop very finely.

Place the peppercorns on a board and crush with the blade of a strong knife.

Stir the white wine vinegar with the lemon juice, white wine, salt to taste and sugar until the salt has completely dissolved. Coarsely chop the capers and add them. Beat in the olive oil a tablespoon at a time.

Mix the chervil and peppercorns into the vinaigrette.

Spoon the chervil vinaigrette over the salmon and serve the carpaccio immediately, with wheatgerm rolls or wholemeal bread and butter.

Serves 4

Per Portion
about 300 calories
3 g carbohydrate
15 g protein · 25 g fat

Cook's Tip
For a slightly stronger flavour you can replace the chervil with snipped fresh chives.

Fish Soup with Vegetables and Cress

1.5 kg/3 lb mixed fish (eg cod, halibut, turbot, salmon trout or salmon)
750 g/1½ lb fish trimmings (bones and heads of salmon, turbot and sole)
1 onion
1 leek
1 stick celery
400 g/14 oz carrots
bunch of fresh parsley
sprig of fresh thyme
few celery leaves
4 white peppercorns
2 juniper berries
1 bay leaf
1 piece lemon rind
500 ml/17 fl oz dry white wine
750 ml/14 mins water
2 shallots
1–2 cloves garlic
1 fennel bulb (about 250 g/9 oz)
250 g/9 oz ripe tomatoes
3 tablespoons olive oil
100 g/4 oz sorrel or spinach

3 tablespoons dry vermouth
250 ml/8 fl oz single cream
salt
freshly ground white pepper
2 boxes of mustard and cress

You will probably need to order the fish and trimmings in advance. Have the fishmonger skin and fillet the fish but ask him to give you the heads and bones for the stock.

Cut the gills off the heads because these will give the stock an oily taste. Make sure you get rid of the gills themselves as well as the outer gill covering. Place all the trimmings in a saucepan.

Peel and quarter the onion. Trim the leek and celery. Peel 2 carrots. Wash these vegetables and cut into fairly large pieces. Wash the parsley, thyme and celery leaves and shake dry. Add the vegetables, parsley, thyme, celery leaves, peppercorns, juniper berries, bay leaf and lemon rind to the fish pan. Pour on the wine and water, bring to the boil and then simmer for 25 minutes.

While the stock is cooking, rinse the fish fillets in cold water, pat dry and cut into bite-sized pieces. Peel and finely chop the shallots and garlic. Halve the fennel bulb and cut out the stalk. Wash and dry the halves and cut across into strips. Peel and wash the remaining carrots and cut into sticks. Blanch the tomatoes in boiling water for 30 seconds and then rinse in cold water. Peel and dice the tomatoes, removing the core and the seeds.

Strain the fish stock (without pressing the fish trimmings and vegetables as this would make the stock cloudy) and discard all the solid ingredients.

Heat the olive oil in a clean saucepan. Fry the shallots and garlic until transparent. Add the fennel, carrot and tomato and fry for a few minutes. Add the fish stock and bring to the boil, then cover the pan and simmer over a low heat for 8 to 10 minutes until the vegetables are tender but still firm to bite.

Meanwhile, wash and dry the sorrel or spinach and coarsely chop. Add to the soup. Stir in the vermouth and cream. Add the pieces of fish, cover the pan and cook over a very low heat for about 3 minutes. Season to taste.

Snip off the cress with scissors and sprinkle over the soup before serving.

Serves 6

Per Portion
about 490 calories
20 g carbohydrate
40 g protein · 20 g fat

Steamed Cod on Vegetables

1 lemon
bunch of fresh dill
250 g / 9 oz young carrots
250 g / 9 oz kohlrabi
bunch of spring onions
250 ml / 8 fl oz water
1 bay leaf
3 white peppercorns
1 juniper berry
4 cod cutlets, about 4 cm / 1½ in
*   thick*
herb salt
freshly ground white pepper
1 egg yolk
100 g / 4 oz chilled butter

Wash the lemon under hot running water, dry and cut in half. Cut a thin slice off one half for the stock. Then squeeze the two halves and keep the juice in reserve for the sauce.

Rinse the dill in cold water and shake dry. Break off the ends of the stalks for the stock. Keep the leaves for the sauce but do not chop yet.

Trim, scrape and wash the carrots. Peel the kohlrabi, cut out any tough parts and then wash. Cut the roots and limp leaves off the spring onions. Wash well and shake dry. Cut the carrots and kohlrabi first into 0.5 cm / ¼ in slices and then into thin sticks. Cut the spring onions, including about half the length of the green leaves, into 1 cm / ½ in pieces.

Bring the water to the boil with the lemon slice, the dill stalks, bay leaf, peppercorns and juniper berry in a fish kettle or steamer.

Rinse the cod cutlets in cold water, wipe dry and season both sides with herb salt and pepper. Arrange the vegetables on the rack in the steamer and top with the cutlets. Cover and steam the fish and vegetables for about 20 minutes.

Arrange the fish and vegetables on heated plates and keep hot in the oven.

Finely chop the dill leaves.

To make the sauce fill a frying pan with hot water and place on the hob. Keep the

water hot over a low heat. Stand a deep container, preferably stainless steel, in the water. Into this container pour 3 tablespoons of the steaming liquid, the lemon juice and egg yolk and beat with a hand or electric whisk to a thick, frothy mixture. The water should be hot throughout but not boiling or the egg yolk will separate.

Cut the butter into small pieces and gradually whisk into the sauce. Stir in the chopped dill and season to taste with pepper.

Pour the sauce over the fish cutlets and vegetables and serve at once with jacket-boiled potatoes.

Serves 4

Per Portion
about 415 calories
9 g carbohydrate
37 g protein · 23 g fat

Cook's Tip

The cooking times given for fish may be shorter than you are used to. But try this modern, time-saving and delicious way of cooking fish. When fish fillets or cutlets are properly cooked the flesh should still look transparent at the thickest point, usually the centre. With whole fish the backbone should be pinkish in colour with the flesh still attached to it. Fish is overcooked if the backbone pulls away easily or if the flesh falls apart as you serve it. Remember that fish will continue to cook when kept hot.

Plaice Fillets in Herb Sauce

2 plaice (600 g/1¼ lb each)
300 g/11 oz fish heads and bones
2 shallots
bunch of fresh parsley
1 carrot
1 small leek
1 stick celery
4 white peppercorns
1 bay leaf
250 ml/8 fl oz water
250 ml/8 fl oz dry white wine
½ bunch of fresh dill
2 handfuls of fresh chervil
5 leaves fresh sorrel
handful of wild herbs (eg dandelion leaves, nettle and salad burnet)
2 tablespoons lemon juice
salt
freshly ground white pepper

Have your fishmonger skin and fillet the plaice, but take the heads and bones with you to add to the other fish trimmings for the stock. Cut the gills off all the fish heads (the fishmonger will do this if you ask him) for they give the stock an oily taste. Make sure you remove the whole gill and not just the gill covering.

Peel and halve the shallots. Wash the parsley and shake dry. Strip the leaves off the stalks and keep to one side for the sauce. The stalks are used in the stock.

Peel and wash the carrot and halve it lengthways. Cut the roots and limp leaves off the leek. Cut a cross through the leaves down as far as the white, open the leaves and wash well. Cut the leek into two pieces. Wash the celery and cut in half.

Tie the parsley stalks, carrot, leek and celery into a bundle with cooking string.

Put the fish heads and bones, the bundle of vegetables, the peppercorns, bay leaf, water and half the wine in a saucepan and bring to the boil. Cover the pan and simmer over a low heat for 25 minutes. Do not overcook the stock or it will have a bitter taste.

Strain the stock into another pan, wide enough to take the plaice fillets side by side, through a sieve lined with absorbent kitchen paper. Do not squeeze out the fish trimmings or seasonings as this would make the stock cloudy.

Pick over the herbs and remove any tough stalks. Rinse, shake dry and chop fairly coarsely with the parsley leaves.

Add the remaining wine and the lemon juice to the fish stock and bring to the boil. Reduce by about half over a high heat, stirring frequently.

Season the plaice fillets. Add the herbs to the stock, then add the fillets and cook over a low heat for about 2 minutes.

Lift the fish gently out of the pan on to warmed plates and spoon on the herb sauce. Serve with potatoes or wholemeal French bread and salad.

Serves 4

Per Portion
about 225 calories
8 g carbohydrate
30 g protein · 2 g fat

Cook's Tip
The sauce will be richer, but higher in calories, if you whisk in a little butter. Arrange the cooked plaice fillets on warmed plates. Cut about 50 g/2 oz chilled butter into small pieces and whisk into the herb sauce.

Trout with Cream and Herbs

4 cleaned fresh trout, about
   300 g/11 oz each
salt
freshly ground white pepper
1 box of mustard and cress
large bunch of fresh parsley
few leaves fresh lemon balm
350 ml/12 fl oz double cream
1 bay leaf

Rinse the trout inside and out in cold water and wipe thoroughly dry. On a plate mix a little salt with plenty of pepper and rub into the inside and outside of the trout. Place the trout side by side in a baking dish.

Snip off the cress with scissors. Wash the parsley, strip the leaves off the stalks, pat dry and finely chop. Wash and dry the lemon balm and cut into strips. Stir the herbs into the cream, pour over the trout and add the bay leaf.

Bake the trout in a moderately hot oven (200 C, 400 F, gas 6) for 20 to 25 minutes, basting repeatedly with the herb cream.

Transfer the cooked trout to a warmed plate. Pour the herb cream into a saucepan. Remove the bay leaf. Boil to reduce the cream over a high heat until thickened.

Serve the trout and sauce separately, with jacket-boiled potatoes and salad.

Serves 4

Per Portion
about 450 calories
5 g carbohydrate
27 g protein · 33 g fat

Cook's Tip
Instead of lemon balm you can use a piece of thinly cut lemon rind. Cut this into fine strips and stir into the cream with the cress and parsley.

Fish with Vegetables

750 g / 1½ lb skinned firm-fleshed
white fish fillets
1 tablespoon cornflour
1 tablespoon dry sherry
2 tablespoons soy sauce
1 clove garlic
bunch of spring onions
2 sticks celery
handful of mung bean sprouts
5 tablespoons vegetable oil
125 ml / 4 fl oz freshly made vege-
table stock
salt
cayenne pepper

Remove any bones in the fish fillet with tweezers. Rinse the fish under cold running water and wipe thoroughly dry. Using a sharp knife cut the fish into 3 cm / 1¼ in cubes. Try to get them all the same size so that they cook evenly.

Beat the cornflour with the sherry and soy sauce, pour over the fish and stir to mix in. Cover and leave to stand while you prepare the vegetables.

Peel and very finely chop the garlic. Cut the roots and limp leaves off the spring onions. Wash the onions well, shake dry and cut into 0.5 cm / ¼ in rings, including about one third of the green leaves. Using a small sharp knife peel off any tough threads from the celery. Wash and dry, then cut off the leaves (reserve for the garnish) and cut the celery sticks into 0.5 cm / ¼ in pieces. Tip the bean sprouts into a sieve, wash under cold water and drain.

Heat 1 tablespoon oil in a frying pan. Cook the garlic over a low to moderate heat, stirring, until transparent. Do not allow it to brown or it will be bitter.

Add all the vegetables and turn up the heat. Stirring continuously, fry the vegetables over a moderate to high heat for 2 to 3 minutes.

Add the vegetable stock and season to taste with salt and cayenne. Cover the pan and cook over a moderate heat for 1 minute until the vegetables are tender but still firm to bite.

Transfer the vegetables to a shallow warmed dish and keep hot while you cook the fish.

Heat 2 tablespoons oil in the frying pan and fry the fish in batches for 3 to 4 minutes, turning them continually and keeping them hot with the vegetables until they are all cooked. You will need to heat more oil for each batch. When all the fish is cooked stir it gently into the vegetables and serve at once, scattered with the celery leaves.

Serve with rice, wholemeal bread or wholemeal French bread.

Serves 4

Per Portion
about 260 calories
9 g carbohydrate
18 g protein · 16 g fat

Cook's Tip
You must use a firm-fleshed fish for this dish, such as cod, huss, haddock or halibut. Even with firm fish the cubes tend to fall apart to some extent during cooking. You can avoid this by deep-frying the fish but this adds extra calories and makes the fish harder to digest. Instead of fish you could use fresh or frozen cooked shelled prawns. You will find how to prepare prawns in the recipe for Prawns in herb sauce.

Steamed Fish with Ginger

2 cleaned trout
salt
4 spring onions
piece of fresh root ginger, about
*   6 cm/2½ in long*
1–2 cloves garlic
4 tablespoons dry sherry
2 tablespoons soy sauce
½ teaspoon caster sugar
1 tablespoon sunflower oil

Rinse the fish and wipe thoroughly dry. Place the fish flat on the worktop and season sparingly with salt, inside and out.

Cut the roots and limp leaves off the spring onions, wash well and cut into strips. Finely shred about a quarter of the spring onions and shred both ends of two pieces to set aside for the garnish. Peel the root ginger like a potato, wash, dry and cut into very thin slices. Peel and finely chop the garlic.

Beat the sherry with the soy sauce, sugar and sunflower oil. Stir in the ginger and garlic.

Cover the bottom of a fish kettle or steamer with water. Place the spring onions and fish on the rack, sprinkling the fine shreds of onion on top of the fish. Pour on the marinade.

Steam the fish for 15 to 20 minutes. Bone the steamed fish and serve on heated plates, garnished with the reserved spring onions. Brown rice or wholemeal French bread and a salad can be served with the fish.

Serves 4

Per Portion
about 230 calories
7 g carbohydrate
27 g protein · 8 g fat

Cook's Tip
Instead of spring onions you can use thin strips of leek.

Prawns in Herb Sauce

12 uncooked Mediterranean or
  Dublin Bay prawns
1 onion
1 leek
2 carrots
½ celeriac
½ bunch of fresh parsley
1 tablespoon butter
125 ml/4 fl oz dry white wine
2 white peppercorns
1 bay leaf
½ bunch of fresh dill
125 ml/4 fl oz double cream
1 teaspoon lemon juice
salt
freshly ground white pepper

Rinse and peel the prawns, then
remove the black thread-like
intestine.

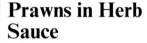
Peel and quarter the onion.
Trim and thoroughly wash the
leek. Peel and wash the carrots
and celeriac. Coarsely chop the
leek, carrots and celeriac. Wash
the parsley, strip off the leaves.
Keep 3 stalks for the stock.

Melt the butter in a saucepan
and fry the prawn shells and
vegetables until the shells are
red in colour. Add the wine and
stir well to mix. Add the parsley
stalks, peppercorns and bay
leaf.
 Simmer for 30 minutes, then
strain. Bring the stock back to
the boil in a clean pan. Add the
prawns and simmer for about 8
minutes.
 Wash the dill and finely chop
with the parsley leaves.
 Lift the prawns out of the
stock and keep hot on four
warmed plates.
 Boil to reduce the stock by
half. Gradually add the cream
and continue boiling until
creamy and saucelike, stirring
continuously. Stir in the herbs
and lemon juice and season to
taste with salt and pepper. Pour
over the prawns.

Serves 4

Per Portion
about 270 calories
2 g carbohydrate
22 g protein · 16 g fat

Grilled Prawns

12 uncooked Mediterranean or
  Dublin Bay prawns in the shell
½ lemon
3 cloves garlic
bunch of fresh parsley
3–4 tablespoons olive oil
salt
freshly ground black pepper

Preheat the grill or barbecue.
Cutting on the in-curving side,
cut the prawns in half lengthways without cutting right the
way through. Open up the
prawns so that the shells crack
and the prawns lie as flat as
possible on the worktop.
 Squeeze the juice from the
lemon. Peel the garlic and
squeeze in a garlic press, or
chop to a pulp. Wash the parsley. Strip the leaves off the
stalks, pat dry and finely chop.
 Beat the lemon juice with the
garlic, parsley and olive oil to
form a paste. Spread the paste
on to the flesh side of the
prawns. Place under a
preheated grill, or on the hot

grid of the barbecue, and cook
for about 10 minutes.
 Transfer to warmed plates,
season to taste and serve at
once with wholemeal French
bread and a mixed salad.

Serves 2

Per Portion
about 220 calories
2 g carbohydrate
22 g protein · 12 g fat

Cook's Tip

The quantities will also
serve 4 as a starter.

Herring Fillets with Potatoes and Quark Sauce

1 kg/2¼ lb small new potatoes
1 tart eating apple
1 red onion
bunch of fresh dill
bunch of fresh chives
250 g/9 oz Quark or other soft
  cheese (20 percent fat)
125 ml/4 fl oz single cream
1–2 tablespoons freshly grated
  horseradish
salt
freshly ground white pepper
8 matjes herring fillets

Scrub the potatoes well under cold running water so that they can be eaten in their skins. Bring a little water to the boil in a saucepan, add the potatoes, cover and cook over a low heat for 20 to 30 minutes, until tender.

Meanwhile, peel, core and dice the apple. Peel and chop the onion. Wash the dill and chives and pat dry. Chop the dill and cut up the chives.

Stir the Quark with the cream until smooth. Mix in the apple, onion, herbs and horseradish. Season to taste with salt and pepper.

Cover the bottom of a shallow dish with ice cubes.

Wash the herring fillets under cold running water to remove some of the salt. Wipe dry and arrange on the ice. Drain the cooked potatoes and allow the steam to evaporate. Serve with the Quark sauce and herring fillets. Accompany with green beans tossed in a little butter.

Serves 4

Per Portion
about 690 calories
57 g carbohydrate
31 g protein · 36 g fat

Fish and Cucumber Stew

100 g/4 oz shallots or very small
  onions
1 (400 g/14 oz) cucumber
1 tablespoon butter
1 tablespoon lemon juice
125 ml/4 fl oz freshly made vege-
  table stock
salt
freshly ground white pepper
600 g/1¼ lb white fish fillet
1 teaspoon made English
  mustard
bunch of fresh dill

Peel the shallots and cut into wedges. Wash the cucumber. Cut it in half across and then into quarters lengthways. Scrape out the seeds with a teaspoon. Cut the cucumber into 1 cm/½ in pieces.

Heat the butter in a large saucepan without allowing it to brown. Cook the shallots and cucumber in the butter, stirring, until transparent. Add the lemon juice and stock. Season to taste and bring to the boil, then cover the pan and simmer over a low heat for 8 to 10 minutes.

Meanwhile, rinse the fish fillet, wipe thoroughly dry and cut into 2 cm/¾ in cubes.

Stir the mustard into the vegetables. Tip the fish on to the vegetables, season to taste, cover the pan again and cook over the lowest possible heat for about 8 minutes.

Meanwhile, wash, dry and finely chop the dill, discarding any tough stalks.

Transfer the fish stew to a heated dish and serve at once, sprinkled with dill. Accompany with jacket-boiled potatoes or rice, and tomato salad generously seasoned with fresh herbs.

Serves 4

Per Portion
about 230 calories
9 g carbohydrate
28 g protein · 9 g fat

Stuffed Chicken

3 bunches of fresh parsley
2 cloves garlic
1 large lemon
1 tablespoon pine nuts
100 g/4 oz Emmental cheese,
  grated
100 g/4 oz low fat Quark or
  other soft cheese
3 tablespoons single cream
salt
freshly ground black pepper
1 chicken, about 1.4 kg/3 lb
1 tablespoon olive oil
1½ teaspoons ground ginger
3 tablespoons dry white wine

To make the stuffing, wash the parsley under cold running water. Strip the leaves from the stalks, wipe thoroughly dry and finely chop. Peel and finely chop the garlic. Wash the lemon well in hot water, wipe dry and grate the rind. Then halve the lemon and squeeze the juice. Keep the juice in reserve to brush over the chicken.

Mix together the parsley, garlic, lemon rind, pine nuts, Emmental, Quark and cream and season to taste.

Remove the giblets from the chicken, if any, and use for some other dish. Rinse the chicken well inside and out under cold running water, making sure you remove any bits of lung or blood from the inside for these have a bitter taste. Drain the chicken and wipe dry inside and out. Mix salt and pepper in a bowl. Sprinkle it over the chicken inside and out and rub into the skin.

Stuff the chicken with the cheese mixture, but do not overfill as the stuffing expands during cooking and could split the skin if too tightly packed. Close the opening with four wooden cocktail sticks, or skewers, threading them horizontally through the skin. Wind a piece of cooking string around the sticks like a shoe lace and tie in a knot.

Mix the lemon juice with the olive oil and ginger. Brush the chicken all over with the oil mixture. Place the chicken breast uppermost in a roasting tin and pour 2 tablespoons cold water around it.

Place in a moderately hot oven (200 C, 400 F, gas 6) and roast for about 1 hour, turning once and basting repeatedly with the juices in the tin to make the skin brown and crisp.

Remove the chicken from the oven, transfer to a roasting rack and return to the oven with the roasting tin beneath to catch the juices. Brown the chicken on the rack for a further 15 minutes.

To make the sauce, soak up the fat from the top of the cooking juices with absorbent kitchen paper. Add the white wine and stir over a low heat to work in the sediment from the bottom of the tin.

Remove the string and sticks from the chicken. Carve either in the kitchen or at the table, as pictured. Arrange the chicken on a warmed plate and serve with the stuffing and gravy. Serve with mixed salad and wholemeal French bread or brown rice.

Serves 4

Per Portion
about 595 calories
6 g carbohydrate
65 g protein · 30 g fat

Cook's Tip

For a different stuffing, halve the amount of Quark and add 1 large fairly tart apple, peeled, cored and finely diced, and a generous pinch of dried marjoram.

Chicken with Sage

1 young chicken, about 1 kg/
  2¼ lb
salt
freshly ground white pepper
1 lemon
2 cloves garlic
2 sprigs of fresh sage
1 tablespoon butter
1 tablespoon olive oil

Remove the giblets, if any. Wash the chicken well and remove any bits of lung or blood from the inside. Wipe thoroughly dry. Mix salt and pepper on a saucer, sprinkle over the chicken inside and out and rub into the skin.

Wash the lemon in hot water and wipe dry. Grate the rind and keep in reserve. Halve the lemon and squeeze the juice from one half. Peel the remaining half and dice the flesh. Peel and finely chop the garlic.

Wash the sage, shake dry, strip the leaves off the stalks and mix with the chopped lemon and garlic. Use to stuff the chicken. Close the opening as described in the recipe on the opposite page.

Melt the butter over a low heat and mix with the olive oil and lemon rind. Brush the chicken with half the seasoned butter and place breast uppermost in a roasting tin. Place the tin in a moderately hot oven (200 c, 400 f, gas 6), on the second shelf from the bottom. Roast for about 1 hour, turning once and basting with the remaining seasoned butter.

Transfer the chicken to a roasting rack, replace in the tin, brush with the lemon juice and roast for a further 15 minutes.

Serve with mixed salad.

Serves 2

Per Portion
about 645 calories
2 g carbohydrate
76 g protein · 33 g fat

Braised Chicken with Vegetables

1 (200 g/7 oz) leek
1 (250 g/9 oz) fennel bulb
3 sticks celery
200 g/7 oz carrots
bunch of fresh parsley
1 young chicken, about 1.6 kg/
* 3½ lb*
salt
freshly ground white pepper
25 g/1 oz butter
250 ml/8 fl oz dry white wine
1 bay leaf

Cut the roots and limp green leaves off the leek. Cut a cross into the leaves down as far as the white so that you can open the leaves and wash to remove all the dirt. Cut the leek into 2 cm/¾ in lengths. Trim the fennel and cut out the wedge-shaped stalk with a sharp knife. Wash and dry the fennel and cut across into 1 cm/½ in slices. Peel off any tough threads from the celery, wash and cut into 1 cm/½ in lengths.

Peel and wash the carrots and cut into sticks or cubes. Wash the parsley and shake dry. Remove the stalks and finely chop them, keeping the leaves in reserve to sprinkle over the chicken later.

Remove the giblets from the chicken, if any, and use in another dish. Wash the chicken well inside and out under cold running water and remove any bits of lung or blood from the inside. Wipe dry. Place the chicken, breast uppermost, on a wooden board and with a large, heavy knife joint into the drumsticks, thighs, wings and breasts. You can use the backbone which has little meat to make a stock. Rub the chicken pieces all over with salt and pepper.

Heat the butter in a large pan without allowing it to brown. Seal the drumsticks, thighs and wings over a moderate heat for about 10 minutes until the skin is nice and brown. Add the breasts and brown for 5 minutes. Remove the chicken from the pan.

Add the vegetables and stir until coated in fat. Add the wine and stir in the sediment from the bottom of the pan.

Arrange the chicken pieces over the vegetables, add the bay leaf and cover the pan. Braise the chicken and vegetables over a low heat for about 30 minutes. Test both a leg and a breast by pricking with the point of a knife to check if they are cooked. If the juice runs clear the chicken is cooked.

Coarsely chop the parsley. Arrange the braised chicken and vegetables on a warmed plate, spoon on the cooking liquid and serve sprinkled with the parsley. Serve with rice, wheatgerm rolls or wholemeal French bread and Sprouted salad.

Serves 4

Per Portion
about 580 calories
13 g carbohydrate
62 g protein · 25 g fat

Cook's Tip
This recipe is just as good made with lamb leg steaks instead of chicken. The meat is sealed for about 5 minutes on each side and then braised over the vegetables with a little garlic and the grated rind and juice of ¼ lemon.

Chicken Breasts in Savoy Cabbage

8 chicken breasts
8 large Savoy cabbage leaves
salt
freshly ground white pepper
100 g/4 oz Parmesan cheese, grated
bunch of fresh parsley
250 ml/8 fl oz crème fraîche

Skin and bone the chicken breasts and wipe dry.

With a knife trim the thick stalks of the cabbage leaves to flatten them, without damaging the leaves. Wash the leaves and blanch in plenty of boiling salted water for 3 to 4 minutes to make them easier to roll up. Lift the leaves out of the pan on a slotted spoon and plunge into iced water so that they keep their fresh green colour.

Sprinkle the chicken breasts with pepper to taste and the Parmesan. Put the breasts together in pairs and wrap each pair in 2 cabbage leaves. Tie up with cooking string.

Wash the parsley, strip the leaves off the stalks, pat dry and finely chop. Mix the crème fraîche with the parsley and season to taste.

Place the cabbage parcels on a sheet of extra-strong aluminium foil and bend up the edges. Pour the crème fraîche mixture over the parcels and seal the foil together firmly at the top and sides.

Cook the chicken breasts in a moderately hot oven (200 C, 400 F, gas 6) for about 40 minutes.

Open the foil, lift the parcels carefully out of the sauce and remove the string. Arrange the chicken breasts on a warmed plate and serve topped with the sauce.

Serves 4

Per Portion
about 500 calories
5 g carbohydrate
68 g protein · 24 g fat

Chicken Rissoles

1 rye or wholemeal bread roll
300 g/11 oz chicken meat
1 onion
handful of fresh chervil or bunch of fresh parsley
75 g/3 oz shelled walnuts
1 egg
1 teaspoon grated lemon rind
salt
freshly ground white pepper
2 tablespoons sunflower oil

Soak the bread roll in lukewarm water, then squeeze out well and fluff up with a fork.

Remove any skin, fat or gristle from the chicken. Wipe dry and finely dice. On a board, finely chop the diced chicken using a large, heavy knife, forming it into a pile and chopping repeatedly.

Peel and finely chop the onion. Wash the chervil or parsley and shake dry. You can chop the chervil on the stalks but parsley leaves should be stripped from the stalks first.

Finely chop the walnuts.

Mix the chicken with the onion, chervil or parsley, walnuts, egg, bread and lemon rind. Season to taste. Using wet hands, shape the mixture into rissoles of similar size.

Heat the oil in a frying pan. Seal the rissoles on either side over a high heat, then reduce the heat to moderate and fry the rissoles for about 7 minutes longer.

Serve with wholemeal French bread and potato salad with herbs.

Serves 4

Per Portion
about 330 calories
31 g carbohydrate
21 g protein · 22 g fat

Chicken with Apricots

250 ml/9 oz dried apricots
250 ml/8 fl oz dry white wine
1 young chicken, about 1.3 kg/
2¾ lb
salt
freshly ground black pepper
2 onions
2 cloves garlic
1 tablespoon vegetable oil
sprig of fresh rosemary

Wash the apricots well in hot water, drain and soak in the white wine in a covered bowl for about 5 minutes.

Cut the chicken into 8 pieces. Rinse in cold water and dry. Rub all over with salt and pepper.

Peel and finely chop the onions and garlic.

Heat the oil in a shallow **flameproof casserole. Brown the chicken in batches over a moderate to high heat and transfer each batch to a plate as it is done.** When you have browned all the chicken, pour off the fat to leave only a thin film on the base of the casserole. Add the onion and garlic and fry for a few minutes, stirring continuously.

Drain the apricots, reserving the soaking wine. Pour the wine into the casserole and stir in the sediment from the bottom.

Return the chicken to the casserole with the juice that has collected on the plate.

Wash the rosemary, strip the leaves from the stalk and add to the chicken. Cover the casserole and braise in a moderately hot oven (200 C, 400 F, gas 6) for about 30 minutes.

Add the drained apricots and cook for a further 20 to 25 minutes, uncovered, to brown the chicken.

Serve with brown rice.

Serves 4

Per Portion
about 620 calories
49 g carbohydrate
52 g protein · 17 g fat

Exotic Chicken

1 young chicken, about 1.25 kg/
  2½ lb
salt
1 onion
5 cloves garlic
2 tomatoes
3 tablespoons vegetable oil
4 tablespoons water
5 tablespoons soy sauce
1 tablespoon honey
2 tablespoons lemon juice
cayenne pepper

Joint the chicken, rinse, wipe dry and rub with salt.

Peel and finely chop the onion and garlic. Blanch the tomatoes in boiling water for 30 seconds, rinse in cold water, then peel and quarter. Remove the core and the seeds.

Heat the oil in a shallow flameproof casserole. Brown the chicken joints in batches over a moderate to high heat, placing each batch on a plate as it is done. When you have browned all the chicken pour off the fat to leave only a thin film.

Fry the onion and garlic for a few minutes in the fat over a moderate heat. Add the water and stir in the sediment from the bottom of the casserole.

Return the chicken to the casserole. Add the tomatoes. Cover and place in a moderate oven (180 C, 350 F, gas 4). Cook the chicken for about 45 minutes.

Stir the soy sauce, honey and lemon juice together in a saucepan to warm them until the honey is fluid. Season to taste with cayenne and pour over the chicken. Cook for a further 30 minutes, turning the chicken frequently and basting with the sauce.

Serves 4

Per Portion
about 455 calories
14 g carbohydrate
48 g protein · 20 g fat

Chinese-style Chicken

4 chicken breasts
2 tablespoons dry sherry
2 tablespoons soy sauce
1 clove garlic
3 sticks celery
200 g / 7 oz mushrooms
1–2 bunches of fresh basil
1 tablespoon vegetable oil
3 tablespoons chopped walnuts
gomasio

Skin and bone the chicken breasts. Cut the meat across the grain into thin strips. Pour the sherry and soy sauce over the chicken and leave to marinate for 15 minutes, stirring occasionally.

Peel and finely chop the garlic. Wash and dry the celery. Pull off any tough threads and cut across into thin slices. Trim the mushrooms, rinse under cold running water and thinly slice. Wash the basil, strip the leaves from the stalks, pat dry and cut into strips.

Take the chicken out of the marinade, drain and pat dry. Reserve the marinade.

Heat the oil in a wok or frying pan and fry the garlic over a moderate heat until transparent. Add the strips of chicken and stir-fry for about 2 minutes. Remove the meat from the pan and keep to one side.

Add the celery and mushrooms to the fat and stir-fry for about 2 minutes. Pour on the sherry marinade and cook the vegetables over a low heat for a further 4 minutes.

Return the chicken to the pan and stir to heat through. Stir in the basil and walnuts. Sprinkle with gomasio to taste and serve at once with brown rice.

Serves 4

Per Portion
about 240 calories
8 g carbohydrate
24 g protein · 10 g fat

Stuffed Shoulder of Lamb

1 (100 g/4 oz) piece celeriac
1 carrot
1 small leek
bunch of fresh parsley
3 sprigs of fresh thyme
50 g/2 oz each sesame and
*   sunflower seeds*
2 shallots
2 cloves garlic
4 tablespoons cold-pressed olive
*   oil*
1 kg/2¼ lb boned shoulder of
*   lamb*
salt
freshly ground black pepper
125 ml/4 fl oz dry white wine

Trim, peel and wash the celeriac and carrot. Cut the roots and about two thirds of the green leaves off the leek and then cut a cross in the leaves down to the white. Open the leaves and wash the leek to remove all the dirt. Cut the celeriac, carrot and leek into fairly large pieces.

Rinse the parsley under cold running water, strip the leaves from the stalks and pat dry. Keep a few stalks to go in the stock and finely chop the leaves for the stuffing. Wash the thyme, shake dry and strip off the leaves.

Crush the sesame seeds and coarsely chop the sunflower seeds. Peel the shallots and garlic and chop to a pulp. Stir the herbs, sesame seeds, sunflower seeds, shallots and garlic with 2 tablespoons olive oil to make a smooth spreadable paste.

Pat the shoulder of lamb dry with a cloth and place on the worktop with the fat side underneath. Remove as much fat as you can from the inside of the shoulder.

Mix salt with plenty of pepper in a small dish. Rub into the inside of the shoulder and spread with the herb paste. Starting at the long side, roll up the meat and tie into shape with cooking string. This keeps the meat in shape as it cooks and prevents the stuffing escaping. Season the outside of the joint

with pepper only and rub into the meat with the ball of your hand.

Heat the remaining oil in a large stewpan with a lid. Seal the lamb over a moderate to high heat to form a crust which will keep the meat moist as it cooks.

Add the celeriac, carrot, leek and parsley stalks and fry for a few minutes. Pour the white wine around the sides of the pan. The liquid will loosen the sediment from the bottom of the pan so that you can scrape it off with a wooden spatula. Cover the pan and braise the meat over a low heat for about 1 hour.

Remove the meat from the pan, wrap tightly in aluminium foil and leave in the warm place for about 10 minutes.

Meanwhile, strain the stock into a saucepan, pressing the vegetables and seasonings with a spatula to squeeze out the liquid. Discard the solids in the sieve. Skim any fat from the stock or soak it up with absorbent kitchen paper.

Unwrap the lamb, remove the string and, using a sharp knife, carve the meat into slices against the grain. Arrange the slices on a warmed plate and spoon on the stock, or serve the stock separately.

Serve with jacket-boiled potatoes or crispy wheatgerm rolls and salad.

Serves 6

Per Portion
about 590 calories
8 g carbohydrate
27 g protein · 44 g fat

Herby Lamb Steaks

4 lamb leg steaks, about 1.5 cm/
½ in thick
4 sprigs of fresh thyme
sprig of fresh rosemary
5 cloves garlic
5 tablespoons cold-pressed olive
* oil*
750 g/1½ lb spinach beet (stalks
* with leaves)*
1 shallot
1 large lemon
salt
freshly ground black pepper

Rub the lamb steaks on each side with a damp cloth to remove any splinters of bone.

Rinse the thyme and rosemary under cold running water and shake thoroughly dry. Strip the leaves from the stalks and coarsely chop on a board. Peel 2 cloves of garlic and either squeeze through a garlic press or chop to a pulp. Mix the garlic with the herbs and 2 tablespoons olive oil.

Brush the lamb steaks on both sides with the oil mixture, place one on top of the other and cover with foil or a bowl. Marinate in a cool place overnight or for 8 hours.

The following day, remove the coarse stalks from the spinach beet and separate the leaves. Wash the spinach beet well under cold running water, shake dry and cut into 1 cm/½ in pieces.

Peel the shallot and the remaining garlic and finely chop. Squeeze the juice from the lemon.

Heat 1 tablespoon oil in a frying pan and cook the shallot over a moderate to low heat until transparent. Add the garlic and stir until it begins to colour. Do not allow it to brown as this gives a bitter taste.

Add the spinach beet, pour on the remaining olive oil and the lemon juice and cook over a low heat for about 3 minutes until tender but still firm to bite. Season to taste and keep to one side. The spinach beet is served lukewarm.

Wipe the herbs and garlic off the lamb steaks with a cloth (they would burn during frying). Using a very sharp knife cut through the outer skin and fat at regular intervals to prevent the meat curling up as it cooks. Make sure you do not cut into the meat itself.

Heat a heavy frying pan without adding any fat. Fry the lamb steaks over a high heat, then over a moderate heat for about 5 minutes each side. You don't need any oil or fat in the pan as the lamb will have absorbed sufficient oil from the marinade. Do not turn the lamb when frying until a crust has formed on the underside, ie when it comes away easily from the pan.

Remove the fried lamb steaks to warmed plates and season to taste. Serve the spinach beet separately. You can also serve wheatgerm rolls or jacket-boiled potatoes and an uncooked vegetable salad.

Serves 4

Per Portion
about 460 calories
6 g carbohydrate
25 g protein · 35 g fat

Cook's Tip
Instead of spinach beet you can use dandelion leaves which are available in early summer.

Lamb Cutlets in Thyme Sauce

bunch of fresh thyme
3 cloves garlic
1 lemon
4 double lamb cutlets, about
  180 g/6 oz each
2 tablespoons sunflower oil
salt
freshly ground white pepper
125 ml/4 fl oz double cream

Wash the thyme under cold running water and shake dry. Strip the leaves off the stalks. Peel and very finely chop the garlic. Squeeze the lemon and keep the juice in reserve for the sauce.

Wipe the lamb cutlets with a damp cloth to remove any splinters of bone. Using a sharp knife, cut through the fat around the edge at 2 cm/¾ in intervals to prevent the chops curling up during cooking. Make sure you do not cut into the meat itself.

Heat the oil in a frying pan.

Seal the chops on both sides over a high heat. Reduce the heat and cook the chops for a further 2 to 3 minutes on each side.

Transfer the chops to warmed plates, season to taste and keep hot.

Add the thyme leaves and garlic to the pan and stir over a low to moderate heat until the garlic is transparent. Add the lemon juice and stir in the sediment from the bottom of the pan.

Stir in the cream and boil over a high heat, stirring, until the sauce is creamy. Season to taste with pepper and pour over the cutlets. Serve with wheatgerm rolls or potatoes and salad.

Serves 4

Per Portion
about 705 calories
3 g carbohydrate
23 g protein · 63 g fat

Lamb Medallions with Rosemary Potatoes

750 g/1½ lb small new potatoes
salt
4 cloves garlic
4 sprigs of fresh rosemary
4 tablespoons cold-pressed olive
  oil
12 medallions of lamb, about 2–
  3 cm/1 in thick
freshly ground black pepper

Scrub the potatoes well under cold running water and boil in the skins in salted water until tender. This will take 20 to 30 minutes depending on size.

Peel the garlic. Rinse the rosemary in cold water, strip the leaves off the stalks and pat dry.

Drain the potatoes, evaporate some of the steam and peel.

Heat 3 tablespoons olive oil in a frying pan. Fry 1 garlic clove over a low to moderate heat until transparent, then remove from the pan and discard. (The garlic is used only to flavour the oil.)

Add the potatoes and rosemary to the oil and over a moderate heat brown the potatoes, stirring frequently. Transfer the potatoes to a heated plate and keep hot.

Wipe the lamb medallions dry. Heat the remaining oil and fry the 3 remaining garlic cloves until transparent, then remove from the pan and discard. Increase the heat and fry the medallions over a moderate to high heat on both sides, for 5 to 6 minutes in all. They should remain pink on the inside.

Serve the medallions on heated plates with the rosemary potatoes. Season to taste. Serve with green beans in butter and tomatoes.

Serves 4

Per Portion
about 480 calories
28 g carbohydrate
26 g protein · 27 g fat

Fried Lamb with Tomatoes

600 g/1¼ lb boneless lamb from
  the leg
500 g/18 oz ripe tomatoes
1 onion
3 cloves garlic
bunch of fresh basil
4 tablespoons sunflower oil
pinch of caster sugar
salt
freshly ground black pepper
125 ml/4 fl oz double cream

Remove any fat or gristle from the lamb and cut across the grain into 2 cm/¾ in slices, then into strips.

Blanch the tomatoes in boiling water for 30 seconds, rinse in cold water and peel. Finely dice the tomatoes, removing the core and the seeds. Peel and finely chop the onion and garlic. Wash the basil, strip the leaves off the stems, pat dry and cut into strips.

Heat 1 tablespoon oil in a frying pan and fry the lamb, in batches, over a high heat for about 30 seconds. Add only enough lamb in each batch to cook without overlapping in the pan, and use more oil as necessary. As each batch of lamb is cooked transfer it to a sieve over a basin to catch the juice; this will prevent the meat continuing to cook in the juice and keep it tender.

Add the remaining oil, reduce the heat and fry the onion and garlic over a moderate heat until transparent. Add the tomato, stir until warmed through and season with the sugar and salt and pepper to taste.

Return the meat and juice to the pan and stir until heated through. Stir in the cream and heat through. Stir in the basil and serve at once, with brown rice or just with bread.

Serves 4

Per Portion
about 545 calories
10 g carbohydrate
25 g protein · 43 g fat

Lamb Ragoût with Yogurt

600 g/1¼ lb boned shoulder of lamb
1 onion
1 clove garlic
bunch of fresh parsley
1 tablespoon vegetable oil
150 ml/¼ pint natural yogurt
freshly ground black pepper
1 red pepper
1 tablespoon crème fraîche
50 g/2 oz walnuts, chopped

Dry the meat, remove any fat and gristle and cut into 2 cm/¾ in cubes. Peel and finely chop the onion and garlic. Wash the parsley in cold water, strip the leaves off the stalks, pat dry and finely chop. Keep one third of the parsley in reserve to garnish.

Heat the oil in a frying pan. Seal the meat, in batches, over a moderate to high heat. As each batch is sealed, transfer it to a sieve over a basin to collect the juice.

When all the lamb is cooked, fry the onion and garlic in the fat until transparent, stirring continuously.

Return the meat and juice to the pan. Stir in the parsley and yogurt and season to taste with pepper. Stir the sediment on the bottom of the pan into the sauce. Cover and simmer over a low heat for 1 hour.

Just before the end of the cooking time, quarter the pepper lengthways and remove the stalk, white pith and seeds. Wash, wipe dry and finely chop. Stir the red pepper and crème fraîche into the ragoût and heat through.

Serve at once, sprinkled with walnuts and the remaining parsley, with brown rice.

Serves 4

Per Portion
about 555 calories
10 g carbohydrate
24 g protein · 44 g fat

Lamb Stew with Quinces

750 g/1½ lb boned shoulder of lamb
1 large onion
2 cloves garlic
1–2 pieces preserved stem ginger
1 lemon
1 tablespoon vegetable oil
250 ml/8 fl oz dry white wine
300 g/11 oz quinces
250 ml/8 fl oz double cream
2 teaspoons mustard powder
½ teaspoon ground cinnamon
salt
cayenne pepper

Cut the meat into cubes. Peel and finely chop the onion and garlic. Chop the ginger. Cut a thin piece of rind from the lemon and cut into very thin strips. Squeeze the juice.

Heat the oil in a frying pan and seal the meat, in batches, over a moderate to high heat. Fry the onion and garlic in the fat until transparent.

Return the meat and juice to the pan. Add the lemon juice and white wine and stir the sediment on the bottom of the pan into the sauce. Add the ginger and lemon rind. Cover and simmer for 1 hour.

Quarter, peel and core the quinces and cut into 1-cm/½-in wedges. Add to the meat and simmer, covered, for a further 30 minutes.

Remove the meat and quinces from the pan to a serving dish and keep hot. Add the cream to the sauce and boil to reduce by about half over a high heat. Season the sauce with the mustard, cinnamon, and salt and cayenne to taste and pour over the meat.

Serves 6

Per Portion
about 560 calories
16 g carbohydrate
19 g protein · 41 g fat

Lamb Curry

500 g / 18 oz boneless lamb
3 cloves garlic
300 ml / ½ pint natural yogurt
3 tomatoes
piece of fresh root ginger, about
    2 cm / ¾ in long
1 large onion
1 teaspoon each turmeric and
    cumin
½ teaspoon ground coriander
generous pinch of hot chilli
    powder
3 tablespoons vegetable oil
piece of cinnamon stick
2 cloves · 2 cardamom pods
salt · bunch of fresh parsley

Cut the lamb into 2.5-cm/1-in
cubes. Peel and finely chop the
garlic. Mix the lamb with the
garlic and yogurt, cover and
marinate for 2 hours.

Blanch the tomatoes in boiling water for 30 seconds, rinse
in cold water and peel. Dice the
tomatoes, removing the seeds.
Peel the ginger and cut into thin
strips. Peel and finely chop the
onion.

In a bowl, mix together the
turmeric, cumin, coriander and
chilli powder.

Heat the oil in a frying pan
and fry the cinnamon, cloves
and cardamoms for 1 minute,
stirring continuously. Add the
ginger and onion and fry until
the onion is transparent.

Add the lamb and its
marinade and cook for about
10 minutes, stirring continuously. Stir in the tomatoes and
the turmeric mixture and
season to taste with salt. Cover
the pan and simmer the lamb
curry over a low heat for 1¼
hours.

Chop the parsley and use to
garnish the curry.

Serves 4

Per Portion
about 390 calories
7 g carbohydrate
19 g protein · 28 g fat

Lamb Stew with Oranges

1 kg / 2¼ lb boned shoulder of
    lamb
1 kg / 2¼ lb small onions
4 juicy oranges
3–4 tablespoons olive oil
scant 1 tablespoon caster sugar
salt
freshly ground black pepper
piece of cinnamon stick
4 cloves
250 ml / 8 fl oz dry white wine

Remove skin and gristle from
the lamb, pat dry and cut into
2.5 cm / 1 in cubes. Peel the
onions. Wash and dry 1 orange
and thinly cut off half the rind;
set aside. Completely peel and
segment the orange, removing
all the white pith. Halve the
segments. Squeeze the remaining oranges and keep the juice
to one side for the stock.

Heat 1 tablespoon of the
olive oil in a frying pan and seal
the lamb, in batches. As they
are sealed transfer them to a
sieve over a basin to catch the
juice, and add more oil to the
pan as necessary.

Fry the onions in batches.
Arrange the lamb and onions
in layers in a stewpan and top
with the pieces of orange. Add
the sugar, and season to taste
with salt and pepper. Add the
piece of orange rind, cinnamon
stick and cloves. Pour on the
orange juice and wine.

Cover the pan and bring
slowly to the boil, then cook
over a low heat for about 1
hour. Remove the lid and simmer over a moderate heat for a
further 30 minutes to thicken
the sauce.

Serves 8

Per Portion
about 450 calories
16 g carbohydrate
18 g protein · 30 g fat

Fennel Salad with Sesame Dressing

50 g/2 oz tofu
2 tablespoons lemon juice
125 ml/4 fl oz water
herb salt
2 tablespoons tahini (sesame paste)
500 g/18 oz fennel
2 tablespoons chopped fresh mixed herbs (eg parsley, dill, chives, lemon balm, chervil)
freshly ground white pepper
2 tablespoons shelled walnuts

Drain the tofu and blend with the lemon juice and water in a liquidiser. Stir in a little herb salt and the tahini.

Halve the fennel bulbs lengthways, wash and drain. Cut out the wedge shaped stalk. Cut off the feathery leaves and keep to one side to garnish the salad. Cut the fennel across the grain into strips.

Arrange the fennel strips on four plates and sprinkle with the chopped herbs. Pour the sesame dressing over the fennel and season to taste with pepper.

Using a sharp knife, coarsely chop the walnuts. Finely chop the reserved fennel leaves. Scatter the fennel salad with the walnuts and leaves and serve.

Serves 4

Per Portion
about 160 calories
14 g carbohydrate
6 g protein · 8 g fat

Cook's Tip
Dressings with tahini need quite a lot of liquid because if the sesame paste comes into contact with undiluted acids, such as vinegar or lemon juice, it forms lumps that you can't get rid of. So always mix all the other dressing ingredients before adding the tahini.

Spinach Salad with Pine Nuts

100 g/4 oz fresh young spinach
handful of young nettle leaves
2 tablespoons raspberry vinegar
pinch of sugar
herb salt
freshly ground white pepper
1 teaspoon Dijon mustard
4 tablespoons cold-pressed olive oil
2 tablespoons pine nuts

Pick over the spinach and nettles. The nettles must be really young and tender or they are not suitable for salad. (Older nettles can be blanched and served like spinach as a hot vegetable.) Wash the spinach several times in plenty of water. Then wash the nettles and shake both dry.

Stir the raspberry vinegar with the sugar and herb salt and pepper to taste until the salt has dissolved. Add the mustard and beat in the olive oil a tablespoon at a time.

Add the spinach, nettles and pine nuts to the dressing, mix gently and serve immediately while the leaves are still nice and crisp.

Serve with garlic bread or crispbread and butter.

Serves 4

Per Portion
about 165 calories
4 g carbohydrate
2 g protein · 15 g fat

Cook's Tip
In late spring when the first fresh herbs reappear, leave out the spinach and make up the salad only with wild and garden herbs. You can use parsley, chervil, burnet and dandelion as well as the nettles.

Carrots with Nut Vinaigrette

500 g/18 oz young carrots
75 g/3 oz shelled hazelnuts or
  walnuts
juice of 1 lemon
2 tablespoons mild herb vinegar
1 pinch of sugar
salt
freshly ground white pepper
2 tablespoons cold-pressed olive
  oil
2 tablespoons chopped fresh
  parsley

Trim and scrape the carrots. Rinse under cold running water, dry and finely grate.

On a board coarsely chop the nuts using a strong knife.

Mix the lemon juice with the herb vinegar. Add the sugar and salt and pepper to taste and stir until the salt and sugar have dissolved. Beat in the oil a tablespoon at a time. Stir the nuts and 1 tablespoon parsley into the vinaigrette.

Pour over the carrots and stir in. Serve immediately, sprinkled with the remaining parsley. Makes a delicious starter or, with wholemeal bread and butter, a light supper.

Serves 4

Per Portion
about 220 calories
14 g carbohydrate
4 g protein · 17 g fat

Variation
Beetroot with Apple
Peel and grate 300 g/11 oz beetroot. Core 1 large (125 g/ 4½ oz) fairly tart apple, then peel and grate. Stir 3 tablespoons mild raspberry vinegar with a pinch of sugar and salt and freshly ground white pepper to taste until the salt and sugar have dissolved. Beat in ½ tablespoon cold-pressed olive oil. Mix the grated beetroot and apple with the vinaigrette. Fold in 250 ml/8 fl oz natural yogurt or soured cream and serve.

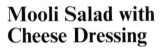

Mooli Salad with Cheese Dressing

2 mooli or daikon (white
*   radishes)*
herb salt
bunch of fresh chives
20 g/¾ oz Gorgonzola or
*   Roquefort cheese*
125 ml/4 fl oz single cream,
*   crème fraîche or soured cream*
2 tablespoons lemon juice
freshly ground white pepper
pinch of caster sugar
1 tablespoon sunflower oil
handful of watercress or 1 box
*   mustard and cress*

Trim, peel and coarsely grate
the mooli. Place in a bowl,
sprinkle with herb salt and
leave to stand for about 5 minutes. This draws some of the
moisture out of the mooli so
that the salad is not watery.

Meanwhile, rinse the chives
in cold water, pat dry and cut
up. Crush the Gorgonzola or
Roquefort with a fork and
work in the cream to make a

smooth paste. Stir in the lemon
juice and season the cheese
dressing with pepper to taste
and the sugar. Add the chives
and oil and mix gently.

Pour off any liquid that has
formed in the mooli bowl.
Squeeze dry the mooli by hand
and transfer to a clean bowl.
Pour the cheese dressing over
the mooli and fold in (or serve
the dressing separately).

Pick over the watercress,
wash well and pat dry. Chop
thick stems and scatter over the
salad with the leaves. If using
mustard and cress, snip off with
scissors and scatter over the
salad.

Serves 4

Per Portion
about 175 calories
7 g carbohydrate
4 g protein · 14 g fat

Uncooked Vegetable Salad

1 green and 1 red pepper
1 carrot
½ cucumber
1 large beef tomato
bunch of spring onions
bunch of radishes
bunch each of fresh chives and
*   dill or 3 tablespoons chopped*
*   mixed fresh herbs*
1 clove garlic
salt
3 tablespoons red wine vinegar
1 tablespoon dry red wine
pinch of caster sugar
freshly ground black pepper
5 tablespoons cold-pressed olive
*   oil*

Remove the stalks from the
peppers, cut lengthways into
quarters and cut out the white
pith with the seeds. Wash in
cold water, wipe dry and cut
into strips or squares.

Peel the carrot and cucumber
and then slice or dice. Wash,
dry and dice the tomato, re-

moving the core and seeds.
Wash, dry and trim the
spring onions and radishes. Cut
the onions with about one third
of the green leaves into rings
and thinly slice the radishes.
Mix the salad ingredients
together in a bowl.

Wash the chives and dill and
shake dry. Cut up the chives
and chop the dill. Peel and chop
the garlic and crush with a little
salt.

Beat the red wine vinegar
and red wine with the sugar,
and salt and pepper to taste.
Gradually beat in the oil. Add
the herbs and garlic.

Pour the dressing over the
salad, stir in gently and serve
immediately.

Serves 4

Per Portion
about 155 calories
7 g carbohydrate
1 g protein · 13 g fat

Bean Sprout Salad with Prawns

200 g/7 oz cooked fresh or frozen prawns, peeled
1 lemon
1 small red pepper
2 spring onions
400 g/14 oz mung bean sprouts
3 tablespoons sunflower oil
125 ml/4 fl oz freshly made vegetable stock
2 tablespoons soy sauce
1 tablespoon dry sherry
pinch of sugar
salt

If using frozen prawns, allow to thaw first and drain well. Squeeze the lemon and sprinkle half the juice over the prawns.

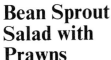

Remove the stalk from the red pepper, cut in half and scrape out the white pith and seeds. Rinse in cold water to get rid of the remaining seeds, then wipe dry and cut across into very thin strips.

Trim, wash and dry the spring onions and then cut into thin rings with about two thirds of the green leaves.

Tip the bean sprouts into a sieve, rinse well in cold water and shake dry. Heat 1 tablespoon oil in a frying pan and add the bean sprouts. Cook for 30 seconds, stirring continuously. Add the stock and soy sauce and cook for 1 minute.

Tip the bean sprouts and the cooking liquid into a bowl and mix in the prawns, red pepper and spring onions.

Beat the remaining lemon juice with the sherry, sugar, remaining oil and salt to taste. Stir gently with the salad.

Marinate for 30 minutes at room temperature before serving.

Serves 4

Per Portion
about 160 calories
8 g carbohydrate
12 g protein · 9 g fat

Leek Salad with Chicken and Almonds

4 boneless chicken breasts (450 g/1 lb total weight)
2 tablespoons chopped fresh parsley
2 tablespoons dry sherry
2 tablespoons cold-pressed olive oil
400 g/14 oz leeks
2 teaspoons chopped fresh thyme
125 ml/4 fl oz freshly made vegetable stock
salt
freshly ground white pepper
2 tablespoons wine vinegar
2 tablespoons lemon juice
1 teaspoon walnut oil
1 teaspoon butter
3 tablespoons chopped almonds

Skin the chicken breasts. Mix the parsley with the sherry and 1 tablespoon olive oil. Brush on to the chicken and leave to marinate.

Trim and wash the leeks and cut into 1-cm/½-in lengths.

Cook the leeks and thyme in the stock for 2 to 3 minutes until the leeks are tender but still firm. Drain, reserving 3 tablespoons stock. Season the reserved stock to taste. Stir in the wine vinegar, lemon juice, the remaining olive oil and the walnut oil. Arrange the leeks on four warmed plates and spoon on the dressing.

Heat the butter and fry the almonds until golden. Remove from the pan and set aside.

Pat the chicken breasts dry. Fry the breasts over a high heat for about 2 minutes on each side or until cooked. Season the chicken, cut into thin slices and arrange over the leeks. Sprinkle with the almonds and serve.

Serves 4

Per Portion
about 245 calories
16.5 g carbohydrate
16.5 g protein · 12 g fat

Couscous Salad

75 g/3 oz couscous
2 small courgettes, about 100 g/
    4 oz each
5 tablespoons sunflower oil
500 g/18 oz ripe tomatoes
1 onion
1 clove garlic
1 small red pepper
3 tablespoons herb vinegar
4 tablespoons chopped fresh
    mixed herbs (eg parsley, dill,
    chives, lemon balm, chervil,
    borage and mint)
salt

Soak the couscous in hot water
for 1 hour, then drain
thoroughly.
   Wash and dry the courgettes.
Trim off the ends. Cut lengthways into 1 cm/⅓ in slices and
then into sticks 1 cm/⅓ in wide.
   Heat 3 tablespoons sunflower
oil in a frying pan. Fry the
courgette pieces over a moderate heat until lightly browned
and beginning to soften. Drain
on absorbent kitchen paper and
leave to cool slightly.

Meanwhile, wash, dry and
dice the tomatoes, removing the
core and seeds. Peel and finely
dice the onion and garlic.
   Remove the stalk from the
red pepper, cut in half and
scrape out the white pith and
seeds. Wash the peppers in cold
water and cut into fine strips.
   Mix the courgettes, tomatoes, onion, garlic and red
pepper with the couscous. Add
the vinegar, herbs, remaining
oil and salt to taste. Cover the
bowl and leave to marinate at
room temperature for 45
minutes.
   Stir through with a fork before serving.

Serves 4

Per Portion
about 230 calories
31 g carbohydrate
4 g protein · 13 g fat

Bean Salad with Tomato Vinaigrette

300 g/11 oz green beans
bunch of fresh savory
1 red onion
1 tablespoon mild herb vinegar
1 tablespoon balsam vinegar
salt
freshly ground black pepper
1 teaspoon whole grain mustard
3 tablespoons cold-pressed olive
    oil
1 large beef tomato

Wash and drain the beans. Top
and tail the beans and pull off
any strings.
   Wash the savory and keep
two sprigs to one side for the
vinaigrette.
   In a saucepan, bring about
two fingers depth of water to
the boil. Add the beans and savory, cover the pan and cook
over a low to moderate heat for
about 5 to 8 minutes until the
beans are tender but still firm.

Meanwhile, peel and finely
chop the onion. Stir the two
vinegars with salt and pepper to
taste. Add the mustard and
beat in the olive oil a tablespoon at a time. Add the
chopped onion.
   Wash, dry and dice the tomato, removing the core and
seeds. Finely chop the reserved
savory.
   Drain the beans, rinse in cold
water and drain well.
   Mix the diced tomato and
chopped savory into the vinaigrette. Arrange the warm beans
on a flat dish and pour on the
vinaigrette. Serve with garlic
bread.

Serves 4

Per Portion
about 100 calories
6 g carbohydrate
2 g protein · 8 g fat

Rice Salad with Chicken and Bean Sprouts

1 (1.3 kg/2½ lb) chicken
150 g/5 oz celeriac
1 carrot
1 leek
1 onion
1 clove garlic
2 cloves
sprig of fresh thyme
4 black peppercorns
1 bay leaf
salt
2 litres/3½ pints water
1 teaspoon instant vegetable
    stock granules
500 g/18 oz long-grain brown
    rice
2 bunches of spring onions
1–2 cucumbers (about 700 g/
    1½ lb)
bunch of fresh parsley
1 lemon
300 g/11 oz mung bean sprouts
herb salt
2 tablespoons cold-pressed olive
    oil

Place the chicken in a large saucepan. Add sufficient cold water just to cover and bring slowly to simmering point over a moderate heat.

As soon as small bubbles begin to form, reduce the heat. The chicken should cook at just below boiling point if the meat is to be tender and moist. Half cover the pan and keep checking that it is not boiling. If necessary add more hot water to keep the chicken just covered throughout. Cook in this way for 30 minutes.

Meanwhile, peel the celeriac and carrot and cut into fairly large pieces. Trim the leek, wash well and halve lengthways. Peel the onion and garlic. Halve the onion and stick the cloves into it.

Add all the vegetables, the garlic, thyme, peppercorns and bay leaf to the chicken. Increase the heat until the stock begins to simmer again. Season to taste with salt. Cook the chicken for another hour, until cooked.

Meanwhile, bring the water

to the boil with the instant vegetable stock. Add the rice, cover the pan and cook over the lowest possible heat for 25 to 30 minutes or until the rice is tender and has absorbed all the liquid. Transfer the rice to a large bowl and leave to cool.

Lift the chicken out of the stock. Remove the meat from the carcass, discarding all skin and bones, and cut the meat into bite-sized pieces. Remove fat and gristle as you go.

Strain the stock through a sieve lined with muslin. Squeeze the liquid out of the vegetables and flavourings before discarding them. Measure off 375 ml/ 13 fl oz stock and set aside.

Cut the spring onions into thin rings. Peel the cucumber. Cut in half across and then lengthways and scrape out the seeds using a teaspoon. Cut into small cubes.

Wash the parsley, pluck off the leaves, pat dry and finely chop. Squeeze the juice from the lemon.

Wash the bean sprouts well in cold water. Bring the re-

served stock to the boil and cook the bean sprouts for 3 minutes.

Add the chicken meat and the bean sprouts with their stock to the cooled rice. Add the spring onion rings, diced cucumber and parsley.

Stir the lemon juice with herb salt to taste until the salt has dissolved, then beat in the olive oil. Pour the dressing over the salad and stir in.

Serves 10

Per Portion
about 360 calories
42 g carbohydrate
24 g protein · 9 g fat

Romanian-style Marinated Vegetables

500 g / 18 oz fennel
250 g / 9 oz carrots
3 tomatoes
3 cloves garlic
juice of ½ lemon
250 ml / 8 fl oz dry white wine
125 ml / 4 fl oz freshly made vegetable stock
3 black peppercorns
1 bay leaf
6 sprigs of fresh thyme
6 sprigs of fresh parsley
salt
6 tablespoons cold-pressed olive oil

Trim the feathery leaves from the fennel and set aside. Halve the fennel bulbs lengthways. Wash the halves, drain and cut lengthways twice more.

Peel the carrots and cut into sticks about 5 cm/2 in long and 1 cm/½ in thick.

Blanch the tomatoes in boiling water for 30 seconds, rinse in cold water and peel. Quarter the tomatoes lengthways and remove the core and the seeds. Peel the garlic.

Put the lemon juice, wine, vegetable stock, peppercorns and bay leaf in a saucepan and bring to the boil. Wash the thyme and parsley and add to the pan.

Add the fennel, carrots and garlic. Return to the boil, cover and cook gently for about 8 minutes until half cooked.

Add the tomatoes and cook for a further 2 minutes. Remove all the vegetables from the stock with a slotted spoon and transfer to a serving dish. Season lightly with salt.

Strain the stock and then boil to reduce by half, stirring continuously. Add the olive oil and reheat. Pour over the vegetables.

Finely chop the reserved fennel leaves and sprinkle over the vegetables. Leave to cool, then cover and marinate at room temperature.

Serves 4

Per Portion
about 230 calories
16 g carbohydrate
4 g protein · 16 g fat

Asparagus with Two Sauces

3 kg/6½ lb asparagus
2 shallots
4 white peppercorns
bunch of fresh tarragon
handful of fresh chervil
2 tablespoons dry white wine
3 tablespoons tarragon vinegar
200 g/7 oz butter
2 egg yolks
2 tablespoons hot water
salt
cayenne pepper
pinch of caster sugar
250 ml/8 fl oz crème fraîche
750 ml/1¼ pints natural yogurt
2 tablespoons chopped mixed
    fresh herbs (eg parsley, dill,
    nettles, salad burnet, cress,
    borage and lemon balm)
1 teaspoon chive mustard
2 tablespoons lemon juice
1 teaspoon sunflower oil
freshly ground white pepper

Thinly peel the bottom end of the asparagus stalks and cut off any woody parts. Wash the as-paragus and wrap in a tea towel.

To make the Béarnaise sauce, peel and very finely chop the shallots. Crush the peppercorns in a mortar. Rinse the tarragon and chervil in cold water and shake dry. Strip the leaves from the stalks and keep in reserve. Coarsely chop the stalks.

Put the white wine into a saucepan and add the vinegar, shallots, crushed peppercorns and herb stalks. Bring to the boil. Reduce over a moderate heat, stirring continuously, until you have about 1 tablespoon of liquid left. Strain the liquid, squeezing or pressing the shallots and herbs before discarding them. Keep the liquid hot.

Melt the butter over a low heat until liquid but not on any account brown. Skim off the white foam that forms. Pour the clear or clarified butter into another pan leaving the white sediment behind. Keep the butter hot.

Fill a saucepan with hot water and keep hot on the hob without allowing it to boil. Put the egg yolks and hot water into a heatproof bowl and place in the pan of hot water. Whisk to a thick, frothy cream.

Whisk in the warm clarified butter, a teaspoon at a time initially and then in a thin trickle. The butter should be warm but not hot or the egg yolks will separate.

Whisk in the warm herb liquid a teaspoon at a time. Finely chop the tarragon and chervil leaves and stir in. Season the sauce to taste with salt and cayenne and keep lukewarm until ready to serve.

Fill a large frying pan three quarters full with water. (The pan must be large enough to take the asparagus flat.) Add the sugar and a pinch of salt and bring the water to the boil. Place the asparagus in the boiling water and cook over a moderate heat for 8 to 10 minutes until tender but still firm to bite.

Meanwhile, mix the crème fraîche with the yogurt. Stir in the chopped herbs, mustard, lemon juice and sunflower oil. Season to taste with pepper.

Gently lift the asparagus out of the water on a skimmer, drain and serve with the Béarnaise and herb sauces, and with jacket-boiled new potatoes.

Serves 8

Per portion
about 425 calories
18 g carbohydrate
12 g protein · 33 g fat

Dried Winter Vegetables

100 g/4 oz dried vegetables (carrots and/or leeks)
1 onion or 2 shallots
1 tablespoon butter
herb salt
freshly ground white pepper
200 ml/7 fl oz double cream
bunch of fresh parsley or dill, or handful of fresh chervil

Tip the vegetables into a bowl, cover with lukewarm water and soak for 4 hours.

Drain the soaked vegetables (which now weigh around 300 g/11 oz) very thoroughly. You can use the soaking water in a soup, although carrot water is very sweet and will need to be highly seasoned.

Peel and finely chop the onion or shallots. Melt the butter in a saucepan without allowing it to brown. Fry the onion or shallot until transparent, stirring frequently.

Add the soaked vegetables and stir until completely coated in fat. Season to taste with herb salt and pepper. Add the cream. Bring to the boil, then cover the pan and cook over a low heat for 10 to 15 minutes.

Meanwhile, wash the herbs, shake dry and finely chop. If using parsley, it should be stirred in a few minutes before the end of the cooking time. Chervil and dill should be sprinkled on at the end for they lose some of their flavour if cooked.

Serve with fried meat or with rice and salad for a vegetarian main course, in which case you should increase the amount of cream.

Serves 4

Per Portion
about 225 calories
10 g carbohydrate
2 g protein · 20 g fat

Tomatoes Stuffed with Wheat

350 ml/12 fl oz water
200 g/7 oz whole wheat grains
  (wheat berries)
8 large, firm tomatoes (about
  2 kg/4½ lb)
1 onion
3 cloves garlic
bunch of fresh parsley
2 sprigs of fresh thyme
½ tablespoon butter
salt
freshly ground black pepper
200 g/7 oz Emmental or Gruyère
  cheese
pinch of caster sugar
150 g/5 oz mozzarella cheese

Bring the water to the boil in a saucepan, add the wheat, cover and cook over a low heat for 1 hour. Remove from the heat and leave to soak, covered, for 1 further hour.

Meanwhile, wash and dry the tomatoes. Cut a lid from each tomato and cut out the core with a sharp knife. Remove the insides of the tomatoes with a teaspoon, trying to get rid of all the seeds. Finely chop the flesh you have removed and the lids and place in a sieve lined with muslin to drain.

Peel and finely chop the onion and garlic. Rinse the parsley and thyme in cold water. Strip the parsley leaves from the stalks, pat dry, finely chop and keep for the filling. Strip the thyme leaves from the stems and dry.

Drain the soaked wheat. Melt the butter in a frying pan over a moderate heat until slightly frothy but not brown. Fry the onion and garlic until transparent. Add the thyme and fry for a few minutes: the hot fat will bring out its full flavour. Add the wheat and stir in well.

Add half the chopped tomato and cook over a high heat until the liquid has completely evaporated. Remove the pan from the heat and season to taste. Leave to cool slightly.

Meanwhile, finely dice the Emmental or Gruyère cheese. Stir the diced cheese and chopped parsley into the wheat mixture.

Lightly salt the inside of the tomatoes and fill with the wheat mixture.

Season the remaining chopped tomato with the sugar and salt and pepper to taste and tip into a baking dish large enough to take all the tomatoes side by side. Place the filled tomatoes in the dish.

Drain and thinly slice the mozzarella and place on top of the tomatoes. Place the dish in a hot oven (220 C, 425 F, gas 7), on the second shelf from the bottom, and bake the stuffed tomatoes for 15 to 20 minutes, or until the mozzarella is melted and slightly browned. Serve with fresh rye or wholemeal bread.

Serves 4

Per Portion
about 610 calories
50 g carbohydrate
34 g protein · 30 g fat

Cook's Tip
Whole wheat grain takes quite a long time to prepare. To save time you can use a pressure cooker. If you often serve cooked wheat it is worth boiling and soaking double the quantity. In a container with a tight lid, cooked wheat will keep in the fridge for up to 1 week.

181

Courgette Gratin

1 kg/2¼ lb small courgettes
2 large ripe tomatoes
bunch of spring onions
10 black olives
about 250 g/9 oz mozzarella
  cheese
bunch of fresh parsley
herb salt
freshly ground black pepper
125 ml/4 fl oz double cream

Wash the courgettes in cold
running water and wipe dry.
Top and tail them and cut in
half lengthways.

Blanch the tomatoes in boiling water for 30 seconds, rinse
in cold water and peel. Dice the
tomatoes, discarding the core
and seeds.

Trim the spring onions, wash
well and cut into thin rings with
about one third of the onion
leaves.

Halve, stone and finely chop
the olives. Drain and dice the
mozzarella. Wash the parsley,
strip the leaves off the stalks,
pat dry and finely chop.

Mix the tomato with the
onion rings, olives, mozzarella
and parsley and season to taste
with herb salt and pepper.

Place the courgette halves in
a baking dish, sprinkle with a
little salt and cover with the
tomato mixture. Pour the
cream around the sides of the
dish.

Bake in a moderately hot
oven (200 C, 400 F, gas 6), on the
second shelf from the bottom of
the oven, for about 30 minutes
until the cheese has melted and
is nice and brown.

Serve with potatoes boiled in
their jackets and a salad.

Serves 4

Per Portion
about 360 calories
22 g carbohydrate
15 g protein · 23 g fat

Stuffed Cucumber

2 (500 g/18 oz) cucumbers
1 shallot
350 g/12 oz tomatoes
½ avocado
1½ bunches each of fresh dill and
  parsley
100 g/4 oz minced lamb
salt
freshly ground white pepper
cayenne pepper
1 tablespoon vegetable oil
100 g/4 oz Edam cheese
1 tablespoon pine nuts
250 ml/8 fl oz crème fraîche or
  soured cream
4 tablespoons single cream
30 g/1¼ oz butter

Peel the cucumbers and cut in
half across then lengthways.

Peel and coarsely chop the
shallot. Wash and dry the
tomatoes and cut out the core.
Stone the avocado and scoop
the flesh out of the skin. Purée
the tomatoes with the avocado
in a liquidiser or food
processor.

Wash and dry the herbs;
chop finely. Mix about half the
herbs into the purée with the
shallot and lamb. Season with
salt, pepper and cayenne.

Brush a baking dish with the
oil. Place the cucumber in the
dish and fill with the lamb
mixture.

Blend the Edam with the pine
nuts in a liquidiser or food processor. Add the crème fraîche
and cream and blend again to a
smooth paste. Stir in the remaining herbs and season to
taste. Pour the mixture over the
cucumbers and dot with the
butter. Bake in a hot oven
(220 C, 425 F, gas 7), for about
40 minutes.

Serves 4

Per Portion
about 405 calories
31 g carbohydrate
12 g protein · 8 g fat

Stuffed Peppers

750 ml / 1¼ pints water
1–2 teaspoons instant vegetable
   stock granules
150 g / 5 oz long-grain brown rice
1 kg / 2¼ lb ripe tomatoes
6 green peppers of similar size
1 red pepper
1 large onion
4 cloves garlic
bunch each of fresh parsley and
   basil
few sprigs of fresh salad burnet
sprig of fresh rosemary
2 tablespoons olive oil
500 g / 18 oz minced lamb
salt
freshly ground black pepper
pinch of cayenne pepper

Bring the water and vegetable stock granules to the boil in a saucepan and add the rice. Reduce the heat, cover the pan and cook the rice over a low heat for 30 minutes.

Meanwhile, blanch the tomatoes in boiling water for 30 seconds, rinse in cold water and peel. Halve the tomatoes so that you can remove the seeds with a teaspoon. Remove the core. Finely chop about one-third of the tomatoes, then purée the rest and keep in reserve for the sauce.

Wash and dry the peppers. Cut round the green peppers about 1 cm / ½ in below the stalk to make a lid. Carefully twist off the lid. Most of the seeds should come out with it. Remove the white pith and rinse the peppers in cold water to remove any remaining seeds. Dry well inside and out.

Halve the red pepper lengthways and remove the stalk, pith and seeds. Rinse the halves, wipe dry and chop very finely. Peel and finely chop the onion and garlic.

Wash the parsley, basil, burnet and rosemary and shake dry. Strip the parsley and basil leaves from the stalks and finely chop with the burnet. Strip the rosemary leaves from the stalk.

Heat the olive oil in a frying pan. Fry the onion and garlic until transparent. Add the minced lamb and stir until it is crumbly in texture and grey in colour.

Mix the lamb with the rice, chopped tomato, red pepper, parsley, basil and burnet. Season with salt and pepper to taste and a generous pinch of cayenne.

Season the insides of the green peppers with salt and fill with the lamb stuffing. Replace the lids on top.

Pour the puréed tomato into a saucepan large enough to take all the stuffed peppers side by side. Stir the rosemary leaves into the tomato. Stand the stuffed peppers in the pan and cover.

Bring the tomato to the boil, then reduce the heat to low and cook the peppers for about 40 minutes.

Lift the peppers carefully out of the tomato sauce and arrange on a warmed plate. Season the sauce to taste and reduce slightly over a high heat. Pour the sauce over the peppers before serving.

Serves 6

Per Portion
about 440 calories
37 g carbohydrate
21 g protein · 20 g fat

Cook's Tip

For a creamier sauce stir in about 125 ml / 4 fl oz crème fraîche after the peppers have cooked and stir until reduced.

Crispy Gratins with Potatoes and Vegetables

Potato and Tomato Gratin

500 g/18 oz floury potatoes
400 g/14 oz ripe tomatoes
salt
freshly ground black pepper
250 ml/8 fl oz double cream
100 g/4 oz cheese (Bel Paese, Emmental, Gruyère or mature Gouda), grated
about 30 g/1¼ oz butter

Peel the potatoes, wash and wipe dry. Using a mandolin, cut into 1 mm/$\frac{1}{16}$ in slices. Wipe the slices dry on absorbent kitchen paper, for the less moisture they contain, the crispier the gratin.

Wash and dry the tomatoes and cut out the cores. Cut downwards into 0.5 cm/¼ in slices. Arrange the potato and tomato slices in layers in a gratin dish and season each layer.

Pour the cream around the edge of the dish. Sprinkle with the grated cheese and dot with the butter.

Bake in a hot oven (220 C, 425 F, gas 7), on the second shelf from the bottom, for 20 to 25 minutes until the cheese is nice and brown, the potatoes tender and the liquid absorbed. If necessary add a little more cream to the edge of the dish. It is impossible to give an exact quantity of liquid for this depends on the variety of potato and the amount of moisture in the tomatoes.

Serve the gratin at once for if left to stand the cheese will become tough.

Serves 4

Per Portion
about 460 calories
25 g carbohydrate
11 g protein · 34 g fat

Spinach Beet Gratin with Garlic Bread

500 g/18 oz spinach beet
salt
125 g/4½ oz tofu
125 ml/4 fl oz freshly made vegetable stock
1 tablespoon lemon juice
2 tablespoons rye breadcrumbs
2 tablespoons sesame seeds
6 tablespoons olive oil
4 cloves garlic
bunch of fresh parsley or box of mustard and cress
freshly ground black pepper
4 slices rye bread (40 g/1½ oz each)

Wash the spinach beet, shake dry and coarsely chop. Place in a gratin dish and season to taste with salt.

Blend the drained tofu with the vegetable stock and lemon juice in a liquidiser or food processor and pour over the spinach beet. Scatter with the breadcrumbs and sesame seeds and sprinkle with 1 tablespoon olive oil.

Bake in a hot oven (220 C,

425 F, gas 7) for 35 to 40 minutes until browned.

Peel the garlic and squeeze through a garlic press or chop very finely. Wash the parsley, strip the leaves from the stalks, pat dry and chop very finely (snip cress with scissors). Mix the garlic with the parsley or cress, pepper to taste and the remaining olive oil.

Toast the rye bread, spread with garlic paste and serve hot with the gratin.

Serves 4

Per Portion
about 370 calories
26 g carbohydrate
10 g protein · 22 g fat

Potato Fingers with Sage Butter

1 kg/2½ lb floury potatoes
6 tablespoons wholemeal flour
4 tablespoons cornflour
salt
freshly grated nutmeg
freshly ground white pepper
handful of fresh sage leaves
100 g/4 oz butter

Scrub the potatoes well in cold running water. Cook in the skins, in a little boiling water until soft, then drain. Evaporate some of the steam, peel and mash well until smooth. Add the flour, cornflour, and salt, nutmeg and pepper to taste and work in to give a uniform mixture.

Sprinkle the worktop with flour and tip out the potato mixture. Shape the mixture into long rolls about the thickness of your thumb. Cut into 1 cm/½ in lengths and shape into fingers.

Drop the potato fingers into a large pan of boiling salted water and simmer gently over a moderate heat until they rise to the surface. Remove from the pan on a slotted spoon, rinse in cold water and drain thoroughly. Leave the fingers to dry for about 3 hours.

Rinse the sage leaves in cold water, pat dry and cut into narrow strips.

Melt the butter in a large frying pan. Fry the sage over a low to moderate heat to bring out its full flavour. Add the potato fingers and brown all over, turning them continuously.

Serve hot with a mixed salad.

Serves 4

Per Portion
about 460 calories
59 g carbohydrate
7 g protein · 21 g fat

Potato Tortilla

250 g/9 oz floury potatoes
1 large onion
4 tablespoons vegetable oil
salt
freshly ground black pepper
4 eggs
½ bunch of fresh chives

Peel, wash and dry the potatoes. Cut into slices about 2 mm/⅛ in thick. Dry the slices well on absorbent kitchen paper. Peel and halve the onion and cut into thin rings.

Heat the oil in a heavy frying pan and fry the onions over a moderate heat until transparent, stirring frequently.

Reduce the heat, add the potatoes and spread them evenly. Season to taste and cook over a low heat for about 10 minutes, turning them frequently, until they are tender and brown.

Meanwhile, beat the eggs until frothy.

Pour the eggs over the potatoes and shake the pan to distribute the mixture evenly. Cook over a low heat for about 10 minutes until the egg has set.

Loosen the tortilla from the pan with a spatula, slide on to a plate and return to the pan the other way up. Cook on the second side for a further 5 minutes.

Rinse the chives in cold water, pat dry and snip.

Halve the tortilla and serve at once on warmed plates, sprinkled with chives. Serve with tomato salad with spring onions and chopped fresh herbs.

Serves 2

Per Portion
about 470 calories
27 g carbohydrate
18 g protein · 30 g fat

Boiled Potatoes with Mushroom Sauce

20 g / ¾ oz dried cèpes or morels
250 ml / 8 fl oz lukewarm water
750 g / 1½ lb small new potatoes
salt
1 tablespoon wholemeal flour
75 g / 3 oz hard cheese
 (Emmental, mature Gouda or
 Gruyère)
½ bunch of fresh parsley
125 ml / 4 fl oz double cream
1 tablespoon butter
freshly ground white pepper
freshly grated nutmeg
1–2 tablespoons lemon juice
salt or gomasio

Soak the dried mushrooms in the water in a covered bowl for 2 hours.

Tip the soaked mushrooms into a sieve, reserving the soaking water, and wash well under cold water to remove any grit or soil (sand tends to collect in the caps of morels). Never wash dried mushrooms before soaking as this loses some of the flavour.

Strain the soaking water through a coffee filter paper to remove any bits of dirt. Set aside.

Scrub the potatoes well under cold running water. Cook, in the skins, in a little boiling salted water until tender. This will take 20 to 30 minutes depending on size.

Meanwhile, heat the flour in a dry pan over a high to moderate heat, stirring continuously, until it gives off a slight aroma. Gradually add the mushroom soaking water, whisking vigorously to avoid lumps. Bring to the boil and continue whisking to form a smooth, velvety sauce. Reduce the heat, cover the pan and simmer over a low heat for 5 minutes, stirring frequently for the sauce burns easily.

While the sauce is cooking, grate the cheese. Wash the parsley, strip the leaves from the stalks, pat dry and finely chop. Add the drained mushrooms, cream and cheese to the sauce and stir to melt the cheese. Whisk in the butter. Finally, stir in the parsley and season to taste with pepper, nutmeg, lemon juice and salt. (If you prefer to use gomasio instead of salt, sprinkle it over the potatoes at the end.) Keep the sauce hot until ready to serve.

Drain the potatoes, evaporate some of the steam, peel and serve in the mushroom sauce with a wild herb or mixed salad.

Serves 4

Per Portion
about 385 calories
35 g carbohydrate
11 g protein · 19 g fat

Cook's Tip
Cèpes: a prized mushroom found in woods in spring and autumn. They are the size of a large common mushroom, with a shiny brown top and spongy gills. They are collected all through the summer in France and they are dried for use in soups and sauces.
Morels: these have either a yellowish or black cap (smaller varieties) and some are pointed. They are gathered in the woods in the spring and used fresh or they can be dried for winter use.

Broccoli and Potatoes with Cheese Sauce

600 g / 1¼ lb floury potatoes
salt
100 g / 4 oz Cheddar cheese
1 kg / 2¼ lb broccoli
250 ml / 8 fl oz double cream
20 g / ¾ oz butter
freshly ground white pepper
freshly grated nutmeg
3 tablespoons chopped mixed
*   fresh herbs*

Scrub the potatoes well under cold running water and cook in the skins in a little boiling salted water until soft. This will take 30 to 40 minutes depending on size.

Meanwhile, finely dice the cheese. Wash the broccoli. Cut off large leaves and the tough ends of the stalks. Using a small pointed knife peel off the skin from the bottom of the stalks towards the top. Cut off the florets for they cook quicker than the stalks.

Bring a large pan of salted water to the boil. Add the broccoli stalks and cook for about 3 minutes. Then add the florets and cook for a further 3 minutes. Remove from the pan with a slotted spoon. Drain well and keep hot in a warmed dish.

Drain the potatoes, evaporate some of the steam and peel. Cut into slices or cubes and add to the broccoli.

Bring the cream to the boil with the butter. Over a moderate heat stir the diced cheese into the cream until melted. The cream should not be too hot or it will not bind with the cheese and will be lumpy. Also the sauce burns easily if it is not stirred continuously.

Season the sauce with a little salt – the cheese already contains salt – and pepper and nutmeg to taste. Stir the herbs into the sauce.

Pour the cheese sauce over the broccoli and potatoes and serve at once.

Serves 4

Per Portion
about 695 calories
47 g carbohydrate
20 g protein · 40 g fat

Flat Bread Cakes

500 g/18 oz wholemeal flour
salt
½ teaspoon freshly ground
caraway
1 teaspoon freshly crushed
coriander
150 ml/¼ pint natural yogurt
250 ml/8 fl oz lukewarm water

In a bowl, mix the wholemeal flour with a generous pinch of salt, the caraway and coriander.

Beat the yogurt with the water and pour on to the flour. Work the ingredients together, then knead the dough vigorously until smooth. Shape into a ball, wrap in greaseproof paper and leave to rest for at least 8 hours.

Divide the dough into about 15 equal portions. Knead each piece vigorously once more, and then roll out on a lightly floured worktop into thin rounds.

Heat a heavy griddle or cast iron frying pan over a low to moderate heat without allowing it to get too hot. Add the bread cakes, one at a time, and cook on both sides until lightly browned and slightly bubbly.

Serve the bread cakes with either avocado cream and/or olive cheese or simply with melted butter, flavoured with a little garlic if liked.

Makes 15

Per Portion
about 130 calories
24 g carbohydrate
5 g protein · 1 g fat

Avocado Cream

50 g/2 oz Roquefort or Gorgon-
zola cheese
1 tablespoon blanched almonds
1 ripe avocado
juice of ½ lemon
freshly ground white pepper

Cream the cheese with a fork until as smooth as possible.

Tip the almonds on to a board and finely chop using a strong knife or grind in a nut mill or coffee grinder.

Halve the avocado and remove the stone. Peel the avocado halves using a small, sharp knife and sprinkle immediately with lemon juice to prevent discolouring. Mash the avocado with a fork.

Add the cheese and almonds and mix to a smooth paste. Season to taste with pepper.

Serves 6

Per Portion
about 245 calories
3 g carbohydrate
2 g protein · 23 g fat

Olive Cheese

100 g/4 oz black olives
1 clove garlic
small bunch of fresh basil
1 tablespoon natural yogurt
125 g/4½ oz cream cheese
1 tablespoon gomasio
freshly ground white pepper

Drain the olives well, remove the stones and chop very finely. Peel and chop the garlic. Wash the basil in cold water, shake dry and chop the leaves.

Stir the yogurt into the cream cheese until smooth. Stir in the olives, garlic and basil. Season to taste with gomasio and pepper.

Serves 6

Per Portion
about 195 calories
3 g carbohydrate
5 g protein · 18 g fat

Home-made Curd Cheese with Herbs and Pumpkin Seeds

3.5 litres/6 pints milk
150 ml/¼ pint lemon juice
100 g/4 oz cottage cheese
1 tablespoon single cream or
    crème fraîche
pinch of caster sugar
freshly ground white pepper
1 onion
1 box of mustard and cress
½ bunch each of fresh parsley,
    dill and chives
handful of fresh chervil
few young leaves of dandelion,
    nettle, sorrel and lemon balm
1–2 tablespoons pumpkin seeds
1 teaspoon sunflower oil

There are two methods of making curd cheese. The first uses untreated milk which is left to sour naturally over a period of several days. Untreated milk is difficult to obtain, and this method calls for careful cleaning of all utensils.

The second method, which is used in this recipe, uses pasteurised milk and a souring agent – lemon juice – to produce the curds.

Heat the milk slowly to 48.5c/120f. Add the lemon juice and stir well, then leave for about 15 minutes or until the milk has separated. Line a colander with clean muslin and drain the curds through it. Tie the corners of the cloth together and hang the cheese over a bowl to drain completely; this should take about 1 hour.

Mix the resulting curds with the cottage cheese and cream or crème fraîche and season with the sugar and pepper to taste.

Peel and finely chop the onion. Snip off the cress with scissors. Pick over the herbs and leaves, remove any tough stalks and wash well under cold running water. Shake until dry and finely chop.

Tip the pumpkin seeds on to a wooden board and chop using a large heavy knife.

Mix the onion, cress, herbs, leaves, pumpkin seeds and sunflower oil into the curds.

Serve with radishes, cucumber and tomatoes and fresh wholemeal bread.

Serves 6

Per Portion
about 235 calories
7 g carbohydrate
21 g protein · 12 g fat

Variations
The following ideas can all be used to make simple curd cheese spreads or dips.

Tomato and Basil
Peel and chop some tomatoes, then mix them into the curd cheese. Add some chopped fresh basil and freshly ground white pepper.

Minted Garlic Dip
Crush one or two cloves of garlic and mix into curd cheese. Add some chopped fresh mint and a little olive oil. Season with a little salt and freshly ground white pepper. Serve well chilled.

Walnut Spread
Finely chop some walnuts and mix them into curd cheese. Add some chopped fresh parsley and freshly ground white pepper. Stir in a little celery salt and press the mixture into a dish. Chill well before serving.

Cucumber Dip
Grate a large piece of cucumber and leave it to drain in a sieve or colander for 30 minutes. Squeeze all the liquid out of the cucumber. Stir the grated cucumber into the curd cheese and add some chopped fresh mint. Season lightly with freshly ground white pepper and a little garlic salt. Chill for 10 minutes before serving but do not leave for too long or the dip will become very runny.

Dips with Vegetables

200 g/7 oz tofu
125 ml/4 fl oz single cream
½ tablespoon lemon juice
1 tablespoon salted shelled
  pistachios
bunch of fresh basil
freshly ground white pepper
2 tablespoons sesame seeds
1 box of mustard and cress
250 g/9 oz cream cheese
125 ml/4 fl oz soured cream
salt
250 g/9 oz ripe tomatoes
1 onion
1 clove garlic
freshly ground black pepper
pinch of caster sugar
Tabasco sauce

To make the tofu dip, finely dice the drained tofu and blend with the cream and lemon juice in a liquidiser or food processor. Finely chop the pistachios. Wash the basil, shake dry and finely chop. Mix the pistachios and basil into the dip and season to taste with white pepper.

To make the cream cheese dip, first toast the sesame seeds in a dry frying pan, stirring continuously. Snip off the cress. Stir the cream cheese with the soured cream until smooth and mix in the sesame seeds and cress. Season to taste with salt and white pepper.

To make the tomato dip, first blanch the tomatoes in boiling water for 30 seconds, and then rinse in cold water. Peel the tomatoes, remove the core and seeds and blend in a liquidiser or food processor. Peel and very finely chop the onion and garlic and mix into the tomato purée. Season to taste with salt, black pepper, sugar and Tabasco sauce.

Serve the dips with fresh vegetables cut into sticks. Try kohlrabi, carrot, cucumber, celery, mushrooms and strips of green pepper. Also serve wholemeal or wheatgerm bread or rolls.

Per Portion
about 465 calories
11 g carbohydrate
16 g protein · 39 g fat

Artichokes with Tofu Sauce

salt
1 lemon
4 globe artichokes
100 g/4 oz tofu
150 ml/¼ pint natural yogurt
1 tablespoon crème fraîche or
   soured cream
1 clove garlic
freshly ground white pepper
1 teaspoon vegetable oil
5 tablespoons chopped mixed
   fresh herbs (chives, parsley,
   dill, borage, lemon balm, tarragon and basil)

Bring plenty of salted water to
the boil in a pan which is large
enough to take all the arti-
 chokes at once.
  Meanwhile, halve the lemon.
Squeeze one half and keep the
juice to one side. Wash the artichokes well in cold water. Cut
off the artichoke stalks close to
the base. Using kitchen scissors
snip off the top half of each
leaf. Rub all the cut edges with

the second lemon half to prevent discolouring. Then squeeze
the lemon half into the fast-
boiling water.
  Add the artichokes. Return
to the boil and cook for 20 to
30 minutes over a low to moderate heat. They are cooked
when the leaves come away
easily.
  Meanwhile, make the sauce
by blending the tofu with the
yogurt and crème fraîche in a
liquidiser or food processor to
give a smooth, creamy consistency. Peel the garlic and
squeeze through a garlic press
into the tofu paste. Season to
taste. Stir in the reserved lemon
juice, oil and herbs.
  Serve the drained artichokes
with the tofu sauce.

Serves 4

Per Portion
about 135 calories
16 g carbohydrate
6 g protein · 5 g fat

Fried Mozzarella

about 250 g/9 oz mozzarella
   cheese
1 egg
1 tablespoon wholemeal flour
3–4 tablespoons stale rye
   breadcrumbs
1–2 tablespoons olive oil

Drain the mozzarella, pat dry
and cut into 4 slices.
  Beat the egg in a dish with a
fork until the white and yolk
are completely mixed. Put the
wholemeal flour and rye
crumbs into dishes.
  Coat the mozzarella slices
first in wholemeal flour, then in
egg and finally in breadcrumbs.
  Heat the olive oil in a frying
pan. Fry the mozzarella slices
over a moderate heat for about
2 minutes on each side until the
cheese is soft and the crumbs
golden brown.
  Serve immediately on individual warmed plates, garnished with sliced tomato, and
sprinkled with fresh herbs and a
little olive oil.

Serves 4

Per Portion
about 200 calories
8 g carbohydrate
11 g protein · 13 g fat

Cook's Tip

Mozzarella is a soft Italian cheese made from
cow's or buffalo's milk.
When it is fresh it is soft
and slightly sticky at the
centre. Slices of tomato
and mozzarella arranged
alternately on a plate and
sprinkled with chopped
fresh basil and cold-
pressed olive oil make a
delicious light starter for
summer.

Tofu Schnitzel with Green Rye and Mushrooms

300 g/11 oz tofu
4 tablespoons soy sauce
200 ml/7 fl oz freshly made vege-
  table stock
100 g/4 oz rye grain
1 slice stale rye or wholemeal
  bread (about 40 g/1½ oz)
2 bunches of fresh parsley
1 onion
400 g/14 oz fresh mushrooms
  (button, oyster or mixed)
2 tablespoons wholemeal flour
freshly grated nutmeg
1 egg
5 tablespoons sunflower oil
salt
freshly ground white pepper

Drain the tofu and cut into
slices scant 1 cm/½ in thick.
Place the slices side by side in a
shallow dish, sprinkle with the
soy sauce and marinate for 2
hours, turning frequently so
that they soak up the soy sauce.

Bring the stock to the boil in
a saucepan. Add the rye, reduce
the heat to low, cover the pan
and simmer gently for 25 minutes. Remove the pan from the
heat and leave the rye to soak
in the open pan for 1 hour.

Finely grate the rye or
wholemeal bread or whizz to
crumbs in a liquidiser. Wash
the parsley, strip the leaves
from the stalks, dry well and
finely chop. Peel and finely
chop the onion. Trim the mushrooms, rinse, if necessary, and
thinly slice.

Transfer the tofu slices from
the bowl to a thick layer of absorbent kitchen paper. If they
are too wet the coating will not
stick.

To make the coating, put the
wholemeal flour into a shallow
dish and mix in nutmeg to
taste. Beat the egg with a fork
in a second dish and tip the
breadcrumbs into a third dish.

First dip the tofu slices in
flour, then in egg and finally in
breadcrumbs.

Heat 4 tablespoons oil in a
frying pan. Fry the tofu slices

over a moderate heat for about
5 minutes until golden brown
on each side. Keep hot in the
oven.

Heat the remaining oil in the
pan and fry the onion until
transparent. Add the mushrooms and rye and heat
through over a high heat, stirring continuously. You need
the temperature really high to
prevent the mushrooms pro-
ducing juice. Stir in the
chopped parsley and season to
taste.

Serve the tofu schnitzel and
rye and mushrooms separately.
Serve with a mixed salad with
sunflower or pumpkin seeds in
a garlic and herb vinaigrette.

Serves 4

Per Portion
about 300 calories
37 g carbohydrate
16 g protein · 17 g fat

Cook's Tip

If you can't get rye, use
whole wheat grain (wheat
berries) which you boil
for 1 hour and leave to
soak for 1 further hour.

You can, if you like,
add some sesame seeds to
the breadcrumbs which
coat the tofu.
Alternatively add some
poppy seeds or very fine-
ly chopped nuts to vary
the flavour and texture.

Vegetable Rissoles with Tofu

350 g / 12 oz celeriac
200 g / 7 oz carrots
200 g / 7 oz leeks
1 onion
2 cloves garlic
bunch of fresh parsley
100 g / 4 oz tofu
2 eggs
5 tablespoons wholemeal
  breadcrumbs
salt
freshly ground white pepper
about 6 tablespoons vegetable oil
  for frying

Peel the celeriac and carrots and wash under cold running water. Dry them and then finely grate. Trim the leek, cut a cross down through the green leaves to the white part and wash. Cut across the leek into thin slices including about two thirds of the green leaves. Place the prepared vegetables in a tea towel and squeeze well.

Peel and finely chop the on-ion and garlic. Wash the pars-ley, strip the leaves from the stalks, pat dry and finely chop. Drain and dice the tofu or crush with a fork.

Place all the prepared ingre-dients in a bowl and mix with the eggs and breadcrumbs to make a firm, smooth and mal-leable mixture. Season to taste, cover and leave to stand for 10 minutes.

With moist hands shape the mixture into rissoles. Heat about half the oil in a frying pan. Fry the vegetable rissoles over a high to moderate heat for about 10 minutes, turning once. Add a little more oil to the side of the pan as and when necessary.

Serve hot, with mixed salad with sunflower seeds.

Serves 4

Per Portion
about 295 calories
16 g carbohydrate
8 g protein · 20 g fat

Vegetable Omelette

200 g / 7 oz courgettes
salt
1 clove garlic
2 sprigs of fresh thyme or
  5 leaves fresh sage
250 g / 9 oz potatoes
4 eggs
1 tablespoon wholemeal flour
75 g / 3 oz Parmesan cheese,
  grated
freshly ground white pepper
1 tablespoon vegetable oil
25 g / 1 oz butter

Wash, dry, top and tail the courgettes. Grate them, place in a bowl and sprinkle with salt to get rid of excess moisture. Leave to sweat for about 30 minutes.

Peel and finely chop the gar-lic. Rinse the thyme in cold water, strip off the leaves and pat dry. If you use sage, wash and dry the leaves and cut into fine strips.

Peel, wash and grate the po-tatoes. Place the grated pota-toes and courgettes in a tea towel and squeeze well.

Beat the eggs with a fork. Stir the courgettes, potatoes, garlic, herbs, flour and cheese into the egg and season to taste.

Divide the oil and butter be-tween two heavy frying pans and heat. Pour the egg mixture into the pans, cover and cook over a low to moderate heat for 10 minutes, until set. When the omelettes are brown under-neath, turn them and fry on the other side for about 5 minutes.

Serves 2

Per Portion
about 570 calories
29 g carbohydrate
29 g protein · 37 g fat

Rye Rissoles

1 onion
3 tablespoons vegetable oil
200 g/7 oz rye grain, crushed
*   medium-fine*
375 ml/13 fl oz cold water
2 eggs
1–2 tablespoons chopped fresh
*   parsley*
salt

Peel and finely chop the onion.
Heat 1 tablespoon oil in a
saucepan and fry the onion until transparent, stirring continuously. Add the rye and stir until
completely coated in fat. Add
the water, cover the pan and
simmer over a low heat for 10
minutes.

Remove from the heat and
leave the rye to soak in the
covered pan for 50 minutes.
 Then uncover the pan and al-
low to cool to lukewarm.

Beat the eggs with a fork and
mix into the rye with the parsley. Season to taste with salt.

Using wet hands, shape the
mixture into 8 equal rissoles.

Heat the remaining oil in a
frying pan and fry the rissoles
over a moderate heat for about
10 minutes until golden brown,
turning once.

Serves 4

Per Portion
about 305 calories
36 g carbohydrate
10 g protein · 13 g fat

Cook's Tip
If you can't get rye grain,
cook 300 g/11 oz coarsely
crushed whole wheat
(wheat berries) in about
750 ml/1¼ pints boiling
water, stirring frequently
to prevent it burning.
Leave the wheat to soak
and cool as in the recipe.
Mix 1 chopped onion and
2 eggs into the wheat and
season. Shape and cook
as above.

Buckwheat Dumplings in Gorgonzola Cream

300 ml/½ pint water
150 g/5 oz buckwheat grain,
*   coarsely crushed*
150 g/5 oz wholemeal or
*   wheatmeal flour*
50 g/2 oz wholemeal semolina
2 eggs
2 tablespoons soured cream
3 tablespoons chopped fresh
*   parsley*
3 tablespoons snipped fresh
*   chives*
salt
freshly ground white pepper
freshly grated nutmeg
30 g/1¼ oz butter
150 g/5 oz gorgonzola cheese
250 ml/8 fl oz double cream

Bring the water to the boil in a
saucepan, add the buckwheat,
cover the pan and simmer for
20 minutes. Remove from the
heat and soak for 1 hour.

Mix the buckwheat with the
flour, semolina, eggs, soured
cream and herbs to a fairly soft
but malleable dough. Season to
taste with salt, pepper and
nutmeg.

Using 2 wet teaspoons, shape
the mixture into dumplings and
cook in a large pan of boiling
salted water until they rise to
the surface. Remove them from
the water with a slotted spoon,
drain well and arrange in a
buttered baking dish. Crumble
the gorgonzola. Tip into a
saucepan and add the cream.
Stir over a low heat until the
cheese has melted. Season to
taste with pepper and nutmeg
and pour over the dumplings.
Dot with the remaining butter.

Place the dish in a hot oven
(220 C, 425 F, gas 7), and cook
for 12 to 15 minutes.

Serves 4

Per Portion
about 780 calories
60 g carbohydrate
24 g protein · 50 g fat

Vegetable Stew with Chickpea Balls

500 g / 18 oz dried chickpeas
1 onion
4 cloves garlic
bunch each of fresh chives and
 parsley
½ teaspoon turmeric
1 teaspoon ground anise or
 cumin
½ tablespoon ground coriander
pinch of hot chilli powder
salt
freshly ground black pepper
2 tablespoons wholemeal flour
600 g / 1¼ lb mixed seasonal vege-
 tables (eg carrots, fennel,
 white cabbage, leeks, broccoli,
 aubergines, courgettes, green
 peppers and tomatoes)
1 Spanish onion
few leaves fresh sage and 1 leaf
 fresh lovage (optional)
250 ml / 8 fl oz sunflower oil
125 ml / 4 fl oz freshly made vege-
 table stock
1 teaspoon dried thyme

Wash the chickpeas, cover with water and soak for 12 hours.

The following day, peel the onion and 2 cloves garlic. Quarter the onion. Rinse the chives and parsley in cold water and shake dry. Cut up the chives. Strip the parsley leaves off the stalks and finely chop.

Drain the chickpeas and blend in a liquidiser or food processor with the onion quarters and peeled garlic. Add the chives, parsley, turmeric, aniseed or cumin, coriander, chilli powder and salt and pepper to taste. Work in the flour to give a firm malleable dough. If the dough is sticky work in a little more flour; if it is too firm work in a few drops of water. Cover the dough and set aside.

Trim all the vegetables, wash and dry. Peel carrots and cut into sticks. Halve fennel, cut out the stalk and cut across into strips. Cut the stalk and thick ribs out of white cabbage and then shred. Cut leeks with about two thirds of the pale green leaves into 2 cm / ¾ in lengths. Separate broccoli into

florets. Slice aubergines and courgettes. Halve peppers, remove seeds and white pith, rinse and cut into strips. Blanch the tomatoes in boiling water for 30 seconds, rinse in cold water and then peel and dice, removing the core and the seeds.

Peel the Spanish onion and cut into rings. Wash the sage and lovage in cold water and shake dry. Peel the remaining garlic.

Using wet hands, shape the chickpea mixture into walnut-sized balls.

Keep 1 tablespoon sunflower oil to one side and heat the rest in a frying pan. Fry the chickpea balls, in batches, for about 4 minutes, turning to brown evenly. Drain the fried balls on absorbent kitchen paper and keep hot in the oven.

While the balls are being fried, place the vegetables in a saucepan with the whole garlic, herbs, vegetable stock and remaining sunflower oil and bring to the boil. Cover the pan and cook over a low heat for 5

to 10 minutes until the vegetables are tender but still firm to bite. Remove the herbs and season the vegetables to taste.

Serve the vegetables and chickpea balls separately.

Serves 6

Per Portion
about 550 calories
63 g carbohydrate
18 g protein · 24 g fat

Baked Courgettes and Tomatoes

1 kg/2¼ lb ripe tomatoes
1 kg/2¼ lb small young
courgettes
1 Spanish onion
2 cloves garlic
bunch of fresh parsley
6 sprigs of fresh thyme
2 sprigs of fresh rosemary
125 ml/4 fl oz olive oil
salt
freshly ground black pepper

Blanch the tomatoes in boiling water for 30 seconds and then rinse in cold water. Peel and quarter the tomatoes and remove the core and the seeds. Wash and top and tail the courgettes. Dry them and cut lengthways into 0.5 cm/¼ in slices.

Peel the onion and garlic. Cut the onion into thin rings and finely chop the garlic. Wash and dry the herbs. Finely chop the parsley leaves. Strip the thyme and rosemary leaves

from the stalks. Heat about half the olive oil in a frying pan and fry the courgette slices, in batches, until golden brown on both sides. Remove them from the pan when they are cooked and drain on absorbent kitchen paper. When you have fried all the courgettes, fry the onion and garlic in the pan until transparent.

Arrange the courgettes and tomato slices in layers in an ovenproof dish, seasoning each layer and scattering with onion, garlic and herbs. Sprinkle with the remaining olive oil. Place in a hot oven (220 c, 425 F, gas 7) and bake for 30 minutes until tender but still firm to bite.

Serves 6

Per Portion
about 285 calories
16 g carbohydrate
5 g protein · 22 g fat

Provençal-style Tofu Ragoût

300 g/11 oz tofu
3 cloves garlic
½ tablespoon fresh rosemary
leaves
3 tablespoons lemon juice
125 ml/4 fl oz olive oil
400 g/14 oz aubergines
salt
400 g/14 oz ripe tomatoes
250 g/9 oz courgettes
8 black olives
125 ml/4 fl oz freshly made vege-
table stock
1 teaspoon dried Provençal herbs
freshly ground black pepper

Dice the tofu. Peel and chop the garlic. Coarsely chop the rosemary. Mix the lemon juice with the garlic, rosemary and 1 tablespoons olive oil. Pour over the tofu, cover and leave for 2 hours.

Wash the aubergines, trim and slice lengthways. Sprinkle with salt and set aside.

Meanwhile, blanch the tom-

atoes in boiling water for 30 seconds. Rinse in cold water, then peel and dice the tomatoes, removing the seeds. Wash, dry and trim the courgettes. Cut into sticks.

Pat the aubergine slices dry. Heat the remaining oil in a frying pan and fry the aubergines until golden brown on both sides, then remove them from the pan. Fry the courgettes until golden and remove from the pan.

Lay the aubergine slices in the pan. Top with the courgettes, tomatoes, olives and tofu. Add the stock, Provençal herbs and salt and pepper to taste. Cover and cook over a moderate heat for about 5 minutes.

Serves 4

Per Portion
about 410 calories
12 g carbohydrate
8 g protein · 34 g fat

Sweet and Sour Vegetables

*225 g/8 oz each broccoli, cauli-
flower, green beans and
carrots*
1 fairly tart apple
1 orange · 1 banana
1 onion
1 clove garlic
2 tablespoons vegetable oil
*250 ml/8 fl oz freshly made vege-
table stock*
bunch of fresh parsley
freshly ground white pepper
1–2 tablespoons cider vinegar
gomasio for sprinkling

Trim and wash all the vegetables. Separate the broccoli and
cauliflower into florets, top and
tail the beans; peel the carrots
and cut into sticks.

Peel and core the apple and
cut into wedges. Peel the
orange, removing all the white
pith, then separate into segments. Peel and slice the banana. Peel and finely chop the
onion and garlic.

Heat the oil in a saucepan.
Fry the onion and garlic, until
transparent. Add the vegetables
and stir well. Add the vegetable
stock and bring to the boil. Reduce the heat, cover and simmer for about 5 minutes.

Stir in the fruit and cook
over a low heat for a further 5
to 7 minutes.

Meanwhile, wash the parsley,
strip the leaves from the stalks,
pat dry and coarsely chop.
Season the sweet and sour vegetables to taste with pepper and
cider vinegar. Stir in part of the
parsley. Serve sprinkled with
the remaining parsley.

Serve the gomasio separately.

Serves 4

Per Portion
about 200 calories
26 g carbohydrate
6 g protein · 6 g fat

Vegetables with Soy Sauce and Sesame

*750 g/1½ lb vegetables (carrots,
kohlrabi, fennel, celery and
spring onions)*
*piece of fresh root ginger, about
2 cm/¾ in long*
1 clove garlic
200 g/7 oz mung bean sprouts
2 tablespoons sunflower oil
*7 tablespoons freshly made vege-
table stock*
1 tablespoon dry sherry
3 tablespoons soy sauce
sambal oelek
4 tablespoons sesame seeds

Peel or trim the vegetables and
then wash them. Cut the carrots
and kohlrabi into sticks. Halve
the fennel, cut out the wedge-
shaped stalk and then cut
across the grain into thin slices.
Cut off the celery leaves and
keep in reserve. Cut the celery
and spring onions into 1-cm/
½-in lengths.

Peel the ginger and garlic.
Thinly slice the ginger; chop the
garlic.

Tip the bean sprouts into a
sieve and rinse in cold water.

Heat the oil in a frying pan.
Fry the ginger and garlic over a
moderate heat until the garlic is
transparent. Add the vegetables
and stir until completely coated
in oil. Add the vegetable stock,
sherry and soy sauce and bring
to the boil. Reduce the heat,
cover the pan and cook over a
low heat for 3 to 4 minutes.

Season to taste with sambal
oelek and stir in the sesame
seeds. Scatter with the reserved
celery leaves and serve at once.

Serves 4

Per Portion
about 180 calories
15 g carbohydrate
7 g protein · 8 g fat

Wholemeal Spaghetti with Cheese and Cream Sauce

salt
400 g/14 oz wholemeal spaghetti
250 ml/8 fl oz double cream
100 g/4 oz pecorino cheese, grated
freshly ground white pepper
freshly grated nutmeg
5 leaves fresh sage

Bring about 4 litres/7 pints salted water to the boil. Allow to boil for about 30 seconds, then add the spaghetti. Stir to avoid it sticking together, then cook until *al dente* (tender but still firm to bite), making sure that the water boils throughout and stirring the spaghetti frequently.

Meanwhile, make the sauce. Pour the cream into a saucepan, bring to the boil and reduce by half on a moderate heat, stirring continuously.

Reduce the heat and stir in the pecorino until melted. You need a really low temperature here or the cheese will form lumps and not bind with the sauce. Make sure you stir throughout for the cheese sauce will burn easily. Season the sauce to taste with salt, pepper and nutmeg.

Wash and dry the sage leaves and cut into strips. Stir into the sauce.

Tip the pasta into a sieve, drain well and stir into the cream sauce. Serve at once on warmed plates with mixed salad in herb vinaigrette.

Serves 4

Per Portion
about 655 calories
66 g carbohydrate
23 g protein · 34 g fat

Variation
Wholemeal Macaroni with Garlic Oil
Cook 400 g/14 oz wholemeal macaroni in a large pan of boiling salted water until *al dente*.

Meanwhile, wash a bunch of fresh parsley, strip the leaves from the stalks, pat dry and chop very finely. Peel and thinly slice 4 cloves garlic. Heat 125 ml/4 fl oz olive oil and fry the garlic over a low to moderate heat until transparent, stirring often. Rub a dried red chilli pepper between your fingers and add to the garlic oil with the parsley. Drain the cooked pasta and stir into the garlic oil at once.

Wholemeal Pasta with Uncooked Tomato Sauce
Cook 400 g/14 oz wholemeal short cut macaroni in a large pan of boiling salted water until *al dente*. Meanwhile, blanch 750 g/1½ lb tomatoes in boiling water for 30 seconds and rinse in cold water. Peel and finely chop the tomatoes, removing the core and the seeds. Peel and very finely chop 1 clove garlic. Wash a bunch of fresh basil, strip the leaves from the stalks, pat dry and cut into fine strips. Mix the chopped tomato with the herbs, garlic, 2 tablespoons cold-pressed olive oil, a pinch of caster sugar and salt and freshly ground black pepper to taste. Drain the pasta and mix with the tomato sauce while very hot.

Cook's Tip
Wholemeal pasta comes in a wide variety of shapes and they can all be substituted for the spaghetti. Children in particular, prefer to eat smaller shapes and find them more attractive.

Polenta Slices with Tomato Sauce

1.25 litres/2¼ pints water
250 g/9 oz cornmeal
salt
300 g/11 oz spinach beet
700 g/1½ lb ripe tomatoes
250 g/9 oz mushrooms
1 onion
1 clove garlic
bunch of fresh basil or parsley
3 tablespoons olive oil
pinch of caster sugar
freshly ground black pepper

Bring the water to the boil in a saucepan, add the cornmeal and a pinch of salt and leave to swell over the lowest possible heat in the open pan for about 45 minutes until the mixture comes away from the sides of the pan.

Meanwhile, strip the beet leaves off the stalks (use the stalks in another dish). Wash, dry and coarsely chop.

When the semolina has been cooking for 30 minutes, stir in the beet leaves.

Spread out the polenta on a baking sheet and leave to dry for about 20 minutes until firm enough to cut. Then cut into pieces about 2 × 5 cm/¾ × 2 in.

Wash and halve the tomatoes, remove the seeds and purée. Trim and slice the mushrooms. Peel and finely chop the onion and garlic. Wash and finely chop the basil or parsley.

Heat 2 tablespoons oil in a frying pan and fry the polenta slices until golden brown on both sides. Remove from the pan and keep hot.

Heat the remaining oil in the pan and fry the onion and garlic until transparent, stirring often. Add the mushrooms and fry for 2 minutes, stirring continuously. Add the puréed tomatoes and season with the sugar and salt and pepper to taste. Cover the pan and heat through.

Stir in the basil or parsley and serve the sauce with the polenta slices.

Serves 5

Per Portion
about 305 calories
50 g carbohydrate
9 g protein · 7 g fat

Cannelloni with Tofu and Spinach

150 g/5 oz wheatmeal flour
salt
1 egg
1–3 egg yolks
1 tablespoon vegetable oil
1 kg/2¼ lb spinach
1 onion
1 clove garlic
500 g/18 oz tofu
freshly ground white pepper
freshly grated nutmeg
250 ml/8 fl oz single cream
100 g/4 oz Parmesan cheese,
  freshly grated
oil for the dish
20 g/¾ oz butter

Work the flour with a pinch of salt, the egg, 1 egg yolk and the oil to make a smooth pasta dough. The dough should not be sticky, but if it is too solid or even crumbly, work in 1 or 2 further egg yolks. Wrap in foil and leave to rest for 30 minutes.

Meanwhile, make the filling. Pick over the spinach, cutting out tough stems, and wash well several times in cold water. Drain the spinach.

Bring plenty of water to the boil with a little salt. Blanch the spinach in batches in the boiling water for about 1 minute. Lift each batch out on a slotted spoon, drain well and then press with a wooden spoon to remove as much liquid as possible. Finely chop the spinach.

Peel and finely chop the onion and garlic.

Drain the tofu. Crush about three quarters of it with a fork or blend in a liquidiser or food processor. Mix the puréed tofu with the spinach, onion and garlic and season to taste with salt, pepper and nutmeg.

Blend the remaining tofu with the cream in a liquidiser or food processor and stir in the grated cheese.

Divide the pasta dough into portions and roll out on a lightly floured worktop. It is much quicker and easier to roll the pasta in a hand-operated pasta machine. This also makes it unnecessary to knead the dough by hand. Set the rollers at the widest setting and roll one piece of dough. Fold one end to the centre and the other end over it, turn the dough through 90 degrees and reroll. Continue in this way until all the dough is smooth. Then reset the rollers at the required thickness and roll out each portion thinly.

Cut the pasta into 10 × 15 cm/4 × 6 in pieces. Spread each with the tofu and spinach mixture and roll up.

Brush a shallow baking dish with the oil and place the cannelloni side by side in the dish. Pour on the tofu cream and dot with the butter. Bake in a hot oven (220 C, 425 F, gas 7), on the second shelf from the bottom, for about 45 minutes until the top is nice and brown.

Serves 6

Per Portion
about 490 calories
28 g carbohydrate
21 g protein · 32 g fat

Cook's Tip

If you can't get fresh spinach, use 2 packets frozen spinach (about 900 g/2 lb). After thawing, squeeze it out very well and finely chop.

The cannelloni are just as good made with spring greens, prepared in the same way as the spinach. Or mix the tofu with peeled, seeded puréed tomatoes. Season this filling with fresh basil or, in winter, dried oregano.

Ravioli with Herbs and Ricotta

*400 g/14 oz wholemeal or
    wheatmeal flour*
salt
4 eggs
1 tablespoon vegetable oil
1–3 egg yolks
*about 500 g/18 oz mixed fresh
    herbs and wild leaves (eg
    parsley, basil, nettle, dande-
    lion leaves, wild garlic and
    wild marjoram)*
1 onion
1 clove garlic
125 g/4½ oz butter
500 g/18 oz ricotta cheese
freshly ground white pepper
freshly grated nutmeg
cayenne pepper
6 sprigs of fresh thyme

To make the dough, mix the flour with a pinch of salt, the eggs, oil and 1 of the egg yolks. The dough should be firm and smooth and not at all crumbly. If necessary, work in the other egg yolks or a few drops of cold water. It is a good idea to mix pasta doughs made with refined wheat flour with your hands so that you can feel the consistency. Wrap the dough in foil and allow to stand for at least 1 hour.

For the filling, pick over the herbs, wash, shake dry and coarsely chop. Peel and finely chop the onion and garlic. Heat 1 tablespoon butter in a frying pan without allowing it to brown. Fry the onion and garlic over a moderate heat until transparent, stirring often. Add the herbs and stir until they produce juice. Remove the pan from the heat and allow to cool slightly.

Tip the herb mixture into a liquidiser or food processor and add the ricotta. Blend until smooth. Season to taste with salt, pepper, nutmeg and a generous pinch of cayenne.

Cut the pasta dough into portions and roll out very thinly on a floured worktop. Cover every other sheet of pasta with teaspoons of filling at 5-cm/2-in intervals. Brush between the piles with water to stick the layers of pasta together. Cover with a second sheet of dough and press down well between the piles of filling with your fingertips. Then cut out the ravioli with a pastry wheel.

Bring a large pan of salted water to the boil. When the water has been boiling for about 2 minutes, add the ravioli and cook for 3 to 6 minutes until *al dente* (tender but still firm to bite). It is impossible to give the time exactly for it depends on the consistency of the pasta and how long the ravioli has stood around and dried before cooking. Moist doughs cook quickest, but if the dough has become dry it will take longer.

While the ravioli is cooking, wash the thyme, shake dry and strip the leaves from the stalks.

Heat the remaining butter in a small pan until slightly brown. Add the thyme to the butter and fry slightly.

Scoop the ravioli out of the water on a slotted spoon and drain well. Mix at once with the thyme butter.

Serves 6

Per Portion
about 660 calories
58 g carbohydrate
27 g protein · 34 g fat

Cook's Tip
Pasta machines usually have ravioli-making attachments. These machines can be used to roll the dough, then the ravioli attachment can be used to fill and cut the dough. Alternatively, a ravioli tin similar to the one shown in the picture can be used. Lift a sheet of pasta over the tin, easing it into the hollows. Put the filling in the hollows, brush between with water and top with pasta. Press down and cut between the hollows. Cook as above.

Wholemeal Noodles with Sesame

150 g / 5 oz wholemeal or
*   wheatmeal flour*
salt
1 egg
1–3 egg yolks
1 tablespoon sunflower oil
2 cloves garlic
½ bunch of fresh parsley
4 tablespoons olive oil
4 tablespoons sesame seeds

To make the pasta, work the flour with a pinch of salt, the egg, 1 egg yolk and the sunflower oil. If the dough is too dry, gradually work in the remaining yolks and keep checking the consistency. If it is too soft add a little more flour.

Wrap the dough in foil and leave to rest for 30 minutes.

Thinly roll out the dough on a floured worktop or in a pasta machine and cut into noodles. Spread on a tea towel and leave to dry for about 1 hour.

Peel and finely chop the garlic. Wash the parsley, strip the leaves from the stalks, pat dry and finely chop.

Heat the olive oil in a frying pan. Fry the sesame seeds over a moderate heat, stirring continuously, until golden brown. Add the parsley and garlic and cook until the garlic is transparent. Remove the pan from the heat to prevent the garlic browning and becoming bitter.

Cook the noodles in a large pan of boiling salted water, stirring frequently, for 2 to 4 minutes until *al dente* (tender but still firm to bite). Drain well and mix at once with the sesame mixture.

Serves 4

Per Portion
about 370 calories
28 g carbohydrate
11 g protein · 20 g fat

Herb Spätzle

100 g / 4 oz mixed young dande-
*   lion and nettle leaves*
3 bunches of fresh parsley
500 g / 18 oz wheatmeal flour
salt
5 eggs
1–3 egg yolks
400 g / 14 oz onions
300 g / 11 oz Emmental cheese
75 g / 3 oz butter

Wash the dandelion, nettle and parsley leaves, shake dry and finely chop.

Mix the flour with the herbs, a pinch of salt, the eggs and 1 egg yolk to give a batter thick enough for marks made with a wooden spoon to disappear only slowly. If the batter is too thick, work in more egg yolk, if it is too runny, work in a little more flour. Cover and leave to stand for 30 minutes.

Meanwhile, peel the onions and cut into thin rings. Grate the Emmental.

Melt the butter in a frying pan and fry the onions until soft and golden brown. Remove from the heat and keep warm.

Bring a large pan of salted water to the boil. Scrape the herb batter off a board into the boiling water, in batches to make squiggly noodles. Remove the noodles or spätzle from the water as soon as they rise to the surface, drain and place in a warmed dish. Sprinkle with a layer of grated cheese and keep hot.

Cook the next batch, transfer to the bowl and sprinkle with cheese. Continue in this way until you have used all the batter and cheese.

Serve topped with the onion rings.

Serves 6

Per Portion
about 720 calories
65 g carbohydrate
33 g protein · 35 g fat

Potato Gnocchi in Herb Sauce

500 g/18 oz floury potatoes
salt
150 g/5 oz wholemeal flour
50 g/2 oz wholemeal semolina
1 egg
1 egg yolk
freshly ground white pepper
freshly grated nutmeg
125 ml/4 fl oz crème fraîche
125 ml/4 fl oz double cream
40 g/1½ oz Parmesan cheese,
*   grated*
4 tablespoons chopped mixed
*   fresh herbs (eg parsley,*
*   chervil, little thyme)*
cayenne pepper

Scrub the potatoes well in cold running water. Cook, in the skins, in a little boiling salted water until tender. This will take 30 to 40 minutes depending on size.

Peel the potatoes and mash while still hot. Mix the potato with the flour, semolina, egg, egg yolk, salt to taste and a generous pinch each of pepper and nutmeg to make a fairly soft malleable mixture. If the mixture is too soft, work in a little more semolina. If it is too dry add 1 more egg yolk.

To make the sauce, boil the crème fraîche and cream over a high heat to reduce by about one-third. Add the grated cheese and stir over a low heat until melted. Do not have the heat too high or the sauce will separate. Stir in the herbs and season to taste with nutmeg and a generous pinch of cayenne. Cover the sauce and keep hot.

To make the gnocchi, shape the potato mixture into balls using 2 teaspoons dipped in water. Cook in a large pan of boiling salted water until they rise to the surface. Lift out on a slotted spoon, drain, cover with the herb sauce and serve.

Serves 4

Per Portion
about 380 calories
53 g carbohydrate
15 g protein · 15 g fat

Buckwheat Pancake with Scorzonera

250 g/9 oz buckwheat flour
250 ml/8 fl oz sour milk or
buttermilk
250 ml/8 fl oz mineral water
3 tablespoons sunflower oil
salt
1–2 tablespoons vinegar
500 g/18 oz scorzonera
1 tablespoon lemon juice
1 tablespoon butter
3 tablespoons crème fraîche or
soured cream
freshly ground black pepper
2 tablespoons chopped fresh
parsley

Whisk the buckwheat flour
with the sour milk or butter
milk, mineral water, 3 table
spoons oil and a little salt to
make a smooth batter. Leave to
stand for 45 minutes.

Fill a bowl with cold water
and add the vinegar. Peel and
wash the scorzonera. Cut into

2 cm/¾ in pieces and place at
once in the acidulated water to
keep them white.

Bring about 600 ml/1 pint
water to the boil with the lemon
juice and a little salt. Add the
scorzonera to the boiling water
and cook over a moderate heat
for about 15 minutes until
tender but still firm to bite.
Drain. Keep the cooking water
to use in some other dish such
as soup.

Heat the remaining oil in a
heavy frying pan. Pour in the
buckwheat batter and cook
over a moderate heat until solid
around the edge. Turn the pancake and cook on the other
side. Break into pieces using
two forks and cook the pancake pieces for a further 2 minutes, stirring often. Remove
from the pan and keep hot.

Heat the butter in the pan
without allowing it to brown.
Stir in the scorzonera over a
moderate heat until coated in
fat. Stir in the crème fraîche
and season to taste. Stir in the
chopped parsley, and serve with
the buckwheat pancake.

Serves 4

Per Portion
about 485 calories
69 g carbohydrate
11 g protein · 17 g fat

Variation
Wholemeal Pancakes
with Leeks
Beat 250 g/9 oz wholemeal flour
with salt and 250 ml/8 fl oz each
milk and uncarbonated mineral
water until smooth. Beat in
2 eggs and leave the batter to
stand for 30 minutes to allow
the flour to swell. Meanwhile,
cut the roots and any limp
leaves from 500 g/18 oz leeks.
Cut a cross in the leaves down
as far as the white. Open the
leaves, wash well and shake
dry. Cut the leeks, including
about two thirds of the pale
green leaves, into 1 cm/½ in
lengths. Peel and finely chop 2
cloves garlic. Pick over, wash
and dry 2 handfuls of fresh
chervil. Heat 2 tablespoons
vegetable oil in a frying pan,
pour in the batter and cook the
pancake as described above.

Keep hot. Heat another tablespoon oil in the pan and fry the
leeks for 2 minutes, stirring
continuously. Add the garlic
and fry for a few more minutes.
Add scant 125 ml/4 fl oz vegetable stock, bring to the boil,
then cover and cook over a low
heat for 8 to 10 minutes until
the leek is tender but still firm
to bite. Meanwhile, finely chop
the chervil. Stir the chervil into
the leeks with 2 tablespoons
cream and season with salt and
freshly ground white pepper.
Serve the leeks with the pancake pieces.

Wholemeal Pancakes with Vegetables

bunch of fresh parsley
250 g/9 oz wholemeal flour
salt
250 ml/8 fl oz milk
250 ml/8 fl oz mineral water
2 eggs
250 g/9 oz celery
1 shallot
250 g/9 oz mung bean sprouts
about 6 tablespoons vegetable oil
*   for frying*
25 g/1 oz butter
250 ml/8 fl oz crème fraîche or
*   soured cream*
2 tablespoons lemon juice
1 tablespoon dry sherry
freshly ground white pepper
handful of fresh chervil

Wash the parsley, shake dry and finely chop.

Whisk the flour with a pinch of salt, the milk and mineral water. Whisk in the eggs and parsley. Cover and leave to stand for 20 minutes.

Meanwhile, wash and trim the celery and cut into 1 cm/½ in lengths. Keep the leaves to sprinkle over the vegetables. Peel and finely chop the shallot. Wash and drain the bean sprouts.

Heat 1 tablespoon oil in a heavy frying pan. Tip 1 ladle of batter into the pan and cook the first pancake. Keep hot. Heat more oil and add more batter. Continue in this way until you have used all the batter. Keep the pancakes hot.

To cook the vegetables, melt the butter in a frying pan without allowing it to brown. Fry the shallot on a moderate heat, stirring continuously. Add the celery and bean sprouts and fry for 2 minutes. Stir in the crème fraîche, lemon juice and sherry. Season to taste, cover and cook gently for about 4 minutes.

Meanwhile, pick over and wash the chervil, shake dry and finely chop. Scatter over the vegetables with the celery leaves.

Fill the pancakes with the vegetables and serve at once.

Serves 4

Per Portion
about 685 calories
49 g carbohydrate
18 g protein · 44 g fat

Tomato Quiche

300 g/11 oz wholemeal or
   wheatmeal flour
6 eggs
1 tablespoon vegetable oil
salt
3–4 tablespoons water (if
   necessary)
1 kg/2¼ lb ripe tomatoes
bunch each of fresh chives and
   basil
6 sprigs of fresh thyme
125 ml/4 fl oz milk
250 ml/8 fl oz crème fraîche or
   soured cream
75 g/3 oz Parmesan cheese,
   freshly grated
freshly ground white pepper
pinch of cayenne pepper
freshly grated nutmeg
butter for the baking sheet
flour for rolling

Mix the flour with 2 eggs, the
oil, salt to taste and a little
water to make a smooth pasta
dough. After kneading the
dough should not be sticky or it
will be difficult to roll later. If it
is too dry work in more water a
few drops at a time.

Shape the dough into a ball,
wrap in greaseproof paper and
leave to rest for 30 minutes to
allow the flour to swell.

Meanwhile, blanch the tomatoes in boiling water for 30
seconds, rinse in cold water and
peel. Using a sharp knife cut
out the cores and slice the tomatoes crossways. Carefully
scrape out all the seeds for they
contain a lot of moisture and
would make the quiche too
soft.

Wash the herbs and shake
dry. Snip the chives into short
lengths. (You should never
chop chives: the delicate stems
need a clean cut if they are to
give their full flavour.) Strip off
the basil leaves and cut into
thin strips. Strip the thyme
leaves from the stalks and leave
whole.

Whisk the remaining eggs
with the milk, crème fraîche or
soured cream and Parmesan.
Stir in the herbs and season to
taste with salt, pepper, cayenne
and nutmeg.

Grease a 23 × 33-cm/9 × 13-
in, deep Swiss roll tin or a
roasting tin with butter.

Divide the dough into 4 to 6
pieces. On a lightly floured
worktop, roll out the dough as
thinly as possible. Line the baking tin with dough, overlapping
the pieces by about 0.5 cm/¼ in
and making a rim 1–2 cm/½ to
¾ in high around the edge.

Arrange the tomato slices on
the dough base. Pour over the
egg and milk mixture.

Place the baking sheet in a
moderately hot oven (200 c,
400 F, gas 6), on the second
shelf from the bottom, and
bake for 30 to 40 minutes until
the egg mixture has set and the
top is golden brown.

Delicious as a starter or, with
a colourful mixed salad, as a
light lunch,

Serves 6

Per Portion
about 470 calories
43 g carbohydrate
19 g protein · 22 g fat

Cook's Tip
The thinner the dough
the better the quiche will
taste. You can make
really thin sheets of
dough in a hand-operat-
ed pasta machine. To use
this, you do not need to
knead the dough for so
long. Instead allow the
dough to rest, then divide
it into pieces and pass
them through the ma-
chine several times until
really smooth. Then roll
the sheets of dough on
the thinnest setting. If
you have any dough over
you can make noodles,
spaghetti or vermicelli. If
you are not intending to
use the pasta immedi-
ately, spread out on tea
towels until completely
dry.

Wholemeal Pizza with Tomato and Mushrooms

300 g/11 oz wholemeal or
  wheatmeal flour
30 g/1¼ oz fresh yeast
125 ml/4 fl oz lukewarm water
1 tablespoon vegetable oil
1 egg yolk
1 tablespoon low-fat Quark or
  other soft cheese
salt
750 g/1½ lb ripe tomatoes
about 400 g/14 oz mozzarella
  cheese
250 g/9 oz mushrooms
bunch of fresh basil
sprig of fresh thyme
3 tablespoons olive oil
flour for rolling
2 tablespoons freshly grated
  Parmesan
2 teaspoons dried oregano
freshly ground black pepper

To make the yeast dough, tip the flour into a bowl, make a well in the centre and crumble in the yeast. Sprinkle about 2 tablespoons lukewarm water over the yeast. Mix a little of the flour into the yeast, cover the bowl and leave to rise in a warm place for 15 minutes.

Work in the remaining luke-warm water, the oil, egg yolk, Quark and a pinch of salt. Knead the dough until elastic and then beat it to work in air. Cover the bowl with a tea towel and leave the dough to rise in a warm place for a further 30 minutes.

Meanwhile, blanch the tomatoes in boiling water for 30 seconds, rinse in cold water, peel and core. Finely chop half the tomatoes and slice the rest from the stalk end downwards. Remove the seeds.

Drain and slice the mozzarella. Trim the mushrooms, rinse if necessary and thinly slice. Rinse the mushrooms under cold running water only if absolutely necessary (if you can't remove dirt with a damp cloth) for they easily absorb water and lose their flavour. For this reason mushrooms should never be left to soak in water.

Rinse the basil and thyme in cold water and shake dry. Chop the basil finely and strip the thyme leaves from the stems. Grease a baking sheet with a little olive oil.

Cut the yeast dough into two portions and roll out each portion on a lightly floured worktop into a thin round. Place the rounds side by side on the baking sheet, cover with a tea towel and leave to rise for a further 10 minutes.

Prick the dough rounds several times with a fork so that they cook evenly without forming bubbles. Cover the dough with the chopped tomatoes, then the sliced tomatoes and mushrooms. Scatter with the Parmesan, basil, thyme, oregano and salt and pepper to taste. Top with the mozzarella slices and sprinkle with the remaining olive oil.

Bake the pizza in a moderately hot oven (200 C, 400 F, gas 6), on the second shelf from the bottom, for 15 to 20 minutes until crisp around the edges and the mozzarella is soft and slightly browned. Serve with a colourful mixed salad.

Serves 4

Per Portion
about 760 calories
67 g carbohydrate
30 g protein · 39 g fat

> **Cook's Tip**
> Try making pizza with sliced aubergine and courgette fried in oil, diced green pepper and spring onion rings. Any pizza should automatically include tomato and mozzarella.

Bean Sprout Pie

FOR THE WHEATMEAL PASTRY
350 g/12 oz wheatmeal flour
175 g/6 oz margarine
about 4 tablespoons water
beaten egg to glaze
FOR THE FILLING
400 g/14 oz mushrooms
1 onion
300 g/11 oz mixed sprouted
mung beans and chickpeas
25 g/1 oz butter
3 tablespoons chopped fresh
parsley
salt
freshly ground black pepper

To make the pastry, put the flour in a bowl and add the margarine, cut into pieces. Rub the fat into the flour until the mixture resembles fine bread-crumbs. Work in just enough water to bind the dough.

Roll out two-thirds of the pastry and use to line a 23-cm/ 9-in ovenproof pie dish.

Trim and wash the mushrooms if necessary and cut into thin slices. Peel and finely chop the onion. Wash the sprouted beans in cold water and drain.

Heat the butter in a frying pan and fry the onion until transparent. Add the mushrooms and cook over a high heat, stirring continuously, until the liquid that forms has evaporated again. Stir in the sprouts and parsley and season.

Turn the filling into the lined pie dish and brush the edges of the pastry with a little water. Roll out the remaining pastry to cover the pie. Lift it over the filling, press the edges together well and trim off excess pastry. Make a hole in the middle of the pie and decorate with re-rolled pastry trimmings.

Brush the top of the pie with a little beaten egg and bake in a moderate oven (180 C, 350 F, gas 4) for about 45 minutes or until the pastry is golden.

Serves 5

Per Portion
about 590 calories
15 g carbohydrate
7 g protein · 35 g fat

Variations
For a change why not flavour the pastry used to make the pie? You can use a variety of herbs or other ingredients.

Herb Pastry
Add 2 tablespoons chopped fresh herbs to the pastry when the fat has been rubbed in.

Cheese Pastry
Add 50 g/2 oz grated matured cheese to the pastry when the fat has been rubbed in.

Sesame Crust
When you have made the pie, brush it with the glaze and sprinkle with some unroasted sesame seeds.

Walnut Pastry
Grind 50 g/2 oz walnuts to a powder and mix them into the pastry once the fat has been rubbed in.

Sunflower Pastry
Add 50 g/2 oz finely chopped sunflower seeds to the pastry once the fat has been rubbed in.

Cook's Tip

To line a pie dish with pastry, roll out the pastry, then carefully fold it over the rolling pin and lift it over the dish. Gently ease the pastry down into the dish using your fingers, at the same time lifting the edge of the dough over the rim of the dish to prevent it from cracking.

When adding the decoration to the pie, you may find it easier to cut leaves and strips from the pastry trimmings if you use a pair of kitchen scissors. Once you have completed the pie, leave it in the refrigerator to chill the pastry for at least 30 minutes, or longer if you have the time.

Vegetable Pasties

*double quantity wheatmeal pas-
  try*
beaten egg to glaze
FOR THE ONION FILLING
175 g/6 oz onions
1 tablespoon vegetable oil
4 tablespoons soured cream
1 egg
½ teaspoon caraway seeds
½ teaspoon dried thyme
freshly ground white pepper
FOR THE QUARK FILLING
2 cloves garlic
*250 g/9 oz Quark or other soft
  cheese (20 percent fat)*
*2 tablespoons chopped mixed
  fresh herbs*
1 tablespoon single cream
freshly ground black pepper
FOR THE COURGETTE FILLING
175 g/6 oz courgettes
4 sprigs of fresh thyme
2 cloves garlic
2 tablespoons sesame seeds
2 tablespoons olive oil
FOR THE TOMATO FILLING
250 g/9 oz ripe tomatoes
100 g/4 oz feta cheese
1 clove garlic

*2 tablespoons chopped fresh
  parsley*
*2 tablespoons fresh wholemeal
  breadcrumbs*
FOR THE MUSHROOM FILLING
2 bunches of fresh basil
1 clove garlic
2 tablespoons pine nuts
*2 tablespoons freshly grated
  pecorino or Parmesan cheese*
5 tablespoons vegetable oil
175 g/6 oz mushrooms
FOR THE KOHLRABI FILLING
200 g/7 oz kohlrabi
2 tablespoons soured cream
1 egg
*1 tablespoon freshly grated
  Emmental cheese*
freshly grated nutmeg

Make the pastry according to
the recipe instructions.

To make the onion filling,
peel and thinly slice the onions.
Heat the oil and fry the onions
until transparent. Leave to
cool. Stir in the remaining
ingredients.

To make the Quark filling,
peel and finely chop the garlic.
Mix the Quark with the garlic,
herbs, cream and pepper.

For the courgette filling,
wash, dry and top and tail
the courgettes. Cut into
matchsticks. Wash and dry the
thyme and pull the leaves off
the stems. Peel and finely chop
the garlic. Mix all these ingredients with the sesame seeds and
oil and season to taste.

For the tomato filling,
blanch the tomatoes in boiling
water for 30 seconds, rinse in
cold water and peel. Dice the
tomatoes, removing the core
and the seeds. Mash the cheese.
Peel and finely chop the garlic.
Mix the tomatoes with the
cheese, garlic, parsley and
breadcrumbs.

For the mushroom filling,
wash and dry the basil and
chop the leaves. Peel and finely
chop the garlic. In a mortar
work the basil, garlic, pine nuts,
cheese and 4 tablespoons oil to
a paste. Trim and chop the
mushrooms and fry in the remaining oil over a high heat.
Season to taste and stir into the
basil paste.

For the kohlrabi filling, peel
and grate the kohlrabi and mix

with the soured cream, egg and
cheese. Season to taste with
salt, pepper and nutmeg.

Cut the pastry into 12 pieces.
Roll out each piece into a
15-cm/6-in circle. Divide the
fillings between the pastry circles and dampen the edges.
Fold the pieces of pastry in half
and press the edges with a fork
to seal in the filling. Brush with
beaten egg and bake in a moderately hot oven (200 C, 400 F,
gas 6) for 25 to 30 minutes.

Makes 12

Per Portion
about 755 calories
73 g carbohydrate
23 g protein · 39 g fat

White Beans Provençal

300 g/11 oz dried white haricot
  beans
sprig of fresh rosemary
2 sprigs of fresh thyme
1 bay leaf
400 g/14 oz ripe tomatoes
1 onion
3 cloves garlic
6 tablespoons olive oil
salt
freshly ground black pepper
1–2 tablespoons raspberry
  vinegar
3 tablespoons chopped fresh
  parsley
2 tablespoons capers

Wash the beans and soak in
cold water for 12 hours.

The following day, wash the
rosemary and thyme and shake
dry. Tip the beans and soaking
water into a saucepan and add
the herbs and bay leaf. Bring to
the boil, then reduce the heat to
low, cover the pan and cook for
1¾ hours.

Blanch the tomatoes in boiling water for 30 seconds, rinse
in cold water and peel. Dice the
tomatoes, removing the core
and the seeds. Peel and finely
chop the onion and garlic.

Heat 2 tablespoons olive oil
in a saucepan and fry the onion
and garlic until transparent.
Add the tomatoes and the
beans with their cooking water.
Discard the bay leaf and herbs.
Cover the pan and cook over a
low heat for a further 15 minutes until the beans are tender.

Season to taste with salt,
pepper and raspberry vinegar
and mix with the remaining
olive oil, the parsley and capers.

Transfer the beans to a
warmed dish and serve with
lamb chops or wholemeal bread
and butter.

Serves 4

Per Portion
about 440 calories
50 g carbohydrate
18 g protein · 17 g fat

Red Beans with Apple

400 g/14 oz dried red kidney
  beans
400 g/14 oz fairly tart apples
250 g/9 oz onions
2 cloves garlic
2 tablespoons vegetable oil
250 ml/8 fl oz cider
1 teaspoon dried marjoram
salt
freshly ground black pepper
cayenne pepper

Tip the beans into a sieve and
rinse in cold water. Soak in cold
water for 12 hours.

The following day, tip the
beans and soaking water into a
saucepan and bring to the boil.
Boil hard for 3 minutes. Cover
the pan, reduce the heat and
simmer gently for 1½ hours.

Peel, core and coarsely chop
the apples. Peel the onions and
cut into rings. Peel and chop
the garlic.

Heat the oil in a saucepan.
Fry the apples, onions and gar-

lic until transparent, stirring
often.

Drain the beans, add to the
apples and cook for a few minutes, stirring continuously. Add
the cider and marjoram. Bring
to the boil, cover the pan and
simmer over a low heat for
about 30 minutes or until the
apples are very soft.

Season the beans to taste
with salt, black pepper and a
pinch of cayenne and transfer
to a warmed dish. Serve with
lamb or poultry, or for a vegetarian meal, serve with brown
rice.

Serves 4

Per Portion
about 485 calories
74 g carbohydrate
23 g protein · 7 g fat

Black Beans and Sweetcorn

300 g/11 oz dried black beans
2 leeks
½ celeriac
3 carrots
bunch of fresh parsley
bunch of fresh savory
1 bay leaf
4 white peppercorns
2 shallots
2 (325 g/11½ oz) cans sweetcorn
  kernels
2 tablespoons vegetable oil
salt
freshly ground white pepper
250 ml/8 fl oz crème fraîche or
  double cream
hot chilli powder

Wash the beans then soak in cold water for 12 hours.

The following day, trim and wash the leeks. Peel and wash the celeriac and carrots. Chop these vegetables coarsely. Wash the herbs and shake dry. Strip the parsley leaves from the stalks and chop.

Tip the beans and soaking water into a saucepan and add the leeks, celeriac, carrots, parsley stalks, savory, bay leaf and peppercorns. Bring to the boil, cover and simmer for about 1¼ hours until the beans are tender.

Drain the beans and discard the vegetables, herbs and peppercorns.

Peel and finely chop the shallots. Drain the sweetcorn.

Heat the oil in a saucepan and fry the shallots until transparent. Add the beans and sweetcorn and season to taste. Stir in the crème fraîche, bring back to the boil, cover and cook gently for 5 minutes. Season with a pinch of chilli powder and garnish with chopped parsley.

Per Portion
about 665 calories
84 g carbohydrate
23 g protein · 26 g fat

Nut Curry

300 g/11 oz cashew nuts
250 g/9 oz fresh peeled coconut
350 ml/12 fl oz warm water
1 onion
1 clove garlic
1 red pepper
1 teaspoon turmeric
½ teaspoon ground ginger
½ teaspoon ground anise or
  cumin
pinch of ground cinnamon
salt
3 tablespoons sunflower oil

Tip the cashew nuts into a bowl, cover with warm water and soak for 4 hours.

Break the coconut into pieces and blend with the water in a liquidiser. Pour the puréed coconut through a muslin-lined sieve placed over a bowl, pressing it well with a wooden spoon. Discard the coconut in the sieve and keep the milk in reserve for the curry.

Peel and finely chop the onion and garlic. Halve the red pepper and remove the stalk, pith and seeds. Rinse in cold water, dry and cut into fine strips.

In a bowl mix the turmeric, ginger, anise or cumin, cinnamon and salt to taste.

Drain the nuts.

Heat the oil in a frying pan and fry the onion and garlic until transparent. Add the nuts and red pepper and fry until the liquid has evaporated.

Sprinkle the spices over the nuts and pour on the coconut milk. Stir well, bring to the boil, cover the pan and cook over a low heat for 5 minutes.

Serve with brown rice.

Serves 4

Per Portion
about 755 calories
30 g carbohydrate
16 g protein · 63 g fat

Wholemeal Savarin with Stewed Fruit

300 g / 11 oz wheatmeal flour
30 g / 1¼ oz fresh yeast
scant 125 ml / 4 fl oz lukewarm
  milk
90 g / 3½ oz butter
3 tablespoons honey
½ lemon
2 eggs
1 egg yolk
1 teaspoon vanilla sugar
salt
250 g / 9 oz prunes
  (unsulphurised)
2 liqueur glasses plum brandy
250 ml / 8 fl oz dry white wine
2 tablespoons orange marmalade
½ cinnamon stick
butter and flour for the tin
250 g / 9 oz cooking apples
2 teaspoons ground cinnamon
250 ml / 8 fl oz double or whipping
  cream

To make the savarin, put the flour into a mixing bowl. Make a well in the centre and crumble in the yeast. Stir the yeast with 2 tablespoons milk and a little of the flour in the bowl. Cover the bowl and leave to stand in a warm place for 15 minutes.

Meanwhile, pour the remaining milk into a pan and add the butter and 1 tablespoon honey. Warm over a low heat until the butter and honey have melted.

Wash the lemon in hot water, dry and then grate the rind. Squeeze the juice and keep to one side for the stewed apple.

Add the butter and honey mixture, the grated lemon rind, the eggs, egg yolk, vanilla sugar and a pinch of salt to the yeast mixture and mix until smooth, beating the mixture with a wooden spoon until light and airy and coming away from the sides of the bowl.

Cover and leave to rise in a warm place for 30 minutes.

Rinse the prunes under hot running water and drain. Put into a bowl and pour on the plum brandy.

Keeping 2 tablespoons in reserve for the stewed apple, heat the white wine with the marmalade, 1 tablespoon honey and the cinnamon stick over a low heat until the honey is fluid. Pour over the prunes, cover and leave to soak until the savarin is cooked.

Grease and flour a savarin or ring tin. Fill with the dough, cover and leave to rise again until it has more or less doubled in volume. This takes around 30 minutes.

Bake the savarin in a moderately hot oven (200 C, 400 F, gas 6), on the second shelf from the bottom, for 30 to 35 minutes.

Meanwhile, peel and core the apples and cut into thick slices. Put the apples in a saucepan with the lemon juice and the remaining wine. Bring to the boil, then cover and cook over a low heat until tender but not mushy. Stir in the remaining honey and the ground cinnamon.

Drain the prunes, reserving the juice; discard the cinnamon stick. Gently mix the prunes with the apple.

Turn the savarin out on to a plate and prick all over with a cocktail stick. Using a teaspoon, spoon the juice from the prunes over the savarin so that it is absorbed evenly. Leave until lukewarm.

Whip the cream and fold into the prunes and apple. Spoon into the centre of the savarin before serving.

Serves 6

Per Portion
about 700 calories
79 g carbohydrate
12 g protein · 32 g fat

Cook's Tip
The savarin is just as delicious filled with fresh fruit.

Pudding with Nuts and Sprouts

100 g/4 oz mixed dried fruit
40 g/1½ oz unsalted shelled
   pistachios
2 tablespoons orange liqueur
butter and fine wholemeal breadcrumbs for the basin
1 tablespoon sprouted chickpeas
½ orange
100 g/4 oz butter, softened
1 tablespoon honey
generous pinch each of ground
   cloves, cardamom and nutmeg
½ teaspoon ground cinnamon
salt
2 tablespoons vanilla sugar
4 eggs, separated
1 tablespoon sprouted whole
   wheat grain (wheat berries)
50 g/2 oz cornflour

Finely chop the dried fruit and pistachios. Put into a bowl, stir in the orange liqueur, cover and leave to soak for 30 minutes.

Butter a 900-ml/1½-pint pudding basin or mould and sprinkle with breadcrumbs. Crush the chickpea sprouts. Grate the orange rind.

Cream the butter with the honey until light and fluffy. Stir in all the spices, orange rind, a pinch of salt and the vanilla sugar. Beat the egg yolks a little at a time into the butter mixture. Stir in the dried fruit and pistachio mixture, chickpeas and wheat grain sprouts.

Whisk the egg whites until very stiff. Spoon on to the pudding mixture, sprinkle on the cornflour and fold in gently. Pour the mixture into the pudding basin and cover with a lid or greaseproof paper and foil tied on with string. Place the basin in a saucepan and pour in boiling water to come two thirds of the way up the sides of the basin. Cover and steam for about 70 minutes or until a skewer inserted into the middle comes out clean.

Lift the basin out of the water and leave to stand, covered, for 10 minutes. Serve hot, with custard flavoured with finely chopped orange rind.

Serves 6

Per Portion
about 735 calories
130 g carbohydrate
4 g protein · 20 g fat

Quark and Cherry Strudel

250 g/9 oz wheatmeal flour
salt
125 ml/4 fl oz lukewarm water
5 tablespoons vegetable oil
1 egg yolk
1 kg/2¼ lb Morello cherries or
600 g/1¼ lb bottled or canned
Morello cherries
3 slices stale wholemeal bread
1 orange
500 g/18 oz low-fat Quark or
other soft cheese
125 ml/4 fl oz crème fraîche or
soured cream
2 eggs
3 tablespoons maple syrup
2 tablespoons vanilla sugar
75 g/3 oz butter for coating
flour for rolling

Strudel dough should always be
left to stand in a warm place for
a while to make it smooth
enough to stretch. The best way
is to bring a little water to the
boil in a pan. Then tip away the
water, cover the empty pan

and leave it in a warm place so
that it is warm rather than hot.

To make the dough, mix the
flour with a pinch of salt, the
water, oil and egg yolk. The
dough should be soft and
smooth but not sticky. If
necessary you can add a few
more drops of lukewarm water
or a little more flour to give the
right consistency. Wrap the
dough in greaseproof paper and
stand in the warm pan for
about 30 minutes.

To make the filling, wash and
drain the cherries. Remove the
stalks and stones. If you are
using bottled or canned cherries
they should be thoroughly
drained.

Grate the wholemeal bread
in a nut mill, or make into fine
crumbs in a liquidiser or food
processor. Set aside.

Grate about half the orange
rind and squeeze out the juice.

Beat the Quark with the
orange rind and juice, the
crème fraîche or soured cream,
eggs, maple syrup and vanilla
sugar. Stir in the prepared
cherries.

Place the butter in a baking
tin large enough to take two
strudels side by side and place
the tin in a hot oven (220 C,
425 F, gas 7) to melt the butter.

Halve the strudel dough.
Roll out one portion on a
floured worktop and then place
on a floured tea towel and
stretch as thin as possible by
hand. The easiest way to do this
is to drape the dough like a
cloth over the backs of your
lightly clenched fists and to
stretch it gently from the centre.
Then spread it on the tea towel
again and stretch the edges between your fingertips.

Brush the stretched dough
with a little of the melted
butter. Sprinkle with half the
breadcrumbs and cover with
half the filling, making sure you
leave 1–2 cm/½–¾ in clear
around the edge to prevent the
filling spilling out as you roll
the strudel. Fold the shorter
sides of the dough in a little
way. Lift the edge of the tea
towel and roll up the strudel
away from you. Lift the rolled
strudel on the cloth and gently

slide it into the baking tin. Repeat the whole process with the
second portion of strudel
dough.

Brush the strudels well with
melted butter. Pour the remaining butter into a small pan and
keep warm.

Place the tin on the second
shelf from the bottom of the
oven and bake for about 25
minutes, brushing frequently
with the remaining melted
butter to make it nice and
brown.

Serves 6

Per Portion
about 635 calories
70 g carbohydrate
22 g protein · 29 g fat

214

Cheese Dumplings

500 g/18 oz home-made curd
cheese
120 g/4½ oz wholemeal semolina
25 g/1 oz wholemeal or
wheatmeal flour
1 egg
1 teaspoon caster sugar
salt
grated rind of ¼ lemon
50 g/2 oz butter
1 tablespoon stale wholemeal
breadcrumbs
1 tablespoon caster sugar mixed
with 1 teaspoon ground
cinnamon

For these dumplings you need
dry, well-drained curd cheese.

Mix the cheese with the
semolina, flour, egg, sugar, a
pinch of salt and the grated
lemon rind to make a dough.
Cover and leave to stand for 30
minutes.

Bring a large pan of salted
water to the boil. Using 2 tablespoons, make a test dumpling
and drop into the fast boiling
water. If it does not fall apart

the dough is the right consistency and you can make and
cook the remaining dumplings.
If it does fall apart the dough is
too soft and needs a little more
semolina added. Reduce the
heat and cook the dumplings
gently for 10 to 15 minutes.

Heat the butter in a frying
pan and fry the breadcrumbs
until crisp.

Remove the dumplings from
the water, drain and arrange on
a warm plate. Sprinkle with the
cinnamon-sugar and pour on
the buttered crumbs.

Serves 4

Per Portion
about 380 calories
36 g carbohydrate
25 g protein · 13 g fat

Peaches with Nut Meringue

4 ripe peaches (preferably
white)
2 tablespoons lemon juice
2 tablespoons Cassis
(blackcurrant liqueur)
3 egg whites
pinch of salt
75 g/3 oz shelled hazelnuts,
finely ground
3 tablespoons maple syrup

Blanch the peaches in boiling
water for 30 seconds, rinse in
cold water and peel. Halve,
stone and slice the peaches.
Cover the bottom of a shallow
baking dish with the peaches
and sprinkle with the lemon
juice and Cassis.

Whisk the egg whites with
the salt until very stiff. Fold the
hazelnuts and maple syrup
gently into the whites using a
metal spoon or a spatula.
Mix very gently at this stage for
if you beat vigorously the
meringue will lose air.

Spoon the meringue over the
peaches and smooth the top.
Bake in a hot oven (220 C, 425 F,
gas 7) for about 10 minutes until the meringue is lightly
browned. Serve hot or the
meringue will become soft.

Serves 4

Per Portion
about 225 calories
24 g carbohydrate
6 g protein · 12 g fat

Bilberry Pudding

250 g/9 oz bilberries
250 ml/8 fl oz lukewarm milk
3 eggs
pinch of salt
1 teaspoon caster sugar
20 g/¾ oz fresh yeast
175 g/6 oz wholemeal or
*   wheatmeal flour*
50 g/2 oz butter
125 ml/4 fl oz double or whipping
*   cream*
2 tablespoons honey

Pick over the bilberries, rinse
under cold running water if
necessary and drain very well.

Beat the milk with the eggs,
salt and sugar. Crumble in the
yeast. Gradually whisk in the
flour and continue whisking
until completely smooth.

Place the butter in a shallow
baking dish and place in a moderate oven (180 c, 350 f, gas 4)
to melt.

Pour the batter into the dish
and scatter with the bilberries.
Bake in the oven for 10
minutes.

Whip the cream with the
honey and pour over the bilberry pudding. Bake for a further 10 minutes until the top is
nice and brown.

Serves 4

Per Portion
about 540 calories
50 g carbohydrate
13 g protein · 30 g fat

> **Cook's Tip**
> The pudding is delicious
> made with fresh Morello
> cherries, or in winter with
> frozen berries.

Strawberries with Dates

400 g/14 oz strawberries
100 g/4 oz fresh dates
100 g/4 oz shelled walnuts
1 tablespoon lemon juice
250 ml/8 fl oz double or whipping
*   cream*
½ tablespoon maple syrup
2 tablespoons rum

Wash the strawberries well, pat
dry, remove the stalks and cut
into slices. Arrange decorat-
ively on six plates.

Stone the dates and halve or
quarter them. Coarsely chop
the walnuts on a board using a
heavy knife.

In a basin, mix the walnuts
and dates with the lemon juice,
and leave to stand at
room temperature for 15
minutes.

Whip the cream until stiff.
Whisk in the maple syrup and
rum.

Scatter the date and walnut
mixture over the strawberries

and serve the rum cream
separately.

Serves 6

Per Portion
about 330 calories
20 g carbohydrate
4 g protein · 24 g fat

> **Cook's Tip**
> The strawberries are deli-
> cious with a wine sauce
> instead of cream: place 2
> egg yolks in a heatproof
> basin with ½ tablespoon
> maple syrup and 125 ml/
> 4 fl oz dry white wine.
> Whisk over hot water
> with a hand or electric
> whisk until light and
> frothy. Arrange the pre-
> pared strawberries in
> glass dishes, cover with
> the wine sauce and serve
> at once.

Plums with Custard

250 g/9 oz plums
½ orange
2 tablespoons caster sugar
½ vanilla pod
250 ml/8 fl oz milk
salt
1 egg yolk
2 teaspoons cornflour
2 slices (about 80 g/3 oz) stale wholemeal bread
2 tablespoons white rum
125 ml/4 fl oz double or whipping cream
2 tablespoons coarsely chopped walnuts

Halve and stone the plums. Cut off a very thin piece of orange rind about 3 cm/1¼ in long. Squeeze out the juice.

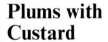

Cook the plums with the orange juice and 1 tablespoon sugar in a covered pan for about 2 minutes until they begin to soften. Set aside.

Slit the vanilla pod open lengthways. Scrape out the seeds and add to the milk with a pinch of salt and orange rind. Bring to just below boiling point.

Meanwhile, beat the egg yolk with the remaining sugar until frothy. Stir in the cornflour. Whisking continuously, add the hot milk, then return to the pan. Cook gently, stirring, until the custard thickens. Leave the custard to cool, stirring from time to time to prevent a skin forming.

Coarsely grate or grind the bread and moisten with the rum.

Whip the cream until stiff and fold into the cooled custard.

Fill 4 glasses with the plums and their juice, then add the breadcrumb mixture and finally the custard. Top with the walnuts.

Serves 4

Per Portion
about 360 calories
40 g carbohydrate
7 g protein · 18 g fat

Honey Ice with Orange Salad

100 g/4 oz honey
2 eggs
pinch of ground ginger
grated rind of ½ orange
250 ml/8 fl oz double or whipping cream
1 kg/2¼ lb oranges
2 liqueur glasses orange liqueur
3 tablespoons unsalted shelled pistachios

Fill a saucepan with hot water and place over a low heat. Tip the honey into a heatproof basin and warm in the water until fluid.

Add the eggs, ginger and orange rind and whisk until thick and frothy.

Tip away the hot water and fill the pan with cold water and a few ice cubes. Place the bowl in the iced water and, stirring continuously, allow to cool. This prevents the ingredients separating out again.

Whip the cream until stiff and fold gently into the honey mixture. Cover the bowl and leave to set in the freezer until firm taking it out and whisking from time to time to prevent ice crystals forming and to keep the ice cream nice and smooth.

Peel the oranges, removing all the white pith, and thinly slice lengthways, removing the pips as you go and catching the juice. Arrange the sliced orange on plates. Stir the liqueur into the orange juice and sprinkle over the oranges. Coarsely chop the pistachios and scatter over the oranges.

Serve with the honey ice cream.

Serves 6

Per Portion
about 330 calories
37 g carbohydrate
6 g protein · 17 g fat

COOKING FOR FRIENDS

Sharing food with friends can be a great pleasure and may require nothing more than a little extra organization and some imagination. This chapter is full of useful and exciting ideas for entertaining at home.

Entertaining today can be as elaborate or informal as you want it to be. For a relaxed occasion, a selection of nibbles and snacks to eat with your fingers may be just the answer when you want to simplify things. It promotes a friendly atmosphere and also saves washing up. Buffets are also a good way to serve food for a large number of people. They can be presented attractively and many of the buffet suggestions that follow can be prepared in advance.

Foreign food can help set a festive mood for informal entertaining. A splendid starter gets a meal off on a lively note, whether followed by a simple roast or one of the exciting international main course ideas certain to make the meal memorable.

Cheese Spirals

350 g/12 oz plain flour
25 g/1 oz fresh yeast, or 15 g/
½ oz dried yeast
150 ml/¼ pint lukewarm milk
100 g/4 oz butter or margarine
1 egg, beaten
1 teaspoon salt
2 egg yolks
100 g/4 oz Emmental or
Cheddar cheese, grated
1 teaspoon paprika pepper
1 tablespoon caraway seeds
1 tablespoon coarse salt

Lightly grease a baking tray.
Sift the flour into a mixing
bowl and form a well in the
centre. Cream the fresh yeast
with a little of the milk, add
the remaining milk, and pour
into the well in the flour.
(Whisk dried yeast into the
milk until dissolved and leave
to stand for 5 minutes before
pouring into the well in the
flour.) Sprinkle a little flour

over either yeast mixture, cover
and leave to stand in a warm
place for 15 minutes until
frothy. Melt the butter or
margarine, and add the fat, egg
and salt to the yeast mixture.
Work in the flour and beat
until smooth. Shape the dough
into a ball, cover, and leave to
rise in a warm place for 20–30
minutes. Roll out into a
rectangle 5-mm/¼-inch thick
Beat the egg yolks with 2
tablespoons water. Coat one
half of the rectangle with egg
yolk and sprinkle with the
grated cheese. Fold over the
other half of the pastry, and
roll out again to 5-mm/¼-inch
thick. Cut into 2.5-cm/1-inch
wide strips, twist into spirals,
and coat with the remaining
egg yolk. Sprinkle the cheese
spirals with paprika, caraway
seeds and salt. Transfer to the
baking tray and bake in a hot
oven (220 C, 425 F, Gas Mark
7) for 15–20 minutes until
golden brown.

Poppy Seed and Cheese Biscuits

1 egg
225 g/8 oz plain flour
50 g/2 oz ground almonds
generous pinch cayenne pepper
½ teaspoon salt
225 g/8 oz Emmental or
Cheddar cheese, finely grated
100 g/4 oz butter or margarine
2 tablespoons poppy seeds
2 tablespoons chopped parsley

Lightly grease two baking
trays. Separate the egg. Sift the
flour into a large mixing bowl,
form a well in the centre, and
into it pour the ground
almonds, cayenne, half the salt
and half the grated cheese, and
the egg white. Cut the butter or
margarine into flakes and dot
round the edge of the well.
Work all the ingredients into a
smooth dough. Divide the
dough into two equal portions

and form one into a long roll,
5 cm/2 inches in diameter, and
the other into a ball. Wrap
both portions in foil and
leave to chill for 1–2 hours.

Beat the egg yolk with
2 teaspoons water. Cut the
pastry roll into 3-mm/⅛-inch
thick slices, and coat the slices
with half the egg yolk. Sprinkle
with poppy seeds and place on
one of the baking trays.

Roll the ball of dough out
thinly to form a long rectangle,
and coat with more of the egg
yolk. Sprinkle evenly with the
chopped parsley, and the
remaining cheese and salt. Roll
up the pastry rectangle
lengthways. Cut into 3-mm/
⅛-inch thick slices, coat with
the remaining egg yolk and
place the slices on the second
baking tray.

Bake the poppy seed and
cheese biscuits in a moderately
hot oven (200 C, 400 F, Gas
Mark 6) for 15 minutes, or
until golden brown.

Cheese Tricorns

225 g/8 oz plain flour
generous pinch salt
1 egg
100 g/4 oz butter or margarine
4 (15-g/½-oz) portions
*   processed cheese, or 50 g/2 oz*
*   Bavarian smoked cheese*
1 egg yolk
2 tablespoons sesame seeds

Sift the flour and salt into a large mixing bowl and form a well in the centre. Tip the egg into the well. Flake the butter or margarine and dot around the edge of the well. Quickly work all the ingredients into a dough, wrap in cooking foil or greaseproof paper and leave to stand in the refrigerator for 1 hour.

  Lightly grease a baking tray. Roll out the dough on a floured surface and cut into 5-cm/2-inch rounds. Slice the processed or smoked cheese and cut into small cubes, dipping the knife frequently into hot water. Place one cheese cube on each pastry round and fold in the edges of the pastry to form a tricorn. Beat the egg yolk with 2 teaspoons water and use to coat the tricorns. Sprinkle with the sesame seeds. Transfer to the greased baking tray and bake in a moderately hot oven (200 C, 400 F, Gas Mark 6) for 15–20 minutes until golden.

Caraway Biscuits

100 g/4 oz plain flour
pinch each salt, sugar and
*   grated nutmeg*
50 g/2 oz butter or margarine
100 g/4 oz matured Gouda
*   cheese, finely grated*
1 egg yolk
2–3 tablespoons caraway seeds

Grease a baking tray. Sift the flour, salt, sugar and nutmeg into a large mixing bowl and form a well in the centre. Flake the butter or margarine and dot around the edge of the flour. Tip the grated cheese into the well, and quickly work all the ingredients together to a dough. Divide the dough into two portions, wrap each in greaseproof paper or cooking foil and chill in the refrigerator for 1 hour.
  On a lightly floured surface, roll out both portions of dough separately until thin. Using a pastry cutter, cut the dough into squares or rectangles. Beat the egg yolk with 2 teaspoons water. Coat the biscuits with egg yolk and sprinkle with caraway seeds. Transfer to the greased baking tray and bake in a moderately hot oven (200 C, 400 F, Gas Mark 6) for 15 minutes.

Crispy Cheese Biscuits

150 g/5 oz butter
180 g/6 oz Gruyère or
   Emmenthal cheese, grated
6 tablespoons single cream
¼ teaspoon salt
1 teaspoon paprika pepper
½ teaspoon baking powder
250 g/9 oz plain flour
1 egg yolk, beaten to glaze
TOPPING
poppy seeds, sesame seeds,
   caraway seeds, chopped
   pistachio nuts, blanched
   almonds

Soften the butter with a wooden spoon. Gradually add the cheese and beat thoroughly. Stir in the cream, salt and paprika. Sift the baking powder with the flour and stir into the mixture. Knead lightly to incorporate all the flour and give a smooth dough. Cut the dough into two or three pieces, wrap in kitchen foil or cling film and leave for 2 hours in the refrigerator.

Preheat the oven to moderately hot (200°C, 400°F, Gas Mark 6). On a floured board roll out the pieces of dough one at a time to a thickness of about 5 mm/¼ inch. Cut into biscuits of any shape, for example rings, hearts, half-moons or stars, and place on greased baking trays. Brush with the beaten egg yolk and while still moist sprinkle with poppy seeds, sesame seeds, caraway seeds or chopped pistachios, or top with a halved almond. Bake the biscuits for

10–15 minutes.

While the cheese biscuits are still hot remove carefully from the baking trays with a palette knife and leave until warm on a wire rack. Serve warm.

Cook's Tip

There is also an Italian variety of these biscuits made with Gorgonzola cheese. Make the biscuits as in the given recipe and sprinkle half with sesame seeds. Bake as above. Finely grate 75 g/3 oz Gorgonzola cheese and mix with 125 g/5 oz cream cheese, 1 egg yolk, a pinch of salt and cayenne pepper, and 1 teaspoon paprika pepper. Fill a piping bag with the cream cheese mixture and with a star nozzle decorate the remaining cooled biscuits.

Cheese Puffs

1 (368-g/13-oz) packet frozen
  puff pastry
80 g/3 oz Gruyère cheese, grated
2 tablespoons milk
1 egg yolk
80 g/3 oz Emmenthal cheese,
  grated
¼ teaspoon paprika pepper

Allow the puff pastry to thaw, then divide in half.

To make cheese bows, sprinkle some of the Gruyère cheese over the pastry board and roll out one-half of the puff pastry on it, to a thickness of 5 mm/¼ inch. Whisk together the milk and egg yolk and use to brush the surface of the pastry. Sprinkle with more of the Gruyère cheese, fold the pastry up and roll it out again. Sprinkle the rest of the cheese over the surface, fold up and finally roll the pastry out to 3 mm/⅛ inch thick. Cut into 7·5-cm/3-inch strips and lay them four strips on top of one another. Cut 5-mm/¼-inch wide slices from these and twist to form bows. Sprinkle a baking tray with cold water, arrange the bows on it and leave to rest for 15 minutes. Preheat the oven to hot (220°C, 425°F, Gas Mark 7), and bake the cheese bows for 8–10 minutes.

Repeat the same process with the second half of the pastry, but this time sprinkle the pastry with the grated Emmenthal and paprika mixed together. Cut into 10-cm/4-inch long narrow strips. Brush these with the rest of the egg yolk glaze and sprinkle with the rest of the cheese. Bake these cheese straws as above.

Cook's Tip

Delicious canapés can be made with a variation of these cheese puffs. Form the cheese pastry into small oval shapes. When cool, sandwich pairs of these together with beaten and piped cream cheese, softened with a little cream. Sprinkle with poppy seeds or caraway seeds and garnish as illustrated.

Ham and Cheese Horns

1 (368-g/13-oz) packet frozen
  puff pastry
1 egg, beaten to glaze
FILLING
75 g/3 oz Gouda cheese
100 g/4 oz ham
1 egg yolk
1 tablespoon finely chopped
  parsley
1 tablespoon finely chopped
  onion
pinch each of pepper and dried
  oregano

Allow the pastry to thaw at
room temperature for 1 hour.

On a floured board roll out
the pastry into a sheet 58 ×
25 cm/23 × 10 inches. Cut into
15 triangles, each with two very
long sides (see illustration).

Finely dice the cheese and
ham and mix with the egg yolk,
parsley, onion, pepper and
oregano. Place about 2 teaspoons of the filling towards
the bottom of each triangle.
Make a small cut in the short
side of the triangle (see illustration) and roll the triangles
into horn shapes; they should
be loosely wrapped.

Sprinkle two baking trays
with cold water and place the
horns on them. Brush with
beaten egg and leave in the
refrigerator for 15 minutes.
Preheat the oven to moderately
hot (200°C, 400°F, Gas Mark
6) and bake the horns towards
the top of the oven for 25
minutes. Serve warm.

Cook's Tip

Instead of horn shapes,
the pastry may be cut
into oblong pieces and
used to make small rolls,
which can be filled with
well-seasoned minced
beef instead of cheese
and ham.

Cheese and Grape Puffs

2 (212-g/7½-oz) packets frozen
  puff pastry
2 eggs
2 tablespoons water
1 teaspoon paprika pepper
¼ teaspoon black pepper
1 teaspoon ground mixed spice
FILLING
225 g/8 oz Red Windsor or
  Cheddar cheese
100 g/4 oz white grapes
100 g/4 oz continental sausage,
  sliced

Allow the pastry to thaw for
1 hour at room temperature.
Preheat the oven to moderately
hot (200°C, 400°F, Gas Mark
6).
  Roll out the pastry on a
floured surface to a rectangle
about 3 mm/⅛ inch thick and
cut into about forty 5-cm/2-
inch squares. Beat the eggs with

the water, paprika, black
pepper and spice, and brush
some of this mixture over the
pastry squares.
  Cut the cheese into small
cubes. Halve the grapes and
remove the pips. Cut the
sausage slices into small pieces.
Place a cube of cheese, a grape
and a piece of sausage on each
pastry square. Bring the corners
of the pastry inwards to form
an envelope, and press together
firmly. Cut small rounds from
the pastry trimmings and press
on the envelopes to seal. Brush
with the remaining egg mixture.
  Place on a baking tray
sprinkled with cold water and
bake in the oven for 15 minutes,
or until lightly browned. Serve
warm.

Surprise Tartlets

1 (368-g/13-oz) packet frozen
  puff pastry
FILLING
125 g/4 oz minced steak
¼ teaspoon salt
¼ teaspoon white pepper
1 egg
50 g/2 oz button mushrooms,
  finely chopped
50 g/2 oz Cheddar cheese, grated
50 g/2 oz liver sausage
50 g/2 oz German sausage, diced
3 tablespoons chopped parsley
75 g/3 oz walnuts, finely chopped

Allow the pastry to thaw for
1 hour at room temperature.
  Sprinkle 12 small boat-
shaped and 18 round patty tins
with cold water. Preheat the
oven to moderately hot (200°C,
400°F, Gas Mark 6). Roll the
pastry out thinly and cut out to
line the patty tins. Prick the
pastry cases with a fork.
  Mix the steak thoroughly

with a little salt and pepper and
the egg. Mix the mushrooms
with the cheese and liver
sausage and season lightly. Mix
the German sausage with the
parsley and walnuts and season
lightly. Use these mixtures to
fill the patty cases.
  Bake the tartlets for 20
minutes and serve hot. Garnish
with tiny parsley sprigs, if
wished.

Cheese Pastry Pockets

*1 (370-g/13-oz) packet frozen
  puff pastry*
25 g/1 oz butter
*100 g/4 oz Cheddar, Gruyère or
  Edam cheese, grated*
2 eggs
2 tablespoons chopped parsley
¼ teaspoon salt
pinch cayenne pepper
juice of 1 lemon
1 egg yolk

Thaw the puff pastry following
the instructions on the packet,
and roll out on a lightly
floured surface. Melt the
butter. Mix together the

cayonne and lemon juice. Stir
the melted butter into the
cheese mixture and leave to
cool.

    Sprinkle a baking tray with
cold water. Cut the pastry into
large rounds, using a 10-cm/
4-inch pastry cutter, and place
one tablespoon of cheese
mixture in the centre of each
round. Brush round the edges
of the pastry with cold water,
fold the rounds in two and
press the edges together. Beat
the egg yolk with 2 teaspoons
water and use to coat the
pastry pockets. Transfer to the
baking tray and leave to stand
for 10 minutes. Bake in a
moderately hot oven (200 C,
400 F, Gas Mark 6) for
12 minutes and leave to cool.

Minced Steak Pasties

PASTRY
275 g/10 oz plain flour
½ teaspoon salt
½ teaspoon baking powder
75 g/3 oz soft butter
1 egg
100 ml/4 fl oz soured cream
FILLING
1 onion
50 g/2 oz mushrooms
40 g/1½ oz butter
225 g/8 oz minced fillet steak
*¼ teaspoon each salt, pepper and
  garlic salt*
2 hard-boiled eggs
beaten egg yolk to glaze

Sift the flour, salt and baking
powder into a mixing bowl.
Form a well in the centre, flake
the butter into the well and
mix with a little of the flour.
Add the egg and soured cream
and knead all the ingredients
together into a smooth dough.
Cover and leave to stand in the
refrigerator for 1 hour.

    To make the filling, peel and
finely dice the onion. Clean,
trim and chop the mushrooms.
Melt the butter and fry the
onion and mushroom together.
Mix with the minced steak and
season with the salt, pepper
and garlic salt. Shell and finely
dice the eggs and stir into the
meat mixture. Roll out the
pastry to 3 mm/⅛ inch thick
and cut into large rounds,
using a 12-cm/4½-inch pastry
cutter. Place one tablespoon of
filling on each round. Brush all
round the edge of the pastry
with beaten egg yolk, fold the
sides over the filling and press
the edges firmly together. Coat
the pasties with the remaining
egg yolk, transfer to a baking
tray and bake in a moderately
hot oven (200 C, 400 F, Gas
Mark 6) for 15–20 minutes.

Cornish Pasties

PASTRY
225 g/8 oz plain flour
pinch salt
1 egg
100 g/4 oz soft butter
FILLING
1 medium potato
1 shallot
150 g/5 oz stewing beef
4 tablespoons meat stock
1 teaspoon salt
½ teaspoon white pepper
1 teaspoon dried thyme
1 egg yolk

Sift the flour and salt into a mixing bowl, form a well in the centre and tip in the egg. Flake the butter round the edge of  the flour and quickly knead all the ingredients together into a dough. Cover in cooking foil and leave to stand in the refrigerator for 1 hour.

To make the filling, peel the potato and shallot and dice

finely. Trim the stewing beef and cut into very small pieces. Mix the potato, shallot and beef with the meat stock, salt, pepper and thyme and divide into four equal portions. Divide the pastry also into four equal portions and roll each into an 18-cm/7-inch round. Beat the egg yolk with 2 teaspoons water. Spoon the filling onto the centres of the rounds and brush all round the edges of the pastry with beaten egg yolk. Fold the rounds in half and press the edges together, making a pattern round the folded edge with a knife, if liked. Coat the tops of the pasties with the remaining egg yolk. Place on a baking tray and bake in a moderately hot oven (190 C, 375 F, Gas Mark 5) for 25 minutes. Turn the oven down to moderate (170 C, 325 F, Gas Mark 3) and bake for a further 20 minutes.

Ham Quiches

PASTRY
225 g/8 oz plain flour
1 egg
1–2 tablespoons cold water
100 g/4 oz soft butter
FILLING
3 medium onions
100 g/4 oz smoked or boiled
  ham
2 tablespoons oil
100 g/4 oz Parmesan or
  Cheddar cheese, grated
2 tablespoons chopped parsley
4 eggs
150 ml/¼ pint double cream
¼ teaspoon salt
pinch white pepper

Sift the flour into a mixing bowl and form a well in the centre. Tip the egg and water into the centre, flake the butter round the edge and work all the ingredients together into a dough. Cover in cooking foil and leave to stand in the

refrigerator for 1–2 hours. Then roll the pastry out on a lightly floured surface and use to line eight 10-cm/4-inch tartlet cases. Prick the bases several times with a fork and bake in a hot oven (220 C, 425 F, Gas Mark 7) for 10 minutes. Leave the tart cases to cool.

Peel the onions and dice finely, together with the ham. Heat the oil and fry the onion until soft, then remove from the pan and leave to cool. Mix together the onion, ham, grated cheese and parsley, and spoon the mixture into the tarts. Beat the eggs with the cream, salt and pepper, and pour over the ham and cheese mixture. Return the tartlets to the oven, turn the oven down to moderately hot (200 C, 400 F, Gas Mark 6) and bake for a further 10–12 minutes. Cover with cooking foil, if necessary, to avoid burning.

Quiche Lorraine

PASTRY
200 g/7 oz plain flour
½ teaspoon salt
100 g/3½ oz butter or margarine,
  cut into flakes
2–3 tablespoons water
FILLING
225 g/8 oz streaky bacon
4 eggs, separated
250 ml/8 fl oz single cream
pinch of white pepper
¼ teaspoon salt
125 g/4½ oz Edam cheese, grated

Grease and flour one loose-bottomed 25-cm/10-inch flan tin or two 18-cm/7-inch tins.

Sift the flour and salt into a mixing bowl and add the butter and water. Knead to a dough. Wrap the pastry in foil or cling film and leave in the refrigerator for 2 hours.

Preheat the oven to moderately hot (200°C, 400°F, Gas Mark 6). Roll out the pastry on a floured surface to about 4 mm/⅙ inch thick and use to line the base and sides of the flan tin. Prick the base of the pastry all over with a fork.

Coarsely chop the bacon rashers and scatter over the pastry base. Whisk the egg yolks with the cream, pepper and salt, and mix in the grated cheese. Whisk the egg whites until stiff and fold into the cheese mixture. Pour into the pastry case, smooth the surface and bake for 30–40 minutes.

When cooked, allow the quiche to cool for a while in the tin, then transfer to a serving plate and cut while still warm. Accompany the quiche with wine – a dry white Alsace is especially good.

Cook's Tip

Bacon, combined with eggs and cream, is the traditional filling for a Quiche Lorraine. Equally delicious quiche fillings include smoked or flaked fresh salmon, mushrooms tossed in a little butter, cooked chopped spinach or drained canned asparagus spears.

Mushroom and Cheese Flan

PASTRY
250 g/9 oz plain flour
125 g/4½ oz butter or margarine,
    cut into flakes
¼ teaspoon salt
2–3 tablespoons water
1 egg yolk
FILLING
1 leek
150 g/5 oz ham
225 g/8 oz button mushrooms
100 g/4 oz Camembert cheese
10 stuffed green olives
2 tablespoons oil
20 g/¾ oz butter
20 g/¾ oz plain flour
300 ml/½ pint milk
2 tablespoons chopped mixed
    herbs
¼ teaspoon each salt and pepper
1 egg yolk

Place the sifted flour in a mixing bowl with the butter or
margarine, salt, water and egg
yolk, and mix until a pastry
dough is formed. Cover and
leave for 2 hours in the
refrigerator.
    Trim and wash the leek. Dice
the ham, leek, mushrooms and
Camembert and slice the olives.
Heat the oil and brown the
diced ham. Add the leek and
mushrooms and simmer for a
further 10 minutes.
    Melt the butter, cook the
flour lightly in it, pour in the
milk and bring to the boil, stirring continuously. Stir the
herbs, seasoning, beaten egg
yolk and diced Camembert
into this sauce. Preheat the
oven to hot (220°C, 425°F, Gas
Mark 7).
    Roll out the pastry to line a
25-cm/10-inch flan tin. Spread
the mushroom filling over the
base, pour on the sauce and
sprinkle with the olives. Bake
for 40–50 minutes and serve
hot.

Country Leek Flan

PASTRY
200 g/7 oz plain flour
pinch of salt
1 egg
1–2 tablespoons water
100 g/3½ oz butter or margarine,
    cut into flakes
FILLING
450 g/1 lb leeks
175 g/6 oz streaky bacon
1 tablespoon oil
salt and freshly ground black
    pepper
pinch of curry powder
225 g/8 oz pork breakfast
    sausage, sliced
2 eggs
250 ml/8 fl oz soured cream

Place the sifted flour in a mixing bowl with the salt, egg,
water and butter, and mix until
a pastry dough is formed.
Cover and leave for 2 hours in
the refrigerator.
    Trim, wash and slice the
leeks. Dice the bacon and
brown in the oil. Add the
leeks, sprinkle with a pinch of
salt, pepper and curry powder
and cook gently for 10 minutes.
Preheat the oven to moderately
hot (200°C, 400°F, Gas Mark
6).
    Roll out the pastry to line a
23-cm/9-inch flan tin. Prick the
base several times with a fork.
Remove the rind from the
breakfast sausage and lay the
slices over the pastry base.
Spread with the leek filling.
Beat the eggs with the soured
cream and seasoning to taste
and pour over the filling. Bake
for 50–60 minutes and serve
hot from the tin.

Bacon Pizza

PIZZA DOUGH
30 g/1 oz fresh yeast
250 ml/8 fl oz lukewarm milk
500 g/1 lb plain flour
pinch of sugar
60 g/2 oz butter
1 egg
½ teaspoon salt
TOPPING
500 g/1 lb streaky bacon
1 tablespoon caraway seeds
  (optional)

Lightly grease two 24-cm/9½-inch flan tins. Cream the yeast with a little of the lukewarm milk. Gradually add all the milk. Sift the flour into a bowl, make a well in the centre and pour in the yeast liquid and sugar. Sprinkle a little of the flour over the liquid and leave to stand in a warm place for 15 minutes, until frothy.

Melt the butter, stir the beaten egg and salt into it then add to the yeast liquid. Gradually mix in all the flour and knead the dough until it is smooth and springy (about 5–10 minutes). Cover and leave to stand in a warm place for 30 minutes.

Cut the bacon into small pieces. Lightly knead the dough then roll out on a floured board and line the flan tins. Spread the bacon pieces over the dough and brush the edges of the pizza with a little oil. Sprinkle with caraway seeds and leave to stand in a warm place for 15 minutes. Preheat the oven to hot (220°C, 425°F, Gas Mark 7). Bake for 25 minutes and serve hot.

Alternatively the dough may be rolled out to line one large baking tray.

Onion Pizza

PIZZA DOUGH
20 g/¾ oz fresh yeast
125 ml/4 fl oz lukewarm milk
300 g/11 oz plain flour
80 g/3 oz butter
1 teaspoon salt
TOPPING
25 g/1 oz butter
100 g/4 oz streaky bacon,
  chopped
1·5 kg/3 lb onions, thinly sliced
150 ml/¼ pint soured cream
2 eggs
pinch of salt
1 tablespoon caraway seeds
  (optional)

Grease a 31-cm/12½-inch square baking tray.

Cream the yeast with a little of the milk. Gradually add the remaining milk. Sift the flour into a bowl and make a well in the centre. Pour the yeast liquid into it and sprinkle with a little of the flour. Cover and leave to stand in a warm place for 15 minutes, until frothy.

Melt the butter and add to the yeast mixture with the salt, then stir in all the flour. Knead the dough until it is smooth and springy (5–10 minutes). Leave the yeast dough to stand in a warm place for 15 minutes. Preheat the oven to moderately hot (200°C, 400°F, Gas Mark 6).

Melt the butter in a frying pan, add the bacon and cook until lightly browned. Add the onion and cook until soft. Roll out the dough on a floured board and line the baking tray. Turn the edges of the dough up to form a rim. Beat the cream with the eggs, salt and caraway seeds. Mix in the onion and bacon and spread the mixture over the pizza dough. Leave to stand in a warm place for a further 15 minutes, then bake for 45 minutes.

Serve hot if possible.

Puff Pastry Pizzas

1 (368-g/13-oz) packet frozen
  puff pastry
TOPPING
1 small onion
1 clove garlic
1 tablespoon oil
1 (425-g/15-oz) can tomatoes,
  drained
1 teaspoon salt
½ teaspoon black pepper
1 tablespoon chopped herbs
200 g/7 oz Emmenthal cheese,
  grated
GARNISH
salami slices, stuffed olives,
  capers and chopped herbs
or mussels, paprika pepper,
  stuffed olives, mushrooms,
  onion rings and freshly
  ground black pepper
or strips of red pepper, black
  olives, cocktail onions and
  anchovy fillets

Allow the pastry to thaw at
room temperature for 1 hour.
  Finely chop the onion and
garlic and cook until soft in the
oil. Cut up the tomatoes and
stir into the onion mixture with
the salt and pepper. Simmer
gently in a covered pan for 15
minutes and finally stir in the
herbs.
  Roll out the pastry and cut
into 10-cm/4-inch squares.
Sprinkle a baking tray with
cold water and place the pastry
squares on it. Top each square
with the tomato mixture and
add the garnishing ingredients
according to taste. Sprinkle
thickly with cheese and leave to
stand for 15 minutes.
  Preheat the oven to hot
(220°C, 425°F, Gas Mark 7)
and bake the squares near the
top of the oven for 15–18
minutes. Serve straight from
the oven.

Baked Roquefort Slices

4 slices white bread
75 g / 3 oz butter
8 slices smoked ham
100 g / 4 oz Roquefort (or other blue cheese)
GARNISH
¼ red pepper
¼ green pepper

Preheat the oven to very hot (240 C, 475 F, Gas Mark 9). Cut the slices of bread in half. Melt the butter in a large pan and fry the bread in it until golden brown on both sides. Remove the bread from the frying pan and leave to cool. Cover each slice of bread with a slice of ham followed by a piece of Roquefort. Transfer to a baking sheet and bake for a few minutes in the oven until the cheese begins to melt but not brown. Remove the slices

from the oven and allow to cool.
    Wash the peppers, remove the seeds and cut into very fine strips. Garnish each slice of bread with a few strips of red and green pepper. *Makes 8.*

Tuscan 'Crostini'

1 (100-g / 4-oz) packet Mozzarella cheese
8 slices white bread
2 cloves garlic
parsley sprigs
40 g / 1½ oz canned anchovy fillets
2 tablespoons capers
6 tablespoons olive oil
¼ teaspoon freshly ground white pepper
100 g / 4 oz black olives

Preheat the oven to very hot (240 C, 475 F, Gas Mark 9). Remove the Mozzarella from its packet of preserving liquid, wipe dry and slice. Remove the crusts from the bread and cut each slice in half. Peel and crush the garlic cloves. Wash, drain and finely chop the parsley. Blend together the anchovy fillets, capers and garlic in a liquidiser, or pass through a sieve to make a

smooth paste. Stir 4 tablespoons of olive oil into the paste, followed by the chopped parsley. Season with pepper. Spread half the bread slices with the paste, top with the cheese and cover with another slice of bread. Sprinkle both sides of the crostini with the remaining oil, place on a baking sheet and bake for a few minutes in the preheated oven until golden brown. Turn once during baking. Remove the crostini from the oven, leave to cool slightly and serve with black olives. *Makes 8.*

Mosaic Loaf

1 small light rye loaf
175 g/6 oz soft butter
2 hard-boiled eggs
½ cooked carrot
50 g/2 oz canned mushrooms
100 g/4 oz ham
1 spring onion
1 tablespoon capers
pinch celery salt
½ teaspoon salt
½ teaspoon pepper
10 stuffed olives, sliced

Cut off one end of the loaf. With a long, sharp knife, cut all round the inside of the loaf 1 cm/½ inch from the crust and, using your hand, scoop out the bread from inside.

Place the butter in a bowl and beat until light and creamy. Shell the hard-boiled eggs, cut them in half and remove the yolks. Sieve the yolks into the butter and mix well. Finely dice the egg whites and the carrot. Drain the mushrooms and chop finely, together with the ham, spring onion and capers. Stir all the chopped ingredients into the butter mixture, followed by the sliced olives. Season with celery salt, salt and pepper. Spoon the mixture into the loaf, filling it completely, and pressing down so that no spaces are left. Replace the piece originally sliced off, wrap the loaf in kitchen foil and leave to stand for a few hours in the refrigerator.

Stuffed Party Rolls

6 Vienna rolls
450 g/1 lb curd cheese
4 drops Tabasco sauce
20 ml/1 fl oz white wine
¼ teaspoon salt
¼ teaspoon white pepper
2 tablespoons chopped fresh mixed herbs, or 2 teaspoons dried mixed herbs
1 green pepper
2 gherkins
225 g/8 oz ham
100 g/4 oz cooked chicken
6 button mushrooms
50 g/2 oz pistachio nuts (optional)
2 teaspoons grated root ginger
1–2 teaspoons chopped mixed peel
20 ml/1 fl oz sherry

Slice off one third of each roll and scoop out all the bread from inside. Place half the curd cheese in a bowl and stir in the Tabasco, white wine, salt, pepper and herbs. Wash the green pepper, remove the seeds and dice the flesh finely, with the gherkins and half the ham. Mix the ham, pepper and gherkins into the curd cheese.

Finely chop the remaining ham, the chicken, mushrooms and pistachios, if used, and mix in a separate bowl with the remaining curd chese. Add the grated root ginger, chopped mixed peel and sherry. Fill three of the rolls with the wine and herb mixture, and the remaining three rolls with the chicken and ginger mixture. Set the two sections of each roll back together again, wrap in cooking foil and leave to stand for a few hours in the refrigerator. *Serves 6*

Cheese Bonnets

100 g/4 oz Cheddar or
  Emmental cheese
bunch parsley
2 tablespoons curd cheese
4 tablespoons mayonnaise
1 tablespoon wine vinegar
12 thin slices salami
12 slices French bread
40 g/1½ oz butter

Dice the cheese very finely.
Wash and dry the parsley, keep
a few sprigs to one side and
finely chop the rest. In a bowl
mix the curd cheese with the
mayonnaise, vinegar and
chopped parsley. Add the
diced cheese.

Cut a straight line to the
centre of each slice of salami

each other to make a bonnet.
Toast the bread and leave to
cool slightly, then spread with
butter. Place spoonfuls of
cheese salad on each slice of

bread and cover each spoonful
with a salami bonnet. Garnish
with parsley sprigs. *Makes 12*

Savoury Butter
Slices

150 g/5 oz soft butter
pinch salt
¼ teaspoon lemon juice
bunch chives
2 tablespoons grated Cheddar
  or Emmental cheese
1 teaspoon paprika pepper
50 g/2 oz smoked ham
2 hard-boiled eggs, shelled
1 tablespoon single cream
50 g/2 oz lobster or crab paste
8 small slices white bread
GARNISH
2 radishes
4 stuffed olives
4 chillies
4 small gherkins

Cream the butter with the salt
and lemon juice and divide
into three equal portions.
Wash, dry and finely slice the
chives, and mix into one
portion of butter. Stir the

grated cheese and paprika into
the second portion. Finely dice
the ham and eggs and stir into
the third portion of butter
followed by the cream. The
lobster or crab paste makes the
fourth topping. Spread two
slices of bread with half of
each, then cut the slices in half
and trim off the crusts.

Slice the radishes and olives.
Cut the gherkins into a fan-
shape by slicing almost to the
bottom of each and spreading
out the sections. Garnish the
chive butter fingers with radish
slices, the cheese and paprika
butter with chillies, the ham
and egg butter with gherkins
and the lobster or crab paste
with olives. *Makes 16*

234

Spicy Cream Cheese Slices

1 (370-g/13-oz) packet frozen
  puff pastry
1 egg yolk
1 tablespoon coarse salt, or
  1 teaspoon table salt
225 g/8 oz full fat cream cheese
225 g/8 oz curd cheese
1 tablespoon brandy
2 tablespoons chopped parsley
2 tablespoons warm water
7 g/¼ oz gelatine
150 ml/¼ pint double cream

Allow the puff pastry to thaw, then roll out evenly on a floured surface to a 30 × 50 cm/12 × 20-inch rectangle. Leave to stand for 15 minutes. Sprinkle a baking tray with cold water. Beat the egg yolk, and brush over the pastry, then prick the pastry several times with a fork and sprinkle one half with the salt. Transfer to the baking tray and bake in a hot oven (220 c, 425 f, Gas Mark 7) for 12–15 minutes. Allow to cool, then cut the pastry in half widthways, dividing the salted half from the unsalted. Slice the salted half into 5 × 10-cm/2 × 4-inch strips. Place the other half on a sheet of cooking foil, and turn up the foil edges all round to make a 5-cm/2-inch lip.

Beat together the cream cheese, curd cheese, brandy and parsley until smooth, and season to taste. Pour the warm water into a bowl and stand it in a pan of hot water. Sprinkle with the gelatine and stir until dissolved, then add to the cream cheese mixture. Whip the double cream until stiff and fold into the mixture. Spread the cheese thickly over the pastry base and top with the strips of pastry. Chill until the cream cheese is firm. Slice before serving.

Cheese Boats

225 g/8 oz plain flour
¼ teaspoon salt
1 egg yolk
1–2 tablespoons water
100 g/4 oz butter or margarine
½ red pepper
100 g/4 oz cooked chicken
1 (200-g/7-oz) packet sliced
  processed cheese
100 g/4 oz canned pineapple
  segments
1 tablespoon canned pineapple
  juice
3 tablespoons mayonnaise
1 teaspoon curry powder
a little mustard and cress

Sift the flour and salt into a large mixing bowl, form a well in the centre and tip in the egg yolk and water. Dot the butter or margarine around the edge of the flour. Quickly knead all the ingredients together to form a dough, wrap in cooking foil and leave to stand in the refrigerator for 1 hour. Roll out the pastry and use to line eight boat-shaped pastry moulds. Prick the pastry with a fork. Bake the boats in a hot oven (220 c, 425 f, Gas Mark 7) for 10–15 minutes, then leave to cool.

Wash the red pepper, remove the seeds and dice, together with the chicken. Cut the cheese into strips. Drain the pineapple segments. Mix together the pepper, chicken, cheese and pineapple. Beat the pineapple juice with the mayonnaise and curry powder and pour over the salad. Mix in gently. Fill the boats with the salad mixture and garnish with mustard and cress.

Savoury Titbits

Gherkins and Smoked Ham
10 thin slices smoked ham
½ teaspoon coarsely ground
  black pepper
10 small gherkins

Dates and Cream Cheese
10 dates
1 hard-boiled egg, shelled
2 tablespoons single cream
1 (75-g/3-oz) packet full fat
  cream cheese
½ teaspoon finely chopped dill
  (optional)
½ teaspoon chopped borage
  (optional)

Olives and Bacon
10 thin slices streaky bacon
10 stuffed olives

Sprinkle the ham with the
pepper. Wrap each gherkin in
a slice of ham and secure with
a cocktail stick.
  Slice the dates open

lengthways and remove the
stones. Cut the egg in half.
Sieve the yolk into a bowl, add
the cream and cream cheese
and stir until smooth. Mix in
the herbs, if used. Transfer the
mixture to a piping bag fitted
with a small star-shaped nozzle
and pipe into the dates. Keep
the stuffed dates in a cool place
until you are ready to serve
them.
  Fry the bacon until cooked
on both sides. Drain for a few
minutes on absorbent kitchen
paper. Wrap a stuffed olive in
each slice of bacon, securing
with a wooden cocktail stick.
Return the bacon rolls to the
frying pan and fry in hot fat
until crisp, turning
occasionally.

Game and Mushroom Croquettes

450 g/1 lb mushrooms
100 g/4 oz ham
bunch parsley
50 g/2 oz butter
100 g/4 oz plain flour
150 ml/¼ pint milk
4 egg yolks
2 egg whites
575 g/1¼ lb game
50 ml/2 fl oz Madeira wine
pinch salt
¼ teaspoon black pepper
1 teaspoon ground allspice
100 g/4 oz dried breadcrumbs
oil for deep-frying

Clean the mushrooms and cut
off the tips of the stalks. Finely
chop the ham and parsley.
Melt half the butter in a
saucepan, sprinkle on 25 g/1 oz
flour and stir over the heat
until golden. Gradually add

the milk and simmer the sauce
for 10 minutes, stirring
continuously. Leave the sauce
to cool slightly, then stir in two
egg yolks.
  Beat the two remaining egg
yolks with the egg whites. Skin
and trim the game, and mince
twice through the finest blade
of the mincer. Mix the mince
with the sauce, ham, parsley,
25 g/1 oz flour, the remaining
butter, the Madeira, salt,
pepper and allspice, and knead
to form a smooth dough. Wet
your hands and surround each
mushroom with a ball of the
mixture, lightly pressing the
meat together. Coat the balls
with the remaining flour, then
the beaten egg and finally the
breadcrumbs. Heat the oil for
deep-frying to 180 c/350 F. Fry
the croquettes for 6–8 minutes
until brown and crispy. Drain
on absorbent kitchen paper
and leave to cool. Serve with
Cumberland sauce or
cranberry jelly.

Prawn Croquettes

225 g/8 oz frozen prawns
25 g/1 oz butter
50 g/2 oz plain flour
150 ml/¼ pint milk
2–3 teaspoons lemon juice
¼ teaspoon salt
¼ teaspoon white pepper
1 tablespoon chopped fresh
  parsley, or 1 teaspoon dried
  parsley
1 egg, beaten
100 g/4 oz dried breadcrumbs
oil for deep frying

Place the prawns in a dish, cover and leave to thaw. Drain and chop finely. Melt the butter in a saucepan. Sprinkle on half the flour and stir over the heat until it becomes golden in colour. Gradually add the milk and, stirring continuously, bring slowly to the boil, when the sauce will thicken. Add the chopped prawns, lemon juice, salt,

pepper and parsley. Continue cooking for about 2 minutes until the mixture becomes firm, again stirring continuously. Chill the prawn mixture.

Wet your hands and, on a lightly floured surface, form the mixture into a long roll. Cut into small pieces and shape into croquettes. Dip the croquettes in the remaining flour, then in beaten egg and finally in breadcrumbs. Heat the oil for deep-frying to 180 c/ 350 f and fry the croquettes for about 6–8 minutes until golden brown. Drain on absorbent kitchen paper and leave to cool. *Makes 18*

Cheese Fritters

350 g/12 oz matured Gouda or
  Cheddar cheese, in slices
  2 cm/1 inch thick
150 g/5 oz thinly sliced smoked
  streaky bacon
2 eggs
25 g/1 oz plain flour
100 g/4 oz dried breadcrumbs
oil for deep-frying
FOR THE SAUCE
1 (500-g/15·9-oz) carton
  natural yogurt
¼ teaspoon salt
pinch celery salt
¼ teaspoon ground white pepper
generous pinch ground ginger
3 tablespoons chopped fresh
  mixed herbs (parsley, chives,
  dill, a little rosemary and
  sage) or 2 teaspoons dried
  mixed herbs

Cut the cheese into 2-cm/ 1-inch cubes. Wrap each cube in a slice of bacon and secure with a wooden cocktail stick.

Beat the eggs. Dip the cheese and bacon cubes in the flour, then in the beaten egg and finally in breadcrumbs. Heat the oil for deep-frying to 180 c/ 350 f and fry the cubes for 4–6 minutes until golden brown. Drain on absorbent kitchen paper and leave to cool.

In a small bowl mix the yogurt with the salt, celery salt, pepper, ginger and mixed herbs. Serve the sauce with the cubes as a dip.

Cheese Sticks

450 g / 1 lb Edam or Emmental
  cheese, in slices 1 cm / ½ inch
  thick
50 g / 2 oz thinly sliced salami
24 stuffed olives
2 small firm tomatoes
GARNISH
parsley sprigs

Cut the cheese into 1-cm/
½-inch cubes. Roll up the
salami slices. Thread each
salami roll onto a cocktail stick
with an olive, a small parsley
sprig and a cheese cube.
   Wash, dry and cut the
tomatoes into eight wedges.
Thread the tomato wedges
onto cocktail sticks, each with
an olive and a cheese cube.
 Thread the remaining cheese
cubes onto sticks, interspersed
with olives, and garnish with
parsley sprigs.

Stuffed Tomatoes

25 g / 1 oz long-grain rice
4 tomatoes
1 tablespoon mayonnaise
1 tablespoon single cream
1 tablespoon chopped fresh
  mixed herbs or 1 teaspoon
  dried mixed herbs
1 tablespoon grated Cheddar
  cheese
salt and white pepper
6 stuffed olives

Cook the rice following the
instructions on the packet,
drain and leave to cool. Wash
and dry the tomatoes. Slice off
the tops to make lids, scoop
out the seeds from inside and
discard. Mix the rice with the
mayonnaise, cream, herbs and
grated cheese. Season with salt
and pepper. Slice the olives
and stir into the rice mixture.
Stuff the tomatoes with the
mixture and replace the lids.
Makes 4

Curried Croquettes

2 onions
parsley sprigs
450 g / 1 lb minced beef, lamb or
  pork
2 eggs
2 tablespoons breadcrumbs
2 teaspoons mild curry powder
½ teaspoon salt
¼ teaspoon black pepper
oil for deep-frying
GARNISH
mandarin segments, pineapple
  segments, maraschino
  cherries, grapes, blue and
  Camembert cheese, a
  sprinkling of chopped nuts,
  stuffed olives, chillies, canned
  baby sweet corn cobs, lettuce
  leaves and parsley

Peel the onions and chop
finely. Wash, dry and chop the
parsley. Place the mince in a
bowl and mix thoroughly with
the chopped onion, parsley,
eggs, breadcrumbs, curry
powder, salt and pepper. Wet
your hands and form the meat
into small balls. Heat the oil
for deep-frying to 180 C/350 F.
Place a few balls at a time in
the hot oil and deep-fry for 5–8
minutes. Remove from the oil
with a draining spoon and
drain on kitchen paper. Thread
the curry balls onto cocktail
sticks and garnish as liked with
pieces of fruit, cheese and
vegetables. Wash and drain the
lettuce, use to line a dish and
arrange the curried croquettes
on top.

Party Nests

225 g/8 oz butter
¼ teaspoon salt
pinch white pepper
1 teaspoon lemon juice
1 punnet mustard and cress
75 g/3 oz shelled walnuts
10 small rounds wholemeal
    bread
pinch each celery salt, garlic
    salt and ground ginger
2 drops Tabasco sauce
3 strips canned pimiento
10 small rounds pumper-
    nickel bread
GARNISH
parsley sprigs

Cream half the butter with the
salt, pepper and lemon juice.
Snip the cress with scissors,
rinse in cold water and leave to
drain. Chop the walnuts.
Spread the wholemeal bread
with the butter and sprinkle
cress round the edges. Place
the chopped walnuts in the
centre of each round.
    Stir the celery salt, garlic
salt, ginger and Tabasco into
the remaining butter. Drain the
pimiento and dice finely. Place
the butter mixture in a piping
bag fitted with a small star-
shaped nozzle and pipe round
the edges of the pumpernickel
bread. Fill the centres with the
diced pimiento. Wash and dry
the parsley, break into sprigs
and use to garnish each round.
(Use a pastry cutter to make
the bread rounds.) Makes 20

Smoked Fish Canapés

bunch chives
100 g/4 oz soft butter
1 tablespoon grated fresh
    horseradish, or bottled
    creamed horseradish
generous pinch each salt and
    garlic salt
4 slices wholemeal bread
400 g/14 oz smoked halibut or
    haddock
2 firm tomatoes
GARNISH
dill or parsley sprigs
2 lettuce leaves
coarsely ground black pepper

Wash the chives, dry well and
slice very finely. Cream the
butter with the horseradish,
salt, garlic salt and chives, and
spread on the bread. Cut each
slice diagonally to form two
triangles. Skin the fish, remove
any bones and cut into pieces
to fit the bread triangles. Place
one piece of fish on each
triangle.
    Wash, dry and slice the
tomatoes. Wash the dill or
parsley and the lettuce and
allow to drain. Place a slice of
tomato on half the pieces of
fish and tuck half a lettuce leaf
under the rest. Garnish with a
dill or parsley sprig. Sprinkle
with pepper before serving.
Makes 8

Party Eggs

10 hard-boiled eggs

Fillings for 4 egg halves at a time:

*2 tablespoons full fat cream
    cheese
1 tablespoon chopped fresh
    mixed herbs
2 tablespoons milk
pinch salt*

*2 tablespoons cottage cheese
1 tablespoon finely grated
    carrot
1 teaspoon ground hazelnuts
pinch each salt and pepper*

*2 tablespoons full fat cream
    cheese
1 teaspoon mild curry powder
1 teaspoon crushed avocado
1 teaspoon lemon juice
1 tablespoon milk
pinch salt*

*2 tablespoons curd cheese
1 teaspoon chopped fresh dill or
    parsley
grated lemon rind
pinch salt*

*2 tablespoons curd cheese
1 tablespoon tomato purée
½ teaspoon paprika pepper
pinch salt*

SUGGESTED GARNISHES
*canned baby sweet corn cobs
    and pickled green
    peppercorns
chillies and parsley
black olives and parsley
rolled anchovies, diced tomato
    and capers
sliced kiwi fruit and maraschino
    cherries
sliced lemon, prawns, and dill or
    parsley
smoked salmon rolls and dill or
    parsley
lumpfish roe and mustard and
    cress
gherkins and sliced mild chillies
stuffed olives and mustard and
    cress*

Shell the eggs and halve
lengthways. Take out the
yolks, mix four yolk halves at a
time with one of the suggested
sets of ingredients for the
fillings, and spoon or pipe the
different fillings into the egg
whites. Garnish as shown.
(A choice of two garnishes is
shown for each of the four
basic fillings.)

Piquant Eggs with Bean Salad

FOR THE EGGS
4 hard-boiled eggs
2 tablespoons mayonnaise
50 g/2 oz soft butter
salt and freshly ground black
    pepper
1 tablespoon brandy
1 teaspoon pickled green
    peppercorns (optional)
FOR THE SALAD
225 g/8 oz young French beans
3 tablespoons oil
225 g/8 oz calf's liver
2 shallots
small bunch parsley
1 tablespoon tarragon vinegar

sprig corn salad or watercress

Shell the eggs and cut in half
widthways. Take out the yolks,
pass through a sieve and beat
with the mayonnaise, butter,
salt, pepper and brandy.

Transfer the mixture to a
piping bag fitted with a star-
shaped nozzle and pipe the
filling into the egg whites.
Garnish with the pickled green
peppercorns, if used.
    To make the salad, trim and
wash the beans, and place in
boiling salted water. Cover and
simmer for 10 minutes, then
drain and leave to cool. Heat
1 tablespoon oil in a pan. Slice
the liver into thin strips and fry
in the oil for 2-3 minutes. Peel
and finely chop the shallots.
Wash, dry and chop the
parsley. Beat the remaining oil
with the vinegar, shallot and
parsley and season to taste.
Place the beans and liver
together in the centre of a
serving platter, sprinkle with
salad dressing and arrange the
eggs all round. Wash the corn
salad or watercress sprig,
shake dry and use to garnish
the platter.

Party Egg Platter

10 hard-boiled eggs
6 tablespoons mayonnaise
salt and pepper
1 tablespoon chopped parsley
juice of ½ lemon
2 tablespoons oil
SUGGESTED GARNISHES
few lettuce leaves, sprigs of corn
    salad or watercress, small
    onion rings, anchovy fillets,
    ham slices, smoked salmon
    slices, prawns, bottled or
    canned mussels, olives, sliced
    cooked carrot, sliced
    radishes, capers, pickled
    green peppercorns, chillies,
    canned baby sweet corn cobs,
    lemon slices, parsley and dill

Shell the eggs and halve
lengthways. Remove the yolks,
pass through a sieve and beat
with the mayonnaise, salt and
pepper. Divide the mixture in
half and stir the chopped
parsley into one of the

portions. Place the portions
separately into piping bags
fitted with star-shaped nozzles,
and fill ten egg whites with
plain mayonnaise and the
other ten with the parsley
mayonnaise. Arrange the eggs
on a serving platter and
garnish with any of the
suggested toppings, as shown
in the photograph.
    Tear the lettuce leaves into
strips and place in a bowl with
any left-over garnishes. Beat
the lemon juice with the oil,
season to taste and stir into the
salad ingredients. Arrange the
salad in the centre of the
platter.

Hard-boiled Eggs with Sauces

Allow two eggs per person

Russian sauce
1 red pepper
1 green pepper
1 yellow pepper
large bunch chives
1¼ (142-ml/5-fl oz) cartons
*   soured cream*
1 teaspoon paprika pepper
dash Tabasco sauce
1 teaspoon horseradish sauce
1 (58-g/2-oz) jar lumpfish roe

Wash, dry and halve the peppers, remove the seeds and pith, and dice. Wash the chives and chop finely. Mix the soured cream with the diced pepper, chives, paprika, Tabasco, horseradish sauce and half the lumpfish roe. Spoon the remaining lumpfish roe on top.

Mushroom sauce
225 g/8 oz mushrooms
2 leeks
2 onions
100 g/4 oz streaky bacon
15 g/½ oz butter

Clean, trim and slice the mushrooms. Wash and slice the leeks. Peel and finely dice the onions. Remove the rinds from the bacon rashers, cut the bacon into pieces and fry until the fat runs. Add the butter, leek and onion and cook for 4-5 minutes. Lastly add the mushroom and continue cooking for 6 minutes. Cool and serve.

Cheese sauce
100 g/4 oz cottage cheese
50 g/2 oz Stilton cheese
juice of 1 lemon
salt
1 teaspoon red currants or
*   cranberry sauce (optional)*

Sieve the cottage cheese and

Stilton into a bowl and beat with the lemon juice until creamy. Season to taste with salt and serve garnished with red currants or cranberry sauce, if liked.

Capri Sauce
large bunch fresh mixed herbs
2 canned anchovy fillets
1 tablespoon capers
10 stuffed olives
2 egg yolks
1 teaspoon strong mustard
3 tablespoons wine vinegar
salt and pepper
6 tablespoons oil
2 tomatoes

Wash and drain the herbs and chop finely, together with the anchovy fillets, capers and olives. Beat the egg yolks with the mustard, vinegar, salt and pepper. Gradually beat in the oil, a few drops at a time, and finally stir in the chopped ingredients. Peel, quarter and

chop the tomatoes and mix into the sauce.

Egg Tartlets with Liver Pâté

4 hard-boiled eggs
bunch fresh mixed herbs (sage, parsley, dill, chives, lovage), or 2 teaspoons dried mixed herbs
50 g/2 oz soft butter
2 tablespoons mild French mustard
salt and pepper
8 small savoury pastry tartlet cases (bought ready-made)
100 g/4 oz smooth liver pâté
GARNISH
2 slices canned truffles (optional)
8 small sprigs dill (optional)

Shell the eggs, slice in half widthways and take out the yolks. Place the yolks in a bowl. Wash, drain and finely chop the fresh herbs, if used. Beat the egg yolks with the butter, mustard, salt, pepper and herbs until smooth and creamy, transfer to a piping bag fitted with a star-shaped nozzle and pipe the mixture into the tartlet cases. Place one egg white half in the centre of each. Beat the liver pâté until light and fluffy and spoon it into the egg whites. Finely dice the truffles, if used, and sprinkle over the pâté. Garnish each tart with a sprig of dill, if liked. *Serves 8*

Egg Tartlets with Ham Salad

225 g/8 oz cooked ham
1 crisp dessert apple
1 banana
2 teaspoons lemon juice
3 tablespoons mayonnaise
2 tablespoons single cream
2-3 teaspoons mild curry powder
pinch each salt and sugar
8 small savoury pastry tartlet cases (bought ready-made)
4 hard-boiled eggs
4 slices smoked salmon
few tarragon leaves (optional)

Finely dice the ham. Peel and halve the apple, remove the core and cut the flesh into strips. Peel and dice the banana and mix the ham, apple and banana together in a bowl. Sprinkle with 1 teaspoon lemon juice.

Beat the mayonnaise with the cream, the remaining lemon juice, the curry powder, salt and sugar, taste and adjust seasoning. Mix the dressing into the salad ingredients, and spoon the salad into the tartlet cases. Shell the eggs, halve lengthways and place one half on top of each tartlet. Cut the slices of smoked salmon in half lengthways and roll up. Top each egg half with a roll of salmon, and garnish with the tarragon leaves, if used. *Makes 8*

243

Luxury Party Loaf

4 eggs
1 long French loaf
5 tablespoons mayonnaise
1 small lettuce
225 g/8 oz sliced ham sausage
1 carrot
1 stick celery
bunch radishes
1 onion
2 tablespoons wine vinegar
4 tablespoons oil
1 tablespoon chopped parsley
salt and pepper
175 g/6 oz frozen peas
225 g/8 oz sliced salami
100 g/4 oz Edam or Cheddar
   cheese
2 tablespoons natural yogurt
¼ teaspoon paprika pepper
GARNISH
few dill and parsley sprigs

Hard-boil the eggs, plunge into
cold water, shell and leave to

cool. Slice the outer crust off
the top of the loaf lengthways,
to within 5 cm/2 inches of each
end. Scoop out some of
the bread, and coat the inside
of the loaf with 4 tablespoons
mayonnaise. Separate the
lettuce into leaves; wash, drain
thoroughly and use to line the
inside of the loaf.

Cut the ham sausage into
fine strips. Wash and scrape
the carrot and slice into small
fingers. Wash the celery and
radishes, chop the celery and
slice the radishes very finely.
Peel the onion and cut into
rings. Place the sausage, carrot,
celery, radishes and onion
rings together in a bowl. Whisk
the vinegar with the oil and
chopped parsley, season with
salt and pepper and stir into
the salad.

Blanch the frozen peas in
boiling water for 5 minutes,
drain and leave to cool. Cut
the salami into fine strips, dice
the cheese, and place the peas,

salami and cheese together in a
bowl. Make a dressing with the
remaining mayonnaise, the
yogurt and paprika, season
with salt and pepper and stir
into the salami mixture. Fill
the inside of the loaf with
alternate spoonfuls of the ham
sausage and salami salads.
Slice each egg into eight
wedges and arrange in the
salad. Garnish with sprigs of
parsley and dill. Serves 8

Cook's Tip

For an evening party
you can prepare the
fillings in advance and
fill the loaf shortly
before you need it. The
lettuce leaves should
prevent the bread from
becoming soggy. Once
filled, keep the loaf
loosely wrapped in cling-
film in a cool place until
you are ready to serve it.

Ham and Egg

For each:
7 g/¼ oz soft butter
50 g/2 oz smoked ham, finely
  chopped
pinch curry powder
1 large slice brown bread
1 hard-boiled egg, shelled
1 teaspoon chopped fresh mixed
  herbs or a generous pinch
  dried mixed herbs
1 tablespoon mayonnaise
GARNISH
parsley sprig

Mix the butter with the ham
and curry powder and spread
the bread with the mixture.
Slice the egg and arrange on
top. Stir the herbs into the
mayonnaise and spoon over
the egg. Garnish with parsley.

Cheese Salad

For each:
2–3 leaves endive
1 large slice wholemeal bread
7 g/¼ oz soft butter
75 g/3 oz Edam cheese
½ hard-boiled egg
4 shelled walnuts
1 teaspoon chopped chives
1 tablespoon mayonnaise
1 teaspoon natural yogurt
salt and pepper
GARNISH
few grapes

Cut the endive into thin strips.
Spread the bread with the
butter and cover with the
endive. Dice the cheese and egg
and chop three of the shelled
walnuts. Mix these with the
chives, mayonnaise and yogurt
and season with salt and
pepper. Spread this mixture
over the endive and garnish
with grapes and the remaining
walnut.

Sausage and Peppers

For each:
1 large slice brown bread
7 g/¼ oz soft butter
½ green pepper, seeded
½ red pepper, seeded
1 small onion
75 g/3 oz ham sausage
1 tablespoon oil
1 teaspoon vinegar
1 teaspoon chopped parsley
salt and pepper

Spread the bread with the
butter. Slice the green pepper
into rings and arrange on the
bread. Finely dice the red
pepper. Peel the onion and
slice into rings and cut the
sausage into small strips. Make
a dressing with the oil, vinegar,
parsley, salt and pepper. Stir
the dressing into the red
pepper, onion and sausage,
and arrange on the sandwich.

Salami and Egg Salad

For each:
1 large slice brown bread
7 g/¼ oz soft butter
6 thin slices salami
1 lettuce leaf
1 hard-boiled egg, shelled
3 mushrooms
½ tomato
1 teaspoon mayonnaise
1 tablespoon single cream
dash of lemon juice
salt and pepper
few capers (optional)

Spread the bread with the
butter and arrange the salami
slices on top. Add the lettuce.
Chop the egg and mushrooms,
dice the tomato, and mix these
ingredients with the
mayonnaise, cream and lemon
juice. Season and arrange on
the lettuce. Sprinkle with
capers, if used.

Vegetarian Special

For each:
75 g / 3 oz frozen peas and carrots
1 tablespoon oil
1 teaspoon wine vinegar
salt and pepper
1 teaspoon chopped parsley
¼ teaspoon strong mustard
7 g / ¼ oz soft butter
1 large slice wholemeal bread
2 leaves red endive or red
  cabbage
1 teaspoon whipped cream

Cook the frozen vegetables following the instructions on the packet and drain. Make a dressing with the oil, vinegar, salt, pepper and parsley and stir into the vegetables. Mix together the mustard and butter and spread over the bread. Arrange the red endive on the bread and top with the vegetables and whipped cream.

Mushroom with Egg

For each:
75 g / 3 oz mushrooms
1 teaspoon lemon juice
1 teaspoon oil
salt and pepper
1 large slice white bread
½ clove garlic, crushed
15 g / ½ oz soft butter
½ hard-boiled egg, chopped
1 teaspoon chopped fresh herbs

Slice the mushrooms very finely. Make a dressing with the lemon juice, oil, salt and pepper and pour over the mushrooms. Rub one side of the bread with the garlic. Melt half the butter in a pan and brown the garlic side of the bread in it. When cool, spread the other side with the rest of the butter and arrange the mushrooms on top. Sprinkle with chopped egg and herbs.

Pinwheels

1 white loaf
1 (225-g / 8-oz) can tuna fish
1 small onion
2 tablespoons fresh grated
  horseradish, or bottled
  creamed horseradish
3 tablespoons whipped cream
¼ teaspoon salt
¼ teaspoon pepper
50 g / 2 oz soft butter
GARNISH
6 small tomatoes
6 twists of lemon
mustard and cress

Remove the crust from the loaf and cut lengthways into six slices. Interleave the slices of bread with greaseproof paper and, with a rolling pin, roll out until thin. Then roll up each slice lengthways as for a sponge roll.

Drain the tuna fish and chop into small pieces. Peel and finely chop the onion. Blend the tuna fish, onion, horseradish, whipped cream, salt and pepper in the liquidiser, taste and adjust the seasoning as necessary. Unroll the bread slices, spread evenly with the butter, followed by the tuna fish mixture, and roll up again. Wrap each of the six rolls of bread in greaseproof paper, then in cooking foil and leave to stand in the refrigerator for 1 hour. Before serving, cut each roll into slices and arrange in a circle on individual plates. Garnish the centre of each plate with a small tomato, a twist of lemon, and a small bunch of cress.
Serves 6.

Gourmet's Delight

For each:
2–3 lettuce leaves
1 large slice brown bread
7 g/¼ oz soft butter
100 g/4 oz cooked chicken breast
1 canned peach half
1 tablespoon mayonnaise
chopped parsley

Wash the lettuce and dry thoroughly. Spread the bread with the butter and place the lettuce on top. Skin the chicken breast, slice thinly and arrange in layers on the lettuce. Drain the peach half, cut into equal slices, and place in a fan-shape on the chicken. Spoon the mayonnaise into a piping bag fitted with a star-shaped nozzle and pipe two swirls onto the peaches. Sprinkle with chopped parsley.

Cook's Tip

When ripe peaches are in season, use one of these in preference to a canned one. Scald the fresh peach by placing it in an ovenproof bowl and pouring on boiling water. Leave for a few seconds, then take out the peach and remove the skin. Cut the peach in half, remove the stone and slice one half as above.

Danish Sandwiches

For each:
25 g/1 oz soft butter
1 slice white bread
1 lettuce leaf
1 slice Tilsit or Cheddar cheese
2 canned sardines
2 large slices tomato
½ onion
salt and coarsely ground black pepper
1 teaspoon grated Emmental or Edam cheese

Melt the butter in a small frying pan and brown the bread in it on both sides. Leave to cool.

Wash the lettuce, dry well and place on the bread. Top with the Tilsit or Cheddar. Drain the sardines, lay them diagonally across the cheese and arrange the sliced tomato on top. Peel and finely dice the onion. Sprinkle on the tomato, followed by the salt, pepper and grated Emmental or Edam cheese.

Cook's Tip

Danish Sandwiches can be topped with canned anchovy fillets cut into strips instead of sardines. Soak the anchovies first in a little milk, as they tend to be very salty.

Mussel and Cress

For each:
*1 large slice brown or white
bread*
7 g/¼ oz soft butter
¼ small onion, peeled
½ punnet mustard and cress
5 canned mussels

Spread the bread with the
butter. Chop the onion very
finely and sprinkle half over
the bread. Snip the cress with
scissors and sprinkle over the
onion in a thick layer. Drain
the mussels thoroughly and
arrange them on the bed of
cress. Garnish with the rest of
the onion.

Smoked trout

For each:
*1 large slice brown or white
bread*
7 g/¼ oz soft butter
*1 (75-g/3-oz) smoked trout
fillet*
2 thin slices honeydew melon
1 teaspoon mayonnaise
*1 teaspoon pickled pink
peppercorns or a sprinkling of
freshly ground white pepper*

Lightly toast the bread and
when cooled, spread with the
butter. Cut the trout fillet in
half and arrange on the bread.
Remove the peel from the
melon slices, scrape away the
seeds and place the slices on
the trout. Spoon over the
mayonnaise and sprinkle with
red peppercorns, if used, or
white pepper.

Swiss Cheese Salad

For each:
2–3 lettuce leaves
1 large slice white bread
7 g/¼ oz soft butter
1 small tomato
½ small green pepper
75 g/3 oz Emmental cheese
1 teaspoon lemon juice
¼ teaspoon French mustard
salt and pepper
1 tablespoon oil
GARNISH
parsley sprig

Cut the lettuce into strips
and arrange on the buttered
bread. Neatly dice the tomato,
pepper and cheese. Stir the
lemon juice, mustard, salt and
pepper into the oil and mix in
the diced ingredients.
  Arrange on the lettuce and
garnish with parsley.

Tomato and Fish

For each:
1 large slice brown bread
7 g/¼ oz soft butter
1 tomato
¼ teaspoon white pepper
2 canned sild or pilchards
*½ hard-boiled egg, cut
lengthways*
1 tablespoon mayonnaise
GARNISH
*½ teaspoon canned lumpfish roe
(optional)*

Spread the bread with the
butter. Slice the tomato and
place on the bread. Sprinkle
with pepper and top with
the fish. Remove the yolk
from the egg, mix with the
mayonnaise and fill the egg
white with the mixture.
Garnish with lumpfish roe, if
used, and place the egg in the
centre of the sandwich.

Smoked Mackerel

For each:
1 large slice rye bread
7 g/¼ oz soft butter
2–3 lettuce leaves
50 g/2 oz curd cheese
1 tablespoon single cream
pinch each salt, sugar and white pepper
½ small pear
½ small banana
few drops lemon juice
100 g/4 oz smoked mackerel fillet
coarsely ground black pepper
GARNISH
dill sprig (optional)

Spread the bread with the butter and top with the lettuce. Mix together the curd cheese, cream, salt, sugar and white pepper. Wash and core the pear and coarsely grate into the mixture. Peel and dice the banana, add to the mixture and sprinkle with lemon juice. Stir well and spoon onto the lettuce. Cut the fish fillet into thick slices and arrange in a fan-shape on top. Sprinkle with coarsely ground black pepper, and garnish with dill, if used.

Spicy Chicken Livers

For each:
100 g/4 oz chicken livers
25 g/1 oz soft butter
¼ teaspoon salt
1 slice white bread
1 large lettuce leaf
1 tablespoon mayonnaise
2 teaspoons red wine
1 teaspoon cranberry sauce
½ red apple
few drops lemon juice
¼ teaspoon sugar
GARNISH
1 wedge lemon

Wash the chicken livers in cold water, trim and dry well. Melt half the butter in a pan and fry the livers for 8 minutes over a moderate heat, turning continuously. Season with salt and when cool, cut into equal slices.

Toast the bread, spread with the rest of the butter and top with the lettuce. Arrange the liver on the lettuce and spoon the mayonnaise on top. Mix the red wine with the cranberry sauce and spoon over the mayonnaise. Wash, core and coarsely grate the apple. Sprinkle with lemon juice and sugar and arrange around one corner of the bread. Garnish with a wedge of lemon.

249

New Yorker

For each:
1 large slice rye bread
40 g / 1½ oz full fat cream cheese
3 thin slices smoked salmon
¼ small red onion, cut
  widthways

Spread the bread thickly with
the cheese. Fold each slice of
smoked salmon in half and
arrange on the bread. Peel the
onion, cut into rings and place
over the smoked salmon.

Cook's Tip

If the onion topping
does not appeal,
you can season the
cheese spread with
freshly grated
horseradish instead.
Mix ½–1 teaspoon
horseradish with the
cream cheese and spread
the bread with this
mixture.

Beef Mayonnaise

For each:
1 large thin slice brown bread
1 tablespoon mayonnaise
3 slices cold roast beef
1 hard-boiled egg
GARNISH
¼ pickled cucumber, sliced

Thickly spread the bread with
the mayonnaise. Fold the slices
of roast beef in half lengthways
and arrange in a fan-shape on
the bread. Shell and slice the
egg lengthways, and place on
the beef. Garnish with the
cucumber slices.

Cook's Tip

Roast beef sandwiches
are just as delicious
made with lightly
toasted bread. In this
case mix the mayonnaise
with 1 teaspoon
cranberry sauce and
omit the pickled
cucumber.

Danish Salami and Cucumber

For each:
1 slice granary bread
top half of 1 sesame roll
15 g/½ oz soft butter
¼ cucumber
salt and pepper
6–8 thin slices salami
chopped parsley

Spread the bread and half roll with the butter. Thinly slice the cucumber and season with salt and pepper. Arrange half the cucumber on the bread, cover with the salami, then follow with the rest of the cucumber. Sprinkle with parsley and top with the half roll.

Cook's Tip

This refreshing and satisfying roll makes an ideal snack for summer rambles. For an outing, wrap these rolls in cling-film or foil. An equally delicious variation would be sliced apple and cold roast pork, garnished with horseradish sauce.

Corned Beef and Egg

For each:
1 bread roll
15 g/½ oz soft butter
7 g/¼ oz cheese spread
2–3 lettuce leaves
2 slices canned corned beef
1 hard-boiled egg, shelled
½ gherkin

Cut the roll in half and spread each half with the butter, followed by the cheese spread. Place the lettuce and corned beef on the bottom half. Cut the egg into slices lengthways and the gherkin into fine strips. Arrange the egg and gherkin over the corned beef and top with the remaining half roll.

Cook's Tip

These rolls are also particularly suitable for picnics. As a variation, substitute cold pork or ham for the corned beef.

Brunch Slices

For each:
¼ teaspoon salt
pinch each black pepper and
    paprika pepper
100 g/4 oz pork fillet
25 g/1 oz dripping
2 large slices white bread
15 g/½ oz soft butter
2–3 lettuce leaves
1 hard-boiled egg
1 small onion, peeled
1 strip canned pimiento
2 tablespoons single cream
1 tablespoon whipped double
    cream
1 teaspoon curry powder
sprig dill (optional)

Rub the salt, black pepper and
paprika into the pork fillet.
Heat the dripping in a frying
pan and brown the fillet well
all over, turning frequently.
Reduce the heat and cook
gently for a further 10 minutes.
Remove the fillet from the pan

and when cool, cut into equal
slices.
   Spread the bread with the
butter. Arrange the lettuce on
one slice of bread followed by
the slices of pork. Shell and
finely chop the egg. Finely dice
the onion and pimiento, and
mix with the chopped egg,
single and double cream and
curry powder. Season to taste.
Spoon the mixture onto the
meat and top with the second
slice of bread. Garnish with a
dill sprig, if used.

Club Sandwich

For each:
2 small slices white bread
1 slice liver sausage
1 small slice wholemeal bread
1 tablespoon mayonnaise
1 slice ham
2–3 lettuce leaves
1 slice Cheddar or Edam cheese
small bunch radishes

Lightly toast the white bread.
Place the liver sausage on one
slice of toast and cover with
the wholemeal bread. Spread
the mayonnaise on top and
add, one after the other, the
ham, lettuce and cheese. Top
with the second slice of toast.
With a sharp knife cut the
sandwich diagonally in half
and secure each half with a
cocktail stick. Serve with the
radishes.

Cook's Tip

As a variation, you
could make this
sandwich using a slice of
cooked chicken instead
of the liver sausage, and
replacing the cheese with
a few tomato slices,
sprinkled with freshly
ground black pepper.

Delicatessen Meat Salads

4 slices brown bread
4 tablespoons curd cheese
2 tablespoons single cream
1 teaspoon paprika pepper
¼ teaspoon salt
¼ teaspoon white pepper
225 g/8 oz meat salad (bought ready made)
GARNISH
1 tomato
8 stuffed olives, sliced
dill or parsley sprigs

Remove the crusts from the bread and cut each slice into two equal triangles. Cream  together the curd cheese, cream, paprika, salt and pepper. Place this mixture in a piping bag fitted with a small star-shaped nozzle and pipe round the edges of the triangles. Fill the centre of each triangle with a spoonful of meat salad. Wash and dry the tomato and cut into eight wedges. Scoop out the seeds and place one wedge on each triangle. Garnish individually with a few slices of olive and a dill or parsley sprig. *Makes 8*

Hawaiian Ham Rolls

3 tablespoons mayonnaise
2 tablespoons curd cheese
2 teaspoons wine vinegar
¼ teaspoon salt
¼ teaspoon white pepper
¼ teaspoon sugar
2 canned pineapple rings
3 hard-boiled eggs
2 slices dark rye bread
15 g/½ oz soft butter
4 large slices ham
GARNISH
1 tomato
parsley sprigs
few lettuce leaves

Cream together the mayonnaise, curd cheese vinegar, salt, pepper and sugar. Drain the pineapple rings and cut into small pieces. Shell and finely chop the eggs, and stir with the pineapple into the mayonnaise mixture.

Remove the crusts from the bread, spread the bread with the butter and cut each slice into quarters. Trim all the fat from the ham and cut each slice in half. Spoon an equal amount of the mayonnaise mixture onto each slice of ham and roll up. Place one roll on each piece of bread.

Wash and dry the tomato, cut into eight wedges and scoop out the seeds with a spoon. Garnish each ham roll with a wedge of tomato and a parsley sprig, and serve on a bed of lettuce. *Makes 8*

253

Salad Buffet with Assorted Dressings

For a large buffet you will need between six and eight different salad ingredients. Choose any of the following, depending on what is in season, and bearing texture and colour in mind: round and cos lettuces, Iceberg or Webb's Wonder lettuce, corn salad, chicory, red endive, curly endive, young spinach, dandelion leaves, watercress, sliced tomatoes and cucumber, radishes, onion rings, green and black olives, hard-boiled eggs, canned sweet corn, green, red and yellow peppers sliced into rings, celery, chopped fresh herbs, cooked peas and diced fruit. Wash and thoroughly drain all salad ingredients, arrange separately in bowls or on platters as liked,

and serve with the following dressings:

Blue Cheese Dressing
100 g/4 oz blue cheese (Stilton, Roquefort, Dolcelatte)
1 tablespoon single or soured cream
1 tablespoon white wine vinegar
2 tablespoons mayonnaise
salt and white pepper

Crush the cheese with a fork and mix with the cream, vinegar, mayonnaise, salt and pepper. Blue cheese dressing goes especially well with all varieties of lettuce.

Egg and Herb Dressing
4 hard-boiled eggs
3 tablespoons oil
1 tablespoon wine vinegar
salt and pepper
2 tablespoons chopped fresh mixed herbs

Shell and finely dice the eggs. Beat the oil with the vinegar, salt and pepper. Stir in the egg and herbs, and serve with tomato or cucumber salad.

French Dressing
3 tablespoons lemon juice
salt and pepper
¼ teaspoon sugar
¼ teaspoon mustard powder
8 tablespoons olive oil

Beat the lemon juice with the salt, pepper, sugar and mustard powder. Gradually mix in the oil, beating continuously. French dressing goes well with chicory, red endive and all kinds of lettuce.

Yogurt Dressing

1 (150-g/5.3-oz) carton natural
*   yogurt*
2 tablespoons lemon juice
1 tablespoon oil
salt and pepper
2 tablespoons chopped fresh
*   mixed herbs*

Mix the yogurt with the lemon
juice and oil and whisk until
creamy. Stir in the salt, pepper
and herbs. Yogurt dressing
goes well with chicory, lettuce
and hard-boiled eggs.

Thousand Island Dressing

2 strips canned pimiento
225 g/8 oz mayonnaise
3 tablespoons tomato ketchup
1 teaspoon finely chopped green
*   pepper*
1 teaspoon grated onion
¼ teaspoon salt
generous pinch paprika pepper

Drain the pimiento and dice
finely. Mix the mayonnaise
with the pimiento, ketchup,
green pepper, grated onion,
salt and paprika. Serve with all
kinds of lettuce, and chicory,
tomato or dandelion salad.

Sherry Dressing
1 egg
2 tablespoons sugar
2 tablespoons dry sherry
¼ teaspoon salt
15 g/½ oz melted butter
4 tablespoons orange juice
2 tablespoons lemon juice
4 tablespoons double cream

Beat the egg. Whisking
continuously, gradually add
the sugar, sherry, salt, butter,
orange and lemon juice and
transfer the mixture to a pan.
Heat very gently, stirring
continuously, until it begins to
thicken, but do not allow to
boil. Remove from the heat
and leave to cool. Then whip
the cream and fold it into the
dressing. Sherry dressing goes
well with celery, red endive,
canned sweet corn and any
kind of fruit salad.

Cook's Tip

You can make your
salad buffet a more
substantial meal by
serving diced Cheddar,
Edam, Emmental or
other kinds of cheeses,
cold ham, beef, chicken
or pork, rolled
anchovies, rollmop
herrings, shrimps or any
kind of smoked fish.
Serve with a selection of
different kinds of bread.

Children's Lunch Party

Children have seemingly insatiable appetites, so offer your young guests plenty to eat and a variety of different fruit juices to drink. You can buy a lot of prepared foods, such as cold meats, continental sausages, various kinds of bread and bread rolls, mixed pickles, sauces, crisps and sweets. Brightly coloured paper plates, cups and napkins add a festive note, and have the added bonus of no washing up. Here are some suggestions for home-made party dishes.
Serves 10-12

Meat Loaf Sandwiches
2 onions
100 g/4 oz fresh white
  breadcrumbs
1.5 kg/3 lb minced beef, lamb or
  pork
4 eggs
1 teaspoon paprika pepper
salt and white pepper
2 tablespoons chopped parsley
12 lettuce leaves
24 slices white bread
3 tomatoes
2 hard-boiled eggs

Peel and dice the onions and mix in a bowl with the breadcrumbs, minced meat, eggs, paprika, salt, pepper and parsley. Mix all the ingredients well together, shape into a long loaf and bake in a moderately hot oven (200 c, 400 f, Gas Mark 6) for 40-45 minutes. Leave the meat loaf to cool and cut into twelve thick slices.
    Wash and thoroughly drain the lettuce leaves, place one leaf on each of twelve slices of

bread and top with a piece of meat loaf. Wash, dry and slice the tomatoes. Shell and slice the eggs. Arrange the tomato and egg over the meat loaf and top each sandwich with a second slice of bread.

Potato and Cucumber Salad
1 kg/2¼ lb new potatoes
2 onions
½ cucumber
100 g/4 oz mayonnaise
4 tablespoons natural yogurt
3 tablespoons wine vinegar
salt and pepper
bunch chives

Wash the potatoes, place in a pan containing boiling salted water and simmer over a moderate heat for 20-25 minutes until tender. Then drain, allow to cool, remove the skins and slice. Peel and finely dice the onions. Wash the cucumber and cut into very thin slices. Mix the potato,

onion and cucumber together in a bowl. Beat the mayonnaise with the yogurt, vinegar, salt and pepper and pour over the salad. Wash, drain and chop the chives and sprinkle over the salad before serving.

Spicy Rice Salad
225 g/8 oz rice
1 tablespoon curry powder
450 g/1 lb boned cooked chicken
2 pears
3 slices canned pineapple
½ (425-g/15-oz) can mandarin
  segments
1 tablespoon chopped pistachio
  nuts (optional)
3 tablespoons lemon juice
salt and pepper
5 tablespoons oil

Cook the rice following the instructions on the packet, adding the curry powder to the cooking water. Rinse through with cold water and leave to drain. Remove any skin from

256

the chicken and dice the meat. Peel, halve, core and dice the pears. Drain and chop the pineapple and mandarins. Mix all these ingredients together in a serving bowl, and add the pistachios, if used.

Beat the lemon juice with the salt, pepper and oil and pour over the rice salad.

Pasta Salad
450 g/1 lb luncheon meat
225 g/8 oz Cheddar or Tilsit
*   cheese*
225 g/8 oz pickled cucumbers
1 red pepper
100 g/4 oz cooked peas
575 g/1¼ lb cooked pasta shells
*   or noodles*
3 tablespoons wine vinegar
salt and white pepper
6 tablespoons oil

Remove the skin from the luncheon meat and dice the meat, together with the cheese. Drain and slice the pickled

cucumbers. Wash and quarter the red pepper, remove the seeds and pith and dice the flesh. Mix the luncheon meat, cheese, cucumber and red pepper together in a bowl and add the cooked peas and pasta shells or noodles.

Beat the vinegar with the salt, pepper and oil and stir the dressing into the salad.

Stuffed French Bread
2 long French loaves
8 tablespoons mayonnaise
100 g/4 oz Mortadella or
*   Cervelat sausage*
100 g/4 oz salami
100 g/4 oz smoked cheese
3 large tomatoes
3 hard-boiled eggs
parsley sprigs
few lettuce leaves
100 g/4 oz blue cheese (Danish
*   Blue, Dolcelatte)*
450 g/1 lb meat salad (bought
*   ready-made, or use any meat*
*   salad from the salad section)*

Cut the loaves in half lengthways and spread the insides with the mayonnaise. Slice the Mortadella or Cervelat, together with the salami and smoked cheese. Fold the slices in half and arrange at intervals along the bottom half of one loaf. Wash and dry the tomatoes. Shell the eggs. Cut 2 tomatoes and 2 eggs into slices, and the remaining tomato and egg into wedges. Arrange the sliced egg and tomato in the intervals between the cold meat and cheese slices. Garnish the loaf with sprigs of parsley and cover with the top half.

Wash the lettuce, drain thoroughly and use to line the bottom half of the second loaf. Slice the blue cheese. Arrange the meat salad in spoonfuls on the lettuce leaves, alternating with slices of blue cheese and the remaining tomato and egg wedges. Top with the other half of the loaf.

Summer Fruit Dessert
225 g/8 oz morello cherries
225 g/8 oz raspberries
225 g/8 oz redcurrants
225 g/8 oz sugar
50 g/2 oz cornflour
250 ml/8 fl oz double cream
¼ teaspoon cinnamon

Pick over the fruit, stone the cherries, place in a pan with 450 ml/¾ pint water, bring to the boil and simmer for 5 minutes. Pass the fruit through a sieve and top up the purée with water to 1 litre/1¾ pints. Add 200 g/7 oz sugar and bring back to the boil. Mix the cornflour with a little cold water, stir into the fruit purée and simmer for 3 minutes, stirring continuously. Pour the fruit mixture into a bowl and leave to set in the refrigerator. Before serving, whip the cream with the remaining sugar until stiff, spoon onto the dessert and sprinkle with cinnamon.

Country Buffet

Serves 6-8

A country buffet calls to mind fresh granary bread, rolls, country butter, crisp radishes, fresh fruit and several varieties of cheese, such as Cheddar, Cheshire, Wensleydale, Stilton. Camembert and Emmental. You can also serve a selection of cold meats (illustrated here are roast pork, smoked ham, liver sausage and salami), a mixed salad, and a herring dish, for contrast. Draught beer and cider are both favourite accompaniments to country fare. Here are some additional recipe ideas.

Cheese and Onion Dip
1 large onion
1 clove garlic
150 ml/¼ pint milk
675 g/1½ lb curd cheese, or sieved cottage cheese
salt
few sprigs fresh mixed herbs (parsley, dill, chives)

Peel and finely dice the onion and garlic. Stir the milk into the curd cheese, or sieved cottage cheese, and add the diced onion, garlic and salt. Transfer the cheese dip to a bowl and garnish with the sprigs of fresh herbs.

Camembert Pâté
½ teaspoon caraway seeds
1 small onion
225 g/8 oz mature Camembert cheese
75 g/3 oz soft butter
1 teaspoon paprika pepper
¼ teaspoon white pepper
1 hard-boiled egg
sprig parsley

Grind the caraway seeds with a mortar and pestle. Peel and finely dice the onion. Place the Camembert in a bowl, crush with a fork and mix with the butter, caraway, diced onion, paprika and white pepper. Arrange the Camembert pâté on a plate. Shell and slice the egg and use to garnish the pâté, together with the parsley.

Redcurrant Dessert Soup
800 g/1¾ lb redcurrants
225 g/8 oz sugar
1 tablespoon cornflour

Wash and drain the redcurrants. Bring 1 litre/1¾ pints water to the boil in a pan with the sugar, stirring continuously. Add the redcurrants, cover the pan and simmer over a low heat for 3 minutes. Dissolve the cornflour in a little cold water and stir into the redcurrants. Bring once more to the boil and simmer gently for 1 minute. Take the pan off the heat, pour the redcurrant soup into a large shallow bowl and chill thoroughly. Serve with cream.

Cheese Platter with Gorgonzola Cream

CHEESE PLATTER
100 g/4 oz Bavarian smoked
  cheese with ham
100 g/4 oz Tilsit or Havarti
100 g/4 oz Stilton
225 g/8 oz Emmental
100 g/4 oz Camembert
GARNISH
black olives
grapes
shelled walnuts
small salted pretzels
GORGONZOLA CREAM
100 g/4 oz Gorgonzola cheese
50 g/2 oz soft butter
1 egg yolk
1 tablespoon single cream
generous pinch cayenne pepper
1 tablespoon chopped fresh
  mixed herbs (optional)
100 g/4 oz ham, unsliced

Cut the Bavarian smoked cheese, the Tilsit or Havarti, the Stilton and half the Emmental into thin slices. Cut the remaining Emmental into cubes and the Camembert into wedges. Arrange the sliced cheese and the Camembert wedges on a cheese board. Thread each Emmental cube onto a cocktail stick, together with an olive or a grape, and place on the board. Arrange the walnuts and pretzels over the cheese.

To make the Gorgonzola cream, place the Gorgonzola in a bowl and mash with a fork. Beat in the butter, egg yolk, cream, cayenne, and the herbs, if used. Finely dice the ham and stir into the mixture, and serve the Gorgonzola cream separately with the platter.
Serves 6

Country Cheese Board

100 g/4 oz mature Camembert
  cheese
100 g/4 oz Emmental cheese
  grated
50 g/2 oz soft butter
1 egg yolk
1 teaspoon paprika pepper
salt and white pepper
1 tablespoon brandy
2 slices pumpernickel bread
3 tablespoons chopped pistachio
  nuts
900 g/2 lb assorted cheeses
  (such as Limburger, Havarti,
  Gouda, Wensleydale,
  Cheshire, Rambol Poivre)
1 Spanish onion
bunch radishes

Place the Camembert in a large bowl and crush it with a fork. Work in the Emmental, butter, egg yolk, paprika, salt, pepper and brandy, and leave to stand in a cool place for 2 hours.

Crumble the pumpernickel very finely. Form the Camembert mixture into balls and dip half the balls in the chopped pistachios and the other half in the pumpernickel crumbs.

Cut your selection of cheeses into thick slices. Peel the onion and cut into rings. Wash the radishes. Arrange the sliced cheese on a large cheeseboard and garnish with the onion rings, radishes and cheese balls. *Serves 6*

Smörgåsbord

Serves 10-12

MEAT PLATTER
1 kg/2¼ lb assorted cold meats
1 hard-boiled egg
HERRING PLATTER
10 pickled herring fillets
5 small cooked carrots
bunch dill
8 maatjes herring fillets
1 onion
2 tomatoes, quartered
RED HERRING SALAD
10 maatjes herring fillets
500 ml/17 fl oz milk
175 g/6 oz pickled beetroot
2 crisp dessert apples
150 ml/¼ pint soured cream
2 tablespoons mayonnaise
1 slice lemon
GREEN HERRING SALAD
10 maatjes herring fillets
*3 tablespoons chopped dill or
  parsley*
juice of 2 lemons
6 tablespoons oil

2 green peppers
*1 (283-g/10-oz) can green
  beans*
*175 g/6 oz pickled cocktail
  onions*
275 g/10 oz canned pimiento
MEATBALLS
50 g/2 oz butter
1 onion
1 tablespoon chopped parsley
450 g/1 lb minced beef
1 egg
*6 tablespoons fresh
  breadcrumbs*
salt
½ teaspoon dried marjoram
1 teaspoon paprika pepper
4 tablespoons oil

Arrange the sliced cold meats
on a serving platter or board.
Shell and quarter the egg and
use to garnish the platter.

For the herring platter,
drain the pickled herring fillets.
Cut the carrots in half
widthways and wrap each half
in a herring fillet. Garnish with
a sprig of dill and arrange in a

circle round the edge of a flat
dish. Drain the maatjes
herrings and place in the centre
of the dish. Wash and quarter
the tomatoes. Peel the onion
and slice into rings. Garnish
the herring platter with the
tomato and onion.

To make the red herring
salad, soak the salted herring
fillets in the milk for 30
minutes, then drain and cut
into pieces. Drain and chop the
beetroot. Wash, quarter, core
and dice the apples. Mix the
herring, beetroot and apple
together in a bowl. Beat the
soured cream with the
mayonnaise, and stir into the
salad ingredients. Garnish the
red herring salad with a sprig
of dill and a slice of lemon.

To make the green herring
salad, chop the salted herrings
and place in a bowl with the
dill or parsley, the lemon juice
and oil. Trim and quarter the
green peppers, remove the
seeds and pith, and dice. Drain

and chop the beans, cocktail
onions and pimiento. Mix all
these ingredients into the
herring and leave to stand.

For the meatballs, melt the
butter in a pan. Peel and finely
dice the onion, and fry in the
butter with the parsley. Place
in a bowl with the minced beef,
the egg, breadcrumbs, salt,
marjoram and paprika, mix
well together and shape into
small balls. Heat the oil in a
frying pan and fry the
meatballs for 8-10 minutes,
turning continuously. Transfer
to a serving bowl and leave to
cool.

Smörgåsbord Favourites

For each:

Egg and Tongue
1 hard-boiled egg
1 large slice brown bread
7 g/¼ oz soft butter
2–3 lettuce leaves
50 g/2 oz sliced smoked tongue
2 stuffed olives
¼ teaspoon capers

Shell and slice the egg. Spread the bread with the butter. Top with the lettuce, smoked tongue, egg, olives and capers.

Mariner's Breakfast
25 g/1 oz soft butter
1 large slice brown bread
2 smoked trout fillets
1 egg
1 teaspoon single cream
salt and pepper
a little chopped fresh parsley

Spread some butter on the bread and top with the trout fillets. Beat the egg with the cream, salt and pepper. Melt the remaining butter in a pan and scramble the egg mixture over a low heat. Spoon onto the trout and sprinkle with parsley.

Prawn and Mock Caviare
50 g/2 oz frozen or canned
  prawns
1 large slice white bread
7 g/¼ oz soft butter
2–3 lettuce leaves
twist of lime
1 teaspoon lumpfish roe

Allow frozen prawns to thaw or drain canned prawns. Spread the bread with the butter and top with the lettuce. Arrange the prawns on top and garnish with a twist of lime and the lumpfish roe.

Roast Beef and Egg
1 large slice brown bread
7 g/¼ oz soft butter
2–3 lettuce leaves
2 slices cold roast beef
1 wedge hard-boiled egg
½ teaspoon grated horseradish
  (optional)
sprig parsley

Spread the bread with the butter. Top with the lettuce, roast beef slices, egg, horseradish and parsley.

Rollmop Herring
1 slice white bread
7 g/¼ oz soft butter
2–3 lettuce leaves
2 rollmop herrings
½ onion, cut widthways
4–5 capers

Spread the bread with the butter and top with the lettuce and rollmop herrings. Slice the onion into rings and place on the rollmops, together with the capers.

Blue Cheese and Walnut
1 slice crispbread
7 g/¼ oz soft butter
1 large tomato, sliced
salt and pepper
2 small slices Stilton cheese
1 shelled walnut

Spread the crispbread with the butter, top with the sliced tomato and season with salt and pepper. Arrange the Stilton on the tomato and garnish with the walnut.

Pâté and Bacon
1 round slice white bread
7 g/¼ oz soft butter
2–3 lettuce leaves
2 slices smooth liver pâté
1 bacon rasher

Spread the bread with the butter and top with the lettuce and liver pâté. Fry the bacon until crisp, cool slightly and place over the liver pâté.

Dips for Vegetables

Serve these dips with strips or slices of raw vegetables, such as fennel, celery, red, green and yellow peppers, chicory and tomatoes.

Tomato Dip

100 g/4 oz tomato purée
1 (150-g/5.3-oz) carton natural
  yogurt
pinch each salt, cayenne pepper
  and sugar
1 teaspoon lemon juice
bunch chives
2 tablespoons pickled green
  peppercorns (optional)

Beat together the tomato purée, yogurt, salt, cayenne, sugar and lemon juice. Wash, drain and finely chop the chives and stir into the mixture. Drain the green peppercorns, if used, crush lightly with a fork and add to the dip.

Herb Dip

1 (150-g/5.3-oz) carton natural
  yogurt
100 g/4 oz full fat cream cheese
1 tablespoon single cream
½ clove garlic
½ teaspoon celery salt
pinch white pepper
4 tablespoons chopped fresh
  mixed herbs

Beat the yogurt with the cream cheese and cream until smooth. Peel and crush the garlic and add to the mixture, together with the celery salt, pepper and chopped herbs.

Orange Dip

100 g/4 oz mayonnaise
2 tablespoons double cream
juice and thinly peeled rind of
  1 orange
1 tablespoon mild French
  mustard
pinch each salt, white pepper
  and sugar

Beat the mayonnaise with the cream, the orange juice and rind (reserving a little for garnishing), the mustard, salt, pepper and sugar. Transfer the dip to a bowl and garnish with the remaining orange rind.

Artichoke Dips

TOMATO DIP
2 tomatoes
100 g/4 oz mayonnaise
3 tablespoons tomato purée
2 tablespoons double cream
5 drops Tabasco sauce
pinch each salt and sugar
1 tablespoon paprika pepper
EGG DIP
3 hard-boiled eggs
8 tablespoons olive oil
3 tablespoons wine vinegar
1 teaspoon mild French mustard
salt and white pepper
1 teaspoon capers
1 tablespoon chopped parsley
1 tablespoon chopped lemon
  balm leaves (optional)
MAYONNAISE DIP
100 g/4 oz mayonnaise
2 teaspoons lemon juice
3 tablespoons double cream

Peel and quarter the tomatoes, remove the seeds and finely dice the flesh. Beat with the mayonnaise, tomato purée, cream, and seasonings.

Shell and halve the eggs. Take out the yolks, pass them through a fine sieve and beat with the oil, vinegar, mustard, salt and pepper. Drain the capers, crush lightly with a fork and stir into the mixture, followed by the parsley and lemon balm, if used. Add the egg whites, chopped very finely.

Beat the mayonnaise with the lemon juice. Whip the cream until thick and fold in.

Cook's Tip

To cook the artichokes: cut a slice off the stalk end of each, place them in boiling salted water and simmer over a low heat for 30 minutes until tender.

Sausage Dips

GARLIC DIP
4 hard-boiled eggs
2 egg yolks
salt and pepper
juice of 1 lemon
4 cloves garlic
150 ml/¼ pint olive oil
GORGONZOLA DIP
50 g/2 oz soft butter
100 g/4 oz Gorgonzola cheese
1 (150-g/5.3-oz) carton natural
  yogurt
CREAM DIP
2 hard-boiled eggs
50 g/2 oz butter
1 tablespoon wine vinegar
salt and white pepper
pinch paprika pepper
few drops Worcestershire sauce
2 tablespoons finely chopped
  chives
150 ml/¼ pint soured cream
150 ml/¼ pint double cream

Shell and halve the hard-boiled eggs. Take out the yolks, pass through a fine sieve and mix with the raw egg yolks, salt, pepper and lemon juice. Peel and crush the garlic and add to the mixture. Gradually beat in the oil, a little at a time, to make a creamy mayonnaise. Chop the hard-boiled egg whites, stir into the dip and serve.

Beat the butter until light and fluffy. Pass the Gorgonzola through a sieve and mix into the butter, together with the yogurt.

For the cream dip, shell and halve the eggs. Pass the yolks through a sieve and finely chop the whites. Beat the butter until light and fluffy, and work in the vinegar, salt, pepper, paprika, Worcestershire sauce, chives, soured cream, egg white and egg yolk. Lightly whip the double cream and fold into the dip.

Steak Tartare Buffet-style

5 large onions
40 stuffed olives
4 pickled cucumbers
8 canned anchovy fillets
large bunch each parsley and
    chives
salt and white pepper
paprika pepper
caraway seeds
tomato ketchup
brandy
capers
9 eggs
1.5 kg/3 lb minced fillet steak

Peel the onions, finely dice four of them and cut the fifth into rings. Chop the olives. Finely dice the pickled cucumbers. Cut the anchovy fillets in half lengthways. Wash, drain and chop the parsley and chives. Arrange the diced onion, olives, cucumber, anchovy, parsley, chives, salt, pepper, paprika, caraway seeds, tomato ketchup, brandy and capers in separate small bowls. Break the eggs and separate, taking care not to break the yolks. Keep the whites to use in another recipe. Return each yolk carefully to its shell. Sprinkle a dish with rock salt and stand eight of the filled shells in the salt.

Place the minced steak on a serving platter, top with the onion rings and garnish with the remaining egg yolk in its shell. Each guest takes a portion of steak tartare and mixes it with the seasonings and accompaniments to taste. Serve with a generous amount of brown bread. *Serves 8*

Individual Steaks Tartare
If you prefer, you can arrange the steak tartare on eight individual plates. Surround each helping of steak tartare with onion rings, and fill the rings with diced onion, olives, capers, paprika, salt, white pepper, caraway seeds, chives and parsley. Add brandy and tomato ketchup. Place an egg yolk in a shell on each portion, and serve with separate bowls containing any of the accompaniments listed in the previous recipe, as well as others such as baby gherkins, canned baby sweet corn cobs, pickled cocktail onions, and mixed pickles.

Cook's Tip

Alternatively, you can mix all the spices, herbs, diced ingredients and egg yolks into the steak tartare in the kitchen, and serve on a large serving dish. Be careful not to over-season though, as guests' tastes are bound to vary. Place extra salt and seasoning on the table so that the guests can help themselves.

Spit Roast Pork with Herb Mayonnaise

*1 kg/2¼ lb neck end of pork,
    boned and rolled, or boned
    knuckle of pork*
½ clove garlic
2 tablespoons oil
1 teaspoon salt
1 tablespoon strong mustard
*½ teaspoon each dried thyme
    and marjoram*
225 g/8 oz mayonnaise
1 gherkin
bunch chives
bunch parsley
*small bunch fresh dill, or
    1 teaspoon dried dill*
2 hard-boiled eggs
GARNISH
*1 tablespoon chopped onion
asparagus (optional)*

Wash the meat in cold water
and wipe dry. Peel and crush
the garlic clove. Beat the oil

with the salt, garlic, mustard,
thyme and marjoram and rub
the mixture well into the meat.
Preheat the grill to moderate
(180 C, 350 F, Gas Mark 4).
Thread the joint onto the spit
and grill for up to 1 hour
40 minutes, until cooked right
through. Remove the pork
from the spit and leave to cool,
then arrange on a flat serving
dish.

Pour the mayonnaise into a
bowl. Finely chop the gherkin.
Wash, dry and finely chop the
chives and parsley, and the
fresh dill, if used. Shell and
chop the eggs. Mix all the
chopped ingredients into the
mayonnaise and serve with the
pork, together with freshly
cooked asparagus, if liked.
Garnish the dish with chopped
onion. *Serves 6*

Braised Veal 'Mostarda'

1 kg/2¼ lb fillet of veal
1 teaspoon salt
*¼ teaspoon each white pepper,
    dried rosemary and dried
    sage*
½ teaspoon paprika pepper
1 onion
*a selection of fresh vegetables in
    season (carrots, celery, leek)*
4 tablespoons oil
100 ml/4 fl oz hot meat stock
100 ml/4 fl oz white wine
225 g/8 oz crystallised fruits

Rinse the meat in cold water
and wipe dry. Mix together the
salt, pepper, herbs and
paprika, and rub the mixture
into the meat. Peel the onion
and cut into quarters. Wash
and trim the fresh vegetables,
allow to drain and chop
coarsely. Heat the oil in a
flameproof casserole, add the

meat and brown in the oil for
10 minutes, turning from time
to time. Add the onion and the
chopped mixed vegetables and
continue frying for a few
minutes. Pour the meat stock
and white wine into the
casserole, cover with a tightly
fitting lid, and place in a hot
oven (220 C, 425 F, Gas
Mark 7). Braise the veal for
60–70 minutes, basting often
during cooking. Remove from
the casserole and leave to cool.

Before serving, carve the
meat into thin slices and
arrange on a platter. Serve the
crystallised fruits separately.
Serves 6

Ham and Salad Platter

175 g/6 oz frozen peas
1 large avocado
1 teaspoon lemon juice
½ red pepper
1 gherkin
100 g/4 oz ham sausage,
    unsliced
4 tablespoons mayonnaise
salt and white pepper
¼ teaspoon curry powder
few sprigs dill
1 crisp dessert apple
2 tablespoons fresh grated
    horseradish, or bottled
    creamed horseradish
250 ml/8 fl oz double cream
generous pinch sugar
400 g/14 oz smoked or boiled
    ham
450 g/1 lb smoked or cold roast
    pork
GARNISH
2 hard-boiled eggs
black grapes

2 tomatoes
½ honeydew melon
5 gherkins
5 chillies
canned baby sweet corn cobs
parsley sprigs

Cook the peas following the
instructions on the packet,
drain and leave to cool. Wash
and dry the avocado, cut in
half lengthways and remove
the stone. Scoop the flesh out
of each half, to within ½ cm/
¼ inch of the shell, and dice.
Sprinkle the diced avocado
and the inside of the shells with
lemon juice.

Wash and dry the red
pepper, remove the seeds and
pith and cut the flesh into
strips. Drain the gherkin and
cut also into strips, together
with the ham sausage. Place
the peas, diced avocado, red
pepper, gherkin and ham
sausage together in a bowl and
mix well. Beat the mayonnaise
with the salt, pepper and curry

powder, and stir into the salad.
Fill the avocado halves with
the salad and garnish each with
a sprig of dill.

Peel, quarter, core and finely
grate the apple, and place in a
bowl with the horseradish.
Whip the cream with the sugar
until stiff and fold into the
horseradish and apple mixture.
Taste and adjust seasoning,
then transfer the horseradish
and apple cream to a piping
bag fitted with a large plain
nozzle. Cut six slices from the
smoked or boiled ham, roll up
the slices and pipe horseradish
cream into each. Cover a large
serving platter with the
smoked or roast pork. Arrange
the ham rolls on top. Cut a few
more slices of ham, fold in half
and place at one end of the
dish, together with the
remaining uncut piece of ham.
Arrange the stuffed avocado
halves at the other end of the
dish.

Shell and slice the eggs.

Wash and drain the grapes.
Quarter the tomatoes. Cut the
melon into wedges and remove
the seeds. Drain the gherkins,
and slice into a fan-shape, if
liked. Garnish the platter with
the egg, grapes, tomato
quarters, melon wedges,
gherkins, chillies, baby sweet
corn cobs and parsley. Serve
with toasted white bread,
brown bread, rye bread and
butter. *Serves 6-8*

Giant Meat Platter

225 g/8 oz ham
225 g/8 oz smoked ham
100 g/4 oz smoked Parma ham
100 g/4 oz salami
225 g/8 oz tongue sausage or
  cooked tongue
225 g/8 oz ham sausage or
  Mortadella sausage
100 g/4 oz meat loaf
100 g/4 oz liver sausage
450 g/1 lb brawn sausage
400 g/14 oz finely minced fillet
  steak
2 onions
salt and white pepper
¼ teaspoon paprika pepper
2 egg yolks
few lettuce leaves
2 tablespoons oil
2 teaspoons wine vinegar
1 tablespoon caraway seeds
2 hard-boiled eggs
2-4 tomatoes
bunch radishes

coarsely ground black pepper
GARNISH
parsley sprigs
a selection of pickled vegetables
  such as baby gherkins,
  canned pimiento, canned
  baby sweet corn cobs and
  olives

Arrange all the cold meats
except for the brawn sausage
on a large serving platter or
board, as shown.

Place the minced steak in a
bowl. Peel and dice one onion
and mix half into the minced
steak with the salt, white
pepper, paprika and one egg
yolk. Wash the lettuce, drain
thoroughly and arrange in one
corner of the meat platter. Top
with the minced steak tartare.
Make a well in the centre of
the meat and carefully tip in
the second egg yolk. Place the
rest of the diced onion next to
the egg and sprinkle with a
little paprika.

Arrange the brawn sausage

on a separate flat dish. Peel the
remaining onion, slice into
rings and arrange over the
brawn. Beat the oil with the
vinegar, pour over the brawn
and sprinkle with the caraway
seeds.

Shell and slice the hard-
boiled eggs. Wash and dry the
tomatoes and cut each into
eight wedges. Wash the
radishes and leave to drain.
Arrange the sliced egg and a
few tomato wedges on the
platter, and sprinkle the egg
with coarsely ground black
pepper. Serve the remaining
tomato wedges and the
radishes separately. Garnish
the platter with parsley and a
selection of pickled vegetables,
and serve with various kinds of
bread, rolls and crispbreads.
Serves 8-10

Cook's Tip

You can of course serve
any kind of cold meat at
a buffet and the ones
listed are intended only
as suggestions. The steak
tartare can be replaced
with a meat or sausage
salad, a Waldorf or even
a crab salad. Slices of
pâté, terrine or cold
roast meat can be
substituted for the
brawn sausage, and you
can vary the garnishes
with sliced fresh
cucumber, celery and red
and green peppers,
depending on what is in
season.

Stilton Spread

175 g/6 oz Stilton cheese (or
   other blue cheese)
100 g/4 oz sliced salami
3 small gherkins
10 pickled cocktail onions
4 shelled walnuts
1 teaspoon grated horseradish
1 tablespoon natural yogurt
3 tablespoons mayonnaise
pinch salt
5 drops Tabasco sauce

Place the cheese in a large bowl
and break up with a fork. Cut
the salami into thin strips.
Finely dice the gherkins. Drain
and chop the cocktail onions.
Chop the walnuts. Stir salami,
gherkins, onions and walnuts
into the cheese, together with
the horseradish, yogurt,
mayonnaise, salt and Tabasco
sauce. Adjust the seasoning.

Egg and Pepper Spread

5 hard-boiled eggs
200 g/7 oz soft butter
½ red pepper
1 small onion, peeled
¼ teaspoon salt
pinch each celery salt, white
   pepper, curry powder and
   cayenne pepper

Cut the eggs in half and
remove the yolks. Place the egg
yolks and butter in a bowl and
mix together until smooth.
Finely dice the egg whites.
Wash the pepper, remove the
seeds and dice the flesh finely,
together with the onion. Stir
the diced egg white, pepper
and onion into the butter and
egg yolk mixture. Season with
salt, celery salt, pepper, curry
powder and cayenne.

Emmental Spread

225 g/8 oz Emmental cheese
4 canned baby sweet corn cobs,
   drained
10 stuffed olives
½ clove garlic
small bunch fresh mixed herbs
   (dill, chives, parsley and
   rosemary) or a generous
   pinch of each herb in its dried
   form
175 g/6 oz soft butter
1 teaspoon pickled green
   peppercorns (optional)
salt and pepper

Finely dice the cheese. Finely
chop the sweet corn cobs and
olives. Peel and crush the
garlic, and wash, dry and chop
the fresh herbs, if used.
   Beat the butter until light
and fluffy. Work in the cheese,
sweet corn, olives, garlic and
herbs. Drain and add the

peppercorns, if used. Season to
taste, cover and leave to stand
in the refrigerator for
1–2 hours.

Savoury Cream Cheese Layer

1 (370-g/13-oz) packet frozen
    puff pastry
1 teaspoon pickled green
    peppercorns (optional)
900 g/2 lb full fat cream cheese,
    or curd cheese
2 teaspoons mild French
    mustard
8 drops Tabasco sauce
1 medium onion, grated
1 teaspoon each salt and
    Worcestershire sauce
2 teaspoons tomato purée
1 teaspoon paprika pepper
2 tablespoons chopped fresh
    mixed herbs, or 2 teaspoons
    dried mixed herbs
1 (57-g/2-oz) packet flaked
    almonds
GARNISH
10 chillies
10 pickled cocktail onions
10 thin slices smoked ham

Thaw the puff pastry following
the instructions on the packet.
Sprinkle a large baking tray
with cold water. Roll the
pastry out into three rounds,
each 25 cm/10 inches in
diameter, and place the rounds
individually on the baking
tray. Leave to stand for
15 minutes, then bake in a hot
oven (220 c, 425 f, Gas
Mark 7) for 12–15 minutes and
leave to cool.
    Chop the green peppercorns,
if used. Beat the cream or curd
cheese with the mustard,
Tabasco sauce, onion, salt and
Worcestershire sauce until
smooth and divide into three
portions. Stir the tomato
purée and paprika into the
first portion, and the green
peppercorns, if used, and herbs
into the second. Spread the
first pastry round with the
tomato mixture, the second
with the herb mixture and the
third with half the remaining
cream or curd cheese. Stack
the rounds one on top of
another, beginning with the
tomato round, then the herb
round and topping with the
plain cheese round. Lightly
toast the almonds and press
round the edge of the cake.
Transfer the rest of the cheese
to a piping bag fitted with a
star-shaped nozzle and pipe
rosettes round the top of the
cake. Garnish with the chillies,
onions and rolls of ham.

Chicken and Vegetable Mould

1 onion
2 large raw carrots
1 (1.25-kg/2½-lb) boiling
  chicken
1 teaspoon salt
20 g/¾ oz gelatine
2 tablespoons vinegar
¼ teaspoon Worcestershire
  sauce
pinch pepper
100 g/4 oz canned asparagus
  tips
50 g/2 oz canned sliced
  mushrooms
2 hard-boiled eggs
2 tomatoes
1 large cooked carrot
1 large gherkin
150 g/5 oz peas, cooked

Peel the onion and cut it in half. Wash and trim the carrots. Place the chicken in a large saucepan, cover with water and add the onion halves, carrots and salt. Bring to the boil, cover and simmer for an hour. Remove the chicken, strain the stock and leave both to cool.

Reheat 1 litre/1¾ pints chicken stock, but do not allow to boil. Pour 2 tablespoons of the hot stock in a bowl and stand in a pan of hot water. Sprinkle with the gelatine and stir until dissolved, then return to the rest of the stock. Add the vinegar, Worcestershire sauce and pepper. Rinse out a 1.15-litre/2-pint soufflé or gratin dish with a little of the gelatine liquid and place in the refrigerator to set.

Remove the skin and bones from the chicken and cut the meat into small pieces. Drain the asparagus tips and sliced mushrooms. Shell and slice the eggs. Wash, dry and slice the tomatoes, together with the cooked carrot and the gherkin. Mix all the ingredients together, add the cooked peas and place in the dish on top of the layer of jelly. Pour over the remaining jelly and leave to set in the refrigerator. *Serves 4–6*

Ham and Vegetable Mould

275 g/10 oz frozen mixed
vegetables
3–4 large carrots
1 tablespoon bone marrow jelly
generous pinch each salt and
grated nutmeg
20 g/¾ oz gelatine
250 ml/8 fl oz fat-free meat
stock
250 ml/8 fl oz white wine
3 tablespoons vinegar
1 hard-boiled egg, sliced
few chives and celery leaves
225 g/8 oz sliced ham

Bring 450 ml/¾ pint salted
water to the boil in a pan, add
the frozen vegetables and cook
for 12 minutes. Remove the
vegetables from the water and
allow to cool.

Wash, trim and peel the
carrots, place together with the
bone marrow jelly in the
vegetable water and simmer
for 20 minutes. Drain the
carrots, blend in the liquidiser
and season with the salt and
nutmeg. Heat the carrot purée
gently and sprinkle with a
quarter of the gelatine, stirring
until the gelatine has dissolved.

Heat the meat stock, wine,
and vinegar together in a pan.
Pour 2 tablespoons of the hot
liquid in a bowl and stand in a
pan of hot water. Sprinkle
with the remaining gelatine,
stir until dissolved and return
to the rest of the stock. Line a
1.15-litre/2-pint mould with
a thin layer of the meat aspic
and allow to set. Arrange the
egg slices, chives and celery
leaves on top. Pour over
another layer of aspic and
leave to set. Spread this layer
with the carrot purée and allow
to set. Build up the rest of the
mould in layers of mixed
vegetables and slices of ham,
pouring aspic between the
layers and allowing each layer
to set before adding the next.
Place the finished aspic in the
refrigerator to set completely.

Salmon in Riesling

10 peppercorns
juice of 1 lemon
4 (150-g/5-oz) fresh salmon
  cutlets
450 g/1 lb fresh or canned
  asparagus
25 g/1 oz gelatine
20 g/¾ oz truffles (optional)
6 small tomatoes
1 egg white, whisked
500 ml/17 fl oz dry Riesling

Bring 750 ml/1¼ pints salted water to the boil in a pan with the peppercorns and lemon juice. Add the salmon cutlets and poach very gently for 10 minutes. Remove the salmon from the water, dry and wrap in cooking foil.

Lightly scrape the lower stems of the fresh asparagus; cut into 2-cm/1-inch lengths. Simmer in the salmon stock until the asparagus is soft.

Lift out of the stock, drain and allow to cool. Drain the canned asparagus, if used. Unwrap the salmon cutlets, place each on a plate and sprinkle with asparagus and chopped truffle, if used. Cut the tomatoes in half and place three halves on each plate. Clarify the salmon stock with the whisked egg white by bringing the stock to the boil, adding the egg white and simmering for 2 minutes. Take off the heat and leave to stand until the egg white gathers on top of the stock. Strain through a piece of clean muslin or a sieve lined with a treble thickness of absorbent kitchen paper. Measure out 750 ml/8 fl oz of stock into a bowl and stand in a pan of hot water. Sprinkle with the gelatine and stir until dissolved. Add the wine and pour the gelatine liquid into the individual soup plates. Place in the refrigerator until set. *Serves 4*

Haddock Mould

450 g/1 lb white fish (coley,
  whiting) and fish trimmings
½ teaspoon salt
juice of 1½ lemons
a selection of fresh vegetables in
  season, chopped
800 g/1¾ lbs haddock fillet
1 (177-g/6¼-oz) can shrimps
3 hard-boiled eggs
200 g/7 oz carrots
150 g/5 oz cooked peas
1 egg white, whisked
100 ml/4 fl oz dry white wine
20 g/¾ oz gelatine
few dill or parsley sprigs

For the stock, place the white fish and the fish trimmings in a large pan and cover with 2 litres/3½ pints water. Add the salt, half the lemon juice, and chopped vegetables and simmer for 20-30 minutes.

Sprinkle the haddock with the remaining lemon juice and poach in 1 litre/1¾ pints salted water for 10 minutes. Drain the haddock and leave to cool, then remove the skin and cut the fish into large pieces.

Rinse the shrimps and dry. Shell the eggs and cut each into six wedges. Cut the carrots into fine strips, blanch in a little boiling water for 2 minutes, then drain. Mix together the haddock, shrimps, egg, peas and carrots and divide between four soup plates. Strain the fish stock, clarify with the egg white (see Salmon in Riesling) and strain again, then boil until reduced to 750 ml/1¼ pints. Take the pan off the heat and pour in the wine. Pour 2 tablespoons warm water into a bowl and stand in a pan of hot water. Sprinkle with the gelatine and stir until dissolved, then add to the stock. Pour the liquid into the four soup plates and place in the refrigerator to set. Garnish with dill or parsley. *Serves 4*

272

Summer Salad Mould

8 white peppercorns
large bunch fresh mixed herbs
    (parsley, sage, chervil,
    tarragon, thyme)
small bunch dill or chives
bunch parsley
1 small cauliflower
225 g/8 oz frozen peas
25 g/1 oz gelatine
450 ml/¾ pint white wine
generous pinch each salt, white
    pepper and sugar
few drops lemon juice
2 hard-boiled eggs
½ red or yellow pepper
few mint sprigs

Bring 250 ml/8 fl oz salted
water to the boil in a pan and
add the peppercorns. Wash
and dry all the herbs. Place the
mixed herbs in the boiling
water, cover the pan, and
simmer over a low heat for

10 minutes. Strain the liquid
and transfer to another pan.
Wash the cauliflower and
break into florets, cutting off
any excess stalk. Place the
florets in the herb stock, cover
and simmer over a low heat for
15 minutes. Take the florets
out of the pan, plunge into
cold water, drain and cool.

Place the peas in the stock,
cover and cook over a low
heat for about 3 minutes.
Remove from the pan, plunge
into cold water, drain and
leave to cool. Take the pan off
the heat, sprinkle with the
gelatine and stir until
thoroughly dissolved. Add
enough white wine to make the
stock up to 750 ml/1¾ pints,
topping up with water if
necessary. Season with the salt,
pepper, sugar and lemon juice
and leave to cool.

Rinse out a 1.4-litre/2½-pint
jelly mould with cold water
and pour 'aspic' into it up to
5 mm/¼ inch high. Place in the

refrigerator to set. Shell and
slice the eggs. Wash the
pepper, remove the seeds and
cut into thin strips. Finely
chop all but a few of the
chives, if used. Arrange the
egg, strips of pepper, dill sprigs
or chopped chives on top of
the mould, keeping back a few
dill sprigs or chives for the
garnish. Pour over a little more
'aspic' and return to the
refrigerator to set, then add
half the peas followed by all
the cauliflower. Cover with
more 'aspic' and return to the
refrigerator to set. Remove the
parsley sprigs from the stems,
keeping a few sprigs on one
side for the garnish. Place the
parsley on top of the
cauliflower layer, top with the
remaining peas and pour on
the remaining gelatine liquid.
Return to the refrigerator for
3-4 hours to set completely.
Before serving, loosen the
edges with a sharp knife. Dip
the mould in hot water for a

few seconds and turn out the
salad mould onto a plate.
Garnish with the remaining
parsley, dill or chives, and the
mint sprigs.

Classic Oysters

For each:
12–16 oysters
2–3 wedges lemon

Clean the oysters under cold running water and dry them. Hold one oyster at a time in a damp cloth with the domed side of the shell in the palm of your hand and, with a sharp movement of the oyster opener or a strong knife, open the pointed edge or 'hinge' of the oyster. Make sure that any sea water trapped inside the shell does not escape, as this adds to the flavour. With a kitchen knife, loosen the muscle all round the edge inside the shell. Remove the top half of the shell, leaving the oyster in the bottom half, and place all the half-shells containing oysters on a dish. If you do not have a special oyster plate, sprinkle a layer of rock salt 1 cm/½ inch

thick over an ordinary plate and arrange the oysters on this. It will prevent the oysters tipping and losing any of their precious liquid. Eat the oysters directly from the shells, seasoned to taste with a little lemon juice or freshly ground pepper. Serve with fresh white bread or caraway bread and a dry white wine.

Mussels with Saffron Sauce

1 onion
1 small leek
250 ml/8 fl oz white wine
250 ml/8 fl oz water
2.25 litres/2 quarts mussels
2 tablespoons olive oil
1 shallot
½ teaspoon powdered saffron
3 tablespoons single cream
2 lettuce hearts
1 tablespoon lemon juice
GARNISH
1 stick celery
2 teaspoons chopped chives
few tarragon leaves (optional)

Peel and dice the onion. Wash, trim and cut the leek into fine strips. Pour the wine and water into a large pan, add the chopped vegetables and bring to the boil. Scrub the mussels under cold, running water, cut away the 'beards' and add the

mussels to the boiling liquid. Cover the pan and simmer over a high heat for 10 minutes until all the shells have opened. Remove the mussels from the liquid, discarding any that have not opened fully; drain and leave to cool. Shell the mussels and place in an ovenproof bowl.

Strain the mussel juice, retaining 250 ml/8 fl oz on one side. Heat the oil in a pan. Peel and dice the shallot and brown in the oil. Add the saffron, cream and mussel juice. Boil for 1 minute. Pour over the mussels and leave to cool.

Wash the celery, slice into thin strips and blanch for 2 minutes in a little boiling water. Drain and leave to cool. Place half a lettuce heart on each of four plates and sprinkle with the lemon juice. Arrange the mussel salad around the lettuce and garnish each plate with celery, chopped chives and tarragon, if used.
Serves 4

Scampi with Aniseed Cream

16 fresh or frozen scampi
1 teaspoon aniseed
¼ teaspoon salt
20 ml/1 fl oz Pernod
6 tablespoons clear meat stock
2 teaspoons wine vinegar
2 egg yolks
100 g/4 oz unsalted butter
GARNISH
1 teaspoon pickled red or green
  peppercorns (optional)

Rinse fresh scampi in cold running water and leave to drain. Place frozen scampi in a dish, cover and leave to thaw, then drain. Crush a quarter of the aniseed and leave on one side. Bring 450 ml/¾ pint water to the boil in a pan, together with the remaining aniseed and the salt. Add the fresh scampi and simmer over a very low heat for 5 minutes. If frozen scampi are used, place in the boiling water, remove the pan immediately from the heat and leave to stand for 5 minutes. Drain the scampi in a sieve and allow to cool, then remove the shells from the fresh scampi.

Bring the Pernod, stock and vinegar to the boil in a pan and simmer until reduced to 40 ml/1½ fl oz (two tablespoons) liquid. Leave to cool. Beat the egg yolks into the cooled liquid. Reheat the pan over a very low heat and gradually stir in the butter to form a thick cream. Stir in the crushed aniseed. Taste and adjust seasoning. Crush some ice cubes, place on a large dish and arrange the scampi on top. Sprinkle the aniseed cream with red or green peppercorns, if used, and serve separately.
Serves 4

Marinated Dublin Bay Prawns with Sole Fillets

675 g/1½ lb sole fillet
1–2 tablespoons flour
1 tablespoon cooking oil
1 tablespoon currants
2 onions
4 tablespoons olive oil
250 ml/8 fl oz white wine vinegar
1 bay leaf
salt and pepper
25 g/1 oz pine kernels or flaked
  almonds
8 cooked Dublin Bay prawns

Wash and dry the sole fillet, cut into four portions and dip each in flour. Heat the cooking oil and fry the sole until golden brown on both sides. Drain on absorbent kitchen paper.

Soak the currants in lukewarm water. Peel the onions and cut into rings. Heat the olive oil and fry the onion rings until golden brown. Add the vinegar and bay leaf, and season with salt and pepper. Bring to the boil and simmer gently for 2 minutes. Drain the currants. Place the sole fillets, pine kernels or almonds, currants and prawns together in a bowl. Take the oil and vinegar marinade off the heat, allow to cool slightly and pour over the fish mixture. Leave to stand in the refrigerator for 5–6 hours. Then strain the marinade, arrange the prawns and sole mixture on a flat dish, and sprinkle with a little of the marinade before serving.
Serves 4

Chicken Breasts and Kiwi Fruit with Orange Sauce

4 cooked chicken breasts
3 kiwi fruit
25 g/1 oz butter
2 tablespoons sugar
150 ml/¼ pint fresh orange juice
grated rind of ½ orange
1 tablespoon brandy

Skin the chicken breasts and thinly slice the meat. Arrange the meat in a fan shape on four individual plates, or on a large serving platter. Thinly peel and slice the kiwi fruit, and arrange the slices alongside the meat. Melt the butter in a small pan, sprinkle with the sugar and stir over the heat until the sugar has dissolved. Gradually add the orange juice, blending the juice thoroughly into the mixture with each addition, and sprinkle in the orange rind. Bring the sauce to the boil and simmer over a low heat, stirring continuously, until the liquid is reduced by half. Take it off the heat, stir in the brandy and leave to cool. Pour some of the orange sauce over the chicken and kiwi fruit and serve the rest separately. *Serves 4*

Melon with Parma Ham and Piquant Mayonnaise

1 tablespoon pickled green
  peppercorns
4 tablespoons mayonnaise
1 teaspoon lemon juice
pinch salt
1 small Ogen melon
100 g/4 oz thinly sliced Parma
  ham

Drain the peppercorns, crush half of them with a fork or a mortar and pestle, and beat these into the mayonnaise, followed by the lemon juice and salt. Taste and adjust seasoning, arrange the sauce in a bowl and sprinkle with the remaining peppercorns.

  Slice the melon into wedges and scoop away the seeds with a teaspoon. Remove the rind from each wedge with a sharp knife. Wrap the wedges individually in slices of ham and arrange on a platter. Serve the piquant mayonnaise separately. *Serves 4*

Cook's Tip

Ogen melon is suggested here because it is particularly good with Parma ham. But you can of course serve honeydew or Charentais melon instead.

Smoked Beef with Kumquat Sauce

2 tablespoons mayonnaise
salt and white pepper
2 teaspoons lemon juice
4 preserved kumquats
150 ml/¼ pint double cream
225 g/8 oz thinly sliced
  pastrami (smoked beef)

Beat the mayonnaise with the salt, pepper and lemon juice. Drain the kumquats, finely dice three of them and stir them into the mayonnaise. Slice the fourth kumquat very thinly. Whip the cream and fold into the mayonnaise, then transfer the sauce to a glass bowl and garnish with the kumquat slices. Roll up the smoked beef and arrange on a serving platter. *Serves 4*

Cook's Tip

If you cannot obtain smoked beef, smoked ham will also taste very good in this recipe. As a variation, try serving smoked ham with fresh fig sauce, or mandarin sauce, following the above recipe but substituting fresh figs or mandarins for the kumquats. Any of these combinations are delicious both as starters and as side dishes to the main buffet meal.

Avocados with Mussels

2 avocados
2 teaspoons lemon juice
1 small grapefruit
1 (250-g/8¾-oz) can mussels
2 tablespoons mayonnaise
1 tablespoon natural yogurt
1 teaspoon ground almonds
generous pinch each salt, white
  pepper and curry powder.

Wash, dry and halve the avocados lengthways. Remove the stones and sprinkle the flesh immediately with half the lemon juice to prevent it from discolouring. Peel the grapefruit, divide into segments and remove the skin from each segment. Drain the mussels. Mix the grapefruit and mussels together and arrange in the avocado halves.

Beat the mayonnaise with the yogurt, ground almonds, the remaining lemon juice, the salt, pepper and curry powder and spoon the dressing over the avocados. *Serves 4*

Cook's Tip

Before arranging the grapefruit and mussels in the avocado, you could scoop out some of the avocado flesh with a teaspoon and mix it into the mayonnaise dressing.

Avocado and Ham Salad

4 avocados
juice of 1 lemon
100 g/4 oz smoked or boiled
  ham, thinly sliced
1 (312-g/11-oz) can mandarin
  segments
3 tablespoons oil
1 tablespoon brandy
generous pinch salt
3–4 lemon balm leaves
  (optional)

Cut the avocados in half and remove the stones. Scoop out the flesh with a melon baller, place in a bowl and sprinkle with a little lemon juice. Slice the ham into very fine strips. Drain the mandarin segments, retaining the juice on one side, and mix the mandarin, avocado and ham together. Beat the remaining lemon juice with 1 tablespoon canned mandarin juice, the oil, brandy and salt. Stir into the salad, cover and leave to stand for a few minutes.

Wash the lemon balm, if used, drain well and cut into strips. Arrange the salad on a serving dish and sprinkle with the lemon balm. *Serves 4*

Angelo's Chicken Salad

3 cooked chicken breasts
¼ cucumber
4 tomatoes
1 apple
juice of ½ lemon
1 tablespoon mild or wholegrain
  mustard
5 tablespoons mayonnaise
bunch dill or parsley
1 tablespoon castor sugar
2 tablespoons wine vinegar
3 tablespoons orange juice
grated rind of ½ orange

Skin the chicken breasts, if necessary, and carve the meat into thin slices. Wash and dry the cucumber, cut in half lengthways and scoop out the seeds with a spoon. Slice the cucumber very finely. Peel and quarter the tomatoes, remove the seeds and dice the flesh. Peel, quarter, core and slice the apple, and sprinkle with the lemon juice. Mix all the salad ingredients together in a bowl.

Beat the mustard into the mayonnaise. Wash, drain and finely chop the dill or parsley. Mix the sugar thoroughly into the vinegar, and orange juice, and stir into the mayonnaise together with the dill, or parsley, and grated orange rind. Arrange the salad in four individual glasses and top each with a tablespoon of the dressing. *Serves 4*

Chicken Salad Tomatoes

100 g/4 oz frozen or canned
  prawns
8 tomatoes
salt and white pepper
1 fresh peach or 2 canned peach
  halves
1 roast chicken breast
2 tablespoons mayonnaise
1 tablespoon soured cream
1 tablespoon tomato purée
dash Worcestershire sauce
pinch cayenne pepper
1 teaspoon brandy

Place frozen prawns, if used, in
a dish, cover and leave to
thaw, then drain. Rinse
through canned prawns with
cold water and leave to dry.
Wash and dry the tomatoes
and cut a third off the bottom
of each to make a lid. Scoop
the seeds out of the tomatoes
with a teaspoon and discard.

Sprinkle the insides of the
shells with salt and pepper.
Peel, halve and stone the fresh
peach, if used. Drain canned
peach halves, and dice the
fresh or canned peach. Remove
any skin from the chicken
breast and chop the meat into
small pieces. Mix the peach,
chicken and prawns together in
a bowl.

Beat the mayonnaise with
the soured cream, tomato
purée, Worcestershire sauce,
cayenne and brandy and stir
into the mixed ingredients.
Cover and leave to stand at
room temperature for 15
minutes, then fill the tomatoes
with the mixture and place the
lids on top. *Makes 8*

Cheese and Peppers on Tomato

2 medium green peppers
175 g/6 oz full fat cream cheese
  or curd cheese
1-2 tablespoons soured cream
salt and white pepper
1 small onion
4 tomatoes
$\frac{1}{2}$ teaspoon paprika pepper

Wash and halve the green
peppers and remove the seeds
and pith. Finely dice two of the
halves. Beat the cheese with the
soured cream to a smooth,
creamy paste, add the diced
green pepper and season with
salt and white pepper to taste.
Fill the two remaining pepper
halves with the cheese mixture
and place the halves together.
Wrap in cling-film and stand in
a cool place for 30 minutes.

Peel and finely dice the
onion. Wash and dry the
tomatoes and cut into thick
slices. Place the tomato slices
individually on a kitchen
board and sprinkle each with
salt, pepper and diced onion.
Unwrap and separate the
pepper halves, cut into slices
and place each slice on top of a
slice of tomato. Sprinkle with
paprika before serving.

Stuffed Persimmons

4 persimmons
2 teaspoons lemon juice
1 teaspoon pickled green
  peppercorns, or ½ teaspoon
  freshly ground white pepper
225 g/8 oz full fat cream cheese
  or curd cheese
150 ml/¼ pint single cream
generous pinch each sugar and
  salt
GARNISH
4 lemon or orange slices

Wash the persimmons in cold
water and rub dry. Using a
sharp knife, cut a third off each
nearest the stalk end and scoop
the flesh out of the persimmon
shells with a teaspoon. Finely
dice the flesh, discarding the
seeds. Sprinkle the persimmon
shells and the diced fruit with
lemon juice.
  Drain and crush the

peppercorns, if used, with a
fork, or a mortar and pestle.
Beat the cheese with the cream,
sugar, salt and crushed
peppercorns or white pepper
until smooth. Taste and adjust
seasoning. Mix the diced
persimmon into the cheese
cream and spoon the mixture
into the persimmon shells.
Garnish each with a slice of
lemon or orange. *Serves 4*

Lychee Cocktail

1 (312-g/11-oz) can lychees or
  450 g/1 lb fresh lychees
350 g/12 oz cooked chicken
4 tablespoons mayonnaise
3 tablespoons canned lychee
  juice, or apple juice
salt and white pepper
3 tablespoons single cream
grated rind of ½ orange
few lettuce leaves
2 teaspoons lemon juice
¼ teaspoon cayenne pepper
GARNISH
4 chillies (optional)

Drain the canned lychees, if
used, keeping the juice on one
side. Peel, halve and stone
fresh lychees. Dice the chicken.
Beat the mayonnaise with the
canned lychee juice or the
apple juice, the salt, pepper,
cream and orange rind.
  Wash the lettuce, drain
thoroughly and use to line four
plates. Mix the lychees with the

chicken, arrange on the beds of
lettuce and pour the
mayonnaise dressing over the
top. Cover the cocktails and
leave to stand in the
refrigerator for 30 minutes.
Mix the lemon juice with the
cayenne and sprinkle over the
cocktails just before serving.
Garnish each portion with a
chilli, if liked. *Serves 4*

Stuffed Leeks

2 large leeks
1 tablespoon lemon juice
2 hard-boiled eggs
5 canned anchovy fillets
50 g/2 oz canned baby sweet
   corn cobs, or canned sweet
   corn
1 tablespoon chopped parsley
3 tablespoons oil
1 tablespoon wine vinegar
pinch salt
dash Tabasco sauce

Wash and trim the leeks and slice each into two 10-cm/ 4-inch lengths. Bring 450 ml/ ¾ pint salted water to the boil in a pan and blanch the leeks for 10 minutes. Remove from the pan, plunge into cold water and drain thoroughly. Leave to cool.

Slice the leek pieces in half lengthways and sprinkle with the lemon juice. Cut a 1-cm/ ½-inch strip off the end of each leek piece and finely slice the strips. Shell and dice the eggs. Rinse the anchovy fillets in cold water, allow to dry and dice finely. Drain the sweet corn cobs, or sweet corn, and cut the cobs, if used, into thin slices. Mix the strips of leek, diced egg, anchovy, sweet corn and parsley together in a bowl. Beat the oil with the vinegar, salt and Tabasco and pour over the salad ingredients. Cover and leave to stand at room temperature for 10 minutes, then divide the salad between the leek halves.
Makes 8

Carrot Boats

4 large carrots
¼ teaspoon salt
¼ teaspoon sugar
1 tablespoon lemon juice
2 large crisp dessert apples
10 baby gherkins
225 g/8 oz ham
small bunch parsley
4 tablespoons soured cream
4 tablespoons mayonnaise

Wash the carrots, peel thinly and cut in half lengthways. Bring 750 ml/1¼ pints water to the boil in a pan with the salt and sugar, add the carrot halves and simmer over a low heat for 15-20 minutes. Drain the carrots, plunge into cold water and leave to dry. Carefully hollow out a channel along each carrot half with a teaspoon, dice the scooped out flesh and place in a bowl. Sprinkle the carrot halves with lemon juice.

Wash, quarter, core and finely dice the apples. Drain the gherkins and chop as finely as possible, together with the ham. Wash, drain and chop the parsley. Mix the apple, ham, gherkin and parsley with the diced carrot, fill each carrot half with the salad and leave to stand in the refrigerator for 10-15 minutes.

Whip the soured cream with the mayonnaise, season to taste and serve separately with the carrot boats. *Makes 8*

Stuffed Cucumber

1 large cucumber
175 g/6 oz canned golden plums
¾ root celeriac
1 large red dessert apple
225 g/8 oz freshly cooked or
*   canned asparagus tips*
1 small lettuce
3 tablespoons mayonnaise
3 tablespoons natural yogurt
1 teaspoon lemon juice
¾ teaspoon salt
pinch sugar

Wash and dry the cucumber and cut out a wedge running down the centre lengthways, leaving a gap measuring a third of the whole cucumber. Scoop the seeds out of both parts and discard. Take out the cucumber flesh and cut into pieces. Drain, halve and stone the plums. Peel and wash the celeriac, and dice as finely as possible. Wash, quarter, core and dice the apple. Drain the canned asparagus tips, if used. Wash the lettuce, separate the leaves and allow to dry. Mix the cucumber, plums, celeriac, apple and canned or fresh asparagus tips together in a bowl. Beat the mayonnaise with the yogurt, lemon juice, salt and sugar and stir the dressing into the salad ingredients. Line the hollowed out cucumber with lettuce and arrange the salad inside.

Fennel with Blue Cheese Dressing

2 heads fennel
1 tablespoon lemon juice
bunch dill
1 tablespoon capers
2 tomatoes
50 g/2 oz soft blue cheese
   (Roquefort, Dolcelatte)
100 g/4 oz cottage cheese
3 tablespoons double cream
salt and black pepper
pinch garlic salt
dash vinegar

Wash and trim the fennel, keeping the tender leaf shoots on one side. Bring 250 ml/ 8 fl oz salted water to the boil in a pan with the lemon juice. Place the fennel in the pan, cover and simmer for 15 minutes, then drain and leave to cool.

Wash the dill and chop finely, together with the fennel leaves. Drain and chop the capers. Peel and halve the tomatoes, remove the seeds and dice the flesh. Crumble the blue cheese into a bowl. Pass the cottage cheese through a sieve and add to the blue cheese, followed by the cream, salt, pepper, garlic salt, vinegar, chopped capers, dill and fennel leaves. Blend all the ingredients well together.

Place the fennel flat on a kitchen board, and slice each in half horizontally along the length of the head. Top each half with blue cheese cream and garnish with diced tomato.
Serves 4

Stuffed Artichokes

8 canned artichoke bottoms
1 (198-g/7-oz) can tuna
2 hard-boiled eggs
3 tablespoons mayonnaise
salt and pepper
few drops lemon juice
generous pinch cayenne pepper
1 (142-g/5-oz) can prawns
few lettuce leaves
GARNISH
1 (58-g/2-oz) jar lumpfish roe
few small lemon slices

Drain the artichoke bottoms and tuna. Shell and finely dice the eggs. Work the egg into the tuna with a fork, or blend together in the liquidiser. Gradually add the mayonnaise and season with salt, pepper, lemon juice and cayenne.

Drain the prawns, rinse through with cold water and leave to dry. Wash the lettuce, drain thoroughly and use to line a flat serving dish. Arrange the artichoke bottoms on the bed of lettuce, and spoon the tuna mayonnaise into the centre of each. Top the artichokes with the prawns and garnish each with a lemon slice and some lumpfish roe.
Makes 8

Zurich Chopped Veal

1 onion
350 g/12 oz button mushrooms
1 tablespoon flour
15 g/½ oz butter
675 g/1½ lb fillet of veal
4 tablespoons oil
150 ml/¼ pint dry white wine
200 ml/7 fl oz single cream
1 teaspoon salt
⅛ teaspoon white pepper

Peel and dice the onion. Trim the mushrooms and slice them thinly. Work the flour into the butter. Cut the veal into bite-sized pieces. Heat the oil and brown the veal, a few pieces at a time. Remove from the pan and place in a sieve over a basin. Fry the onion in the oil until transparent. Add the mushrooms and fry. Then add the wine and cream, stir in the flour and butter and cook the sauce for a few minutes. Season with the salt and pepper. Mix the veal, and juices from the basin, into the sauce. Heat through and serve with rösti, and a green or cucumber salad. *Serves 4*

Cook's Tip

Rösti or roesti is a national potato dish in Switzerland. Boil or bake potatoes until half-cooked, then slice the hot potatoes. Fry the slices in hot lard; as the potato cooks it will soften and form a potato cake. Cook until a golden crust forms on the cake.

Cheese Fondue

1 clove garlic
350 ml/12 fl oz white wine
350 g/12 oz Gruyère cheese
350 g/12 oz Emmental cheese
1 teaspoon cornflour
3 tablespoons kirsch
pinch each of grated nutmeg
  and white pepper
500 g–1 kg/1–2 lb white bread

Peel and halve the garlic and rub the inside of a *caquelon* – an earthenware, flameproof dish specifically designed for cheese fondue – with the cut side of the garlic. Alternatively, chop the garlic very finely and sprinkle it in the pot. Add the wine and warm slightly. Dice the cheeses and melt in the warm wine, stirring continuously over a moderate heat. Mix the cornflour with the kirsch and stir into the melted cheese. Season with the nutmeg and white pepper. Then place the dish over a spirit burner and regulate the flame to keep the cheese just below boiling point.

Cut the white bread into 4-cm/1½-in cubes and serve separately, with the fondue. At the table each guest sticks a piece of bread on to his fondue fork, dips it into the cheese and leaves the bread to soak up as much cheese as possible before removing and eating it. The crust at the bottom of the dish is considered a great delicacy; when this is reached, lift it out and divide it between the guests. *Serves 4*

Each Swiss canton has its own cheese fondue recipe, using the local cheeses. Depending on availability, you can try making the recipe with other Swiss cheeses. French bread is excellent with fondue – the small slices have a lot of crust and they are especially easy to pierce on to the fork. To drink, serve the same wine that you used to melt with the cheese or, better still, serve hot black tea and kirsch. Traditionally, anyone who loses a piece of bread in the fondue must provide the company with a bottle of wine!

Cook's Tip
Another Swiss national dish is meat fondue. The pot is filled with hot oil and guests put small pieces of fillet steak on their forks to cook in the oil. French bread and an assortment of salads and sauces are traditionally served as well, to accompany the meat: horseradish sauce, mustard pickles, black olives and thinly sliced onion rings are all popular.

Pork with Mussels

1 kg/2 lb (2 pints) live mussels
salt and white pepper
450 g/1 lb loin of pork
15 g/½ oz lard
2 onions
4 tomatoes
1 clove garlic
3 tablespoons oil
1 tablespoon flour
250 ml/8 fl oz white wine
1 tablespoon chopped parsley
½ teaspoon each dried thyme
*   and dried basil*
sprig of basil to garnish

Soak the mussels for 2 hours in several changes of salted water. Scrape the shells clean, and pull out and cut off the beards. Rinse the mussels in cold water.

Set the oven at hot (220c, 425f, gas 7). Rub the pork with salt and pepper and place it in a roasting tin. Heat the lard, pour it over the loin and bake in the heated oven for 25 minutes. Meanwhile, peel and dice the onions. Peel, deseed and chop the tomatoes. Peel the garlic.

Heat the oil in a large pan and fry the onions and garlic until transparent, then remove the garlic. Add the tomatoes and cook until soft. Mix the flour with a little of the wine. Add the remaining wine to the tomatoes and boil gently.

Add the mussels to the sauce, cover the pan and cook over a high heat for 10 minutes, until the shells have opened. Discard any that have not done so. Remove most of the mussels from the shells, leaving a few intact, and set aside. Add the blended flour, parsley, dried herbs and a little salt to the sauce and bring back to the boil. Cut the pork into cubes and add them to the sauce with the shelled mussels. Heat through gently without allowing to boil. Arrange the mussels still in their shells on top of the sauce and serve, garnished with the sprig of basil. *Serves 4*

Genoese Fish Stew

1 kg/2 lb mixed sea fish (red snapper, squid, mackerel)
1 clove garlic
1 onion
2 anchovy fillets
450 g/1 lb tomatoes
6 tablespoons olive oil
450 ml/¾ pint water
3 tablespoons chopped parsley
bay leaf
1 teaspoon salt
50 g/2 oz chopped walnuts
450 ml/¾ pint dry white wine
4 slices white bread

Clean, rinse and dry the fish, and cut into small pieces. To prepare squid, reach inside the sack and pull away the head and tentacles. Pull off and discard the mottled skin from the sack, then separate the 'backbone' from the flesh at the opening of the sack, carefully draw it out and discard it. Separate the two flaps from the sack. Cut the tentacles from the head, then discard the head. Rinse the squid thoroughly. Cut the sack into rings, slice the flaps in broad strips and cut up the tentacles.

Peel the garlic. Peel and dice the onion. Chop the anchovy fillets. Peel, deseed and chop the tomatoes.

Heat the oil in a large, flameproof serving pan or dish. Gently fry the onion with the garlic for a few minutes, stirring continuously, then remove the garlic. Add the chopped anchovies and tomatoes, with the water. Stir in the parsley, bay leaf and salt, cover, and simmer for 10 minutes. Add the fish pieces to the pan with the nuts and wine, and simmer for a further 20 minutes over a very low heat. Serve with the toasted bread. *Serves 4*

Scampi in Garlic Oil

900 g/2 lb unpeeled cooked scampi or 450 g/1 lb frozen peeled scampi
2 cloves garlic
250 g/8 fl oz olive oil
½ teaspoon salt
GARNISH
lemon wedges
parsley sprigs

If using fresh scampi, peel them. Remove frozen scampi from the packet, cover and leave to thaw, preferably in the refrigerator.

Set the oven to very hot (240c, 475f, gas 9). Peel and finely chop the garlic. Heat the olive oil in a frying pan and add the garlic and salt. Place the scampi in an ovenproof dish, pour on the garlic oil and bake in the heated oven for 5 minutes. Serve, garnished with lemon wedges and parsley sprigs. *Serves 4*

Cook's Tip

True Italian scampi are caught only in the Adriatic Sea and are characterized by their large size and delicious flavour. If you can't get scampi, Dublin Bay prawns are a good substitute: zoologically they are the same, although they seldom grow to the same size.

Grilled Lobster

2 (675-g/1½-lb) live lobsters
1 carrot
1 onion
3 tablespoons salt
250 ml/8 fl oz white wine
juice of 1 lemon
6 black peppercorns
4 tablespoons olive oil
BUTTER
150 g/5 oz softened butter
2 cloves garlic
2 tablespoons finely ground
    almonds
2 tablespoons finely chopped
    shallots
2 tablespoons finely chopped
    parsley
½ teaspoon salt
generous pinch of white pepper
pinch of cayenne
SAUCE
175 ml/6 fl oz crème fraîche or
    half double cream and half
    soured cream
1 teaspoon tarragon mustard

1 tablespoon chopped mixed
    herbs (chervil, chives,
    tarragon)
1 teaspoon cornflour
generous pinch each of salt and
    pepper
pinch of cayenne
4 tablespoons calvados

Rinse the lobster under cold
running water. Peel and finely
chop the carrot. Peel the onion
and cut it into wedges. Bring 6
litres/10 pints of water to the
boil with the salt, wine, lemon
juice, carrot, onion and peppercorns. You will need a
saucepan deep enough to allow
the lobster to be completely
submerged. Plunge one lobster,
head first, into the boiling
water and hold it under the
water with the handle of a
wooden spoon for 5 minutes.
Then simmer gently for a
further 10 minutes, remove it
from the liquid and leave it to
cool. Repeat the process with

the second lobster.
  Halve the lobsters lengthways. Remove the orange
coral and the creamy contents
of the head and place in a
bowl. Break off and crack
open the claws, dice the claw
meat and add it to the bowl.
Break off the empty head
section. Brush the lobster
halves containing the tail meat
with oil and place them on a
greased baking sheet, cut side
up. Set the oven at hot (220c,
425f, gas 7).
  Place the softened butter in
a bowl. Peel the garlic cloves
and squeeze them through a
garlic press into the butter,
then cream the butter with the
almonds, shallots, parsley and
seasonings. Place the lobster in
the oven and immediately
reduce the temperature to
moderate (180c, 350f, gas 4).
Remove the lobster from the
oven after 5 minutes and
spread the lobster meat with

some of the seasoned butter.
Return to the oven and bake
for a further 5 minutes.
  Mix the lobster meat which
you kept to one side with the
remaining seasoned butter,
spread this mixture on the
lobster halves and bake on the
top shelf for 5 minutes more.
Remove and keep hot.
  To make the sauce, heat the
crème fraîche and stir in the
mustard and herbs. Blend
together the cornflour, seasonings and calvados and stir this
mixture into the sauce. Bring
to the boil once, then transfer
the sauce to a sauceboat and
serve it with the lobster.
Serves 4

Creole Fillet Steak

BLACK BEANS
200 g/7 oz black beans
½ green pepper
1 clove garlic
½ onion
2 tablespoons olive oil
½ teaspoon salt
FILLET STEAKS
4 (200-g/7-oz) fillet steaks
2 onions
675 g/1½ lb tomatoes
3 tablespoons olive oil
1 teaspoon salt
generous pinch of ground cumin
RICE
200 g/7 oz long-grain rice
3 tablespoons olive oil
½ onion
1 green chilli pepper
500 ml/17 fl oz boiling water
1 teaspoon salt
GARNISH
4 unripe bananas
3 tablespoons oil

Soak the beans in water for 12 hours, then boil them in the soaking water in an open pan for 1–1¼ hours, adding a little more water if necessary. Remove the seeds and pith from the ½ green pepper, then chop it finely with the garlic. Dice the ½ onion. Heat the 2 tablespoons of olive oil and fry the pepper, onion and half the garlic until the onion is transparent. Season with the ½ teaspoon of salt and add to the beans. Cover the pan and simmer the beans for a further 15 minutes.

To cook the steaks, preheat the grill and grill the steaks for 4 minutes on each side. Cut the meat into thin strips and set aside. Peel and coarsely chop the 2 onions. Peel, deseed and quarter the tomatoes. Heat the 3 tablespoons of olive oil and fry the onion and the remaining garlic. Add the tomatoes, salt and cumin, mix well and simmer for 30 minutes. Place the steak pieces on top of the vegetables, cover the pan and keep warm over a very low heat.

Set the oven to very cool (120c, 250f, gas ½). Wash the rice in a sieve. Heat the 3 tablespoons of olive oil in a flameproof casserole. Peel the ½ onion and chop coarsely. Deseed and coarsely chop the chilli pepper. Add both to the oil and fry for 5 minutes. Stir in the drained rice and fry for 5 minutes, stirring continuously. Pour the boiling water over the rice, season with the salt, stir, cover the casserole and transfer to the oven. Cook for 20 minutes, until the rice has swollen and is just cooked. Remove the onion and chilli pepper from the rice, cover the rice and keep it warm in the oven.

For the garnish, peel the bananas, halve them lengthways and cut each half into three. Fry in the oil until brown on both sides.

Pour the vegetables and fillet steak on to a warm serving dish, add alternate portions of rice and black beans and arrange the banana over the meat. *Serves 4*

Couscous with Stewed Beef

COUSCOUS
400 g/14 oz couscous
1 teaspoon salt
250 ml/8 fl oz water
2 teaspoons olive oil
STEW
225 g/8 oz onions
450 g/1 lb potatoes
2 carrots
2 beetroots
375 g/13 oz white cabbage
2 large tomatoes
225 g/8 oz courgettes
225 g/8 oz pumpkin
400 g/14 oz canned chick peas
450 g/1 lb braising steak
6 tablespoons oil
1 teaspoon salt
½ teaspoon ground cayenne
½ teaspoon ground cumin
*2 generous pinches ground
   allspice*
6 tablespoons water

Spread the couscous on a pastry board. Dissolve the salt in the water and sprinkle over the couscous, with the oil. Rub the couscous between the palms of your hands to form small balls, cover and leave to swell.

To make the stew, peel and dice the onions. Peel or scrape the potatoes and other vegetables and cut into 5-cm/2-in pieces. Drain the chick peas. Chop the meat into 2-cm/¾-in pieces. Heat the oil in a large, deep pan. Fry the meat and onion for 10 minutes, stirring frequently. Add the salt and other spices and the water. Stew the meat over a gentle heat for 30 minutes, stirring frequently. Then add the vegetables and sufficient water just to cover, and continue to simmer until the meat and vegetables are tender.

Meanwhile, line a steamer with muslin and place it on top of the pan. Seal any space left between the steamer and the sides of the pan with a damp tea-towel. Rub a handful of couscous between your palms into the steamer. As soon as it begins to steam add a second handful. Continue in this way until you have used all the couscous. Steam for 20 minutes, then transfer the couscous to a dish. Spread it out and leave it to dry.

Remove the cooked meat and vegetables from the pan and keep warm. Return the couscous to the steamer and steam it for a further 10–15 minutes over the stock, until the couscous is soft but still in grains. Transfer to a dish and keep warm. Heat the meat and vegetables through in the stock. Strain off the stock and arrange the meat and vegetables round the couscous. Boil the stock to reduce it, and serve separately. *Serves 6*

Cook's Tip

There is a special cooking pan for making this North African speciality, called a *couscoussier*. The pan is divided into two parts: the bottom half looks like a deep stewpan and is used to cook the meat and vegetables, while the couscous is cooked in a perforated steamer which sits snugly on top of the stewpan. The lid of the steamer has about eight holes in it; the holes allow some of the steam to escape which aids the cooking of the couscous.

Pot-au-feu

2 beef marrow bones
2.5 litres/4½ pints water
2 bay leaves
1½ teaspoons salt
1 (1.5-kg/3-lb) boiling chicken
675 g/1½ lb top rump of beef
2 carrots
4 parsnips
2 onions
4 leeks
generous pinch of black pepper
1½ tablespoons brandy
4 tablespoons chopped parsley

Put the bones into a pan,
cover with water and boil for 5
minutes, then pour the water
away. Bring the 2.5 litres/4½
pints of water to the boil in a
large pan. Add the bay leaves
salt, bones, chicken and beef
and bring back to the boil.
Remove any scum as it forms,
and when no more scum rises
to the surface cover the pan
and simmer over a low heat
for 2½ hours.

Peel the carrots and cut
them into eight pieces lengthways. Peel the parsnips and cut
them into quarters or eighths.
Peel the onions and cut them
into wedges. Trim the leeks,
halve them lengthways,
and cut into 5-cm/2-in lengths.
After about 2 hours cooking
time add the carrots and
parsnips to the pan and cook
for a further 10 minutes. Then
add the onions and leeks and
continue cooking.

Slice the meat and arrange it
on a large serving dish. Divide
the chicken into joints and
arrange them on the dish, too.
Arrange the vegetables around
the meat, or serve them separately. Strain the stock and
season it with the pepper and
brandy. Serve the parsley and
stock separately, with the meat
and vegetables. *Serves 6*

Pigeon Pancake Pie

PANCAKES
450 g / 1 lb flour
1 teaspoon salt
375–500 ml / 13–17 fl oz water
FILLING
3 onions
4 (450-g / 1-lb) oven-ready
   young pigeons, with giblets
salt and pepper
200 g / 7 oz butter
3 tablespoons chopped parsley
2 teaspoons grated fresh root
   ginger
½ teaspoon ground cumin
½ teaspoon cayenne
⅛ teaspoon ground turmeric
¼ teaspoon powdered saffron
250 ml / 8 fl oz water
6 eggs
2 egg yolks
150 g / 5 oz shelled almonds
ground cinnamon
25 g / 1 oz sugar

3 tablespoons oil
icing sugar for dusting

The pancakes for the pie are
best baked the previous day.
Sift the flour and salt into a
bowl and gradually stir in
sufficient water to form a thin
batter. Leave to stand for at
least 6 hours. Fry the batter
without fat to make 18–20 very
thin pancakes. Fry one side
only and do not allow them to
brown.

To make the filling, peel and
dice the onions. Chop the
pigeon giblets. Season the
pigeons with salt and pepper.
Melt 100 g / 4 oz of the butter in
a saucepan and brown the
pigeons. Remove them from
the pan and set aside. Fry the
onion and giblets in the remaining fat. Add the parsley,
ginger, cumin, cayenne, turmeric, saffron and water and
bring to the boil. Return the
pigeons to the pan, cover and

simmer for about 50 minutes,
until tender.

Remove the pigeon meat
from the bones and chop it.
Pour half the cooking liquor
into a basin and keep it to one
side. Reduce the liquor left in
the pan over high heat to
about 4 tablespoons, skim off
the fat and set aside.

Reheat the cooking liquor
from the basin. Beat the eggs
and egg yolks and stir in to
thicken the sauce; do not boil.
Add the reduced liquor.

Melt 50 g / 2 oz of the butter
and brown the almonds, then
drain and chop them and mix
them with 1 teaspoon ground
cinnamon and the sugar.

To make the pie crust ar-
range 6 pancakes on a piece of
foil in a circle. Cover with 6
more pancakes and then put 4
pancakes one on top of the
other in the centre of the
circle. Cover these pancakes
with the almond mixture. Stir

the pigeon meat into the sauce
and pour over the almonds.
Fold the edges of the top layer
of pancakes over the filling
and cover with the remaining
pancakes. Fold up the edges of
the bottom layer of pancakes.

Heat the remaining butter
with the oil in a large frying
pan. Slide the pie into the hot
fat and fry for about 5 minutes, until golden brown. Use
a saucepan lid to help turn the
pie and fry the other side until
golden brown. Slide the pie on
to a plate. Sift together a little
icing sugar and cinnamon.
Sprinkle over the pie and cut it
into portions, as for a cake.
Serve hot. *Serves 6*

Blintzes

225 g/8 oz potato flour
pinch of salt
2 eggs
450–600 ml/¾–1 pint water
FILLING
225 g/8 oz cooked beef or
    poultry
2 small onions
oil for frying
½ teaspoon salt
generous pinch each of black
    pepper and hot paprika
1 egg

Sift the potato flour and salt into a bowl. Beat in the eggs and gradually add sufficient water to give a thin batter. Leave to stand for 30 minutes.

Prepare the filling. Mince the meat, using the finest blade of the mincer. Peel and dice the onions and brown them in 1 tablespoon of hot oil. Stir the diced onion, salt, pepper, paprika and egg into the meat.

Heat 1 teaspoon of oil in an 18-cm/7-in frying pan. Pour in 1 tablespoon of the batter to make a thin pancake, frying it on one side only until the underside is golden and the top firm. Continue in this way until all the batter is used. Cover the top side of each pancake with a little of the meat mixture. Fold in half and then into quarters. Fry the filled pancakes in hot oil until golden brown on both sides.
Makes 16

Cook's Tip
These pancakes can also be served stuffed with a mixture of curd cheese, honey and chopped almonds, for dessert.

Beef Satay with Peanut Sauce

450 g/1 lb rump steak
4 small red onions
2 cloves garlic
1 teaspoon grated lemon rind
1 teaspoon each ground
   coriander, ground caraway
   seeds and ground ginger
½ teaspoon salt
generous pinch of sugar
5 tablespoons oil
PEANUT SAUCE
6 tablespoons groundnut oil
1 tablespoon dried onion flakes
1 clove garlic, crushed
¼ teaspoon shrimp paste
1–2 teaspoons sambal oelek
   (hot chilli sauce)
4 tablespoons peanut butter
6 tablespoons water
½ teaspoon salt
1 tablespoon soy sauce
2 teaspoons cane or palm sugar
1 tablespoon lemon juice

Cut the meat into small pieces.
Peel the onions and garlic,
grate them and mix with the
grated lemon rind, ground
spices, salt and sugar. Rub
into the meat and marinate for
1 hour.

Heat the grill. Thread the
meat pieces on to oiled
wooden skewers and grill for
4–6 minutes, turning them
frequently and brushing repeatedly with the oil. Serve
hot, with peanut sauce.

To make the sauce, heat the
oil and fry the dried onion
flakes until golden, then drain.
Remove all but 2 tablespoons
of oil from the pan and fry the
crushed garlic, shrimp paste
and sambal oelek. Add the
peanut butter and water and
boil until the sauce is thick and
smooth. Season with the salt,
soy sauce, sugar and lemon
juice. Leave to cool, then stir
in the onion flakes.

Cucumber and raw onion
slices are also served as an
accompaniment to the beef
satay. *Serves 4*

Tempura

6 fresh or frozen Dublin Bay
  prawns or scampi
2 dried Japanese mushrooms
¼ green pepper
1 aubergine
oil for deep frying
1 slice lotus root, 1 cm/½ in
  thick (optional)
40 g/1½ oz flour
2 egg yolks, beaten
2 tablespoons water
few thin Japanese rice noodles

Thaw the prawns or scampi if frozen. Peel them, leaving the ends of the tails intact, de-vein them and cut in half lengthways (cut very thick prawns into three slices). Soften the mushrooms for 30 minutes in hot water. Cut the piece of green pepper in half. Halve the aubergine crossways and cut almost through each half several times to make thin fan-shaped slices, attached at one end.

Heat the oil in a wok or deep frying pan to 180c, 350f. Dip the prawns, pepper pieces, aubergine fans, the lotus root if used, and the drained mushrooms in a little flour. Sift the remaining flour into a bowl and stir in the beaten egg yolks and water, to make a thin batter. Dip the prawns and vegetables in the batter and fry in the hot oil until golden. Tie the noodles together in a bunch like a brush, dip into the batter and fry for a few minutes. Use as a garnish.

Serve Tempura with a sauce made from 6 tablespoons of Japanese rice wine (sake) or dry sherry, 6 tablespoons of soy sauce, 475 ml/16 fl oz of water in which 4 seaweed leaves have been soaked, and 1 teaspoon of salt. Bring all the ingredients to the boil, then leave to cool. When cold, pour into two small bowls. Mix one with grated white radish and root ginger and the other with 1 teaspoon of monosodium glutamate and a little salt. Lemon wedges may also be served. *Serves 2*

Duck with Pineapple Sauce

2 oven-ready young ducks
1 tablespoon corn oil
6 tablespoons canned pineapple
*   juice*
250 ml/8 fl oz red wine
½ teaspoon salt
generous pinch of white pepper
juice of ½ lemon
1 tablespoon cornflour
juice and grated rind of 1
*   orange*
6 tablespoons water
4 tablespoons chopped fresh
*   pineapple*

Set the oven to moderately hot
(200c, 400f, gas 6). Cut the
ducks in quarters, brush with
the oil and place in a roasting
tin. Mix the pineapple juice
with the red wine, salt, pepper
and lemon juice. Pour over the
duck joints and roast near the
bottom of the oven for about
40 minutes, or until cooked.
During the cooking baste
repeatedly with the juices in
the tin. Transfer the duck
joints to a serving dish and
keep warm.

To make the pineapple
sauce, blend together the
cornflour and orange juice.
Skim off the fat from the juices
in the roasting tin and stir into
the cornflour mixture. Add the
water and heat on top of the
stove in a small pan, stirring
continuously, until the sauce
begins to thicken. Add the
grated orange rind and
chopped pineapple, cook for a
few more minutes, then pour
over the duck joints. Serve
with sweet potatoes. *Serves 4*

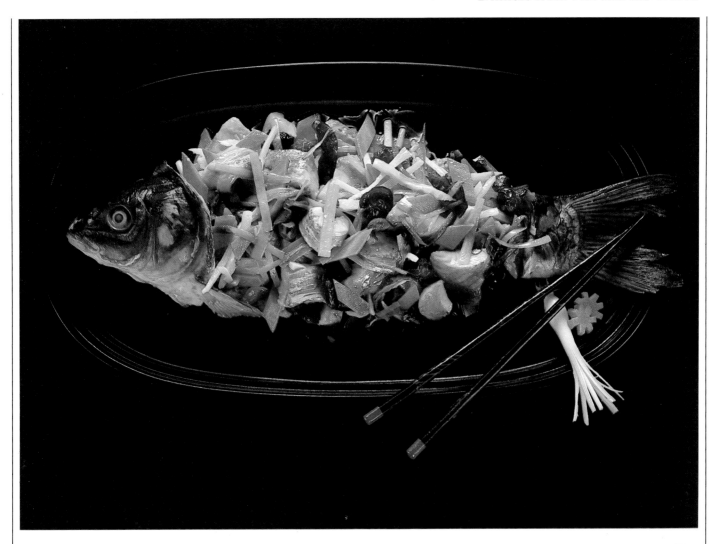

Carp

3 carrots
1 leek
100 g/4 oz canned bamboo
    shoots
100 g/4 oz canned bean sprouts
50 g/2 oz dried Chinese
    mushrooms
1 (1-kg/2-lb) oven-ready carp
1 onion
sprig of parsley
bay leaf
2 cloves
salt and pepper
500 ml/17 fl oz white wine
500 ml/17 fl oz water
50 g/2 oz butter
1 tablespoon soy sauce
juice of 1 lemon
½ teaspoon ground ginger

Peel 2 of the carrots and cut
them into small diamond
shapes. Trim and thinly slice
the leek. Drain the bamboo
shoots and cut them into thin
strips. Drain the beans sprouts
Soak the dried mushrooms in
hot water for 30 minutes to
soften them. Fillet the carp,
skin it and cut the fish into 2-
cm/¾-in cubes. Keep the bones
with head and tail intact (see
Cook's Tip below).

To make a stock, peel and
chop the onion. Peel and chop
the remaining carrot and the
parsley sprig. Boil the onion,
chopped carrot and parsley,
with the bay leaf, cloves and 1
tablespoon of salt, in the wine
and water for 5 minutes. Add
the diced carp and simmer for
3 minutes over a very gentle
heat.

Heat the butter in a pan.
Cook the carrot diamond
shapes, bamboo shoots, bean
sprouts and drained mushrooms
for 8–10 minutes, stirring
continuously; do not allow the
vegetables to become too soft.
Mix the soy sauce with the
lemon juice, ½ teaspoon of salt,
¼ teaspoon of pepper and the
ginger. Stir the sauce into the
fish with the vegetables. Then
remove the fish and vegetables
with a slotted spoon and
arrange them carefully along
the reserved backbone of the
fish. *Serves 3–4*

Cook's Tip

The easiest way to fillet
the carp and to keep the
head and tail intact is to
cut along the bones on
each side from head to
tail. Cut behind the gills
to free the fillet at the
head end, lift the fillet
and make short cuts
along the middle bone
to free the fillet entirely.

In China this is one
way of making fish go
further, yet giving the
impression that a whole
fish is being served, as a
courtesy to the guests at
a party.

Crisp-fried Duck

1 (1.5-kg/3 lb) oven-ready duck
salt and white pepper
pinch of monosodium glutamate
piece of fresh root ginger
2 tablespoons dried Chinese
* mushrooms*
2 spring onions
1 leek
1 onion
1 yellow pepper
1 red pepper
100 g/4 oz canned bamboo
* shoots*
50 g/2 oz cornflour
2 egg whites
oil for deep frying
2 tablespoons soy sauce
pinch of sugar

Put the duck in a saucepan
and cover it with water. Add 1
teaspoon of salt, the monosodium glutamate and the
peeled and chopped root
ginger. Bring to the boil and

simmer for 50 minutes. Soak
the mushrooms in hot water
for 30 minutes. Cut the spring
onions, leek and peeled onion
into fine rings. Deseed the
peppers and cut into narrow
strips. Chop the drained bamboo shoots.
   Cut the wings and legs from
the duck and cut the remaining
meat from the carcass in large
pieces. Beat the cornflour and
a little salt and pepper into the
egg whites and coat the pieces
of duck. Heat the oil to 180c,
350F. Deep fry the duck until
crisp, remove from the oil and
keep warm. Fry the chopped
vegetables and drained mushrooms in 3 tablespoons of the
oil. Stir in 6 tablespoons of
duck stock and cook for 8–10
minutes. Season with the soy
sauce, sugar and a pinch of
salt. *Serves 2–3*

Szechwan
Chicken

1 (1-kg/2-lb) chicken
2 tablespoons light soy sauce
1 teaspoon cornflour
3 carrots
3 spring onions
1 red chilli pepper
4 tablespoons oil
1 tablespoon soy sauce
* (optional)*

Halve the chicken and bone it
with a sharp knife. Cut the
chicken into bite-sized pieces,
place them in a shallow bowl
and sprinkle with the light soy
sauce and the cornflour. Stir
well. Cover and marinate for
30 minutes.
   Peel the carrots, trim the
spring onions and cut both
into thin strips. Cut the chilli
pepper into rings. Heat 2
tablespoons of the oil in a wok

or large frying pan and fry the
chicken for 4–5 minutes, stirring continuously. Remove the
meat from the pan with a
slotted spoon. Heat the remaining oil in the pan and fry
the carrot, spring onion and
chilli pepper for 5–6 minutes,
stirring continuously. Return
the chicken to the pan and
heat through with the vegetables, stirring frequently.
Season to taste with soy sauce,
if liked. Serve with boiled long-
grain rice. *Serves 3–4*

Chicken with Rice 'Hai Nan'

1 clove garlic
1 (1.25 to 1.5-kg/2½ to 3-lb) chicken
2 teaspoons salt
1 teaspoon oyster sauce
1 spring onion
100 g/4 oz celery
40 g/1½ oz fresh root ginger
1.5 litres/2¾ pints water
1 red chilli pepper
1 onion
4 tablespoons canned coconut milk
200 g/7 oz long-grain rice

Peel and crush the garlic. Rub the chicken, inside and out, with the garlic, salt and oyster sauce, cover and leave to stand for 1 hour. Trim the spring onion. Trim and slice the celery. Peel and finely chop the root ginger. Bring the water to the boil in a large saucepan with the spring onion, celery, three-quarters of the chopped root ginger, and the chilli pepper. Add the chicken and simmer over a low heat for 45 minutes–1 hour, until tender.

Peel and dice the onion. Bring 250 ml/8 fl oz of the chicken stock (from the pan) to the boil with the coconut milk and add the rice, onion and the remainder of the chopped root ginger. Cook over a gentle heat for 15–20 minutes, until the rice is tender but still firm. Drain.

Remove the chicken from the stock and cut the meat into pieces. You can either bone the chicken and cut all the meat into small pieces, or bone the breasts only, cut them into equal slices and serve on a bed of lettuce, as illustrated.

Serve with the boiled rice, and the vegetables and chicken stock from the pan. Soy sauce is served separately, for individual seasoning. You can also serve chilli sauce and radish sauce. *Serves 3–4*

This recipe, which originated on the island of Hai-Nan-Pao in the South China Sea, has now become very popular throughout China and there are several variations, served throughout the world wherever the Chinese have settled.

Cook's Tip

To make radish sauce, which is not available as a bottled sauce in Europe, finely grate 1 white radish, squeeze out the juice and mix the radish with 3 tablespoons each of wine vinegar and light soy sauce.

Fried Vegetables

1 onion
1 clove garlic
bunch of spring onions
675 g/1½ lb mixed vegetables
    (aubergines, courgettes,
    French beans, peas, Chinese
    leaves, bamboo shoots, bean
    sprouts)
2 tablespoons oil
1 tablespoon fish sauce or
    oyster sauce
generous pinch of black pepper
1 teaspoon salt
½–1 teaspoon light soy sauce

Peel and finely chop the onion.
Peel and crush the garlic, and
trim and chop the spring

the aubergines, courgettes,
French beans, Chinese leaves
and bamboo shoots. Heat the
oil in a wok or large frying
pan and fry the onions, garlic,
fish sauce or oyster sauce,

pepper and salt for 2 minutes.
Add the prepared vegetables,
peas and bean sprouts and
cook over high heat, stirring
continuously, until cooked but
still firm. Season with the soy
sauce. Serve immediately.
Serves 6

In Burma, as in China, vegetables are not boiled or steamed
but stir-fried in a wok. Cooked
in this way each vegetable
keeps its own flavour and its
fresh, appetising appearance.
In Burma fried vegetables are
served with rice as a main
course or to accompany a
meat or fish curry. It is important to cut all the vegetables
into small pieces or thin slices
so that they cook evenly. To
prevent the vegetables losing
their crispness, eat them
immediately after cooking.

Chicken Curry

1 (1.5-kg/3-lb) chicken
1 onion
2 cloves garlic
25 g/1 oz fresh root ginger
1 teaspoon salt
stem of citronella, if available,
    or 1 teaspoon grated lemon
    rind
1 teaspoon ground turmeric
4 dried red chilli peppers
4 tablespoons oil
about 250 ml/8 fl oz water
2 tomatoes
2 potatoes
150 g/5 oz pumpkin flesh
1 teaspoon shrimp paste
1 teaspoon chopped coriander
    leaves or parsley
¼ teaspoon crushed cardamom
    seeds (from cardamom pods)

Cut the chicken into 12–14
pieces. Peel and chop the
onion, garlic and ginger root
and purée them in a blender

with the salt, citronella or
lemon rind, turmeric, chillies
and 2 teaspoons of the oil.
Heat the remaining oil in a
wok or large frying pan and
cook the purée from the blender for 3–4 minutes. Add the
water and chicken pieces and
cook over a gentle heat for 20
minutes.

Peel and dice the tomatoes
and potatoes. Cut the pumpkin
into strips and add to the
chicken with the tomato and
potato. Add the shrimp paste
and, if necessary, a little more
water. Simmer the curry over a
low heat for a further 30–35
minutes, until the chicken is
very tender. Sprinkle with the
chopped coriander or parsley
and the cardamom and serve.
Serves 3–4

Salmon and Pork

200 g/7 oz smoked salmon,
* thinly sliced*
675 g/1½ lb fillet of pork, cut
* into 2-cm/¾-in slices*
675 g/1½ lb spinach
salt and freshly ground black
* pepper*
lemon slices to garnish

Cut the salmon into strips
2 cm/¾ in wide and cut the
meat into 5-cm/2-in squares.
Pick over the spinach. Cut as
many 22-cm/8½-in squares of
foil as you have squares of
pork.

Cover each piece of foil with
a thick layer of spinach and 1
slice of pork. Season the meat
with freshly ground black
pepper and – if the salmon is
very mild – a little salt. Cover
the meat with the strips of
salmon. Fold the foil over and
seal the edges.

Bring a large pan of water
to the boil. Add the foil parcels and boil for 20 minutes. If
necessary, top up with more
boiling water. Serve in the foil
with hot sweet potatoes, garnished with slices of lemon.
Serves 4

Fijian Baked Fish

175 g/6 oz fresh coconut
475 ml/16 fl oz milk
250 ml/8 fl oz single cream
4 (200-g/7-oz) fillets of white
* fish (cod, haddock, coley)*
juice of 1 lemon
salt and white pepper

Grate the coconut. Put the
milk and cream into a saucepan and stir in the coconut.
Bring to the boil and simmer
for 10 minutes. Then set aside
and allow to cool.

Set the oven to moderately
hot (190c, 375f, gas 5).
Sprinkle the fish fillets with the
lemon juice and season them
with salt and pepper. Grease a
shallow baking dish generously
with butter. Place the fish
fillets in the dish, cover with
the coconut mixture and bake
for 30–40 minutes. *Serves 4*

Cook's Tip

Serve Fijian Baked Fish
with the following
sauce: grate the flesh of
1 coconut and soak it
for 1 hour in 6 table-
spoons of water. Mix 1
peeled and chopped
lemon with ½ chopped
onion. Drain the coco-
nut through muslin,
squeezing the coconut
well to extract all the
milk. Stir the milk into
the lemon and onion
mixture with salt and 2
finely chopped chillies.
Serve cold. *Serves 4*

HOME BAKING

Baking is the area of home cooking most likely to be appreciated by your family and friends. Warm, aromatic bread and rolls, fresh from the oven, are well worth the effort and if you have never tried it, you will find breadmaking easier than you imagine.

The array of tea time treats and biscuits, from strudel to shortbread, Bath buns to Florentines is certain to please. Nothing is more welcome than home-made biscuits or cake when the children come in from school, and when you want to spoil your family and friends, a home-baked tart or gâteau shows you really care.

Dessert can make a simple meal special so try the tempting tarts and cakes in this selection. There are fruit cakes and simple loaf cakes, layer cakes and rich tortes, as well as more elaborate gâteaux and cream cakes to bring a luxury air to any meal. For holiday baking, you will find many traditional specialities from all over the world, perfect for parties or for gifts.

Strong Ryebread

STARTER DOUGH
1 tablespoon milk
2 tablespoons water
¼ teaspoon oil
¼ teaspoon dried yeast
1 tablespoon lukewarm water
¼ teaspoon castor sugar
1 teaspoon salt
50 g/2 oz strong plain flour
RYEBREAD DOUGH
750 ml/1¼ pints lukewarm water
750 g/1 lb 10 oz coarse rye flour
250 g/9 oz wheaten flour
2 teaspoons salt

First make the starter dough. Combine the milk, 2 table-spoons water and the oil in a saucepan and bring to the boil. Allow to cool until lukewarm. Blend the yeast with 1 table-spoon lukewarm water and the sugar and leave for 5 minutes. Add to the milk mixture with the salt. Stir this liquid into the flour until well blended then cover and leave to stand for 12–18 hours.

The following day, mix the starter dough with 500 ml/ 17 fl oz of the lukewarm wate Mix the rye flour with the wheaten flour in a large warmed bowl. Make a well in the centre of the flours and pour in the starter dough. Stir half the flour into the starter dough until a thick flowing dough is formed. Cover the bowl with a tea towel and leave to rise overnight in a warm place.

The following day add the remaining lukewarm water and the salt. Mix the rest of the flour into the dough and knead until firm and well bound together. Form the dough into a ball and place in a warmed, lightly floured bowl. Cover it with a tea towel and leave in a warm place to rise for 3 hours.

Line a large baking tray with foil. With floured hands shape the dough into a flat round loaf. Place on the baking tray and once again leave to rise at room temperature for 1½–2 hours. During this time brush the top of the loaf three or four times with lukewarm water so that no crust forms. Cut criss-cross patterns on the top of the risen loaf with a sharp knife. Preheat the oven to moderately hot (200°C, 400°F, Gas Mark 6) and bake the loaf on the bottom shelf for 2 hours.

Turn off the oven, remove the bread, brush with cold water and return to the oven for a few minutes to dry.

Cook's Tip

Rye flour can be bought in most healthfood shops. Bread made from rye flour has an agree-able taste and will keep fresh for longer than ordinary bread.

Wholemeal Breakfast Rolls

500 g / 1 lb plain wholemeal
flour
30 g / 1 oz fresh yeast
1 teaspoon sugar
250 ml / 8 fl oz lukewarm water
½ teaspoon salt
2 tablespoons oil

Lightly grease a baking tray with margarine.

Tip the flour into a bowl and form a well in the centre. Cream the yeast with the sugar and a little of the water. Stir in the remaining water and pour into the flour. Sprinkle a  little of the flour over this liquid, cover and leave in a warm place for 15 minutes, until frothy.

Sprinkle the salt around the edges of the flour, add the oil to the yeast mixture and knead all the ingredients together to make a smooth elastic dough. Cover again and leave to stand in a warm place for 30 minutes. Knead lightly with floured hands and divide the dough into 16 equal pieces. Roll each into a ball, sprinkle with a little flour and place on the baking tray. Leave the rolls to stand in a warm place for a further 15 minutes. Preheat the oven to hot (230°C, 450°F, Gas Mark 8) and bake for 15–20 minutes.

Wholemeal Bread

400 g / 14 oz strong plain white
flour
400 g / 14 oz plain wholemeal
flour
40 g / 1½ oz fresh yeast
500 ml / 17 fl oz lukewarm milk
1 teaspoon salt
7 tablespoons oil

Sift the white flour into a bowl and mix with the wholemeal flour. Form a well in the centre. Cream the yeast with a little of the milk. Add the remaining milk and pour into the flour. Sprinkle with a little of the flour, cover and leave in a warm place for 15 minutes, until frothy. Add the salt and oil and mix all the ingredients to a dough. Knead for 5–10 minutes, until smooth and elastic. Cover and leave to rise for 30 minutes in a warm place.

Knead lightly on a floured board and form into a loaf. Sprinkle a baking tray with flour, place the loaf on it, cover and leave to stand in a warm place for a further 30 minutes. Preheat the oven to moderately hot (190°C, 375°F, Gas Mark 5). Sprinkle the loaf with flour and bake for 50–60 minutes.

Walnut and Banana Bread

150 g/5 oz soft margarine
160 g/5½ oz castor sugar
3 eggs
3 bananas
¼ teaspoon vanilla essence
275 g/10 oz plain wholemeal
  flour
2 teaspoons baking powder
¼ teaspoon salt
100 g/4 oz walnuts, chopped
2 tablespoons milk

**Grease a 1-kg/2-lb loaf tin
with margarine. Preheat the
oven to moderate (180°C,
350°F, Gas Mark 4).**

Beat the margarine with the
sugar until pale and creamy
then beat in the eggs. Peel the
bananas and mash with a fork,
or press through a nylon sieve.
Stir the banana purée and
vanilla essence into the
creamed mixture. Mix the

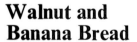

flour and baking powder with
the salt and walnuts. Fold into
the creamed mixture together
with the milk. Turn into the
prepared loaf tin, smooth the
surface and bake for 1¼ hours.
Test with a skewer to make
sure the loaf is cooked through.

Turn out on to a wire rack
and leave to cool.

Wheatgerm Loaf

60 g/2 oz fresh yeast
750 ml/1¼ pints lukewarm water
2 teaspoons salt
5 tablespoons thick honey
2 tablespoons oil or melted
  margarine
900 g/2 lb wholemeal flour (or
  450 g/1 lb wheatmeal and
  450 g/1 lb wholemeal flour)
150 g/5 oz wheatgerm

Cream the yeast with a little of
the water, add the salt, honey
and oil or melted margarine.
Stir in half the flour. Beat well,
cover and leave to stand in a
warm place for 30 minutes.
Stir in the remaining flour and
the wheatgerm then knead well
to give a smooth elastic dough.
Add a little more flour if the
dough is too wet. Cover and
leave to stand in a warm place
until doubled in size, about 30
minutes.

Knead the dough thoroughly

again and form into two
loaves. Place on greased
baking trays and leave loosely
covered in a warm place for a
further 15 minutes. Preheat
the oven to moderately hot
(200°C, 400°F, Gas Mark 6).

Using a sharp knife, lightly
cut a cross on the top of each
loaf and brush with water.
Sprinkle with a little flour and
bake for 50 minutes. Leave the
baked bread to cool on a wire
rack.

Aniseed Marble Bread

PLAIN DOUGH
350 g/12 oz plain flour
20 g/¾ oz fresh yeast
6 tablespoons lukewarm milk
pinch of sugar
50 g/2 oz butter
2 eggs
½ teaspoon salt
RYE DOUGH
350 g/12 oz rye flour
20 g/¾ fresh·yeast
6 tablespoons lukewarm milk
pinch of sugar
50 g/2 oz butter
2 eggs
½ teaspoon salt
½ teaspoon ground aniseed
1 tablespoon aniseed to sprinkle

First make the plain dough.
Sift the flour into a bowl and
form a well in the centre.
Cream the yeast with a little of
the milk, add the remaining
milk and pour into the flour.
Add the sugar and sprinkle a
little of the flour over the
surface. Cover and leave to
stand in a warm place for 15
minutes, until frothy. Melt the
butter, stir in the eggs and salt,
add to the yeast liquid and
mix in the flour to make a
dough. Knead the dough until
smooth and elastic. Cover again
and leave in a warm place to
rise for 1 hour.

Make the rye dough in the
same way, using the rye flour.
Incorporate the ground aniseed
into this dough when adding
the butter. Finally leave the
rye dough in a warm place for
1 hour, as above.

Divide both the plain and
rye dough into two pieces.
Lightly knead a piece of each
dough together and shape into a
loaf. Repeat with the remaining two pieces. Place the two
loaves on a floured baking
tray, cover and leave in a warm
place for a further 30 minutes.
Preheat the oven to hot (220°C,
425°F, Gas Mark 7).

Brush the loaves with water,
sprinkle with aniseed and bake
for 30–40 minutes.

Spiced Flat Cakes

375 g/13 oz rye flour
375 g/13 oz plain wholemeal
  flour
25 g/1 oz fresh yeast
250 ml/8 fl oz lukewarm water
125 ml/4 fl oz lukewarm milk
1 teaspoon salt
2 teaspoons caraway seeds
2 teaspoons crushed coriander
  seeds

Grease a baking tray with oil.
  Combine the flours in a bowl
and form a well in the centre.
Cream the yeast with a little of
the water. Add the remaining
water and the milk then pour
into the flour. Sprinkle a little
of the flour over the liquid,
cover and leave in a warm
place for 15 minutes, until
frothy.
  Mix in all the flour, the salt,
caraway and coriander, to

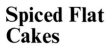

make a dough. Knead the
dough until smooth, cover and
leave to stand in a warm place
until doubled in size, about 30
minutes.
  Divide the dough into four
equal pieces. Roll out each
piece to give a large round
flat cake. Place on the baking
tray, sprinkle with flour and
leave to stand in a warm
place for 30 minutes. Preheat
the oven to hot (230°C, 450°F,
Gas Mark 8), and bake for
15–20 minutes, until crisp and
golden.

Herb Ring Loaf

50 g/2 oz butter
300 ml/10 fl oz lukewarm water
25 g/1 oz fresh yeast
300 g/11 oz rye flour
300 g/11 oz plain wholemeal
  flour
2 teaspoons salt
1 tablespoon chopped mixed
  herbs (marjoram, sage,
  tarragon, basil)
3 tablespoons chopped parsley

Melt the butter and mix with
the water. Cream the yeast with
a little of this liquid, add the
remaining liquid and leave in a
warm place for 15 minutes.
Place the rye flour in a bowl
and add the wholemeal flour,
salt, mixed herbs and parsley.
Pour the yeast liquid into the
flour and mix to a dough.
Knead the dough for about 5
minutes until smooth, cover
and leave to rise in a warm
place for 30 minutes.

Form the dough into a round
flat loaf. Make a hole in the
centre of the loaf with a
wooden spoon and rotate the
spoon to make the hole larger
until you have a ring. Place
on a greased baking tray, cover
and leave in a warm place for
30 minutes.
  Preheat the oven to hot
(220°C, 425°F, Gas Mark 7).
Brush the loaf with water and
sprinkle lightly with flour.
Make slight slashes in the top
of the loaf with a knife and
bake for 30 minutes.

Flowerpot Loaves

500 g / 1 lb plain flour
30 g / 1 oz fresh yeast
pinch of sugar
175 ml / 6 fl oz lukewarm milk
2 onions
1 clove garlic
50 g / 2 oz butter, melted
2 large eggs, beaten
¼ teaspoon salt
pinch of grated nutmeg
1 teaspoon ground aniseed
¼ teaspoon dried fennel
2 tablespoons dried dill
¼ teaspoon dried rosemary
ground aniseed to sprinkle

Grease two new 10 cm/4 inch earthenware flower pots.

Sift the flour into a bowl and form a well in the centre. Cream the yeast with the sugar and a little of the milk. Stir in the remaining milk and pour into the flour. Sprinkle over a little of the flour, cover and leave in a warm place for 15 minutes, until frothy.

Peel the onions and garlic. Finely chop the onions and crush the garlic. Mix the melted butter with the beaten eggs, salt, nutmeg, aniseed, fennel and dill. Pound the rosemary in a mortar, add to the yeast liquid with the butter mixture, onion and garlic and mix all the ingredients well together. Knead the dough until smooth and elastic. Cover and leave to stand in a warm place until doubled in size, about 30 minutes.

Knead the dough lightly and put half in each of the flowerpots. Leave to stand in a warm place for a further 20 minutes. Preheat the oven to moderately hot (200°C, 400°F, Gas Mark 6).

Brush the surface of the loaves with water and sprinkle lightly with aniseed. Bake for 35–40 minutes.

French Bread

1 kg / 2 lb strong plain flour
40 g / 1½ oz fresh yeast
600 ml / 1 pint lukewarm water
4 teaspoons salt

Sprinkle a large baking tray with flour.

Sift the flour into a bowl and make a well in the centre. Cream the yeast with a little of the water then add the remaining water and pour into the flour. Sprinkle a little of the flour over the liquid, cover and leave to stand in a warm place for 15 minutes. Sprinkle the salt on to the flour and mix all the ingredients to a dough. Knead the dough until smooth and elastic, about 5–10 minutes. Sprinkle well with flour so that the surface does not form a crust, cover and leave to stand for 2–3 hours at room temperature.

Quickly knead the dough again on a floured board and divide into four pieces. Form each piece into a long roll and place on the floured baking tray. Cover and leave to stand in a warm place for a further 30 minutes. Preheat the oven to hot (220°C, 425°F, Gas Mark 7).

Slash the loaves diagonally several times with a fine sharp knife and brush with lukewarm water. Bake for 15 minutes then reduce the oven temperature to moderate (180°C, 350°F, Gas Mark 4) and bake for a further 15–20 minutes.

Milk Crescents

500 g / 1 lb plain flour
30 g / 1 oz fresh yeast
250 ml / 8 fl oz lukewarm milk
30 g / 1 oz butter or margarine
1 teaspoon sugar
½ teaspoon salt
1 egg
1 egg yolk, beaten to glaze

Sift the flour into a bowl and make a well in the centre. Cream the yeast with a little of the milk, add the remaining milk and then pour into the flour. Sprinkle a little of the flour over the yeast liquid, cover and leave in a warm place for 15 minutes, until frothy.

Melt the butter or margarine and mix with the sugar, salt and egg. Add to the yeast liquid and flour and mix all together to give a dough. Knead until smooth and elastic then leave in a warm place until doubled in size.

Divide the dough into pieces weighing approximately 50 g/ 2 oz and shape into balls. Roll out each into a triangular shape, with sides approximately 15 cm/6 inches long. Press the point of each triangle firmly on to a baking tray and, starting at the other end, roll up with both hands. Finally seal the point of the triangle with a little beaten egg yolk. Curve each roll into a crescent shape, arrange on a baking tray and brush with beaten egg yolk. Cover and leave to rise for 15–20 minutes in a warm place. Preheat the oven to hot (230°C, 450°F, Gas Mark 8).

Bake the crescents for 10–15 minutes until golden brown and serve fresh from the oven.

Poppy Seed Plaits

500 g / 1 lb plain flour
30 g / 1 oz fresh yeast
250 ml / 8 fl oz lukewarm water
1 teaspoon salt
1 egg
poppy seeds to sprinkle

Sift the flour into a bowl and make a well in the centre. Cream the yeast with a little of the water, add the remaining water and pour into the flour. Sprinkle over a little of the flour, cover and leave in a warm place for 15 minutes, until frothy.

Sprinkle the salt on the flour, add the egg to the yeast liquid and mix the ingredients to a dough. If it is too stiff, add a little more lukewarm water. Knead until smooth and elastic. Cover and leave to rise in a warm place, until doubled in size, about 30 minutes.

Divide the mixture into 50-g/2-oz pieces. Form three long thin strands from each piece, about 15 cm/6 inches in length, and weave into small plaits. Brush these plaits with water and sprinkle with poppy seeds. Arrange on a greased baking tray, cover and leave to rise in a warm place for about 15 minutes. Preheat the oven to hot (230°C, 450°F, Gas Mark 8).

Bake the poppy seed plaits for 10–20 minutes and serve fresh from the oven.

Dinner Rolls

500 g / 1 lb strong plain white
flour
30 g / 1 oz fresh yeast
250 ml / 8 fl oz lukewarm milk
pinch of sugar
1 teaspoon salt
1 egg
1 egg yolk, beaten to glaze
sesame seeds and poppy seeds to
sprinkle

Sift the flour into a bowl and make a well in the centre. Cream the yeast with a little of the milk and the sugar. Add the remaining milk and pour into the flc . Sprinkle a little of the flour er the liquid, cover and leave in a warm place for 15 minutes, until frothy.

Sprinkle the salt on to the edges of the flour, add the egg to the yeast liquid and mix all together to form a dough. Knead the dough until it is smooth and elastic, about 5–10 minutes. Cover and leave to rise in a warm place until doubled in size.

Divide the dough into small portions and form into 20-cm/ 8-inch long rolls, about 2·5 cm/ 1 inch in diameter. From these shape rolls as shown in the illustration. Place the rolls on greased baking trays, cover and leave to rise in a warm place for 20 minutes. Preheat the oven to hot (230°C, 450°F, Gas Mark 8).

Brush the rolls with beaten egg yolk, and sprinkle some with sesame seeds and some with poppy seeds. Bake the rolls for 10–15 minutes, until golden brown.

Croissants

550 g/1 lb 2 oz plain flour
30 g/1 oz fresh yeast
250 ml/8 fl oz lukewarm milk
225 g/8 oz butter
1 egg
1 teaspoon salt
1 egg yolk, beaten to glaze

Sift 500 g/1 lb flour into a bowl and make a well. Cream the yeast with the milk, pour into the flour, cover and leave in a warm place for 15 minutes. Mix in 50 g/2 oz melted butter, the egg and salt, then knead until a smooth, elastic dough. Cover and leave in a warm place for 1 hour.

Knead lightly and roll out to a 20 × 35-cm/8 × 14 inch rectangle. Work the rest of the flour into the remaining butter and chill. Divide into thirds and mark the pastry dough into three lengthways. Dot one-third of the butter over  the top two-thirds of the pastry, leaving a border. Fold the bottom third of pastry over the middle third and the top third over that. Press the edges together, give one turn in a clockwise direction and then roll out to the original size. Repeat this folding and rolling process twice more with the remaining butter, then twice without any butter. Chill for 30 minutes between each rolling.

Finally roll out the dough to a 50-cm/20-inch square. Cut into sixteen 12·5-cm/5-inch squares and roll up each, starting from one corner to the opposite corner. Place on baking trays, brush with egg yolk and leave in a warm place for 30 minutes.

Preheat the oven to hot (220°C, 425°F, Gas Mark 7). Bake the croissants for 5 minutes then reduce to 190°C, 375°F, Gas Mark 5 for a further 15 minutes.

Brioches

500 g/1 lb plain flour
30 g/1 oz fresh yeast
6 tablespoons lukewarm milk
1 teaspoon castor sugar
200 g/7 oz butter
4 eggs
¼ teaspoon salt
1 egg yolk, beaten to glaze

Grease 20 small brioche or patty tins with butter.

Sift the flour into a bowl and make a well in the centre. Cream the yeast with a little of the milk, add the remaining milk and the sugar. Pour into the well in the flour, sprinkle a little of the flour over, cover and leave in a warm place for 15 minutes.

Melt the butter, cool slightly and mix with the eggs and salt. Beat into the yeast mixture with the rest of the flour, kneading with your hand to give a smooth dough. Leave covered in a warm place for 30 minutes.

Knead lightly, take three-quarters of the dough and shape into approximately 20 small balls. Place in the greased tins. Make 20 smaller pear-shaped pieces out of the remaining dough. Make a small indentation in the dough in the tins and place the smaller pieces of dough on top, with the slightly elongated end in the indentation. Brush the brioches with beaten egg yolk and leave to rise in a warm place for 15 minutes. Preheat the oven to hot (220°C, 425°F, Gas Mark 7).

Bake the brioches for about 15 minutes, until well risen and golden brown. Remove from the oven and allow to cool on a wire rack.

Sugar Buns

500 g / 1 lb plain flour
30 g / 1 oz fresh yeast
50 g / 2 oz castor sugar
250 ml / 8 fl oz lukewarm milk
40 g / 1¼ oz butter, melted
2 eggs
1 teaspoon salt
grated rind of ½ lemon
FILLING AND GLAZE
200 g / 7 oz butter, melted
100 g / 4 oz castor sugar
75 g / 3 oz raisins
2 tablespoons granulated sugar

Sift the flour into a bowl and make a well in the centre. Cream the yeast with a little of the sugar and the milk. Pour into the well in the flour and sprinkle over a little of the flour. Cover and leave for 15 minutes in a warm place, until frothy.

Add the butter to the bowl with the remaining sugar, the eggs, salt and lemon rind. Mix everything to a dough and knead on a lightly floured board until smooth and elastic. Leave to rise until doubled in size, about 30 minutes. Divide the dough into 50-g/2-oz pieces and roll these out into 20 × 7·5-cm/ 8 × 3-inch strips. Brush with a quarter of the melted butter and sprinkle with the castor sugar and raisins. Fold over lengthways and roll up, starting from the short side.

Pour 4 tablespoons of the remaining butter into a 23-cm/ 9-inch round cake tin. Place the buns in the tin with the rolled sides uppermost. Cover and leave to rise in a warm place for 15 minutes. Preheat the oven to hot (220°C, 425°F, Gas Mark 7).

Brush the rolls with the remaining melted butter and sprinkle with granulated sugar. Bake for 40–45 minutes then pull apart and serve warm.

Batch Buns

These buns are made using the same dough, omitting the filling. Form 50 g/2 oz pieces of the dough into round bun shapes and place in the butter in the cake tin. Leave to rise then brush with 50 g/2 oz melted butter and bake in a hot oven (220°C, 425°F, Gas Mark 7) for 35 minutes.

Date and Almond Stollen

500 g/1 lb plain flour
30 g/1 oz fresh yeast
250 ml/8 fl oz lukewarm milk
60 g/2 oz castor sugar
2 eggs
150 g/5 oz butter, cut into flakes
50 g/2 oz blanched almonds,
　chopped
grated rind of 1 lemon
pinch of salt
FILLING
25 g/1 oz cornflour
450 ml/¾ pint milk
1 egg yolk
100 g/3½ oz castor sugar
250 g/8 oz dates, finely chopped
15 g/½ oz butter
ICING
200 g/7 oz icing sugar
1 egg white
juice of 1 lemon
2 tablespoons toasted flaked
　almonds

Grease a baking tray with butter or margarine.

Sift the flour into a bowl and form a well in the centre. Cream the yeast with a little of the milk and 1 tablespoon of the sugar. Add the remaining milk and pour into the flour. Sprinkle a little flour over it, cover and leave to stand for 15 minutes in a warm place, until frothy.

Beat the eggs and mix with the remaining sugar, the butter, almonds, lemon rind and salt. Add to the flour and yeast mixture and knead all the ingredients well for 5–10 minutes, to form a smooth elastic dough. Cover and leave to rise for 30 minutes.

Blend the cornflour with a little of the milk, the egg yolk and sugar. Bring the dates to the boil in the remaining milk. Stir the milk and dates into the cornflour mixture then add the butter. Return to the heat and bring to the boil, stirring

continuously until thickened. Leave the mixture to cool, stirring occasionally to prevent a skin forming.

Lightly knead the dough and roll out to 1 cm/½ inch thick on a floured board. Spread the date mixture evenly over it. Turn both side edges over twice towards the centre and press together. Place on the baking tray and leave to stand for a further 20 minutes.

Preheat the oven to moderately hot (200°C, 400°F, Gas Mark 6) and bake the stollen for 1 hour. Sift the icing sugar and beat into the egg white with the lemon juice. Ice the stollen while still warm and sprinkle flaked almonds on to the icing before it sets.

Cook's Tip

This stollen tastes best when eaten fresh. However, if well wrapped in foil, it will keep for 3–4 days.

Hazelnut Stollen

500 g / 1 lb plain flour
30 g / 1 oz fresh yeast
70 g / 2⅔ oz castor sugar
250 ml / 8 fl oz lukewarm milk
100 g / 3½ oz margarine, melted
1 egg
¼ teaspoon salt
grated rind of ½ lemon
FILLING AND ICING
100 g / 4 oz ground almonds
100 g / 4 oz soft brown sugar
100 g / 4 oz ground hazelnuts
2 egg whites, lightly beaten
2 tablespoons rum
½ teaspoon ground cinnamon
1 egg yolk, beaten to glaze
120 g / 4½ oz icing sugar, sifted
1–2 tablespoons lemon juice
50 g / 2 oz toasted hazelnuts

Sift the flour into a bowl and
form a well. Cream the yeast
with a little of the sugar and
the milk. Pour into the well,
cover and leave for 15 minutes,
until frothy. Add the remaining
sugar, the margarine, egg, salt
and lemon rind and mix to a
dough. Knead lightly then
leave to rise for 1 hour.

Mix the almonds, sugar,
hazelnuts, egg whites, rum and
cinnamon. Knead the dough
lightly and roll out to a 45-cm/
18-inch square. Spread over the
filling. Brush the sides with egg
yolk and roll up. Place on a
greased baking tray, brush with
egg and leave for 15 minutes.
Preheat the oven to 220°C,
425°F, Gas Mark 7.

Bake the stollen for 30–40
minutes. Ice with the sugar and
lemon juice and sprinkle with
chopped hazelnuts.

Bohemian Plait

500 g / 1 lb plain flour
30 g / 1 oz fresh yeast
60 g / 2 oz castor sugar
250 ml / 8 fl oz lukewarm milk
100 g / 4 oz margarine
pinch of salt
50 g / 2 oz raisins
1 egg yolk, beaten to glaze
2 tablespoons sugar crystals to
sprinkle

Sift the flour into a bowl and
make a well in the centre.
Cream the yeast with a little
of the sugar and the milk and
pour into the well. Sprinkle the
surface with a little of the
flour. Cover and leave in a
warm place for 15 minutes,
until frothy.

Melt the margarine, add it
to the bowl with the remaining
sugar, the salt and raisins, and
beat all the ingredients to a
dough. Knead on a lightly
floured surface, then cover and
leave to rise for 1 hour.

Halve the dough. Divide one
half into three 35-cm/14-inch
strips and use to make a plait.
Place on a greased baking tray.
From two-thirds of the
remaining dough, make an-
other smaller plait. From the
remaining dough, make two
strips and form a twist. Brush
the larger of the plaits with
beaten egg yolk, place the
smaller one on top and brush
this. Finally place the twist
on top and brush with beaten
egg yolk. Sprinkle with the
sugar crystals and leave in a
warm place to rise for 15
minutes. Preheat the oven to
moderately hot (200°C, 400°F,
Gas Mark 6).

Bake the loaf for 25–30
minutes and allow to cool on a
wire rack.

Apricot Plait

500 g/1 lb plain flour
30 g/1 oz fresh yeast
250 ml/8 fl oz lukewarm milk
60 g/2 oz castor sugar
150 g/5 oz dried apricots, finely
   chopped
100 g/3½ oz blanched almonds,
   chopped
50 g/2 oz candied lemon peel,
   chopped
25 g/1 oz candied orange peel,
   chopped
1 tablespoon arrack or ouzo
2 eggs, beaten
150 g/5 oz butter, cut into flakes
grated rind of 1 lemon
pinch of salt
TOPPING
50 g/2 oz butter
icing sugar to sprinkle

Grease a narrow 1-kg/2-lb
loaf tin and sprinkle with flour.

Sift the flour into a bowl and
form a well in the centre.
Cream the yeast with a little
of the milk and 1 teaspoon of
the sugar. Stir in the remaining
milk and pour into the flour.
Sprinkle a little of the flour
over the liquid and leave for
15 minutes, until frothy.

Mix the apricots with the
almonds, chopped peel and
arrack. To the flour and yeast
mixture add the eggs, remaining
sugar, the butter, lemon rind and
salt, and knead together until
smooth and elastic. Knead in
the fruit mixture, cover and
leave to rise in a warm place
for 30 minutes.

Divide the dough into three
and form into long rolls.
Weave into a plait, place in the
loaf tin, cover and leave to
stand in a warm place for a
further 20 minutes. Preheat
the oven to moderately hot
(190°C, 375°F, Gas Mark 5).

Bake for 30–40 minutes.
While still warm brush with
the melted butter and sift
icing sugar generously over the
top and sides.

Soft Fruit Loaf

500 g/1 lb cottage cheese
500 g/1 lb plain flour
2 teaspoons baking powder
2 eggs
150 g/5 oz castor sugar
1 tablespoon vanilla sugar
pinch of salt
1 tablespoon grated lemon rind
1 tablespoon chopped almonds
1 tablespoon raisins
2 tablespoons chopped mixed
   candied fruit
2 tablespoons chopped mixed
   peel
TOPPING
15 g/½ oz butter, melted
1 tablespoon icing sugar
1 tablespoon vanilla sugar

Grease a baking tray with
butter or margarine and
sprinkle with flour. Preheat the
oven to moderately hot (190°C,
375°F, Gas Mark 5).

Press the cottage cheese
through a sieve or liquidise.
Sift the flour with the baking
powder on to a pastry board
and form a well in the centre.
Add the cottage cheese, eggs,
sugar, vanilla sugar, salt,
lemon rind, nuts, fruit and
peel. Mix to a firm dough,
knead lightly and form into a
loaf. Place on a baking tray
and bake for 50–60 minutes.

Transfer the loaf to a wire
cooling rack and brush with
melted butter while still hot.
Mix the icing sugar and vanilla
sugar and sift generously over
the loaf.

Bremer Fruit Loaf

750 g / 1½ lb plain flour
45 g / 1¾ oz fresh yeast
250 ml / 8 fl oz lukewarm milk
100 g / 4 oz castor sugar
400 g / 12 oz butter
1 tablespoon vanilla sugar
1 teaspoon each salt and ground
    cardamom
150 g / 5 oz blanched almonds,
    chopped
125 g / 4 oz candied lemon peel,
    chopped
grated rind and juice of 1 lemon
500 g / 1 lb raisins

You can bake the Bremer Fruit Loaf either in a loaf tin or on a baking tray. The following recipe uses both ways. Grease a long 1-kg/2-lb loaf tin and a baking tray.

Sift the flour into a bowl and make a well in the centre. Cream the yeast with a little of the milk then add the sugar and the remaining milk. Pour into the flour, cover and leave in a warm place for 15 minutes, until frothy.

Melt the butter, cool slightly and beat with the vanilla sugar, salt and cardamom. Beat the butter mixture into the yeast liquid and flour to obtain a dough. Knead in the almonds, chopped peel, lemon rind and juice and the raisins, until the dough is smooth. Cover and leave to stand in a warm place for a further 40 minutes.

Lightly knead the dough and then halve it. Place one half in the greased loaf tin and leave to stand in a warm place for

30 minutes. Preheat the oven to moderately hot (190°C, 375°F, Gas Mark 5). When the loaf is well risen, place in the oven and bake for 45–50 minutes. Before removing from the oven, test with a skewer. Turn out on a wire rack and leave to cool.

Shape the second half of the dough into a long loaf, place on the greased baking tray and leave to stand in a warm place for 30 minutes. Bake for 45–50 minutes then cool on a wire rack.

Cook's Tip

You can also bake fruit rolls from this dough. When the dough is ready, weigh portions of 40–50 g / 1½–2 oz and roll into balls. Place on a greased baking tray, flatten slightly, cover and leave to stand in a warm place for 15 minutes. Before baking brush with beaten egg yolk. Sprinkle with sugar and bake for 20–30 minutes in a moderately hot oven (190°C, 375°F, Gas Mark 5).

Country Plum Strudel

PASTRY
15 g/½ oz lard
6 tablespoons lukewarm water
1 egg
pinch of salt
250 g/9 oz plain flour
FILLING
1 kg/2 lb plums
140 g/5 oz butter
100 g/4 oz fresh white
* breadcrumbs*
75 g/3 oz castor sugar
icing sugar to sprinkle

Melt the fat and beat with the water, egg and salt. Sift the flour on top and mix everything together to a smooth dough. Roll the dough into a ball, return to the bowl, cover and leave to stand for 1 hour.

Roll out the pastry as thinly as possible on a large floured cloth. Finally stretch the pastry with your hands, working from the middle outwards until it is paper thin. If the pastry tears join it together immediately. Put the pastry back on the cloth. Preheat the oven to moderately hot (200°C, 400°F, Gas Mark 6).

Wash the plums and quarter them, removing the stones. Melt the butter and put 2 tablespoons of it to one side. Mix the rest with the breadcrumbs and spread this over two-thirds of the pastry, leaving the bottom third uncovered. Arrange the plums over the top of the bread-crumbs and sprinkle with the castor sugar. Spread a little butter on the uncovered third of the pastry and, lifting the cloth, roll the pastry up, starting from the covered side. Place the strudel on a greased baking tray and brush with the remaining butter. Bake for 40 minutes and dust with icing sugar before serving warm with cream.

Country Butter Cake

450 g / 1 lb plain flour
40 g / 1½ oz fresh yeast
250 ml / 8 fl oz lukewarm milk
225 g / 8 oz castor sugar
225 g / 8 oz butter
pinch of salt
1 egg, beaten
1 teaspoon ground cinnamon

Grease two baking trays with butter or margarine.

Sift the flour into a bowl and make a well in the centre. Cream the yeast with a little of the milk and 1 teaspoon sugar and pour into the well. Sprinkle over a little of the flour, cover and leave in a warm place for 15 minutes, until frothy.

Melt half the butter and place the remaining butter in the refrigerator. Add 50 g / 2 oz sugar, the salt, egg, melted butter and remaining milk to  the yeast mixture and beat with the flour to form a dough. Knead on a floured surface until smooth and elastic. Leave to rise for 1 hour in a warm place.

Preheat the oven to hot (220°C, 425°F, Gas Mark 7). Roll out the dough to fit two 25 × 30-cm/10 × 12-inch baking trays. Make small wells in the surface of the dough and into these put the remaining butter, cut into flakes. Mix the rest of the sugar with the cinnamon and sprinkle over the cakes. Bake for 25 minutes, leave the cakes to cool and then cut into slices.

Butter Cream Sandwich Fingers

BISCUIT MIXTURE
500 g / 1 lb plain flour
15 g / ½ oz fresh yeast
175 g / 6 oz castor sugar
250 ml / 8 fl oz lukewarm milk
90 g / 3½ oz butter
1 egg
¼ teaspoon grated lemon rind
100 g / 4 oz almonds, chopped
1 tablespoon cold milk
BUTTER CREAM
75 g / 3 oz unsalted butter
175 g / 6 oz icing sugar
¼ teaspoon vanilla essence

Sift the flour into a bowl and make a well in the centre. Cream the yeast with 1 tablespoon of sugar and 2 tablespoons of the milk. Pour into the well in the flour, sprinkle with a little of the flour and leave in a warm place for 15 minutes, until frothy.

Melt 50 g / 2 oz butter in the remaining warm milk and add to the bowl with the egg, 50 g / 2 oz sugar and the lemon rind. Form into a dough and knead. Spread out on a greased baking tray and leave to rise for 1–1½ hours.

Preheat the oven to moderately hot (200°C, 400°F, Gas Mark 6).

Melt the remaining butter, and stir in the remaining sugar and the almonds. Mix in the tablespoon of milk, cool, then spread over the dough. Bake for 40 minutes, cool and cut into fingers.

Split each finger in half horizontally through the centre. Cream the butter with the sifted icing sugar and vanilla essence until light and fluffy. Sandwich together the fingers with this butter cream.

Cream Cheese Crumble Cake

YEAST DOUGH
350 g/12 oz plain flour
20 g/¾ oz fresh yeast
6 tablespoons lukewarm milk
50 g/2 oz butter, melted
50 g/2 oz castor sugar
2 eggs
pinch of salt
FILLING
180 g/6 oz butter, softened
180 g/6 oz castor sugar
3 eggs
575 g/1¼ lb curd or cream
  cheese
25 g/1 oz cornflour
grated rind of 1 lemon
100 g/4 oz raisins (optional)
TOPPING
180 g/6 oz plain flour
50 g/2 oz sugar
pinch of salt
¼ teaspoon ground cinnamon
75 g/3 oz butter

Sift the flour into a mixing
bowl and make a well in the
centre. Cream the yeast with
the lukewarm milk and pour
into the well. Sprinkle the
surface with a little of the
flour. Cover and leave in a
warm place for 15 minutes,
until frothy. Pour the melted
butter into the flour together
with the sugar, eggs and salt.
Work all the ingredients
together to make a dough.
Knead lightly, cover and leave
to rise in a warm place for
1 hour.
 Beat the butter and sugar
until light and creamy. Add
the eggs, cheese, cornflour,
lemon rind and raisins, if used.
 Knead the dough and roll
out to line the base of a
greased 23 × 33-cm/9 × 13-
inch Swiss roll tin. Spread the
cheese mixture on top.
 To make the crumble
topping, mix together the
flour, sugar, salt and cinnamon. Melt the butter and
gradually add to the flour,
rubbing it in with the fingertips. Sprinkle over the cheese
filling and leave to stand for
15 minutes.
 Preheat the oven to
moderately hot (200°C, 400°F,
Gas Mark 6) and bake the
cake for 30–40 minutes.

Marbled Crumble Cake

YEAST DOUGH
350 g/12 oz plain flour
20 g/¾ oz fresh yeast
50 g/2 oz castor sugar
125 ml/4 fl oz lukewarm milk
50 g/2 oz margarine, melted
2 eggs
pinch of salt
FILLINGS
250 ml/8 fl oz milk
20 g/¾ oz margarine
grated rind of ½ lemon
30 g/1 oz semolina
100 g/4 oz ground poppy seeds
50 g/2 oz sugar
1 egg
1 tablespoon rum
¼ teaspoon ground cinnamon
250 g/9 oz curd or cream cheese
3 tablespoons milk
1 egg, separated
100 g/4 oz castor sugar
250 g/9 oz cherry jam
1 tablespoon rum

CRUMBLE TOPPING
75 g/3 oz butter, melted
175 g/6 oz plain flour
90 g/3½ oz castor sugar

Make the dough as for Dresden Slices (see right) and line a greased 23 × 33-cm/9 × 13-inch Swiss roll tin.

Bring the 250 ml/8 fl oz milk to the boil with the margarine, lemon rind and semolina, and leave for 5 minutes. Mix in the poppy seeds, sugar, egg, rum and cinnamon.

Mix together the cheese, milk, egg yolk and sugar. Whisk the egg white until stiff and fold in. Mix the jam and rum together.

Rub the melted butter into the flour and sugar until crumbly. Spread spoonfuls of the poppy seed, cheese and jam mixtures over the dough, and top with the crumble. Leave for 15 minutes then bake in a hot oven (220°C, 425°F, Gas Mark 7) for 20–30 minutes.

Dresden Slices

YEAST DOUGH
225 g/8 oz plain flour
15 g/½ oz fresh yeast
25 g/1 oz castor sugar
6 tablespoons lukewarm milk
25 g/1 oz margarine, melted
1 egg, beaten
pinch of salt
FILLING
350 g/12 oz curd or cream
   cheese
100 g/4 oz castor sugar
1 egg
1 tablespoon plain flour
grated rind of 1 lemon
TOPPING
100 g/4 oz butter
100 g/4 oz castor sugar
1 tablespoon plain flour
2 eggs
100 g/4 oz flaked almonds

Sift the flour into a bowl and make a well in the centre. Cream the yeast with a little of the sugar and the milk. Pour into the well and sprinkle the surface with a little of the flour. Cover the bowl and leave for 15 minutes, until frothy. Add the remaining sugar, the melted margarine, egg and salt, and beat all the ingredients until a dough is formed. Knead lightly, cover and leave to rise for 1 hour.

Mix the cheese with the sugar, egg, flour and lemon rind, beating until light and fluffy.

Lightly knead the dough and roll out to line a greased 33 × 23-cm/13 × 9-inch Swiss roll tin. Spread the cheese filling over it evenly.

Preheat the oven to moderately hot (200°C, 400°F, Gas Mark 6). Beat the butter and sugar until creamy. Add the flour and the eggs, one at a time. Spread over the cheese filling and finally sprinkle with the almonds. Bake the cake for 30–40 minutes. Allow to cool slightly then cut into slices.

Creamy Rice Flan

1 (212-g/7½-oz) packet frozen puff pastry
FILLING
100 g/4 oz short-grain rice
600 ml/1 pint milk
300 ml/½ pint single cream
¼ teaspoon salt
3 tablespoons castor sugar
2 eggs plus 2 egg yolks
40 g/1½ oz chopped mixed peel
50 g/2 oz red and yellow glacé cherries, chopped
25 g/1 oz almonds, chopped
50 g/2 oz raisins
icing sugar to sprinkle

Allow the pastry to thaw for 1 hour at room temperature.

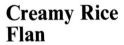

Put the rice, milk, cream, salt and 2 tablespoons of the castor sugar into a saucepan and bring to the boil. Cover and simmer for 20–25 minutes, until the rice is tender and has absorbed all the liquid.
Cool then beat in the eggs and 1 egg yolk.

Preheat the oven to moderately hot (200°C, 400°F, Gas Mark 6). Roll out the pastry to line a 23-cm/9-inch flan ring and bake blind for 10 minutes. Mix all the rice with the candied peel and spread half into the pastry case. Mix the remainder with the cherries, almonds and raisins, spoon over and smooth the top. Whisk the remaining egg yolk with the castor sugar and pour over the rice mixture. Bake in the oven for a further 25 minutes. Cool then sprinkle with icing sugar.

Chelsea Cake

500 g/1 lb plain flour
40 g/1½ oz fresh yeast
60 g/2 oz castor sugar
250 ml/8 fl oz lukewarm milk
100 g/3½ oz margarine, melted
FILLING
200 g/7 oz raisins
2 tablespoons rum
125 g/4½ oz butter, melted
125 g/4½ oz granulated sugar
60 g/2 oz ground almonds
2 teaspoons ground cinnamon
80 g/3 oz chopped mixed peel
GLAZE
1 egg yolk, beaten
2 tablespoons apricot jam

Sift the flour into a bowl and make a well. Cream the yeast with a little of the sugar and the milk and pour into the well. Sprinkle over a little flour, cover and leave in a warm place for 15 minutes, until frothy. Add the margarine with the remaining sugar and mix to a dough. Knead lightly then leave to rise for 1 hour.

Soak the raisins in the rum. Knead the dough again then roll out to 3 mm/⅛ inch thick and brush with the butter. Sprinkle with the sugar, almonds, cinnamon, raisins and chopped peel. Cut the dough into 5-cm/2-inch wide strips. Roll up one strip and place in the centre of a greased 25-cm/10-inch flan tin. Roll the remaining strips around it and leave in a warm place for 15 minutes. Preheat the oven to hot (220°C, 425°F, Gas Mark 7).

Brush with beaten egg yolk and bake the cake for 35 minutes. Cool then spread with the warmed jam.

Fruit Flans

PASTRY
60 g/2 oz soft margarine
45 g/1½ oz icing sugar
few drops of vanilla essence
pinch of salt
1 small egg yolk
125 g/4½ oz plain flour
TOPPING
50 g/2 oz ground almonds
1 tablespoon rum
2 tablespoons sugar syrup
675 g/1½ lb prepared fresh or
drained canned fruit
1 small packet quick-setting jel
mix (lemon)
50 g/2 oz toasted flaked almonds

Knead together the margarine,
sifted icing sugar, vanilla
essence, salt, egg yolk and
sifted flour. Wrap in foil or
cling film and leave for 2 hours
in the refrigerator.

Preheat the oven to moderately hot (200°C, 400°F, Gas
Mark 6). Roll out the pastry on
a floured surface to line the
base of two 15-cm/6-inch flan
tins. Bake blind for 15 minutes
then allow to cool on a wire
rack.

Mix the ground almonds
with the rum and syrup, and
spread over the pastry bases
and sides. Arrange the prepared fruit attractively on top.
Prepare the quick-setting jel
mix, following the instructions
on the packet, and pour over
the fruit. Finally decorate the
sides of the flans with toasted
flaked almonds, pressing them
in well.

Iced Lemon Cake

CAKE MIXTURE
125 g/4½ oz soft margarine
grated rind of 1 lemon
100 g/4 oz castor sugar
2 eggs
3 tablespoons milk
200 g/7 oz self-raising flour
50 g/2 oz cornflour
¼ teaspoon baking powder
SYRUP
2 tablespoons water
juice of 1 lemon
50 g/2 oz sugar
1 tablespoon arrack or ouzo
ICING
100 g/4 oz icing sugar
2 tablespoons lemon juice
strip of lemon peel

Grease a 20 cm/8 inch round
cake tin and sprinkle with fine
breadcrumbs. Preheat the oven
to moderately hot (190°C,
375°F, Gas Mark 5).

Beat together the margarine,
lemon rind and sugar until pale
and creamy. Stir in the eggs
and milk then fold in the sifted
flour, cornflour and baking
powder. Turn into the prepared
cake tin, smooth over the surface, and bake for 40–50
minutes. Turn on to a wire
rack to cool.

Bring the water to the boil
with the lemon juice and sugar.
Add the arrack or ouzo and
pour slowly over the cake,
allowing the syrup to soak well
in.

Mix the sifted icing sugar
with the lemon juice until
smooth and spread thickly on
top of the cake, allowing it to
fall over the sides. Shred the
strip of lemon peel and
sprinkle over the icing before
it sets.

Austrian Hazelnut Cake

100 g/4 oz butter
100 g/4 oz soft brown sugar
2 eggs, separated
1 egg
50 g/2 oz ground hazelnuts
50 g/2 oz self-raising flour
30 g/1 oz candied lemon peel,
  finely chopped
icing sugar to sprinkle

Line the base of a 23-cm/9-inch greased sandwich tin with greaseproof paper. Grease the paper and sprinkle with fine breadcrumbs. Preheat the oven to moderate (180°C, 350°F, Gas Mark 4).

Cream the butter and sugar until light and fluffy, then beat in the egg yolks and egg, one at a time. Grind the hazelnuts with the flour in a liquidiser to give a fine powder and fold into the creamed mixture with the chopped peel. Whisk the egg whites until very stiff and fold into the mixture. Turn into the prepared tin and smooth the surface. Bake for 30 minutes.

Turn on to a wire rack to cool. Place a paper doily on the cake as a stencil and then sift icing sugar over. Remove the doily carefully to leave a pretty pattern.

Walnut Cream Pie

PASTRY
160 g/5½ oz butter
150 g/5 oz castor sugar
pinch of salt
1 egg
300 g/11 oz plain flour
1 egg yolk, beaten to glaze
FILLING
20 g/¾ oz butter
300 g/11 oz granulated sugar
250 g/9 oz walnuts, roughly
  chopped
250 ml/8 fl oz double cream

Cream the softened butter with the sugar, salt and egg. Sift the flour over the top and knead all the ingredients together to make a pastry dough. Cover and leave for 2 hours in the refrigerator.

Roll out two-thirds of the pastry to line the base and sides of a 23-cm/9-inch flan tin, allowing the pastry to overlap the top all the way round. Preheat the oven to moderately hot (200°C, 400°F, Gas Mark 6).

Melt the butter in a pan, add the sugar and cook, stirring continuously, until it caramelises to a light golden brown. Add the walnuts and cream and bring to just below boiling point. Allow to cool then spread into the pastry case. Roll out the remaining pastry to make a lid, brush the overlapping sides with egg yolk and press on to the pastry lid to seal. Brush the top of the pie with egg yolk and prick several times with a fork. Bake for 30–40 minutes then cool on a wire rack.

Linzertorte

200 g/7 oz butter or margarine
200 g/7 oz castor sugar
3 eggs plus 1 egg yolk
pinch each of salt and ground
    cloves
½ teaspoon ground cinnamon
grated rind of ½ lemon
100 g/3½ oz sweet biscuit
    crumbs
150 g/5 oz ground almonds
225 g/8 oz flour
225 g/8 oz raspberry jam
1 egg yolk, beaten to glaze

Grease a 25-cm/10-inch
springform cake tin.

Beat the butter or margarine
with the sugar until light and
creamy. Add the eggs and egg
yolk one at a time with the
salt, cloves, cinnamon and
lemon rind. Mix the biscuit
crumbs with the ground almonds and stir into the
mixture together with the
flour. Chill for 30 minutes in

a refrigerator.

Roll out two-thirds of this
pastry and place in the base of
the cake tin, shaping it so it is
about 1·5/¾ inch high around
the edges.

Preheat the oven to
moderately hot (190°C, 375°F,
Gas Mark 5). Spread the jam
over the pastry base and roll
out the remaining pastry dough.
Cut this into strips, using a
pastry cutter, and arrange in a
lattice pattern over the jam.
Brush with beaten egg yolk and
bake for 35–40 minutes.

Leave to cool in the tin for a
while before turning it on to
a wire rack to cool completely.

Mandorla
Almond Cake

PASTRY
200 g/7 oz plain flour
100 g/3½ oz butter, cut into
    flakes
40 g/1½ oz castor sugar
1 egg yolk
pinch of salt
grated rind of ½ lemon
2 tablespoons water
FILLING
3 tablespoons apricot jam
1 whole egg plus 2 eggs,
    separated
125 g/4½ oz castor sugar
pinch of salt
few drops of vanilla essence
1 tablespoon plain flour
100 g/4 oz ground almonds
60 g/2 oz butter
MERINGUE TOPPING
2 egg whites
100 g/4 oz castor sugar
100 g/4 oz ground almonds

Sift the flour into a bowl and
mix in the butter, sugar, egg
yolk, salt, lemon rind and
water, until a dough is formed.
Cover and leave in the
refrigerator for 2 hours.

Roll out the pastry and use
to line the base and sides of a
23-cm/9-inch sandwich tin.
Spread the jam over the base.
Preheat the oven to moderate
(180°C, 350°F, Gas Mark 4).

Mix together the egg, egg
yolks, half the sugar, the salt,
vanilla essence, flour and
ground almonds. Whisk the
egg whites with the remaining
sugar until stiff and fold into
the mixture. Melt the butter
and fold it in. Pour the filling
on to the pastry base and
bake for 45 minutes.

Whisk the egg whites with
the sugar until stiff and fold
in the almonds. Spread over the
hot cake and bake for a further
15 minutes in a moderately hot
oven (200°C, 400°F, Gas
Mark 6).

Cream Horns

1 (368-g/13-oz) packet frozen
puff pastry
1 egg yolk
1 tablespoon milk
50 g/2 oz flaked almonds
icing sugar to sprinkle
FILLING
150 g/5 oz strawberries
25 g/1 oz icing sugar
150 ml/¼ pint double cream
few drops of vanilla essence

To make these, you will require special cream horn tins. Allow the pastry to thaw for 1 hour at room temperature.

Roll out the pastry on a floured surface to a rectangle 30 × 20 cm/12 × 8 inches. Using a pastry wheel or sharp knife, cut the pastry into eight long strips, each 2·5 cm/1 inch wide. Leave to stand for 15 minutes. Preheat the oven to hot (220°C, 425°F, Gas Mark 7).

Rinse eight cream horn tins in cold water. Beat the egg yolk and milk together. Brush the strips of pastry along one edge with the beaten egg. Starting from the narrow end of the tin, roll the pastry around the tins so that the edge brushed with egg overlaps the unbrushed side by about 5 mm/¼ inch. Press both edges together and brush the pastry horns with the remaining beaten egg. Sprinkle half the horns with flaked almonds. Place them all on a

dampened baking tray and bake for 15 minutes, until puffed up and golden brown.

While still hot, carefully loosen the horns from their tins and cool on a wire rack. Sift icing sugar over those not decorated with almonds.

Wash and hull the strawberries, drain and purée in a liquidiser or press through a sieve. Stir the icing sugar into this strawberry purée. Whip the cream with the vanilla essence until stiff. Put just over half the cream into a piping bag fitted with a star nozzle and pipe into the horns sprinkled with icing sugar. Mix the rest of the cream with the strawberry purée and pipe this into the remaining horns.

Cook's Tip

If you want to make cream horns, but do not have the special tins, the shape can be made using cardboard and covering it with foil. Allow 2–3 minutes longer baking time as foil is not such a good conductor of heat. During these last few minutes of baking, cover the horns with grease-proof paper, so they do not turn too brown on the outside before cooking through completely.

Palmiers

1 (368-g/13-oz) packet frozen
  puff pastry
about 100 g/4 oz castor sugar
1 egg, beaten to glaze

Allow the pastry to thaw for 1
hour at room temperature.

Roll out thinly on sugared
paper into a rectangle 30 × 35
cm/12 × 14 inches. Sprinkle
with a little sugar and roll up
the two shorter edges of the
pastry into the centre, until
they meet. Brush with a little
beaten egg and turn the roll
over. Using a sharp knife, cut
into slices 5 mm/¼ inch thick.
Place well apart on dampened
baking trays, brush with
beaten egg yolk and leave for
15 minutes.

Preheat the oven to
moderately hot (200°C, 400°F,
Gas Mark 6) and bake the
palmiers for 8–12 minutes.

Cook's Tip

Be careful not to brush
the edges of the palmiers
with egg yolk, as this will
cause the layers to stick
together and prevent the
pastry from rising during
baking.

Orange Windmills

1 (368-g/13-oz) packet frozen
  puff pastry
1 egg yolk, beaten to glaze
FILLING
25 g/1 oz ground almonds
1 tablespoon orange jelly
  marmalade
1 teaspoon orange liqueur
ICING
50 g/2 oz icing sugar
1 tablespoon hot water
20 g/¾ oz pistachio nuts, chopped

Allow the pastry to thaw for 1
hour at room temperature.

Roll out on a lightly floured
board into a 37·5-cm/15-inch
square. Divide into sixteen
8·5-cm/3½-inch squares,
leaving two strips of pastry
for later. Cut diagonally in
from the corner of each square
towards the centre, leaving the
pastry joined in the centre for
the filling. Mix the ground
almonds with the marmalade
and orange liqueur and place a
little in the centre of each
square. Fold the points of the
four cut corners to the centre,
to form windmills. Secure
firmly and brush with egg
yolk. Cut out 16 small rounds
from the leftover strips of
pastry and place in the centre
of each windmill. Brush with
beaten egg yolk. Place on a
dampened baking tray and
leave for 15 minutes.

Preheat the oven to hot
(220°C, 425°F, Gas Mark 7)
and bake the pastries for 10–12
minutes. Transfer to a wire
cooling rack. Blend the sifted
icing sugar with the water, use
to ice the windmills and
sprinkle with the chopped
pistachios.

Swiss Choux Rings

CHOUX PASTE
60 g/2 oz butter
250 ml/8 fl oz water
pinch of salt
200 g/7 oz plain flour
4 eggs
ICING
50 g/2 oz apricot jam
100 g/4 oz plain chocolate
FILLING
40 g/1½ oz cornflour
180 g/6 oz castor sugar
4 eggs, separated
500 ml/17 fl oz milk
¼ teaspoon vanilla essence

Preheat the oven to hot (220°C, 425°F, Gas Mark 7). 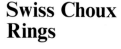 Grease a baking tray.

Heat the butter in the water until melted, add the salt and bring to the boil. Tip in the sifted flour all at once and stir vigorously until the mixture leaves the sides of the pan and forms a smooth ball. Leave to cool slightly then add the eggs one at a time. Pipe 16 small rings on to the baking tray and bake for 20 minutes. Split the rings after cooking to allow steam to escape.

Warm the jam and spread over the top of the rings. Melt the chocolate in a basin over hot water and pour over the jam on the rings.

Blend the cornflour with the sugar, egg yolks and a little of the milk. Heat the remaining milk then pour on to the blended mixture together with the vanilla essence. Return to the pan and bring to the boil, stirring continuously. Boil for a few seconds then cool slightly. Whisk the egg whites until stiff and fold into the cornflour custard which should be just warm. Cool completely, cut the rings in half and fill with the cornflour custard.

Iced Vanilla Slices

1 (368-g/13-oz) packet frozen
  puff pastry
ICING
200 g/7 oz icing sugar
1 tablespoon water
1 tablespoon lemon juice
FILLING
4 eggs, separated
150 g/5 oz icing sugar
50 g/2 oz cornflour
30 g/1 oz castor sugar
¼ teaspoon vanilla essence
500 ml/17 fl oz milk

Allow the pastry to thaw for 1 hour at room temperature. Preheat the oven to hot (220°C, 425°F, Gas Mark 7).

Roll out the pastry to an oblong 60 × 45 cm/24 × 18 inches. Cut it in half widthways and place on a baking tray sprinkled with cold water. Prick with a fork and leave to stand in a cool place for 15 minutes. Bake the pastry for 12–18 minutes then leave to cool on a wire rack.

Mix the sifted icing sugar with the water and lemon juice and ice one of the pastry pieces.

Prepare the filling. Whisk the egg whites with the sifted icing sugar until stiff and glossy. Blend the cornflour with the egg yolks, castor sugar, vanilla essence and a little milk. Bring the remaining milk to the boil and pour on to the cornflour mixture. Return to the heat and cook for a few minutes, stirring until thickened. Fold in the whisked egg whites and leave to cool. Spread this filling thickly over the piece of pastry without icing and put the iced pastry on top.

Leave in the refrigerator until set and then cut into slices.

Cream Slices

1 (368-g/13-oz) packet frozen
puff pastry
100 g/4 oz sugar crystals
FILLING
300 ml/½ pint double cream
few drops of vanilla essence
1 tablespoon castor sugar

Allow the pastry to thaw for 1 hour at room temperature.

Roll out the pastry fairly thinly and cut out oval shapes approximately 13 cm/5 inches long. Rinse a baking tray with cold water, arrange the pastry ovals on it and sprinkle th sugar over them. Leave to stand in the refrigerator for 15 minutes.

Preheat the oven to hot (230°C, 450°F, Gas Mark 8). Bake the pastry for 10 minutes, then leave to cool on a wire rack. Whip the cream with the vanilla essence and castor sugar until stiff. Spread the

cream over half the pastry ovals on the unsugared side, and place a second oval on top, sugar side up.

Lemon Ring Biscuits

150 g/6 oz plain flour
1 teaspoon baking powder
100 g/4 oz cornflour
100 g/4 oz butter
100 g/4 oz castor sugar
2 egg yolks
grated rind of 2 lemons
ICING
125 g/5 oz icing sugar
2 tablespoons lemon juice
50 g/2 oz pistachio nuts, chopped

Sift the flour, baking powder and cornflour into a mixing bowl. Melt the butter and stir into it the sugar, egg yolks and lemon rind. Add to the flour and mix all the ingredients together to give a smooth biscuit dough. Cover and chill in the refrigerator until firm.

Preheat the oven to moderately hot (200°C, 400°F, Gas Mark 6). Roll out the

dough on a floured surface to 3 mm/⅛ inch thick. Using a 6-cm/2½-inch fluted cutter, cut out circles from the dough. Cut out the centre of each biscuit using a 1-cm/½-inch fluted cutter. Roll out the centres to make more biscuits. Place the ring biscuits on to two greased baking trays and bake for about 10 minutes.

Cool slightly on the trays, then lift off with a palette knife and cool on a wire rack.

Blend the sifted icing sugar with the lemon juice and spread over the biscuits. Decorate with the chopped pistachio nuts before the icing sets.

Bath Buns

500 g/1 lb plain flour
30 g/1 oz fresh yeast
185 ml/6 fl oz lukewarm milk
120 g/4 oz butter, melted
2 eggs
80 g/3 oz castor sugar
100 g/4 oz chopped mixed peel
¼ teaspoon salt
¼ teaspoon ground aniseed
pinch of ground cinnamon
grated rind of ½ lemon
80 g/3 oz raisins
GLAZE
1 egg yolk, beaten
60 g/2 oz sugar crystals

Sift the flour into a bowl and make a well in the centre. Cream the yeast with a little of the milk, pour into the well in the flour with the remaining milk, sprinkle over a little flour and leave for 15 minutes, until frothy. Add the melted butter, eggs and sugar and beat all together to a dough. Then work

in the finely chopped peel, salt, spices, lemon rind and raisins. Cover and leave to rise until doubled in size, up to 1 hour.

Knead the dough on a lightly floured board until smooth. Shape into small buns and place well apart on greased baking trays. Leave to rise in a warm place until doubled in size.

Preheat the oven to moderately hot (200°C, 400°F, Gas Mark 6). Brush the buns with beaten egg yolk, sprinkle with sugar crystals and bake for 15–20 minutes.

Shrewsbury Biscuits

530 g/1¼ lb plain flour
300 g/12 oz castor sugar
2 eggs
pinch each of salt and ground cinnamon
300 g/12 oz butter, cut into flakes

Line two baking trays with greased greaseproof paper.

Sift the flour on to a working surface, make a well in the centre and add the sugar, eggs, salt and cinnamon. Dot the butter over the flour and quickly knead all the ingredients to a smooth dough. Wrap the mixture in foil and leave for 2 hours in the refrigerator.

Preheat the oven to moderate (180°C, 350°F, Gas Mark 4). Roll out the biscuit dough on a floured surface to a thickness of about 3 mm/⅛ inch. Cut out

rounds measuring 6–7.5 cm/ 2½–3 inches in diameter. Place on the baking trays and bake for 15–20 minutes.

Allow the biscuits to cool on the trays before removing with a palette knife.

330

Shortbread Fingers

320 g/11 oz butter
180 g/6 oz castor sugar
¼ teaspoon salt
500 g/1 lb 2 oz plain flour
castor sugar to sprinkle

Cream the butter with the sugar and salt until pale and fluffy. Sift the flour and knead into the creamed ingredients to give a workable dough. Cover and leave for 2 hours in the refrigerator.

Preheat the oven to moderately hot (190°C, 375°F, Gas Mark 5). Roll out the mixture on a floured surface until 1·5 cm/¾ inch thick and place on a greased baking tray. Prick several times with a fork and bake for 25–30 minutes.

Whilst still warm, cut the shortbread into fingers with a sharp knife and sprinkle with castor sugar.

Teacakes

Prepare these using the recipe for Bath Buns (see left), but use 1 teaspoon of sugar to sweeten the mixture instead of 80 g/ 3 oz. Leave out the aniseed, cinnamon and lemon rind. Instead of using mixed peel and raisins, add 150 g/5 oz currants. Brush the risen teacakes with egg yolk before baking.

Orange Almond Cookies

250 g/9 oz butter or margarine
250 g/9 oz soft brown sugar
2 eggs
325 g/12 oz plain flour
1 teaspoon baking powder
¼ teaspoon salt
grated rind of 1 large or 2 small oranges
75 g/3 oz blanched almonds, chopped

Beat the butter with the sugar until pale and creamy. Add the eggs one at a time. Sift the flour and baking powder with the salt then stir a spoonful at a time into the creamed mixture. Finally add the orange rind and chopped almonds and mix thoroughly. Form the dough into a roll, 6 cm/2½ inches in diameter. Wrap in foil and leave in the refrigerator for 24 hours.

Preheat the oven to moderately hot (200°C, 400°F, Gas Mark 6). Cut thin slices from the roll of biscuit dough and lay on greased baking trays. Bake the cookies for 8–10 minutes. Leave to cool slightly on the tray then remove to a wire rack.

Cook's Tip

Instead of flavouring the cookies with orange, try using a mixture of lemon and orange rind and substitute desiccated coconut for the almonds.

Macaroon Bars

4 egg whites
225 g/8 oz castor sugar
225 g/8 oz flaked almonds
¼ teaspoon ground cinnamon
grated rind of 1 lemon
50 g/2 oz plain chocolate

Line a 19 × 29-cm/7½ × 11½-inch baking tray with rice paper. Preheat the oven to very cool (110°C, 325°F, Gas Mark ¼).

Whisk the egg whites until stiff. Gradually whisk in half the sugar then fold in the remaining sugar with the flaked almonds, cinnamon and grated lemon rind. Spread the mixture over the baking tray and bake for 3–4 hours. Halfway through the cooking time cut the macaroon mixture into fingers. Cool on a wire rack when completely cooked.

Melt the chocolate in a basin over a pan of hot water. Dip both ends of the macaroons into the chocolate and leave to set.

Cook's Tip

Place small spoonfuls of the macaroon mixture on to the rice paper. When cooked and cooled, sandwich together in pairs with a little melted chocolate.

Aniseed Biscuits

4 eggs, separated
225 g/8 oz icing sugar
pinch of salt
300 g/11 oz plain flour
2 teaspoons ground aniseed

Grease a baking tray and sprinkle with flour.
Cream the egg yolks with the sifted icing sugar and salt until pale and light. Whisk the egg whites until very stiff, then fold into the yolk mixture. Sift the flour and aniseed on to this mixture and fold in quickly but thoroughly. Fill a piping bag fitted with a plain nozzle with the biscuit mixture and pipe in small rounds on to the baking tray. Leave to dry out overnight.
  Preheat the oven to moderate (160°C, 325°F, Gas Mark 3), and bake towards the top of the oven for 20 minutes. Cool on a wire rack.

Cook's Tip
To make Cinnamon Biscuits, substitute 2 teaspoons ground cinnamon for the ground aniseed.

Chocolate Macaroons

100 g/4 oz plain chocolate
4 egg whites
200 g/7 oz castor sugar
225 g/8 oz ground almonds

Line a baking tray with non-stick baking parchment or rice paper. Preheat the oven to moderate (180°C, 350°F, Gas Mark 4).
  Grate the chocolate. Whisk the egg whites until stiff. Add the sugar gradually and continue whisking until the mixture is thick and glossy. Fold in the ground almonds and grated chocolate. Drop spoonfuls of the mixture on to the baking tray, leaving space between each biscuit. Bake for 15–20 minutes. Do not let the macaroons become too dark or they will taste bitter.
  Cool on the baking tray,

then carefully peel the macaroons off the non-stick paper or cut around each biscuit on the edible rice paper.

333

Nutmeg Biscuits

125 g/4 oz butter
125 g/4 oz castor sugar
1 egg
grated rind of ½ lemon
generous pinch of grated nutmeg
pinch each of ground cinnamon
and ground cloves
125 g/4 oz plain flour
125 g/4 oz hazelnuts, finely
chopped
125 g/4 oz fresh white
breadcrumbs
1 egg yolk, beaten to glaze
50 g/2 oz blanched almonds

Beat the butter with the sugar, egg, lemon rind and spices. Mix the sifted flour with the hazelnuts and breadcrumbs, add to the butter mixture and knead all the ingredients quickly to a dough. Cover and leave for 2 hours in the refrigerator.

Preheat the oven to moderately hot (200°C, 400°F,

Gas Mark 6). Roll out the dough to 5 mm/¼ inch thick. Cut out small scalloped arcs 6 cm/2½ inches long and 2·5 cm/1 inch wide. Place on greased baking trays and brush with beaten egg yolk. Place a blanched almond on each biscuit and bake for 10–15 minutes.

> ### Cook's Tip
> If you do not have the proper biscuit cutter, make a cardboard pattern and use it to help you cut out the arcs.

Iced Lemon Bars

150 g/5 oz butter
125 g/4 oz castor sugar
1 egg
generous pinch each of ground
cinnamon, ground cloves and
grated nutmeg
grated rind of 1 lemon
125 g/4 oz plain flour
125 g/4 oz ground almonds
125 g/4 oz fresh white
breadcrumbs
ICING
200 g/7 oz icing sugar
2–3 tablespoons lemon juice
30 g/1 oz candied lemon peel
30 g/1 oz candied orange peel

Beat the butter with the sugar until pale and creamy. Stir in the egg, spices and lemon rind. Sift in the flour, gradually add the almonds and breadcrumbs and knead to a smooth soft dough. Wrap in foil or cling film and leave for 2 hours in the refrigerator.

Preheat the oven to moderately hot (200°C, 400°F, Gas Mark 6). Roll out the dough on a floured board to 5 mm/¼ inch thick and cut out bars 2·5 × 6 cm/1 × 2½ inches. Place on greased baking trays, allowing room between each for spreading. Bake for 10–15 minutes then remove with a palette knife and place on a wire rack.

Sift the icing sugar and stir in the lemon juice until smooth. Use to thickly ice the biscuits when they are slightly cooled. Cut the lemon and orange peel into thin strips and place on the icing while still soft.

Apricot Rings

400 g / 14 oz plain flour
120 g / 4 oz castor sugar
pinch of salt
grated rind of 1 lemon
25 g / 1 oz vanilla sugar
1 egg
2 tablespoons rum
250 g / 9 oz butter, cut into flakes
icing sugar to sprinkle
225 g / 8 oz apricot jam

Sift the flour into a mixing bowl. Make a well in the centre and add the sugar, salt, lemon rind, vanilla sugar, egg and rum. Dot the butter over the flour and knead all the ingredients to a soft dough. Wrap in foil or cling film and leave for 2 hours in the refrigerator.

Preheat the oven to moderate (180°C, 350°F, Gas Mark 4). Roll out the dough a little at a time on a floured board, to a thickness of

3 mm/⅛ inch. Using a plain and ring cutter of the same size, cut out equal quantities of rounds and rings. Place all on greased baking trays and bake for 10–15 minutes.

Remove from the baking tray with a palette knife and leave to cool on a wire rack. Sift icing sugar generously on to the rings. Warm the jam over a low heat and spread smoothly on to the rounds. Place the rings on top. Add a little more jam to the centre of the rings and cool completely before storing in an airtight tin.

Italian Biscotti

150 g / 5 oz butter
200 g / 7 oz castor sugar
few drops of vanilla essence
1 egg yolk
1 tablespoon milk
generous pinch each of ground cardamom and ground cinnamon
grated rind of ½ lemon
75 g / 3 oz ground almonds
150 g / 5 oz plain flour
100 g / 4 oz plain chocolate

Beat the butter in a mixing bowl with the sugar and vanilla essence until pale and creamy. Add the egg yolk, milk, spices, lemon rind and almonds and knead the sifted flour into this mixture. Chill in the refrigerator for 1 hour. Form the dough into rectangular blocks, about 3·5 cm/1½ inches in diameter, wrap in foil and leave in the refrigerator for 2 hours.

Preheat the oven to moderately hot (190°C, 375°F, Gas Mark 5). Cut the blocks of dough into 5-mm/¼-inch slices, place on a baking tray and bake for 15 minutes.

Remove the biscuits with a palette knife and cool on a wire rack. Melt the chocolate in a basin over a pan of hot water. Dip the biscuits into the chocolate so that they are half-coated diagonally and leave to dry on greaseproof paper.

Dutch Zebras

250 g/9 oz butter
200 g/7 oz castor sugar
½ teaspoon salt
4 egg yolks
250 g/9 oz plain flour
100 g/3½ oz cornflour
½ teaspoon baking powder
2 tablespoons rum
4 tablespoons cocoa powder
2 tablespoons sugar crystals

Cream the butter with the sugar and salt until light and fluffy. Add the egg yolks one at a time and beat well until smooth. Sift the flour with the cornflour and baking powder, add to the butter mixture and knead to a firm dough. Halve the dough; mix the rum into one half and the sifted cocoa powder into the other. Cover both portions and leave for 1 hour in the refrigerator.

Preheat the oven to moderately hot (190°C, 375°F, Gas Mark 5). Roll out the light and dark dough separately on a floured board until very thin (1·5 mm/1/16 inch). Halve each portion and place the pieces of light and dark dough alternately one upon the other, to make four striped layers. Press together well and cut into small oblong shapes. Sprinkle each with the sugar crystals and press the sugar in slightly. Place on greased baking trays and bake for 15–20 minutes.

Remove from the baking trays with a palette knife and leave to cool on a wire rack.

French Madeleines

125 g/4 oz castor sugar
125 g/4 oz self-raising flour
125 g/4 oz butter
3 eggs
pinch of salt
60 g/2 oz ground almonds
2 teaspoons orange flower water
¼ teaspoon vanilla essence

For Madeleines you will need the traditional small shell-shaped tins. Grease the tins with butter.

Mix the sugar and sifted flour together in a bowl. Melt but do not brown the butter. Mix the eggs into the flour and sugar with a wooden spoon and gradually add the cooled butter, salt, ground almonds, orange flower water and vanilla essence. Cover and leave to stand for 1 hour in the refrigerator.

Preheat the oven to moderately hot (200°C, 400°F, Gas Mark 6). Half-fill the greased tins with the cake mixture and bake for 10–15 minutes.

Cook's Tip

If you have no Madeleine tins, use individual patty or brioche tins.

Florentines

100 g/4 oz butter
150 g/6 oz castor sugar
50 g/2 oz honey
4 tablespoons double cream
pinch of salt
grated rind of ½ lemon
180 g/7 oz flaked almonds
30 g/1 oz candied orange peel,
  finely chopped
ICING
100 g/4 oz plain chocolate
10 glacé cherries

Grease two baking trays. Pre-heat the oven to moderate (180°C, 350°F, Gas Mark 4).

Mix the butter, sugar, honey, cream, salt and lemon rind together in a saucepan. Lightly boil these ingredients for approximately 4–5 minutes, stirring continuously until the mixture becomes thick and creamy and leaves the sides of the pan. Add the almonds and chopped peel to the pan and stir them well in. Remove the pan from the heat. Place heaped teaspoonfuls of the mixture well apart on the baking trays and flatten slightly with the back of a wet spoon. Bake the florentines for approximately 10 minutes.

Leave to cool on the tray for a few minutes until they are firm enough to be lifted on to a wire rack. Melt the chocolate in a basin over hot water and spread thickly over the under-side of the florentines, marking into ridges with a fork. When set, place a halved cherry on the top of each florentine, to decorate.

Almond Tartlets

1 (368-g/13-oz) packet frozen
  puff pastry
FILLING
125 g/4¼ oz ground almonds
125 g/4¼ oz castor sugar
1 egg
3 tablespoons milk
1 tablespoon rum
grated rind of 1 lemon
12 almonds, halved

Allow the pastry to thaw for 1 hour at room temperature.

Roll out the pastry on a floured surface to a thickness of 3 mm/⅛ inch. Rinse about eight small tartlet or patty tins in cold water. Line each tin with pastry and prick the pastry several times with a fork. Leave to stand in the refrigerator for 15 minutes. Preheat the oven to hot (220°C, 425°F, Gas Mark 7).

Mix the ground almonds, sugar, egg, milk, rum and lemon rind together. Fill the pastry cases with this mixture. Smooth over the surface and put 3 almond halves on top of each. Bake the tartlets for 20 minutes.

Allow to cool for a few minutes in the tins, then turn out carefully on to a wire rack.

Blackberry Meringue Pie

PASTRY
200 g/7 oz plain flour
pinch of salt
100 g/3¾ oz butter, cut into flakes
1 egg
2 tablespoons water
25 g/1 oz castor sugar
FILLING
350 g/12 oz blackberries
75 g/3 oz castor sugar
2 teaspoons cornflour
3 tablespoons gooseberry jam
MERINGUE
3 egg whites
175 g/6 oz castor sugar

bowl. Rub in the butter then stir in the egg, water and sugar. Form into a pastry dough, wrap in foil or cling film and leave for 2 hours in the refrigerator.

Sprinkle the blackberries with the sugar and leave to drain in a sieve over a saucepan. Warm the berry juice. Blend the cornflour with 1 tablespoon water, stir into the berry juice, bring to the boil, stirring, and simmer until thickened. Add the blackberries and allow to cool.

Preheat the oven to moderate (160°C, 325°F, Gas Mark 3). Roll out the pastry to line a 20-cm/8-inch loose-bottomed flan tin. Bake blind for 15–20 minutes then allow to cool. Spread the jam over the pastry base and cover with the blackberry mixture.

Whisk the egg whites until stiff then whisk in half the sugar and fold in the rest. Pipe a lattice work over the filling and bake in a moderate oven (180°C, 350°F, Gas Mark 4) for 15 minutes. Cool before serving.

Fresh Plum Tart

PASTRY
300 g/10 oz plain flour
200 g/7 oz butter, cut into flakes
100 g/3½ oz castor sugar
1 egg
FILLING
1·5 kg/3 lb plums
2 tablespoons sugar crystals

Sift the flour into a mixing bowl. Add the butter, sugar and egg and mix well until a dough is formed. Wrap in foil or cling film and leave for 2 hours in the refrigerator.

Wash the plums, halve and remove the stones and cut the fruit into quarters. Preheat the oven to moderately hot (200°C, 400°F, Gas Mark 6).

Roll out the pastry on a floured surface and use to line a 25-cm/10-inch flan tin. Prick the base of the flan all over with a fork. Arrange the plums in a rosette shape to fill the flan

and sprinkle sugar crystals over the top. Bake the tart for 30–35 minutes; cover with foil if becoming too brown. Leave the tart to cool on a wire rack, sprinkle with extra sugar crystals and serve with whipped cream.

338

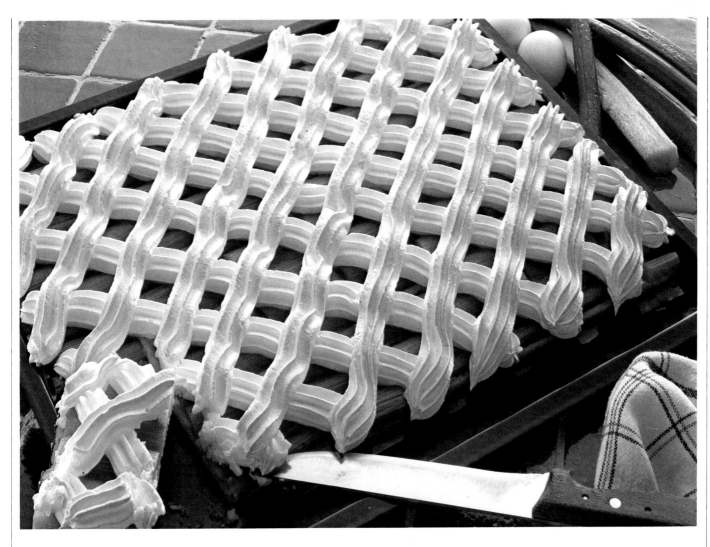

Rhubarb Meringue Tart

PASTRY
300 g/10 oz plain flour
200 g/7 oz butter or margarine,
  cut into flakes
100 g/3½ oz castor sugar
1 egg
TOPPING
1 kg/2 lb rhubarb
sugar to sprinkle
3 egg whites
150 g/5 oz castor sugar

Sift the flour into a mixing bowl. Add the butter, sugar and egg and mix until a dough is formed. Wrap the pastry in foil or cling film and leave for 2 hours in the refrigerator.

Wash the rhubarb, dry on absorbent paper and pull away the thin outer skin from the top downwards. Cut the sticks of rhubarb into 7·5-cm/3-inch lengths. Preheat the oven to moderately hot (200°C, 400°F, Gas Mark 6).

Roll out the pastry on a floured surface into a rectangle approximately 25 × 20 cm/ 10 × 8 inches. Carefully lift the pastry on to a baking tray and prick all over with a fork. Arrange the lengths of rhubarb next to one another on the pastry base and sprinkle with a little sugar to taste. Bake for 30 minutes then allow to cool slightly.

Whisk the egg whites until stiff, whisk in a little of the sugar then fold in the rest.

Put the meringue mixture into a piping bag fitted with a star nozzle and pipe an even, diagonal trellis over the top of the tart. Return to the oven and cook for a further 10 minutes, until the meringue is lightly browned.

Allow the tart to cool a little, cut into even slices and leave to cool on a wire rack.

Cook's Tip

If piping is too time-consuming, spread the meringue over the rhubarb with a palette knife. The tart won't look quite as distinguished, but it will taste just as good. You can also use blackberries, gooseberries or bilberries to make the flan.

Alsace Apple Tart

PASTRY
200 g/7 oz plain flour
100 g/3½ oz butter or margarine, cut into flakes
1 egg yolk
30 g/1 oz castor sugar
pinch of salt
2 tablespoons cold water
FILLING
1 kg/2 lb cooking apples
2 tablespoons lemon juice
100 g/4 oz castor sugar
3 eggs
125 ml/4 fl oz double cream
few drops of vanilla essence

Sift the flour into a mixing bowl. Add the butter, egg yolk, sugar, salt and water and mix until a dough is formed. Wrap in foil or cling film and leave for 2 hours in the refrigerator.

Peel the apples, quarter and remove the cores. Slice each apple quarter very thinly, keeping the quarter in shape, and sprinkle with the lemon juice. Preheat the oven to moderately hot (200°C, 400°F, Gas Mark 6).

Roll out the pastry to 5 mm/¼ inch thick and use to line a 23-cm/9-inch flan tin. Prick the base all over with a fork and arrange the sliced apple quarters on it. Bake for 20–25 minutes.

Meanwhile, beat the sugar with the eggs until frothy and add the cream and vanilla essence. Pour the egg mixture into the half-cooked flan and bake for a further 20–30 minutes.

Allow the flan to cool for a while in the tin then transfer to a wire rack to cool completely.

Apple Lattice Flan

PASTRY
450 g/1 lb plain flour
150 g/5 oz margarine, cut into flakes
25 g/1 oz castor sugar
½ teaspoon salt
150 ml/¼ pint water
FILLING
1 kg/2 lb cooking apples
grated rind and juice of 1 lemon
125 g/4½ oz sugar
1 teaspoon ground cinnamon
100 g/4 oz raisins
100 g/4 oz hazelnuts, chopped
GLAZE
1 egg yolk, beaten
4 tablespoons apricot jam
100 g/4 oz icing sugar
1½ tablespoons lemon juice

Sift the flour into a bowl and rub in the margarine. Add the sugar, salt and water and mix to a dough. Wrap in foil or cling film and leave for 1 hour in the refrigerator.

Peel the apples, chop roughly and mix with the lemon rind and juice, sugar, cinnamon, raisins and hazelnuts. Preheat the oven to moderately hot (200°C, 400°F, Gas Mark 6).

Roll out three-quarters of the pastry to line the base and sides of a 33 × 23-cm/13 × 9-inch Swiss roll tin. Spread the apple mixture over the pastry. Roll out the remaining pastry, cut into thin strips and arrange over the flan in a lattice pattern. Brush with beaten egg yolk and bake the flan for 30–40 minutes. Leave to cool.

Brush the pastry with the warmed apricot jam. Mix the sifted icing sugar and lemon juice together and use to glaze the trellis.

Plum Lattice Tart

PASTRY
300 g/11 oz plain flour
pinch of salt
180 g/6 oz butter, cut into flakes
1 egg yolk
120 g/4 oz castor sugar
FILLING
1 kg/2 lb plums
2 tablespoons cornflour
150 g/5 oz sugar
25 g/1 oz butter
50 g/2 oz walnuts, chopped
icing sugar to sprinkle

Sift the flour into a mixing bowl and add the salt, flaked 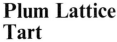 butter, egg yolk and sugar. Mix to a pastry dough, cover and leave in the refrigerator for 1 hour.

Wash, stone and quarter the plums and cook in a little water for 5 minutes. Mix the cornflour with 3 tablespoons

cold water and stir into the plums with the sugar. Continue to cook until thickened, stirring all the time. Remove from the heat and stir in the butter and walnuts. Leave to cool.

Preheat the oven to moderately hot (200°C, 400°F, Gas Mark 6). Roll out the pastry to line a 23-cm/9-inch flan tin, reserving enough pastry to make the lattice. Spread the plum filling into the flan case. Cut the remaining pastry into thin strips and arrange in a lattice pattern over the plums.

Bake for 35–45 minutes. Sprinkle with sifted icing sugar to serve.

Grape Cream Flan

PASTRY
300 g/10 oz plain flour
200 g/7 oz butter, cut into flakes
100 g/3½ oz castor sugar
1 egg
FILLING
600 ml/1 pint milk
50 g/2 oz cornflour
25 g/1 oz castor sugar
2 eggs, separated
500 g/1 lb black grapes, washed and pips removed
150 ml/¼ pint double cream

Place the sifted flour in a mixing bowl with the butter, sugar and egg and mix until a dough is formed. Wrap in foil or cling film and leave in the refrigerator for 2 hours.

Preheat the oven to moderately hot (190°C, 375°F, Gas Mark 5). Roll out the pastry to line a 23-cm/9-inch

flan tin and bake blind for 20 minutes, until cooked. Allow the pastry to cool.

Blend 4 tablespoons milk with the cornflour, sugar and egg yolks. Bring the remaining milk to the boil and pour on to the cornflour. Return to the heat and bring to the boil, stirring until thickened. Allow to cool, stirring frequently to prevent a skin forming. Whisk the egg whites until stiff and fold into the cooled mixture. Place half this filling in the pastry case. Reserve 12 grapes for decoration and place the remainder on top of the filling. Cover with the remaining filling, smoothing evenly. Chill in the refrigerator until set.

Decorate the flan with piped whipped cream and grapes.

French Orange Flan

PASTRY
100 g/4 oz butter
50 g/2 oz icing sugar
1 egg yolk
150 g/6 oz plain flour
FILLING
4 tablespoons orange jelly
    marmalade
250 ml/8 fl oz double cream
100 g/4 oz castor sugar
6 eggs
grated rind of 3 lemons
DECORATION
1 orange
50 g/2 oz sugar
2 tablespoons water
4 cherries

Knead together the butter,
sifted icing sugar and egg yolk.
Sift the flour on to this mixture
and work in quickly with the
fingertips. Cover the dough and
leave for 2 hours in the
refrigerator.

Preheat the oven to moderately hot (200°C, 400°F, Gas
Mark 6). Roll out the pastry to
a thickness of about 3 mm/
⅛ inch and carefully line two
15-cm/6-inch flan dishes.
Spread the base of the flans
with the orange marmalade.
Beat the cream, sugar, eggs and
lemon rind together until
frothy and pour into the flan
cases. Cook for 45–50 minutes.

Peel the orange carefully,
removing all the pith, and slice
thinly. Dissolve the sugar in the
water over a low heat, stirring
continuously until the sugar
has completely dissolved. Place
the orange slices in the hot
sugar syrup, leave for 3 minutes
and then drain. Arrange over
the flans and top with the
cherries, also glazed in the
sugar syrup.

Chinese Gooseberry Cream Tart

1 (368-g/13-oz) packet frozen
    puff pastry, thawed
1 egg yolk, beaten to glaze
FILLING
250 ml/8 fl oz double cream
2 tablespoons castor sugar
1½ teaspoons powdered gelatine
1 tablespoon rum
6 Chinese gooseberries
1½ teaspoons arrowroot

Roll out the pastry quite thinly
and cut out a 20-cm/8-inch
round from the centre. Using a
5-cm/2-inch round cutter, cut
out 12 half-moon shapes from
the surrounding pastry.
Sprinkle a baking tray with
cold water, place the pastry
round on it and brush with
beaten egg yolk. Prick the
pastry all over with a fork.

Place the half-moon shapes
around the edge of the pastry
and brush these with egg yolk.
Leave in the refrigerator for
15 minutes. Preheat the oven to
hot (220°C, 425°F, Gas Mark
7) and bake towards the top of
the oven for 15 minutes. Cool
on a wire rack.

Whip the cream and sugar
together until stiff. Dissolve the
gelatine in 3 tablespoons hot
water over a gentle heat. Allow
to cool then stir into the cream
with the rum. When half-set,
spread the cream over the
pastry base, mounding it up in
the centre, and leave in the
refrigerator until firm.

Peel the Chinese goose-
berries, cut into slices and
arrange overlapping on the
cream. Blend the arrowroot in
a pan with a little water. Add
150 ml/¼ pint cold water and
bring to the boil, stirring continuously. Leave until just
warm then pour over the fruit
to glaze.

Gooseberry Meringue Pie

PASTRY
250 g/9 oz plain flour
125 g/4½ oz butter, cut into flakes
25 g/1 oz castor sugar
1 egg
FILLING
500 g/1 lb gooseberries
450 ml/¾ pint water
25 g/1 oz granulated sugar
25 g/1 oz castor sugar
450 ml/¾ pint milk
2 egg yolks
20 g/¾ oz cornflour
MERINGUE
3 egg whites
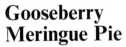

Sift the flour into a bowl. Add the butter, sugar and egg and mix to a dough. Wrap in foil or cling film and chill for 2 hours.

Wash the gooseberries and top and tail them. Cook in the water with the granulated sugar for 15 minutes and allow to cool in a sieve over a basin. Preheat the oven to moderately hot (200°C, 400°F, Gas Mark 6).

Roll out the pastry to line the base and sides of a 23-cm/ 9-inch sandwich cake tin. Prick all over with a fork and bake blind for 20 minutes.

Meanwhile, whisk the castor sugar with 3 tablespoons milk, the egg yolks and cornflour. Bring the rest of the milk to the boil, pour on to the cornflour mixture then return to the saucepan. Bring to the boil, stirring until thickened. Pour into the pastry case and arrange the gooseberries on top.

Whisk the egg whites until very stiff then add the sifted icing sugar and whisk again. Spread this meringue over the gooseberries and cook for 5–10 minutes in a hot oven (220°C, 425°F, Gas Mark 7).

Raspberry Meringue Nest

MERINGUE
6 egg whites
175 g/6 oz castor sugar
150 g/5 oz icing sugar
30 g/1 oz cornflour
FILLING
250 ml/8 fl oz double cream
1 tablespoon brandy
350 g/12 oz raspberries

Line a baking tray with non-stick baking parchment. Preheat the oven to very cool (110°C, 225°F, Gas Mark ¼).

Whisk the egg whites until stiff then gradually whisk in the castor sugar. Fold in the sifted icing sugar and cornflour. Fill a piping bag fitted with a large plain nozzle with the mixture, and pipe in a spiral on to the baking tray to make a 20–23-cm/8–9-inch round base. Form the sides of the meringue nest by piping individual rosettes over the edge. Allow to dry out in the oven for 12 hours, leaving the oven door slightly ajar.

Remove from the oven and leave to cool. Whip the cream with the brandy until thick. Spread this cream into the meringue nest and cover with the raspberries.

343

Gooseberry Meringue Tartlets

PASTRY
160 g/5 oz plain flour
100 g/3 oz butter
60 g/2 oz castor sugar
pinch of salt
1 tablespoon soured cream
2 egg yolks
FILLING
500 g/1 lb gooseberries
60 g/2 oz sugar
4 tablespoons brandy
300 ml/½ pint milk
2 tablespoons cornflour
3 tablespoons double cream
25 g/1 oz icing sugar
MERINGUE

4 egg whites
225 g/8 oz castor sugar

Knead the sifted flour with the butter, sugar, salt, cream and egg yolks, to make a dough.

Cover and chill for 2 hours.

Top and tail the gooseberries, wash them and cook gently in a covered pan with the sugar and brandy, until soft.

Blend 2 tablespoons milk with the cornflour. Bring the remaining milk to the boil with the cream and icing sugar. Stir into the cornflour, return to the pan and bring to the boil, stirring until thickened. Cool.

Preheat the oven to moderately hot (200°C, 400°F, Gas Mark 6). Roll out the pastry to 3 mm/⅛ inch thick and line eight to ten 7·5-cm/3-inch tartlet tins. Bake blind for 10–15 minutes, then cool in their tins.

Fill the tartlet cases with the cream and cover with the gooseberries. Whisk the egg whites until stiff then whisk in half the sugar and fold in the rest. Pipe a meringue lattice over each. Brown the meringue in a hot oven (220°C, 425°F, Gas Mark 7) for a few minutes with the door slightly open.

Raspberry Tartlets

PASTRY
125 g/4 oz plain flour
60 g/2 oz butter
50 g/2 oz icing sugar
few drops of vanilla essence
pinch of salt
1 small egg yolk
FILLING
225 g/8 oz fresh or frozen
    raspberries
150 g/5 oz butter
150 g/5 oz castor sugar
3 egg yolks
grated rind and juice of 3 lemons
1 tablespoon cornflour
DECORATION
3 tablespoons apricot jam
75 g/3 oz toasted flaked almonds
150 ml/¼ pint double cream
1 tablespoon icing sugar

Knead together the sifted flour, butter, icing sugar, vanilla essence, salt and egg yolk, to make a pastry dough. Cover and leave in the refrigerator for 2 hours. Allow the frozen raspberries to defrost.

Preheat the oven to moderately hot (200°C, 400°F, Gas Mark 6). Roll out the pastry thinly and use to line six to eight 7·5-cm/3-inch tartlet tins. Bake blind for 10–15 minutes then remove from their tins and cool on a wire rack.

Place the butter in a saucepan with the sugar, egg yolks, lemon rind and juice and the cornflour. Bring gently to the boil, stirring continuously until smooth and thickened. Cool.

Spread the warmed apricot jam over the sides of the tartlets and sprinkle with the flaked almonds, pressing them on well. Fill the tartlets with the lemon cream and cover with the raspberries. Whip the cream with the sugar until stiff and pipe on to the centre of the tartlets, decorating with a few flaked almonds.

Crumble-Based Fruit Tart

18 digestive or wholemeal
biscuits
25 g/1 oz castor sugar
¼ teaspoon ground cinnamon
75 g/3 oz butter or margarine,
melted
FILLING AND TOPPING
25 g/1 oz cornflour
25 g/1 oz castor sugar
½ teaspoon vanilla essence
450 ml/¾ pint milk
1 (298-g/10½-oz) can goose-
berries
1 (213-g/7½-oz) can peach
slices
1 small packet quick-setting

Grease a 23-cm/9-inch flan tin with butter or margarine. Place the biscuits in a poly-thene bag and crush finely with a rolling pin. Mix the biscuit crumbs with the sugar, cinna-mon and melted butter or margarine. Place the mixture in the tin and press down slightly with the back of a spoon. Chill well.

Mix the cornflour with the sugar, vanilla essence and a little of the milk. Heat the remaining milk and pour on to the cornflour mixture. Return to the heat and bring to the boil, stirring continuously. Leave to cool, stirring occa-sionally to prevent a skin forming.

Drain the gooseberries, reserving the juice, and also drain the peaches. Spread the vanilla sauce over the biscuit base and top with the fruit as illustrated. Prepare the glaze using the gooseberry juice, according to the directions on the packet, cool slightly and pour over the tart.

Date Crumble Cake

350 g/12 oz fresh dates
175 g/6 oz plain wholemeal
flour
¼ teaspoon salt
100 g/4 oz soft margarine
100 g/4 oz castor sugar
¼ teaspoon vanilla essence
100 g/4 oz medium oatmeal

Grease a 23-cm/9-inch spring-form cake tin with margarine. Preheat the oven to moderate (180°C, 350°F, Gas Mark 4).

Stone the dates and dice finely. Mix the flour with the salt. Beat the margarine with the sugar and vanilla essence until pale and creamy. Gradually add the flour and oatmeal and mix with the fingertips until crumbly.

Spread half the mixture over the base of the cake tin, press down over the base, raising the sides slightly. Spread the dates over this base and crumble the rest of the mixture over the top. Bake for 45–50 minutes. Leave to cool slightly in the tin and serve preferably warm.

Viennese Chocolate Cake

CAKE MIXTURE
6 eggs, separated
1 tablespoon vanilla sugar
pinch of salt
150 g/5 oz castor sugar
100 g/3¼ oz plain chocolate, grated
100 g/3¼ oz biscuit crumbs
100 g/3¼ oz ground hazelnuts
FILLING
3 tablespoons sherry
300 g/11 oz apricot jam
ICING
120 g/4 oz plain chocolate
1 egg
200 g/7 oz icing sugar
60 g/2 oz butter

Grease the base of a 25-cm/10-inch springform cake tin. Preheat the oven to moderate (180°C, 350°F, Gas Mark 4).

Whisk the egg yolks, vanilla sugar, salt and sugar together until pale and creamy. Stir in the grated chocolate. Whisk the egg whites until stiff and fold carefully into the yolk mixture. Mix the biscuit crumbs with the hazelnuts and fold in. Turn the mixture into the cake tin, smooth the surface and bake for 50–60 minutes. Turn the cake out on to a wire rack and leave to cool.

Cut the cake through twice to make three layers and soak each layer with sherry. Soften the jam and use to sandwich the layers together.

Melt the chocolate in a basin over a pan of hot water and allow to cool a little. Stir in the egg and sifted icing sugar. Melt the butter and add this to the chocolate, beating well until the mixture is

creamy. Cover the top and sides of the cake with this and use a palette knife to swirl the icing. Allow the icing to set before cutting the cake.

Cook's Tip

This cake may also be filled with almond paste. Knead 225 g/8 oz almond paste, divide it in half and roll out each half into a thin round the size of the cake. Sandwich the cake layers together with the almond paste and apricot jam then ice as in the recipe.

Chocolate Gâteau Alice

140 g/5 oz plain chocolate
140 g/5 oz butter, softened
160 g/6 oz castor sugar
3 eggs, separated
80 g/3 oz ground almonds
80 g/3 oz rye or wheat flour
ICING
100 g/4 oz almond paste
100 g/4 oz plain chocolate
12 almonds
sugar crystals

Grease a 20-cm/8-inch spring-form cake tin and sprinkle with breadcrumbs. Preheat the oven to moderate (180°C, 350°F, Gas Mark 4).

Melt the chocolate in a basin over hot water. Cream the butter with half the sugar until light and fluffy. Stir in the melted chocolate, egg yolks and ground almonds. Whisk the egg whites until stiff and fold in the remaining sugar. Fold into the chocolate mixture and finally fold in the flour. Turn into the prepared tin and bake for 40–45 minutes.

Roll out the almond paste thinly and use to cover the top and sides of the cake. Melt the chocolate in a basin over hot water and coat the cake thinly using a palette knife. Dip the tip of the almonds in a little melted chocolate, turn them in the sugar crystals and decorate the cake as illustrated.

Sachertorte

SPONGE MIXTURE
7 eggs, separated
200 g/7 oz castor sugar
50 g/2 oz cocoa powder
100 g/4 oz plain flour
100 g/4 oz butter, melted
50 g/2 oz biscuit crumbs
ICING
5 tablespoons apricot jam
225 g/8 oz plain chocolate
6 tablespoons double cream
175 g/6 oz icing sugar
chocolate vermicelli to sprinkle

Grease two 23-cm/9-inch sandwich tins and sprinkle with dry breadcrumbs. Preheat the oven to moderately hot (200°C, 400°F, Gas Mark 6).

Whisk the egg yolks with 100 g/4 oz castor sugar until thick and light. Fold in the sifted cocoa powder and flour with the cooled, melted butter. Whisk the egg whites until frothy. Add the remaining castor sugar and whisk until stiff. Fold into the egg yolk mixture with the biscuit crumbs.

Spoon the mixture into the prepared tins and bake in the centre of the oven for 30 minutes. Reduce the heat to moderate (180°C, 350°F, Gas Mark 4) and bake for a further 15–20 minutes. Cool in the oven, with the door slightly open, for 15 minutes, then remove to cool completely.

Warm the jam and use to sandwich the layers and spread thinly over the top and sides of the cake. Melt the chocolate in a basin over hot water. Cool, then beat in the cream and sifted icing sugar. Spread this icing smoothly over the cake and sprinkle a little chocolate vermicelli around the base of the cake, if liked.

Chocolate Slice

CAKE MIXTURE
130 g/5 oz plain chocolate
130 g/5 oz butter
200 g/7 oz castor sugar
pinch each of salt, ground
  cinnamon and grated lemon
  rind
6 eggs, separated
130 g/5 oz plain flour
ICING
200 g/7 oz plain chocolate
2 eggs
400 g/14 oz icing sugar
120 g/4 oz coconut oil or butter
3 tablespoons rum

Line a 25 × 35-cm/10 × 14-inch Swiss roll tin with greased greaseproof paper. Preheat the oven to moderate (180°C, 350°F, Gas Mark 4).

Melt the chocolate in a basin over hot water. Cream the butter with half the sugar until light and fluffy. Add the salt, cinnamon and lemon rind, then beat in the egg yolks, one at a time, with the melted chocolate. Whisk the egg whites until stiff and fold in the remaining sugar. Fold into the creamed mixture with the sifted flour. Spread evenly into the Swiss roll tin and bake in the centre of the oven for 20 minutes.

Turn the cake out on to greaseproof paper sprinkled with sugar, remove the greaseproof lining paper and leave to cool for 2 hours. Cut the cake lengthways into two strips.

Grate the chocolate finely and mix with the beaten eggs, sifted icing sugar, melted coconut oil or butter, and rum. Heat gently in a basin over a pan of boiling water, stirring until the chocolate melts and all the ingredients are thoroughly combined. Cool. Use to sandwich the strips of cake together and spread thickly over the top. Cut into slices when the icing is firm.

Nougat Slice

SPONGE MIXTURE
4 eggs, separated, plus 2 egg
  yolks
100 g/4 oz castor sugar
80 g/3 oz plain flour
20 g/1 oz cornflour
40 g/1½ oz cocoa powder
FILLING AND ICING
25 g/1 oz cornflour
2 egg yolks
50 g/2 oz castor sugar
300 ml/½ pint milk
250 g/9 oz butter
100 g/4 oz nougat
175 g/6 oz plain chocolate
glacé cherries to decorate

Line a 33 × 23-cm/13 × 9-inch Swiss roll tin with greased greaseproof. Preheat the oven to 220°C, 425°F, Gas Mark 7.

Whisk the egg yolks with half the sugar until pale. Whisk the egg whites until stiff and fold in the remaining sugar. Fold into the egg yolks. Sift the flour, cornflour and cocoa powder and fold in. Spread over the Swiss roll tin and bake for 10–12 minutes. Turn out on to clean greaseproof and peel off the lining paper. Cool then cut lengthways into three strips.

Blend the cornflour with the egg yolks, sugar and a little milk. Heat the remaining milk, stir into the cornflour mixture and return to the heat. Bring to the boil, stirring until thickened. Leave to cool. Cream the butter until pale and soft, then gradually beat in the cornflour sauce. Melt the nougat with 50 g/2 oz of the chocolate in a basin over hot water, then beat into the butter cream a tablespoon at a time. Spread this nougat cream over two of the strips of cake, then place the strips on top of each other and spread a thin layer of nougat cream over the top and sides.

Melt the remaining chocolate and ice the cake. Decorate as illustrated.

Brandy Snap Ring

CAKE MIXTURE
175 g/6 oz butter
175 g/6 oz castor sugar
¼ teaspoon salt
3 eggs
1 tablespoon rum
grated rind and juice of ½ lemon
150 g/5 oz plain flour
1 tablespoon baking powder
75 g/3 oz cornflour
ICING
175 g/6 oz butter
350 g/12 oz icing sugar
1 egg yolk
6–8 brandy snaps, crushed
150 ml/¼ pint double cream
8 glacé cherries

Grease a 23-cm/9-inch ring tin. Preheat the oven to moderate (180°C, 350°F, Gas Mark 4).

Cream the butter with the castor sugar until light and fluffy. Beat in the salt, eggs, rum, lemon rind and juice. Fold in the sifted flour, baking powder and cornflour. Pour into the ring tin and bake for 45–60 minutes. Cool slightly in the tin, then turn out on to a wire rack to cool completely. Cut into four layers.

Cream the butter with the sifted icing sugar and egg yolk. Use to sandwich together the four layers and to cover the whole cake. Press on the crushed brandy snaps to cover completely. Decorate with the cream, whipped and piped, and halved glacé cherries.

Chocolate Délice

100 g/4 oz butter
100 g/4 oz castor sugar
100 g/4 oz plain chocolate
6 eggs, separated
100 g/4 oz ground almonds
50 g/2 oz biscuit crumbs
75 g/3 oz plain flour
DECORATION AND ICING
50 g/2 oz slivered almonds
100 g/4 oz plain chocolate

Grease a 30-cm/12-inch long Balmoral cake tin or 1-kg/2-lb loaf tin and dust with flour. Preheat the oven to moderate (180°C, 350°F, Gas Mark 4).

Beat the butter and sugar together until pale and creamy. Break the chocolate into small pieces and melt in a basin over hot water. Add it to the butter mixture together with the egg yolks. Beat the mixture thoroughly until very creamy. Stir in the ground almonds, biscuit crumbs and sifted flour.

Whisk the egg whites until stiff and fold into the cake mixture. Turn into the prepared tin and bake the cake for 50–60 minutes. Turn the cake out on to a wire rack to cool and press the almonds into it as illustrated. Melt the chocolate in a basin over hot water and cover the cake thickly with this icing.

Viennese Cherry Cake

PASTRY
100 g/4 oz butter
60 g/2 oz castor sugar
150 g/6 oz plain flour
1–2 tablespoons water
CAKE MIXTURE
300 g/11 oz butter
300 g/11 oz castor sugar
6 eggs, separated
grated rind of 1 lemon
pinch of salt
150 g/5¼ oz plain flour
150 g/5¼ oz cornflour
450 g/1 lb fresh or 225 g/8 oz glacé cherries
icing sugar to sprinkle

Cream the butter with the sugar, sift over the flour and knead well with the water to form a pastry dough. Cover and leave for 2 hours in the refrigerator.

Preheat the oven to hot (220°C, 425°F, Gas Mark 7). Roll out the pastry to line the base of a 23-cm/9-inch cake tin. Prick the base all over with a fork and bake blind for 15 minutes.

For the cake mixture, cream the butter with half the sugar, the egg yolks, lemon rind and salt, until pale and light. Whisk the egg whites until stiff and fold in the remaining sugar. Carefully fold into the creamed mixture. Sift the flour and cornflour on to this and fold in well. Pour the cake mixture over the pastry and scatter the cherries on top. If using glacé cherries, toss lightly in flour first. Bake the cake for a further 1–1¼ hours in a moderately hot oven (190°C, 375°F, Gas Mark 5), covering with foil if the cake becomes too brown. Allow to cool then dust with sifted icing sugar.

Orange Almond Cake

7 eggs, separated
280 g/10 oz castor sugar
grated rind and juice of 2 oranges
30 g/1 oz plain flour
80 g/3 oz cake crumbs
280 g/10 oz ground almonds
TOPPING
200 g/7 oz orange jelly marmalade
100 g/4 oz toasted flaked almonds
14 candied orange segments

Grease a 23-cm/9-inch spring-form cake tin and sprinkle with fine breadcrumbs. Preheat the oven to moderately hot (200°C, 400°F, Gas Mark 6).

Whisk the egg yolks with half the sugar until creamy, then whisk in the orange rind and juice. Whisk the egg whites until stiff and fold in the remaining sugar. Carefully fold into the egg yolk mixture. Sift the flour over this and fold in with the cake crumbs and ground almonds. Turn into the prepared tin, smooth the surface and bake for 30–40 minutes.

Allow the cake to cool slightly on a wire rack, then spread the top and sides with the warmed orange jelly. Cover with the flaked almonds and finally decorate with the candied orange segments.

Daisy Cake

300 g/12 oz butter
100 g/4 oz ground almonds
6 eggs, separated
grated rind of 1 lemon
few drops of vanilla essence
140 g/5 oz castor sugar
120 g/4½ oz plain flour
80 g/3 oz cornflour
ICING
150 g/5 oz apricot jam
200 g/7 oz icing sugar
1 tablespoon lemon juice
1 tablespoon water

Grease a 23-cm/9-inch round fluted cake tin and sprinkle with fine breadcrumbs. Preheat the oven to moderately hot (190°C, 375°F, Gas Mark 5).

Cream the softened butter with the ground almonds. Stir in the egg yolks, lemon rind and vanilla essence. Whisk the egg whites until stiff then carefully fold in the sugar. Fold the egg whites into the butter mixture. Sift the flour and cornflour together and fold into the mixture. Turn into the prepared cake tin, smooth the surface and bake for 50–60 minutes.

Leave to cool slightly on a wire rack, then spread with the warmed apricot jam. Leave to cool and set for 30 minutes. Mix the sifted icing sugar with the lemon juice and water and spread over the cake.

Hazelnut Loaf Cake

250 g/9 oz soft margarine
200 g/7 oz castor sugar
25 g/1 oz vanilla sugar
4 eggs
250 g/9 oz ground hazelnuts
250 g/9 oz self-raising flour
1 teaspoon baking powder
1 tablespoon brandy
icing sugar to sprinkle

Grease a 1-kg/2-lb loaf tin. Preheat the oven to moderate (180°C, 350°F, Gas Mark 4).

Cream the margarine, sugar and vanilla sugar until light and fluffy. Stir in the eggs, one at a time, then the hazelnuts. Sift the flour and baking powder together and fold into the mixture, making sure all is thoroughly mixed. Finally stir in the brandy. Turn into the tin and bake for 1–1¼ hours.

Allow the cake to cool on a wire rack, then sprinkle with sifted icing sugar.

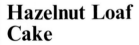

> ### Cook's Tip
> For deeper cakes, test the cooking with a warmed metal skewer. Towards the end of cooking time, insert the warmed skewer into the middle of the cake and then withdraw; if it comes out clean then the cake is cooked.

Crumble Cake

200 g/7 oz soft margarine
200 g/7 oz castor sugar
1 egg
grated rind of 1 lemon
500 g/1 lb 2 oz plain flour
1 teaspoon baking powder
1 (454-g/1-lb) jar cherry jam
50 g/2 oz ground almonds
icing sugar to sprinkle

Grease a 25-cm/10-inch spring-form cake tin with margarine. Preheat the oven to hot (220°C, 425°F, Gas Mark 7).

Beat the margarine and sugar together until creamy. Stir in the egg and lemon rind. Sift the flour and baking powder and fold a few tablespoons into the creamed mixture. Tip the remaining flour on to the mixture and, with the fingertips, work quickly into crumbs. Place half this crumb mixture in the prepared cake tin and spread with the jam. Mix the rest with the almonds and crumble over the jam. Bake the cake for 50–60 minutes.

Leave to cool on a wire rack and dust with sifted icing sugar.

Rum Butter Cake

180 g/6 oz butter
200 g/7 oz castor sugar
5 eggs
250 g/9 oz plain flour
80 g/3 oz maize flour
1 teaspoon baking powder
3 tablespoons rum
1 tablespoon lemon juice
1 tablespoon orange juice
grated rind of ½ lemon
grated rind of ½ orange

Grease a 1-kg/2-lb loaf tin and sprinkle with flour. Preheat the oven to moderately hot (190°C, 375°F, Gas Mark 5).

Beat the butter and sugar until pale and creamy then add the eggs one at a time. Sift the flour, maize flour and baking powder together then carefully fold into the mixture. Gradually fold in the rum, lemon and orange juice and grated fruit rinds. Place the mixture in the tin, smooth over the top and

bake for 1¼ hours. Cover with foil if becoming too brown.

Turn out on to a wire rack to cool.

Royal Fruit Loaf

50 g/2 oz candied lemon peel
100 g/4 oz blanched almonds
200 g/7 oz raisins
175 g/6 oz self-raising flour
175 g/6 oz butter or margarine
100 g/4 oz castor sugar
4 eggs
50 g/2 oz cornflour
1 teaspoon baking powder
1 tablespoon rum

Grease a 0·5-kg/1-lb loaf tin and sprinkle with fine breadcrumbs. Preheat the oven to moderate (180°C, 350°F, Gas Mark 4).

Chop the lemon peel and almonds. Toss the raisins in a little of the flour. Beat the butter or margarine with the sugar until pale and creamy, then beat in one of the eggs. Sift the flour, cornflour and baking powder together and fold in a little of this between adding the remaining eggs.

Fold in the rest of the flour. Add the lemon peel, almonds, raisins and rum and fold into the creamed mixture. Place in the prepared tin, smooth over the surface and bake for about 1 hour 5 minutes.

Turn the cake on to a wire rack to cool.

Arabian Honey Cake

75 g/3 oz butter
3 eggs
125 g/4½ oz castor sugar
few drops of vanilla essence
2 tablespoons double cream
150 g/5 oz plain flour
¼ teaspoon baking powder
TOPPING
100 g/4 oz butter
80 g/3 oz castor sugar
75 g/3 oz thick honey
2 tablespoons double cream
150 g/5 oz flaked almonds
¼ teaspoon ground cinnamon
grated rind of ½ orange

Grease a 25-cm/10-inch
sandwich tin. Preheat the oven
to moderately hot (200°C,
400°F, Gas Mark 6).
　Melt the butter. Whisk the
eggs with the sugar and vanilla
essence until frothy. Stir in the
cooled butter and the cream.

Sift the flour and baking
powder into the mixture and
fold in thoroughly. Turn into
the prepared tin, smooth over
and bake for 10–12 minutes.
　Meanwhile, make the
topping. Melt the butter in a
pan and add the sugar, honey,
cream, almonds, cinnamon and
orange rind. Stir the ingredients
well to mix and bring them to
the boil. Spread this mixture
over the cake and return to the
oven for a further 15–20
minutes. Loosen the cake from
the tin and leave to cool on a
wire rack.

Iced Banana Ring

225 g/8 oz margarine or butter
150 g/5 oz castor sugar
pinch of salt
5 eggs, separated
15 g/½ oz candied ginger,
　chopped
75 g/3 oz desiccated coconut
grated rind of 1 lemon
500 g/1 lb bananas
3 tablespoons lemon juice
1 tablespoon rum
250 g/9 oz plain flour
1 teaspoon baking powder
ICING
200 g/7 oz icing sugar
2–3 tablespoons lemon juice

Grease a fluted 23-cm/9-inch
ring tin. Preheat the oven to
moderately hot (200°C, 400°F,
Gas Mark 6).
　Beat the margarine with the
sugar and salt until light and
creamy. Add the egg yolks one

at a time with the ginger,
coconut and lemon rind. Mix
well. Peel the bananas, dice
and sprinkle with the lemon
juice and rum. Fold into the
egg mixture. Sift the flour with
the baking powder and fold in.
Whisk the egg whites until
very stiff and carefully fold into
　e mixture. Turn into the
prepared tin and bake for
1–1¼ hours. Turn out and
leave to cool on a wire rack.
　Mix the sifted icing sugar
with the lemon juice until
smooth and use to ice the cake.

Classic Sand Cake

3 eggs
180 g/6 oz castor sugar
¼ teaspoon vanilla essence
grated rind of ½ lemon
pinch of salt
125 g/4 oz self-raising flour
125 g/4 oz cornflour
180 g/6 oz butter, melted
icing sugar to sprinkle

Grease a 1-kg/2-lb loaf tin and line with greased greaseproof paper. Preheat the oven to moderately hot (190°C, 375°F, Gas Mark 5).

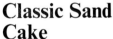Whisk the eggs with the sugar, vanilla, lemon rind and salt in a basin over a pan of hot water, allowing the ingredients to become lukewarm only. Remove the mixture from the heat and whisk until cooled. Sift the flour with the cornflour and fold in well.

Lastly mix in the melted butter. Turn into the prepared tin and bake for 40–45 minutes.

Cool on a wire rack and dredge the top with sifted icing sugar.

Chocolate Cherry Cake

100 g/4 oz glacé cherries, halved
200 g/7 oz butter
250 g/9 oz castor sugar
6 eggs
pinch of salt
grated rind of 1 lemon
½ teaspoon ground cinnamon
200 g/7 oz milk chocolate, grated
100 g/3¼ oz ground hazelnuts
100 g/3¼ oz ground almonds
150 g/5 oz plain flour
1 teaspoon baking powder
DECORATION
2 tablespoons icing sugar
2 tablespoons drinking chocolate powder

Grease a 23-cm/9-inch springform cake tin and sprinkle with fine breadcrumbs. Preheat the oven to moderate (180°C, 350°F, Gas Mark 4).

Wash the cherries and pat dry. Cream the butter and sugar together until pale and light. Add the eggs, salt, lemon rind, cinnamon, chocolate, hazelnuts and almonds and stir well. Finally fold in the cherries with the sifted flour and baking powder. Turn the cake mixture into the tin and smooth over the surface. Bake the cake for 1–1½ hours then leave to cool on a wire rack.

Cut the centre from a paper doily, place it over the centre of the cake and sift icing sugar over the uncovered area. Remove this centre piece, place the rest of the doily over the cake and sift all over with chocolate powder.

Honey Crunch Cake

6–7 tablespoons milk
25 g/1 oz castor sugar
¼ teaspoon salt
25 g/1 oz butter
20 g/¾ oz fresh yeast
2 tablespoons lukewarm water
80 g/3 oz flaked almonds
380 g/13 oz plain flour
1 egg
2 tablespoons raisins
FILLING
25 g/1 oz butter
25 g/1 oz castor sugar
¼ teaspoon ground cinnamon
TOPPING
25 g/1 oz butter
4 tablespoons honey
25 g/1 oz sugar
100 g/4 oz almonds, chopped

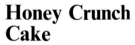

Grease a 23-cm/9-inch spring-form cake tin. Bring the milk to the boil and stir in the sugar, salt and butter. Leave to cool.

Cream the yeast with the lukewarm water. Mix the almonds with the flour, add the milk and yeast mixtures, the egg and raisins. Knead all the ingredients until smooth then cover and leave in a warm place for 20 minutes.

Roll out the mixture to a 30 × 35-cm/12 × 14-inch rectangle. Melt the butter and spread it over the dough, then sprinkle with the sugar and cinnamon. Roll it up from the shorter side and cut into 2·5-cm/1-inch slices.

Melt the butter for the topping with the honey, sugar and almonds, and pour into the prepared tin. Form balls from the slices of dough and arrange them over the honey mixture. Leave to rise in a warm place for 25 minutes. Preheat the oven to moderately hot (190°C, 375°F, Gas Mark 5), and bake for 30–40 minutes. Invert on to a wire rack to cool.

Iced Rum Cake

50 g/2 oz pumpernickel breadcrumbs
2 teaspoons rum
8 eggs
150 g/5 oz castor sugar
120 g/4 oz ground almonds
50 g/2 oz plain chocolate, grated
grated rind of ½ lemon
pinch of ground cloves
50 g/2 oz chopped mixed peel
ICING
200 g/7 oz icing sugar
1 tablespoon rum
1–2 tablespoons water
12 glacé cherries

Grease a 25-cm/10-inch springform cake tin. Preheat the oven to moderately hot (200°C, 400°F, Gas Mark 6).

Mix the breadcrumbs with the rum. Separate 6 of the eggs. Whisk the whole eggs, egg yolks and sugar together until thick and creamy. Stir in the almonds, chocolate, lemon rind, cloves and chopped peel, mixing well. Whisk the egg whites until stiff and fold into the mixture. Finally stir in the soaked breadcrumbs and transfer to the prepared tin, smoothing over the surface. Bake the cake in the centre of the oven for 45–55 minutes, covering with foil if it becomes too brown.

Turn the cake out on to a wire rack to cool. Mix the sifted icing sugar with the rum and water and spread over the cake. Decorate with the glacé cherries.

Iced Orange Loaf Cake

250 g/9 oz soft margarine
250 g/9 oz castor sugar
3 eggs plus 4 egg yolks
100 g/4 oz self-raising flour
pinch of salt
1 tablespoon orange liqueur
grated rind of 2 oranges
grated rind of 1 lemon
2 tablespoons orange juice
1 tablespoon lemon juice
100 g/4 oz cornflour
100 g/4 oz ground almonds
75 g/3 oz candied orange peel,
   finely chopped
ICING
50 g/2 oz orange jelly
   marmalade
200 g/7 oz icing sugar
2 tablespoons orange juice
25 g/1 oz candied orange peel,
   finely chopped

Grease a 1-kg/2-lb loaf tin and sprinkle with fine breadcrumbs.

Preheat the oven to moderate (180°C, 350°F, Gas Mark 4).

Cream the margarine and sugar together until light and fluffy. Stir in the eggs and egg yolks, one by one, along with a few tablespoons of the flour. Mix in the salt, liqueur, fruit rinds and juice. Sift the remaining flour with the cornflour and fold into the cake mixture with the ground almonds and candied peel. Turn into the tin and bake for about 1¼ hours.

Cool on a wire rack then spread the top of the cake with the warmed orange jelly. Mix together the sifted icing sugar and orange juice and spread over the cake. Sprinkle with the candied peel to decorate.

Marzipan Cake

MARZIPAN
120 g/4½ oz almond paste
100 g/4 oz pistachio nuts or
   blanched almonds, grated
1 tablespoon arrack or ouzo
CAKE MIXTURE
250 g/9 oz soft margarine
240 g/8½ oz castor sugar
5 eggs, separated
pinch of salt
1 tablespoon arrack or ouzo
few drops of vanilla essence
230 g/8 oz plain flour
85 g/3 oz cornflour
1 teaspoon baking powder
ICING
175 g/6 oz plain chocolate
25 g/1 oz pistachio nuts, chopped

Grease a 20–23-cm/8–9-inch round fluted cake tin and sprinkle with fine breadcrumbs. Preheat the oven to moderately hot (190°C, 375°F, Gas Mark 5).

Knead the almond paste with the pistachios and arrack, roll out to a thickness of 1 cm/ ½ inch and cut into 1-cm/½-inch cubes.

Beat the margarine with half the sugar, the egg yolks, salt, arrack and vanilla essence until well mixed. Whisk the egg whites until stiff and whisk in the remaining sugar. Fold into the egg yolk mixture. Sift together the flour, cornflour and baking powder and mix in the marzipan cubes. Fold all this thoroughly into the egg mixture. Turn into the cake tin and bake for 1¼–1½ hours. Turn out and cool on a wire rack.

Melt the chocolate in a basin over hot water and spread over the cake. Decorate with the chopped pistachios while still soft and leave the icing to set.

Swiss Carrot Cake

5 eggs, separated, plus 2 egg
    yolks
200 g/7 oz castor sugar
pinch each of salt, ground
    cinnamon and ground cloves
1 tablespoon Kirsch
200 g/7 oz finely grated carrots
100 g/4 oz ground almonds
100 g/4 oz hazelnuts, finely
    chopped
50 g/2 oz fresh white
    breadcrumbs
50 g/2 oz plain flour
1 teaspoon baking powder
ICING AND DECORATION
200 g/7 oz icing sugar
2 tablespoons Kirsch
2 tablespoons lemon juice
2 tablespoons apricot jam
50 g/2 oz toasted flaked
    almonds
100 g/4 oz almond paste
few drops of orange food
    colouring
few pistachio nut pieces

Grease a 25-cm/10-inch
springform cake tin. Preheat
the oven to moderately hot
(190°C, 375°F, Gas Mark 5).
Whisk all the egg yolks with
the sugar, salt, cinnamon,
cloves and Kirsch, until thick
and creamy. Mix together the
carrots, ground almonds,
hazelnuts, breadcrumbs and
the flour sifted with the baking
powder; stir these ingredients
into the egg yolk mixture.
Whisk the egg whites until
stiff and fold in. Turn the cake
mixture into the prepared tin,
smooth over and bake for
45–55 minutes. Turn the cake
out on a wire rack to cool,
cover and leave it for 2 days.

  Mix the sifted icing sugar
with the Kirsch and lemon
juice, and use to ice the top
of the cake. Brush the sides of
the cake with a little warmed
jam and press on the flaked
almonds. Colour the almond
paste and shape into small
carrots. Insert a couple of
pistachio nut pieces into one
end to resemble the carrot's
stalk, and arrange on top of
the cake.

Caribbean Coconut Cake

SPONGE MIXTURE
4 eggs, separated
2 tablespoons lukewarm water
140 g/4½ oz castor sugar
grated rind of ¼ lemon
120 g/4 oz plain flour
60 g/2 oz cornflour
1 teaspoon baking powder
FILLING AND TOPPING
1 coconut or 225 g/8 oz
  desiccated coconut
2 tablespoons coconut milk
40 g/1½ oz sugar
1 tablespoon dark rum
25 g/1 oz cornflour
300 ml/½ pint milk
3 eggs, separated
180 g/6 oz castor sugar
¼ teaspoon vanilla essence
16 glacé cherries

Grease the base of a 20-cm/ 8-inch springform cake tin. Preheat the oven to moderately hot (190°C, 375°F, Gas Mark 5).

Whisk the egg yolks with the water, half the sugar and the lemon rind until creamy. Whisk the egg whites until stiff, fold in the remaining sugar and carefully fold into the egg yolk mixture. Sift the flour with the cornflour and baking powder and fold into the egg mixture. Turn into the prepared tin, smooth the surface and bake for 35–40 minutes. Allow to cool slightly in the tin then turn on to a wire rack to cool completely. Leave overnight if possible, then cut into three layers.

Pierce the coconut twice at the thinnest part of the shell, pour off the milk and reserve. Cut the coconut in half, scoop out the flesh, cover and reserve. Boil 2 tablespoons of the coconut milk with the 40 g/1½ oz

sugar until the sugar dissolves completely. Add the rum and leave to cool. (If using desiccated coconut, 100 g/4 oz of this should be infused in 300 ml/½ pint boiling water overnight, then strained. This liquid may be used instead of the fresh coconut milk.)

Blend the cornflour with 3 tablespoons fresh milk and the egg yolks. Heat the remaining fresh milk with half the castor sugar until almost boiling. Whisk the egg whites until stiff then carefully fold in the rest of the castor sugar. Pour the hot milk on to the cornflour mixture. Return to the heat and bring to the boil, stirring continuously. Remove from the heat, stir in the vanilla essence, cool for 3 minutes and carefully fold in the whisked egg whites.

Allow this vanilla cream to cool slightly then spread thickly over the bottom cake layer. Place the second cake layer on

top, sprinkle over half the coconut milk mixture and allow it to soak in. Spread over a layer of the cream then top with the last cake layer. Sprinkle over the rest of the coconut milk, allowing it to soak in, and then spread the top and sides of the cake with the remaining vanilla cream.

Grate the coconut flesh finely and use to cover the cake thickly all over. Alternatively, use the remaining desiccated coconut. Arrange the glacé cherries around the edge of the cake.

359

Chocolate Faces

CAKE MIXTURE
*4 eggs, separated, plus 2 egg
  whites*
120 g/4½ oz castor sugar
grated rind of ½ lemon
1 tablespoon water
50 g/2 oz plain flour
60 g/2½ oz cornflour
ICING AND DECORATION
100 g/4 oz apricot jam
100 g/4 oz plain chocolate
1 egg white
50 g/2 oz icing sugar
1 tube Smarties

Line a baking tray with non-stick baking parchment. Preheat the oven to moderate (180°C, 350°F, Gas Mark 4).

Beat the egg yolks with 25 g/1 oz sugar, the lemon rind and water until frothy. Whisk the egg whites until stiff, whisk in the remaining sugar and fold into the egg yolk mixture. Sift over the flour and cornflour

and fold in well. Turn this mixture into a piping bag fitted with a large plain nozzle and pipe quite large half-spheres on to the non-stick paper. Bake for 12–15 minutes then leave to cool on a wire rack.

Remove the paper and stick two halves together with a little jam. Melt the chocolate in a basin over hot water and use to cover the cakes. Add sufficient lightly whisked egg white to the sifted icing sugar until the icing is of a piping consistency. Pipe faces on to the cakes, as illustrated, using coloured Smarties to represent the eyes.

Alphabet Biscuits

180 g/6 oz plain flour
1 egg
90 g/3 oz castor sugar
25 g/1 oz vanilla sugar
60 g/2 oz butter, cut into flakes
ICING
200 g/7 oz icing sugar
2–3 tablespoons lemon juice
50 g/2 oz jelly bears

Sift the flour on to a pastry board and knead to a dough with the egg, sugar, vanilla sugar and butter. Wrap in foil or cling film and leave for 2 hours in the refrigerator.

Preheat the oven to moderately hot (200°C, 400°F, Gas Mark 6). Cut small pieces from the biscuit dough and form into sausage shapes about 1 cm/½ inch in diameter. Make a letter from each sausage and flatten slightly.

Place on a greased baking tray and bake in the centre of the oven for 8–10 minutes.

Stir the sifted icing sugar with enough lemon juice to give a thick icing, but thin enough to spread. Ice the letters with it while still warm and stick the jelly bears on to the icing before it sets.

Cook's Tip

When you are making the letters for older children or adults, use candied coffee beans for the decoration.

Birthday Car

1 (326-g/11¼-oz) packet lemon
* sponge cake mix*
175 g/6 oz raspberry jam
ICING AND DECORATION
100 g/4 oz icing sugar
1–2 tablespoons boiling water
1–2 teaspoons cocoa powder
Smarties and silver balls

Line the base of a 33 × 23-cm/
13 × 9-inch Swiss roll tin with
greased greaseproof paper. Preheat the oven to moderately
hot (200°C, 400°F, Gas Mark
6).

Prepare the cake mix according to the instructions on the
packet. Spread evenly over the
Swiss roll tin and bake for 15–
20 minutes. Turn out on to a
wire cooling rack, remove the
greaseproof paper and leave to
cool.

Cut the cake in half widthways and place the two halves
together. Using a cardboard

pattern, cut out the shape of a
car from the cake, cutting
through both cake layers. Cut
windows in one of the layers
and sandwich the cake layers
together with jam. Cut out two
extra wheels from the cake
trimmings and sandwich on to
the car wheels using jam.

Stir the sifted icing sugar
with the water until smooth.
Cover the car with white icing
then stir 1–2 teaspoons sifted
cocoa powder into the re-
mainder. Fill a greaseproof
paper piping bag with the
chocolate icing and decorate
the car as illustrated. Stick the
Smarties and silver balls into
the icing while still soft.

Children's Birthday Cake

1 (326-g/11¼-oz) packet
* chocolate sandwich cake mix*
ICING AND DECORATION
50 g/2 oz butter
75 g/3 oz icing sugar
1 tablespoon cocoa powder
1 tablespoon boiling water
marshmallows
Smarties and coloured sugar
* balls*

Grease and flour two 18-cm/
7-inch sandwich tins. Preheat
the oven to moderately hot
(200°C, 400°F, Gas Mark 6).

Prepare the chocolate cake
mix according to the instructions on the packet. Pour into
the prepared tins, smooth the
surface and bake for 15–20
minutes. Turn out and cool on
a wire rack.

Prepare the chocolate filling
from the packet according to

the instructions. Sandwich the
cake together with this filling.

Cream the butter with the
sifted icing sugar until pale and
soft. Blend the cocoa powder
with the water and stir into the
butter cream. Cover the top
and sides of the cake with this
cream, swirling it with a palette
knife. Make figures from the
marshmallows, as illustrated,
and join together with wooden
cocktail sticks. Before serving
decorate the cake with the
marshmallow figures, Smarties
and coloured sugar balls.

Classical Petits Fours

SPONGE MIXTURE
5 eggs, separated, plus 1 egg yolk
80 g/3 oz ground almonds
grated rind of 1 lemon
120 g/4½ oz castor sugar
120 g/4½ oz plain flour
FILLING
175 g/6 oz apricot jam
225 g/8 oz almond paste
ICING
225 g/8 oz icing sugar
1–2 tablespoons water
1 tablespoon white rum
red and yellow food colouring
DECORATION
glacé cherries, crystallised violets, chopped pistachios silver balls

Line two 28 × 18-cm/11 × 7-inch Swiss roll tins with greased greaseproof paper. Preheat the oven to hot (220°C, 425°F, Gas Mark 7).

Beat all the egg yolks with the ground almonds, lemon rind and half the sugar, until creamy. Whisk the egg whites until stiff, then fold in the remaining sugar. Fold into the egg yolk mixture and finally fold in the sifted flour. Spread the sponge mixture evenly over both Swiss roll tins and bake for 10–12 minutes. Remove the cakes from the tins while still warm, turning out on to clean greaseproof paper, and strip off the lining paper.

Spread one cake with apricot jam and place the second cake on top. Cut the cake into three equal strips, spread these with jam too and place on top of each other, to make six layers in all. Knead the almond paste and roll out to the size of the cake. Place on top of the cake,

cover with foil or greaseproof paper, weigh down with a heavy wooden board and leave for 24 hours. At the end of this time cut the cake into 3·5-cm/1½-inch squares or shapes.

For the icing, beat the sifted icing sugar with the water and rum until smooth. The icing should be of a thick flowing consistency. Use to coat the petits fours, colouring some of the icing with food colouring, if liked. Pipe over pretty decorations with the rest of the icing and decorate with glacé cherries, crystallised violets, chopped pistachios or silver balls, according to taste. Allow to dry out on a wire rack for 1–2 hours, and serve in small paper cases.

Cook's Tip

The key to success with these petits fours is to weigh the sponge cake layers down with a heavy board and leave for several hours. Otherwise the sponge will dry out and the petits fours will lose their delicious moistness.

Traditional Wedding Cake

CAKE MIXTURE
250 g/9 oz butter
250 g/9 oz castor sugar
5 eggs
grated rind and juice of 1 lemon
1 tablespoon rum
250 g/9 oz plain flour
½ teaspoon ground cinnamon
generous pinch of grated
  nutmeg
150 g/5 oz glacé cherries
  washed, dried and roughly
  chopped
400 g/14 oz currants
400 g/14 oz raisins
200 g/7 oz chopped mixed peel
50 g/2 oz blanched almonds,
  chopped
ROYAL ICING
3 large egg whites
675 g/1½ lb icing sugar
1 teaspoon lemon juice
sugar flowers to decorate

Grease a 25-cm/10-inch cake tin with butter or margarine. Line the greased tin with greaseproof paper and grease this thoroughly. Preheat the oven to cool (140°C, 275°F, Gas Mark 1).

Beat the butter with the sugar until pale and creamy. Beat in the eggs one at a time with the lemon rind and juice and the rum. Add a little flour if necessary to prevent the mixture curdling. Sift the remaining flour and mix with the cinnamon, nutmeg, cherries, currants, raisins, chopped peel and almonds. Add to the creamed mixture, folding it all in thoroughly. Pour into the cake tin and smooth the surface. Wrap a double thickness of brown paper or newspaper around the tin and secure it with string. This will prevent the outside of the cake from becoming overcooked before the middle is cooked through.

Bake the cake for 4½–5½ hours. It is essential to test with a skewer before removing the cake from the oven. If necessary continue baking for a little longer. Leave to cool for a short while in the tin then turn out on to a wire rack.

Lightly whisk the egg whites and brush a little over the surface of the cake. Gradually beat the sifted icing sugar and lemon juice into the remaining egg white to give a firm icing. Ice the top and sides of the cake, spreading smoothly with a palette knife. Place the rest of the icing in a piping bag fitted with a small star nozzle and decorate as illustrated.

Cook's Tip

The wedding cake will taste best if baked at least 3–4 weeks before the wedding and kept well wrapped in foil. Ice and decorate it just before using.

If well wrapped, the cake will keep for up to 1 year. In England it is customary in many families to make a two or three-tier wedding cake and to keep the second tier for the christening of the first child.

The traditional wedding cake is often covered with a layer of almond paste before the royal icing; this gives a smoother surface on which to ice.

Festive Chocolate Gâteau

SPONGE MIXTURE
200 g/7 oz castor sugar
4 eggs, separated
3 tablespoons hot water
pinch of salt
200 g/7 oz plain flour
1 teaspoon baking powder
FILLING AND TOPPING
3 tablespoons orange jelly
    marmalade
1 tablespoon Cointreau
250 g/9 oz butter
225 g/8 oz icing sugar
15 g/½ oz cocoa powder
4 eggs
7 candied orange segments
14 glacé cherries
50 g/2 oz chocolate vermicelli or
    chopped chocolate

Line a 23-cm/9-inch spring-form cake tin with greaseproof paper, then grease this with butter or margarine. Preheat the oven to hot (220°C, 425°F, Gas Mark 7).

Reserve 3 tablespoons sugar and whisk the remainder with the egg yolks and hot water until creamy. Whisk the egg whites with the salt until stiff then fold in the remaining sugar. Drop the egg whites on top of the egg yolk mixture. Sift the flour and baking powder on to the egg whites and fold altogether into the yolk mixture. Turn into the prepared tin, smooth the surface and bake for 30 minutes.

Turn on to a wire rack to cool for about 2 hours and remove the greaseproof paper. Mix the orange marmalade and Cointreau together. Beat the butter until pale and creamy. Sift the icing sugar with the cocoa powder. Whisk the eggs and mix in the icing sugar and

cocoa powder. Add this mixture a little at a time to the butter, beating well to incorporate.

Cut the cooled cake horizontally into four layers. Spread three layers thinly with the orange marmalade and a little of the butter cream. Place one on top of the other and spread the top layer and sides with butter cream. Place the remaining cream in a piping bag fitted with a star nozzle. With a sharp knife mark the cake into 14 equal portions and decorate each with a swirl of butter cream ending in a rosette. Halve the orange segments and place on each rosette, topping with a glacé cherry. Decorate the sides of the gâteau with chocolate vermicelli or chopped chocolate.

Cook's Tip

When freezing elaborate cream gâteaux, interleave the slices with greaseproof paper. This way you can take as many slices from the freezer as you want at one time, and there is no wastage.

Coffee Layer Gâteau

CAKE MIXTURE
130 g/5 oz butter
200 g/7 oz castor sugar
pinch each of salt, ground
*   cinnamon and grated lemon*
*   rind*
6 eggs, separated
130 g/5 oz plain chocolate
130 g/5 oz plain flour
FILLING AND TOPPING
300 ml/½ pint milk
25 g/1 oz cornflour
1 tablespoon instant coffee
*   powder*
150 g/5 oz castor sugar
250 g/9 oz butter
15 candied coffee beans
50 g/2 oz toasted flaked almonds

Grease the base of a 23-cm/ 9-inch springform cake tin. Preheat the oven to moderately hot (190°C, 375°F, Gas Mark 5).

Beat the softened butter with half the sugar, the salt, cinnamon and lemon rind, until light and fluffy. Add the egg yolks to the mixture one by one. Melt the chocolate in a basin over hot water but do not allow to get too hot. Stir into the butter mixture. Whisk the egg whites until stiff then whisk in the remaining sugar and fold into the chocolate mixture. Finally fold in the sifted flour. Turn the mixture into the prepared tin, smooth over and bake in the centre of the oven for 50–60 minutes. Turn on to a wire rack to cool for at least 2 hours, then cut into four layers.

Mix 4 tablespoons milk with the cornflour. Bring the rest of the milk to the boil with the coffee and sugar. Stir into the cornflour mixture then pour back into the saucepan and bring to the boil, stirring continuously until smooth and thickened. Remove from the heat and cool completely, stirring often. Beat the butter until light and fluffy then gradually add to it the cooled coffee cream, beating well with each addition.

Spread three cake layers with coffee cream and arrange them one on top of the other. Spread the top and sides of the gâteau with the cream and mark into 14 portions with a sharp knife. Put the rest of the coffee cream into a piping bag fitted with a star nozzle and decorate each portion with a swirl ending in a rosette. Pipe a double rosette in the centre of the gâteau. Top each rosette with a candied coffee bean and sprinkle the centre and sides of the gâteau with flaked almonds.

Cook's Tip

To cut a cream gâteau, dip the longest and sharpest knife you possess into warm water before making each cut.

Cherry Cream Layer Gâteau

1 (368-g/13-oz) packet frozen puff pastry
FILLING AND TOPPING
50 g/2 oz redcurrant jelly
100 g/4 oz icing sugar
1 tablespoon lemon juice
1 (425-g/15-oz) can red cherries
pinch of ground cinnamon
1 tablespoon cornflour
450 ml/¾ pint double cream
40 g/1½ oz castor sugar
12 glacé cherries

Allow the pastry to thaw for 1 hour at room temperature. Sprinkle a baking tray with cold water. Preheat the oven to moderately hot (200°C, 400°F, Gas Mark 6).

Divide the pastry into three portions and roll out each into a 20-cm/8-inch round. Arrange on the baking tray and leave for 15 minutes. Bake for 10–12 minutes, until lightly browned.

Cover the best pastry round with the warmed redcurrant jelly. Mix the sifted icing sugar and lemon juice together and spread this glaze over the jam. Leave to cool then divide the glazed pastry layer into 12 slices.

Drain the cherries, reserving the juice. Heat the juice from the cherries with the cinnamon. Blend the cornflour with a little cold water and add to the cherry juice. Bring to the boil, stirring continuously until slightly thickened. Stir in the stoned cherries and leave to cool. Spread the cooled cherry sauce over the bottom pastry layer.

Whip the cream with the castor sugar until stiff. Put about 5 tablespoons of this cream into a piping bag fitted with a star nozzle. Spread some of the remaining cream over the cherries and put the last uncovered pastry layer on top. Spread the remaining cream thickly over this and around the sides of the gâteau. Arrange the glazed pastry slices on top and decorate each with a rosette of cream and glacé cherry.

Cook's Tip

It is important to cut the glazed pastry layer into slices before placing over the cream filling. If you try to cut it when serving the gâteau, the cream filling will spill out.

Gooseberry Meringue Gâteau

SPONGE MIXTURE
6 eggs, separated
150 g/5 oz castor sugar
120 g/4 oz plain flour
60 g/2 oz cornflour
50 g/2 oz ground almonds
50 g/2 oz butter
FILLING
150 g/5 oz ground almonds
3 tablespoons rum
2 tablespoons icing sugar
3 tablespoons water
TOPPING
500 g/1 lb gooseberries
3 tablespoons granulated sugar
6 tablespoons water
4 egg whites
170 g/6 oz castor sugar
few drops of vanilla essence
100 g/4 oz toasted flaked
  almonds

Grease the base and sides of a 25-cm/10-inch springform cake tin. Preheat the oven to moderately hot (190°C, 375°F, Gas Mark 5).

Whisk the egg yolks with a third of the sugar until creamy. Whisk the egg whites until stiff, then gradually fold in the rest of the sugar. Sift the flour with the cornflour and mix with the ground almonds. Fold the egg whites into the egg yolks then fold in the flour mixture. Melt the butter, cool slightly and stir into the mixture. Turn into the prepared tin and bake for 35–40 minutes. Cool on a wire rack for at least 2 hours then slice through into two layers.

Mix the ground almonds with the rum, icing sugar and water to form a smooth paste. Use to sandwich the cake layers together.

Top, tail and wash the gooseberries. Mix the granulated sugar with the water, bring to the boil, add the gooseberries

and simmer over a gentle heat for 10 minutes. Drain thoroughly in a sieve over a basin.

Preheat the oven to hot (230°C, 450°F, Gas Mark 8). Whisk the egg whites until stiff, then whisk in the sugar and fold in the vanilla essence. Arrange the gooseberries over the cake, reserving 14 whole gooseberries for decoration. Spread the meringue mixture thickly over the top and sides. Pipe 14 meringue garlands on top, working from the centre outwards and ending each in a rosette. Bake the cake for 1 minute only until the meringue is light golden brown on top. Decorate the centre and sides of the gâteau with toasted flaked almonds and top each meringue rosette with a gooseberry.

Cook's Tip

In order to achieve a light sponge, when folding in the ingredients use a metal tablespoon and work quickly and lightly. An uncooked sponge mixture must be put into the preheated oven without delay.

Fruit Layer Gâteau

SPONGE MIXTURE
4 eggs, separated
2 tablespoons lukewarm water
140 g/5 oz castor sugar
grated rind of $\frac{1}{2}$ lemon
120 g/4 oz plain flour
60 g/2 oz cornflour
1 teaspoon baking powder
FILLING
100 g/4 oz nougat
100 g/4 oz ground almonds
1–2 tablespoons Kirsch
2 tablespoons water
1 tablespoon icing sugar
TOPPING
100 g/4 oz apricot jam
75 g/3 oz toasted flaked almonds
675 g/1½ lb mixed fruit or
   1 (825-g/1 lb 13-oz) can
   fruit salad
1 small packet quick-setting jel
   mix

Grease a 25-cm/10-inch spring-form cake tin. Preheat the oven to moderately hot (190°C, 375°F, Gas Mark 5).

Whisk the egg yolks with the water, half the sugar and the lemon rind, until frothy. Whisk the egg whites until stiff, fold in the remaining sugar then fold into the egg yolks. Sift the flour with the cornflour and baking powder and fold evenly into the mixture. Turn into the prepared tin and bake for 40 minutes.

Remove the cake from the tin and cool on a wire rack for at least 2 hours, then cut into three layers.

Melt the nougat in a basin over hot water and spread over one cake layer. Put the next layer on top. Mix the ground almonds with the Kirsch, water and sifted icing sugar and spread over the second layer. Cover with the third cake layer, spread the top and sides with the warmed apricot jam and cover the sides with flaked almonds, pressing in well. Arrange the prepared and drained fruit over the cake and glaze with the jel mix, made up according to the packet instructions.

Fresh Cream Pear Gâteau

SPONGE MIXTURE
6 eggs, separated
150 g/5 oz castor sugar
100 g/3½ oz plain flour
30 g/1 oz cornflour
50 g/2 oz cocoa powder
50 g/2 oz ground almonds
50 g/2 oz butter or margarine
FILLING AND TOPPING
1 kg/2 lb ripe dessert pears
1 litre/1¾ pints water
50 g/2 oz sugar
juice of 1 lemon
225 g/8 oz blackcurrant
    preserve
600 ml/1 pint double cream
60 g/2 oz icing sugar
50 g/2 oz toasted flaked almonds
7 glacé cherries

Grease a 25-cm/10-inch cake tin. Preheat the oven to moderately hot (190°C, 375°F, Gas Mark 5).

Whisk the egg yolks with a third of the sugar until pale and thick. Whisk the egg whites until stiff then add the remaining sugar. Whisk again until stiff and fold into the egg yolks. Sift the flour, cornflour and cocoa powder together, mix with the ground almonds and fold all thoroughly into the egg mixture. Melt the butter or margarine, cool a little and carefully fold into the cake mixture. Turn into the prepared tin, smooth the surface and bake in the centre of the oven for 40–50 minutes.

Cool on a wire rack for at least 2 hours then cut into three layers.

Peel the pears, divide each into eight segments and remove the cores. Bring the water to the boil with the sugar and lemon juice and poach the

pears in this syrup for about 10 minutes, keeping the pan covered. Leave to drain in a sieve over a basin and allow the fruit to cool.

Spread two cake layers with the blackcurrant preserve and arrange the pear segments over, reserving 14 segments for decoration. Whip the cream with the sifted icing sugar until stiff. Spread half the cream over both the cake layers, sandwich them together and finally place the last layer on top. Spread the top and sides thickly with cream, smoothing over carefully. Sprinkle the sides with flaked almonds and mark the top of the gâteau into 14 equal portions. Place the remaining cream in a piping bag fitted with a star nozzle and pipe a rosette on each portion. Finally decorate each with a segment of pear and a halved cherry.

Cook's Tip

Instead of fresh dessert pears, use a large can of pear halves, drained and sliced.

Raspberry Cream Torte

SHORTBREAD BASE
100 g/3½ oz butter or margarine
50 g/2 oz castor sugar
150 g/5 oz plain flour
SPONGE MIXTURE
4 eggs, separated, plus 2 egg
    yolks
100 g/4 oz castor sugar
80 g/3 oz plain flour
25 g/1 oz cornflour
35 g/1½ oz cocoa powder
FILLING
450 g/1 lb fresh or frozen
    raspberries
1 tablespoon raspberry liqueur
    or Kirsch
15 g/½ oz powdered gelatine
450 ml/¾ pint double cream
70 g/2½ oz icing sugar
DECORATION
250 ml/8 fl oz double cream
1 tablespoon icing sugar
25 g/1 oz toasted flaked
    almonds

Cream the butter with the
sugar. Add the sifted flour and
work into a dough. Wrap in
foil or cling film and leave in
the refrigerator for 2 hours.

If using frozen raspberries,
allow to defrost at room
temperature.

Grease a 23 × 33-cm/9 ×
13-inch Swiss roll tin and line
with greased greaseproof paper.
Preheat the oven to hot (220°C,
425°F, Gas Mark 7). Whisk all
the egg yolks with half the
sugar until thick and creamy.
Whisk the whites until stiff
then whisk in the remaining
sugar and fold into the egg
yolk mixture. Sift the flour,
cornflour and cocoa powder
on to the eggs and fold in
carefully using a metal spoon.
Spread this mixture into the
prepared tin and bake for
10–12 minutes. Turn the
sponge out on to clean greaseproof paper sprinkled with
sugar. Remove the lining
paper from the cake, cover

with a damp cloth and leave
to cool.

Reduce the oven temperature
to moderately hot (190°C,
375°F, Gas Mark 5). Roll out
the shortbread dough to line
the base of a 20-cm/8-inch
springform cake tin. Bake for
15–20 minutes and leave to
cool in the tin.

Lightly crush two-thirds of
the raspberries and mix with
the liqueur. Reserve the
remaining fruit for decoration.
Dissolve the gelatine in 3
tablespoons cold water over a
gentle heat. Whip the cream
with the sifted icing sugar until
stiff. Fold in the cooled gelatine together with the raspberries. Spread the sponge
evenly with the fruit and
cream mixture and cut length
ways into 5·5-cm/2¼-inch
strips. Roll up one of the
strips and stand upright on the
centre of the shortbread. Shape
the other strips carefully into
circles around the central roll,

until the whole base has been
covered. Place the cake in the
refrigerator and leave to set.

Whip the cream for decoration with the sifted icing sugar
until stiff. Remove the cake
from the tin and place on a
serving plate. Spread some of
the whipped cream over the
top and sides of the cake,
smoothing with a palette knife.
Place the remainder in a piping
bag and pipe an attractive
design on top of the cake, as
illustrated. Decorate the
rosettes with the reserved
raspberries and sprinkle flaked
almonds over the centre.

Raspberry Cream Roll

SPONGE MIXTURE
4 eggs, separated, plus 2 egg yolks
100 g/4 oz castor sugar
80 g/3 oz plain flour
20 g/1 oz cornflour
FILLING
225 g/8 oz fresh or frozen raspberries
300 ml/½ pint double cream
50 g/2 oz icing sugar

Allow the frozen raspberries to defrost at room temperature. Line a 33 × 23-cm/13 × 9-inch Swiss roll tin with greaseproof paper and grease well. Preheat the oven to hot (220°C, 425°F, Gas Mark 7).

Whisk all the egg yolks with half the sugar until creamy and thick. Whisk the egg whites until stiff, then whisk in the remaining sugar and fold into the whisked egg yolks. Sift the flour and cornflour over this mixture and fold in. Spread evenly in the Swiss roll tin and bake towards the top of the oven for 10–12 minutes.

Turn the sponge out on to a clean sheet of greaseproof paper sprinkled with sugar, with a dampened tea towel underneath. Strip off the lining paper, trim the edges of the sponge and roll up with the clean greaseproof inside. Allow to cool.

Crush the raspberries with a wooden spoon, reserving a few for decoration. Whip the cream and sifted icing sugar together until stiff, place about one-quarter in a piping bag and mix the remainder with the crushed raspberries. Carefully unroll the Swiss roll and remove the greaseproof paper. Spread with the raspberry cream and roll up. Pipe cream rosettes on top and decorate with the reserved raspberries.

Chocolate Cream Roll

SPONGE MIXTURE
4 eggs, separated, plus 2 egg yolks
100 g/4 oz castor sugar
80 g/3 oz plain flour
20 g/1 oz cornflour
40 g/1½ oz cocoa powder
FILLING
100 g/4 oz fresh or frozen strawberries
300 ml/½ pint double cream
50 g/2 oz icing sugar
1 tablespoon drinking chocolate powder

Allow the frozen strawberries to defrost at room temperature. Line a 33 × 23-cm/13 × 9-inch Swiss roll tin with greaseproof paper and grease well. Preheat the oven to hot (220°C, 425°F, Gas Mark 7).

Whisk all the egg yolks with half the sugar until creamy and thick. Whisk the egg whites until stiff, then whisk in the remaining sugar and fold into the whisked egg yolks. Sift the flour, cornflour and cocoa powder over the egg mixture and fold in. Spread evenly in the Swiss roll tin and bake towards the top of the oven for 10–12 minutes.

Turn the sponge out on to a clean sheet of greaseproof paper sprinkled with sugar, with a dampened tea towel underneath. Strip off the lining paper, trim the edges and roll up with the greaseproof paper inside. Allow to cool.

Purée the strawberries in a liquidiser or press through a sieve. Whip the cream with the sifted icing sugar until stiff and mix with the puréed strawberries. Carefully unroll the Swiss roll and remove the greaseproof paper. Spread with the strawberry cream and roll up. Dredge the top with sifted chocolate powder.

Fresh Strawberry Savarin

SAVARIN DOUGH
20 g/¾ oz fresh yeast
250 ml/8 fl oz lukewarm milk
350 g/12 oz plain flour
4 eggs
40 g/1½ oz castor sugar
1 tablespoon vanilla sugar
¼ teaspoon salt
150 g/5 oz butter or margarine
SYRUP
4 tablespoons rum
6 tablespoons white wine
250 ml/8 fl oz water
150 g/5 oz sugar
FILLING
225 g/8 oz strawberries
150 ml/¼ pint double cream
50 g/2 oz castor sugar
1 teaspoon chopped pistachio
    nuts

Grease a 23-cm/9-inch savarin tin and dust with flour.

Cream the yeast with a little of the milk, then add the remaining milk. Sift the flour into a bowl, make a well in the centre and pour in the yeast liquid. Sprinkle with a little of the flour, cover and leave for 15 minutes, until frothy.

Beat the eggs with the sugar until frothy, then mix in the vanilla sugar, salt and melted butter. Add this to the yeast mixture, beating well to an almost pouring consistency. Cover and leave to rise for 10 minutes. Beat the mixture with a wooden spoon and pour into the savarin tin. Cover and leave until the mixture almost reaches the top of the tin.

Preheat the oven to hot (220°C, 425°F, Gas Mark 7). Bake the savarin for 40 minutes then turn out on to a wire rack.

Heat the rum, white wine, water and sugar until the sugar has dissolved. Simmer for 5 minutes. Place a container underneath the wire rack to catch the syrup then pour it over the savarin until completely absorbed. Place on to a serving plate.

Wash, hull and halve the strawberries. Whip the cream with the sugar until stiff. Place most of the strawberries in the centre of the savarin and pipe the cream over them. Use the remaining strawberries and pistachios to decorate.

Strawberry Ring

CHOUX PASTE
60 g/2 oz butter
pinch of salt
grated rind of ½ lemon
250 ml/8 fl oz water
200 g/7 oz plain flour
4 eggs, beaten
FILLING
500 g/1 lb strawberries
2 teaspoons vanilla sugar
450 ml/¾ pint double cream

First wash and hull the strawberries. Reserve three large strawberries and mix the rest with the vanilla sugar; leave for a while for the sugar to be absorbed. Lightly grease a  baking tray and dust with flour. Preheat the oven to hot (220°C, 425°F, Gas Mark 7).

Melt the butter with the salt, lemon rind and water over a low heat, then bring quickly to the boil. Remove from the heat, add the sifted flour, and beat with a wooden spoon until it comes away from the sides of the pan. Return to the heat for 1 minute, stirring continuously. Allow to cool slightly then add the eggs a little at a time, beating in well.

Fill a piping bag fitted with a large star nozzle with the mixture and pipe 11 rosette shapes in a 25-cm/10-inch ring on the baking tray. When risen they will join together to form a circle. Bake just below the centre for 20–25 minutes.

Purée the strawberries through a nylon sieve. Whip the cream until stiff and put 2 tablespoons of the cream into a clean piping bag fitted with a large star nozzle. Mix the remaining cream with the strawberry purée.

While still warm, split the choux ring to allow it to cool more quickly, then fill with the strawberry cream mixture. Decorate with rosettes of cream and segments of strawberry.

Strawberry Curd Cake

PASTRY
250 g/9 oz plain flour
125 g/4½ oz butter, cut into flakes
100 g/4 oz castor sugar
2 egg yolks
FILLING
225 g/8 oz curd cheese
100 g/4 oz castor sugar
1 tablespoon cornflour
grated rind of 1 lemon
4 eggs
450 ml/¾ pint double cream
225 g/8 oz strawberries
1 small packet quick-setting jel mix (red colour)

Knead together the sifted flour, butter, sugar and egg yolks. Wrap the pastry in foil or cling film and leave in the refrigerator for 2 hours.

Preheat the oven to moderately hot (200°C, 400°F, Gas Mark 6). Roll out the pastry on a lightly floured surface and use to line the base and sides of a 28-cm/11-inch springform cake tin. Prick thoroughly all over with a fork and bake blind for 10 minutes. Reduce the oven temperature to moderate (180°C, 350°F, Gas Mark 4).

Beat the curd cheese, sugar, cornflour, lemon rind and eggs together. Whip the cream until stiff and fold into the cheese mixture. Turn into the pastry case and bake for a further 50–60 minutes. Leave to cool slightly.

Wash and hull the strawberries and dry on absorbent paper. Cut each strawberry in half and arrange over the curd cake. Prepare the jel mix according to the instructions on the packet and pour over the strawberries.

Baked Vanilla Cheesecake

PASTRY
250 g/9 oz plain flour
125 g/4½ oz butter, cut into flakes
pinch of salt
30 g/1 oz castor sugar
1 egg
2–3 tablespoons water
FILLING
675 g/1½ lb curd or cream cheese
3 tablespoons oil
275 g/10 oz castor sugar
3 eggs, separated
3 tablespoons cornflour
few drops of vanilla essence
6 tablespoons milk

Sift the flour into a bowl. Add the butter, salt, sugar, egg and water and mix to a dough. Wrap in foil or cling film and leave for 2 hours in the refrigerator.

Preheat the oven to moderate (180°C, 350°F, Gas Mark 4). Roll out the pastry to line the base and sides of a 25-cm/10-inch flan tin. Mix the cheese with the oil, sugar, egg yolks, cornflour, vanilla essence and milk, until smooth. Whisk the egg whites until stiff and fold into the cheese mixture. Pour into the pastry case and bake in the centre of the oven for 50–60 minutes.

Rich Lemon Cheesecake

BISCUIT BASE
175 g/6 oz digestive biscuits
75 g/3 oz margarine, melted
FILLING
575 g/1¼ lb cream cheese
6 eggs, separated
100 g/4 oz castor sugar
1 (142-ml/5-fl oz) carton soured cream
grated rind of 1 lemon
1 tablespoon lemon juice
2 tablespoons cornflour
1 teaspoon baking powder

Crush the biscuits into crumbs and mix with the melted margarine. Press into the base of a greased 25-cm/10-inch springform cake tin. Preheat the oven to moderate (160°C, 325°F, Gas Mark 3).
Beat the cream cheese with the egg yolks, sugar, soured cream, lemon rind and juice, cornflour and baking powder, mixing until smooth. Whisk the egg whites until stiff and fold into the cheese mixture. Pour into the prepared tin and bake in the centre of the oven for 1¼–1½ hours. Cover with foil if becoming too brown. The cheesecake should be firm to the touch, but still slightly springy. Loosen the sides immediately with a knife and allow to cool.

Rich Cream Cheesecake

SHORTBREAD
200 g/7 oz plain flour
120 g/4 oz butter, cut into flakes
70 g/2½ oz castor sugar
1 egg yolk
pinch of salt
grated rind of ½ lemon
FILLING
250 ml/8 fl oz milk
200 g/7 oz castor sugar
pinch of salt
grated rind of 1 lemon
4 egg yolks
25 g/1 oz powdered gelatine
450 ml/¾ pint double cream
450 g/1 lb curd or cream cheese
icing sugar to sprinkle

Sift the flour on to a large board and dot with the flaked butter. Make a well in the centre, add the sugar, egg yolk, salt and lemon rind. Working from the centre outwards, quickly knead all the ingredients to a smooth dough. Shape into a ball, wrap in foil or cling film and leave for 2 hours in the refrigerator.

Preheat the oven to moderately hot (190°C, 375°F, Gas Mark 5). Roll the shortbread out thinly on a floured surface to make two 25-cm/10-inch rounds. Place on greased baking trays and bake for 8–10 minutes, until golden brown. While still warm, cut one round into 12 equal portions and cool on wire rack with the other round.

Place the milk, sugar, salt, lemon rind and egg yolks in the top of a double saucepan or in a basin over a pan of hot water. Heat gently, stirring continuously until smooth and thickened. Remove from the heat. Dissolve the gelatine in 3 tablespoons water over a gentle heat. Stir into the custard and leave to cool. Whip the cream until thick. When the custard begins to set, stir in the beaten cream cheese then carefully fold in the whipped cream.

Line the sides of a 25-cm/10-inch springform cake tin with a strip of greaseproof paper. Place the uncut shortbread round in the base of the tin, spoon over the cheese filling and smooth the surface. Arrange the cut shortbread on top to form a complete round then allow to set in the refrigerator.

Remove the cheesecake from the tin and carefully peel away the greaseproof paper. Finally sprinkle with sifted icing sugar.

Cook's Tip

If wished, fresh or frozen strawberries, raspberries, redcurrants or blackcurrants can be added to the cheese mixture. Make sure the frozen fruit has thawed sufficiently and is drained and sweetened to taste. If fresh fruit is used, wash, pat dry and sprinkle with sugar. Leave for a few minutes before adding to the mixture.

Raspberry Ice Cream Cake

SPONGE MIXTURE
3 eggs
65 g/2½ oz castor sugar
pinch of salt
50 g/2 oz plain flour
25 g/1 oz cornflour
25 g/1 oz ground almonds
25 g/1 oz butter, melted
FILLING AND TOPPING
1 tablespoon Kirsch
225 g/8 oz raspberries
600 ml/1 pint double cream
250 g/9 oz castor sugar
chocolate caraque

Grease and flour a 20-cm/8-inch cake tin. Preheat the oven to moderately hot (190°C/375°F, Gas Mark 5).
Beat the eggs with the sugar and salt until pale and creamy. Sift the flour with the cornflour and fold into the mixture with the ground almonds and butter.

Place in the cake tin and bake for 25–30 minutes.
Turn on to a wire rack to cool for 24 hours then cut into two layers. Line the sides of the cake tin with foil and place one of the layers over the base.
Spoon the Kirsch over the raspberries, cover and leave for 1 hour. Keep a few whole raspberries for decoration and crush the remainder lightly.
Whip the cream with the sugar until stiff. Reserve approximately a quarter of this cream and stir the raspberries into the remainder. Pour into the cake tin and place the second cake layer on top. Freeze for 5–10 hours in a freezer or in the freezing compartment of a refrigerator.
Leave at room temperature for 15 minutes then turn out. Spread a little of the reserved cream thinly over the top and sides of the cake and decorate as illustrated.

Hazelnut Ice Cream Cake

SPONGE MIXTURE
3 eggs
65 g/2½ oz castor sugar
25 g/1 oz plain flour
30 g/1 oz cornflour
75 g/3 oz toasted hazelnuts, finely ground
FILLING AND TOPPING
600 ml/1 pint double cream
225 g/8 oz castor sugar
75 g/3 oz toasted hazelnuts, ground
few whole hazelnuts

Grease and flour a 20-cm/8-inch cake tin. Preheat the oven to moderately hot (190°C/375°F, Gas Mark 5).
Whisk the eggs with the sugar until pale and creamy. Sift the flour with the cornflour and carefully fold in with the ground hazelnuts. Pour into the cake tin and bake for

25–30 minutes.
Turn on to a wire rack to cool. Leave the cake for 24 hours then cut it through into two layers. Line the sides of the cake tin with foil and place one of the layers over the base.
Whip the cream with the sugar until stiff. Reserve a third of this cream then add 50 g/2 oz ground hazelnuts to the remainder. Spread over the cake base and place the second cake layer on top. Freeze the cake for 5–10 hours in the freezer or in the freezing compartment of the refrigerator.
Leave at room temperature for 15 minutes then turn out and decorate. Use a little of the reserved cream to spread thinly over the top and sides of the cake then sprinkle with the remaining grounds nuts. With the rest of the cream, pipe rosettes on the cake and top these with whole hazelnuts. Serve at once.

Baked Alaska

SPONGE BASE
1 egg
25 g/1 oz castor sugar
25 g/1 oz plain flour
TOPPING
50 g/2 oz ground almonds
50 g/2 oz apricot jam
1 tablespoon rum
50 g/2 oz candied lemon peel
4 egg whites
225 g/8 oz castor sugar
1 block each raspberry ripple
*   and raspberry ice cream*
8 glacé cherries
2 teaspoons flaked almonds

Preheat the oven to 190°C, 375°F, Gas Mark 5. Grease and flour a 15-cm/6-inch sandwich tin. Whisk the egg with the sugar until pale. Fold in the sifted flour and turn into the tin. Bake for 20–25 minutes then cool.

Mix the ground almonds with the jam, rum and chopped peel. Whisk the egg whites until stiff, fold in the sugar and place in a piping bag.

Spread the almond mixture over the cake base. Place the raspberry ripple ice cream on the centre and surround with the raspberry ice cream cut into pieces. Smooth over. Place in a freezer for 30 minutes until firm. Preheat the oven to 240°C, 475°F, Gas Mark 9.

Cover the cake completely with the whisked egg white, decorate with glacé cherries and flaked almonds and brown in the oven for 3–4 minutes. Serve at once.

Baked Chocolate Alaska

Make a sponge base as above, using twice the quantity of ingredients, and bake in a 15 × 23-cm/6 × 9-inch shallow tin. Trim to fit a block of Neapolitan ice cream, spread with 2 tablespoons redcurrant jelly and place the ice cream on top. Whisk 4 egg whites with 225 g/8 oz castor sugar as above, adding 1 teaspoon sifted cocoa powder. Pipe all over and brown in a very hot oven (240°C, 475°F, Gas Mark 9) for 3–4 minutes. Sift over chocolate powder before serving at once.

Christmas Stollen

1 kg/2¼ lb plus 200 g/7 oz
   plain flour
100 g/4 oz fresh yeast
450 ml/¾ pint lukewarm milk
100 g/4 oz castor sugar
2 eggs
few drops of vanilla essence
grated rind of 1 lemon
¼ teaspoon salt
400 g/14 oz butter
350 g/12 oz raisins
100 g/4 oz blanched almonds,
   chopped
100 g/4 oz candied lemon peel,
   chopped
50 g/2 oz candied orange peel,
   chopped
1 tablespoon rum
TOPPING
150 g/5 oz butter, melted
150 g/5 oz icing sugar

Line a baking tray with buttered greaseproof paper.

Sift the 1 kg/2¼ lb flour into a large bowl and make a well in the centre. Cream the yeast with a little milk then gradually add the remaining milk. Stir in a little sugar, pour into the well and sprinkle with a little of the flour. Cover and leave in a warm place for 15 minutes, until frothy. Mix the rest of the sugar with the eggs, vanilla, lemon rind and salt, add to the yeast mixture and work in with the rest of the flour to give a dry firm dough. Knead until smooth then cover and leave to rise for 1 hour.

Work the butter and the remaining 200 g/7 oz flour together, knead into the risen dough, cover and leave to stand for a further 15 minutes. Meanwhile, mix the raisins, almonds and chopped peel together, sprinkle with the rum, cover and leave to steep. Then quickly work this fruit

mixture into the dough, cover and leave to stand in a warm place for a further 15 minutes.

Divide the dough into three portions and roll each piece into a 30-cm/12-inch length. Roll gently so that the dough is thinner in the middle than at the ends. Fold the dough over lengthways, making a 15-cm/6-inch length – this gives the typical stollen shape – and place on the baking tray. Repeat using the other two pieces of dough. Cover the loaves and leave to stand for a further 20 minutes, until increased in size. Preheat the oven to moderately hot (200°C, 400°F, Gas Mark 6).

Bake the loaves for 25–30 minutes. While still hot, brush with the melted butter and dredge generously with sifted icing sugar.

Almond Stollen

Omit the raisins, almonds, lemon peel, orange peel and rum. Prepare the dough as for the Christmas Stollen, and after the second rising knead in 250 g/9 oz chopped blanched almonds and 250 g/9 oz chopped candied lemon peel. Leave to stand for a further 15 minutes then continue as for Christmas Stollen.

Italian Panettone

400 g/14 oz plain flour
25 g/1 oz fresh yeast
50 g/2 oz castor sugar
150 ml/¼ pint lukewarm milk
100 g/4 oz butter, melted
3 egg yolks
1 teaspoon salt
pinch of grated nutmeg
grated rind of ½ lemon
100 g/4 oz chopped mixed peel
50 g/2 oz raisins
1 egg yolk, beaten to glaze

Line a deep 18-cm/7-inch cake tin with buttered greaseproof paper.

Sift the flour into a bowl and make a well in the centre. Cream the yeast with a little of the sugar and the milk and pour into the well. Sprinkle with a little of the flour and leave in a warm place for 15 minutes, until frothy. Add the remaining sugar, the melted butter, egg yolks, salt, nutmeg

and lemon rind and beat in all the flour until the mixture forms a soft dough. Knead the dough for about 10 minutes then cover and leave to rise until doubled in size (about 1 hour). Turn on to a lightly floured board and knead in the chopped peel and raisins. Form the dough into a ball, place in the tin, cover and leave to stand until the dough reaches the top of the tin. Preheat the oven to moderately hot (200°C, 400°F, Gas Mark 6).

Brush the cake with beaten egg yolk, cut a cross on the top and bake for 20 minutes. Reduce the oven temperature to moderate (180°C, 350°F, Gas Mark 4) and continue to bake for a further 45 minutes. Allow the cake to cool slightly in the tin, then turn out on to a wire rack and leave until completely cold. Remove the greaseproof paper just before cutting the cake.

Honey Cakes

500 g/1 lb honey
6 tablespoons water
500 g/1 lb black treacle
700 g/1½ lb wholemeal flour
300 g/10 oz rye flour
1 tablespoon baking powder
1 teaspoon bicarbonate of soda
1 tablespoon milk
FILLING
100 g/4 oz almond paste
130 g/4½ oz castor sugar
1 egg white
1 tablespoon rum
100 g/4 oz candied fruit,
* chopped*
100 g/4 oz blanched almonds,
* chopped*
milk to brush
ICING
300 g/11 oz plain chocolate
glacé cherries and angelica

Melt the honey and gradually bring to the boil with the water and treacle. Leave to cool. Work in the flours and the

baking powder. Dissolve the bicarbonate of soda in the milk and stir into the mixture. Wrap in foil and leave for 2 days at room temperature.

Break the almond paste into small pieces and mix with the sugar, egg white, rum, candied fruit and almonds. Stand over a pan of hot water and mix well.

Preheat the oven to moderately hot (190°C, 375°F, Gas Mark 5). Grease three baking trays. Divide the cake dough into three portions. Roll each piece out to a thickness of 1·5 cm/¾ inch and cut out two heart shapes from each portion. Spread the marzipan filling over the centre of half the hearts, brush the edges with milk, top with a second heart and press the edges well together.

Bake the cakes for 30–35 minutes then leave to cool. Melt the chocolate in a basin over hot water, ice the cakes all over and top with cherries and angelica as illustrated.

Gingerbread House

1 kg/2 lb thick honey
250 ml/8 fl oz water
650 g/1¼ lb rye flour
500 g/1 lb plain wholemeal flour
200 g/7 oz chopped mixed peel
1 teaspoon ground ginger
1 teaspoon ground cinnamon
¼ teaspoon grated nutmeg
1 teaspoon bicarbonate of soda
DECORATION
20–30 blanched almonds
2 egg whites
500 g/1 lb icing sugar
1 tablespoon lemon juice
coloured sugar balls

Bring the honey to the boil with the water, stirring continuously, then leave to cool. Place the flours in a large mixing bowl and sprinkle with the mixed peel and spices. Form a well in the centre and pour in the honey which should be almost cold. Knead all the ingredients to obtain a soft dough. Finally mix the bicarbonate of soda into the dough. Place the dough in a polythene bag, seal and leave to stand for 1–2 days; this will make the gingerbread more tasty.

To construct the house it is advisable to cut out a cardboard pattern for the walls and roof, corresponding in size with the illustration. Lightly oil two or three baking trays. Pre-heat the oven to moderately hot (200°C, 400°F, Gas Mark 6). Roll part of the honey dough into 18 long sausage shapes, 40 cm/16 inches long and 1·5 cm/¾ inch in diameter.

Place side by side on one of the baking trays, leaving about 3 mm/⅛ inch between each. They should form a rectangle 40 × 25 cm/16 × 10 inches. During baking the gaps close up and form the walls of the log cabin. Bake in the centre of the oven for 20–30 minutes.

Roll out the rest of the dough to 1 cm/½ inch thick. Cut out one piece of about 25 × 15 cm/10 × 6 inches and a second piece 35 × 28 cm/14 × 11 inches. Place these pieces on the baking tray, prick with a fork and bake for 12–18 minutes in the centre of the oven. From the 40 × 25-cm/16 × 10-inch piece which was baked first, cut out with a sharp knife the front, back and side walls of the house, using the cardboard pattern. Cut out a door and window in the front wall. From the flat pieces of dough cut out a base and two roof pieces using the cardboard pattern as a guide. Roll out

the rest of the dough to 5 mm/¼ inch thick, cut out 20 small biscuits and place an almond on each. Also cut out pieces for the chimney and strips for the fence as illustrated and bake for 12–15 minutes.

Lightly whisk the egg whites until frothy, then gradually beat in the sifted icing sugar until a thick icing is obtained. Finally beat in the lemon juice. Assemble the sections of the house, using the icing to hold the pieces together; leave the icing to dry completely at each stage before constructing the next section. Coat the roof and chimney with icing to resemble freshly fallen snow. Decorate the house as you choose or as illustrated with the ginger biscuits, sugar balls and almonds.

Gingerbread Family

90 g/3¼ oz margarine
275 g/10 oz clear honey
115 g/4½ oz castor sugar
1½ teaspoons ground ginger
¼ teaspoon ground allspice
¼ teaspoon ground cinnamon
7 g/¼ oz cocoa powder
675 g/1½ lb plain flour
1 teaspoon bicarbonate of soda
pinch of salt
2 eggs
ICING
1 egg white
175–225 g/6–8 oz icing sugar
75 g/3 oz plain chocolate
blanched almonds, pistachio
*   nuts, glacé cherries, raisins,*
*   etc., to decorate*

Stir the margarine, honey, sugar, spices and cocoa powder together and warm over a low heat until the sugar is completely dissolved. Leave to cool.

Sift the flour and bicarbonate of soda into a bowl and knead in the salt, eggs and honey mixture to obtain a smooth dough. Cover and leave to stand overnight at room temperature.

Grease two baking trays. Preheat the oven to moderately hot (200°C, 400°F, Gas Mark 6). Roll out the dough to 5 mm/¼ inch thick and cut out figures using a gingerbread cutter. Place on the trays and bake for 12–15 minutes in the centre of the oven. Remove from the baking tray while still warm and cool on a wire rack.

Whisk the egg white stiffly with the sifted icing sugar. Decorate the figures with the piped icing, melted chocolate and the nuts and fruit, as illustrated.

Shortbread Christmas Tree

SHORTBREAD
300 g/11 oz plain flour
100 g/4 oz icing sugar
150 g/5½ oz butter, softened
1 egg
FILLING
250 ml/8 fl oz milk
1 tablespoon sugar
2 tablespoons custard powder
2 egg whites
2 tablespoons icing sugar
DECORATION
4 tablespoons apricot jam
100 g/4 oz desiccated coconut
chocolate and coloured icing,
*   hundreds and thousands,*
*   silver balls and chopped nuts*

Cut out from cardboard a Christmas tree pattern 33 cm/ 13 inches high and 28 cm/11 inches wide at the widest point. Sift the flour and icing sugar into a bowl with the butter

and egg, and mix until a dough is formed. Cover and leave for 2 hours in the refrigerator.

Prepare a custard from the milk, sugar and custard powder, following the instructions on the packet. Leave to cool. Whisk the egg whites until stiff then whisk in the sifted icing sugar. Fold into the cooled custard. Preheat the oven to moderately hot (190°C, 375°F, Gas Mark 5).

Roll out the shortbread dough, cut out two trees, and from the trimmings cut several small shapes for decoration. Bake for 15–20 minutes. While still warm cover one tree with the custard filling and place the second tree on top. Leave to cool.

Warm the jam, spread on the tree and sprinkle generously with desiccated coconut. Ice and decorate the small biscuit shapes and attach to the Christmas tree with jam.

Chocolate Orange Cookies

100 g/4 oz plain chocolate
125 g/4½ oz butter or margarine
125 g/4½ oz castor sugar
pinch of salt
1 egg
grated rind of 1 orange
200 g/7 oz plain flour
1 teaspoon baking powder
ICING
100 g/4 oz icing sugar
1–2 tablespoons orange juice

Coarsely grate the chocolate. Beat the butter or margarine with the sugar, salt, egg and orange rind. Sift in the flour with the baking powder, add the grated chocolate and quickly knead all the ingredients to a workable dough. Form into a ball, wrap in foil or cling film and leave for 2 hours in the refrigerator.

Preheat the oven to 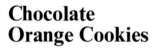 moderately hot (200°C, 400°F, Gas Mark 6). Roll out the dough on a floured board to 5 mm/¼ inch thick and cut out rounds 5 cm/2 inches in diameter. Place on greased baking trays, allowing room for spreading, and bake for 10–15 minutes. Carefully remove from the baking trays with a palette knife and leave to cool on a wire rack.

Sift the icing sugar and stir in the orange juice until smooth. Spread this icing over the top of the cookies and leave to set.

Crumbly Almond Hearts

250 g/9 oz butter
120 g/4½ oz icing sugar
2 egg yolks
100 g/4 oz ground almonds
350 g/12 oz plain flour
40 blanched almonds, halved

Beat the butter with the sifted icing sugar and 1 egg yolk until pale and creamy. Add the ground almonds and sifted flour and knead quickly to a firm dough. Form into a ball, wrap in foil or cling film and leave for 2 hours in the refrigerator.

Preheat the oven to moderately hot (200°C, 400°F, Gas Mark 6). Roll out the dough on a floured board to 5 mm/¼ inch thick and cut out 40 small heart shapes. Place on a large baking tray, beat the second egg yolk, brush the biscuits with this and place two almond halves on each. Bake for 10–12 minutes.

Allow the biscuits to cool slightly on the baking tray, then remove to a wire rack and leave until completely cool.

Norwegian Christmas Rings

3 eggs
1 egg yolk
160 g/5¼ oz icing sugar
250 g/9 oz butter, softened
few drops of vanilla essence
350 g/12 oz plain flour
1 egg yolk, beaten to glaze
sugar crystals to sprinkle

Boil the eggs for 10–12 minutes, plunge into cold water and shell. Press through a fine sieve and stir into the fresh egg yolk with the sifted icing sugar. Gradually work in the softened butter and the vanilla essence. Finally add the sifted flour and knead the ingredients to a soft dough. Wrap in foil or cling film and leave for 3 hours in the refrigerator.

   Preheat the oven to moderately hot (190°C, 375°F,

Gas Mark 5). Divide the dough into small pieces and form each into a roll about 10 cm/4 inches in length. Brush the strips at each end with beaten egg yolk and join into rings. Generously brush the tops with egg yolk and sprinkle with sugar crystals. Place on a baking tray and bake for 10–12 minutes.

   Remove from the baking tray with a palette knife and leave to cool on a wire rack.

Swedish Yule Biscuits

250 g/9 oz butter, softened
125 g/4½ oz castor sugar
1 egg
400 g/14 oz plain flour
1 teaspoon baking powder
½ teaspoon salt
1 egg white, beaten to glaze
¼ teaspoon ground cinnamon
50 g/2 oz granulated sugar

Beat the butter with the sugar and egg until light and fluffy. Sift the flour with the baking powder and mix in the salt. Gradually add the flour to the butter mixture and knead all together. Form the dough into a ball, wrap in foil or cling film and leave for 3 hours in the refrigerator.

   Preheat the oven to moderately hot (200°C, 400°F, Gas Mark 6). Divide the dough into three portions and

knead each in turn. Take each portion of dough from the refrigerator as required and roll out to a thickness of 3 mm/⅛ inch on a floured board. Cut out 6-cm/2½-inch round biscuits and place on a baking tray.

   Brush the biscuits with beaten egg white and sprinkle generously with the mixed cinnamon and sugar. Bake for 8–10 minutes then cool on a wire rack.

Cook's Tip

When sprinkling the biscuits with cinnamon and sugar some will fall on to the baking tray. Before baking remove this with a pastry brush, so it does not burn.

383

Traditional Fruit Loaf

75 g/3 oz dried stoned prunes
175 g/6 oz dried pears
75 g/3 oz dried figs
50 g/2 oz raisins
50 g/2 oz currants
50 g/2 oz chopped mixed peel
300 ml/½ pint hot black tea
50 g/2 oz sugar
¼ teaspoon ground cinnamon
pinch each of ground cloves,
    ground aniseed and salt
2 tablespoons rum
2 tablespoons lemon juice
200 g/7 oz plain flour
50 g/2 oz hazelnuts, finely
    chopped
50 g/2 oz walnuts, finely
    chopped
STARTER DOUGH
2 tablespoons milk
4 tablespoons water
1 teaspoon oil
1 teaspoon dried yeast
2 tablespoons lukewarm water

1 teaspoon castor sugar
2 teaspoons salt
50 g/2 oz strong plain flour
50 g/2 oz rye flour
DECORATION
25 g/1 oz blanched almonds,
    halved
glacé cherries
angelica

First make the starter dough.
Combine the milk, 4 tablespoons water and the oil in a
saucepan and bring to the boil.
Allow to cool until lukewarm.
Blend the yeast with 2 tablespoons lukewarm water and the
sugar and leave for 5 minutes.
Add to the milk mixture with
the salt. Stir this liquid into the
plain and rye flours until well
blended. Cover and leave to
stand for 12–10 hours.

Meanwhile chop the prunes,
pears and figs. Place in a bowl
with the raisins, currants and
mixed peel. Pour on the freshly
made tea, cover and leave to
soak overnight. Add the sugar,

spices, salt, rum and lemon
juice to the fruit. Stir all the
ingredients well, cover and
leave to stand for a further
30 minutes.

Grease a 20-cm/8-inch cake
tin with butter or margarine.
Preheat the oven to moderate
(180°C, 350°F, Gas Mark 4).

Add the fruit mixture to the
starter dough with the sifted
flour and chopped nuts. Mix
all thoroughly until well
combined and place in the cake
tin. Decorate with almond
halves, glacé cherries and strips
of angelica, as illustrated. Bake
for 1 hour 10 minutes.

Cook's Tip

This fruit loaf is
especially delicious made
with the given mixture
of various fruits. Should
you not have one kind of
dried fruit, you can in-
crease the quantity of the
other fruits accordingly.
Take care that your fruit
is made up of a mixture
of light and dark fruits.
Fruit loaves keep fresh
and moist for a long time
if stored in an airtight
container or wrapped
tightly in foil.

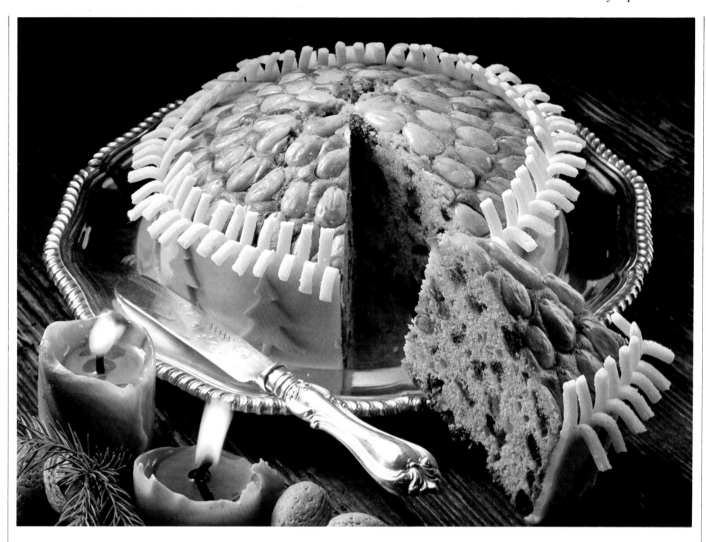

Festive Light Christmas Cake

250 g/9 oz butter
250 g/9 oz castor sugar
¼ teaspoon vanilla essence
generous pinch of salt
1 tablespoon rum
6 eggs
350 g/12 oz plain flour
1 teaspoon baking powder
400 g/14 oz sultanas
50 g/2 oz ground almonds
100 g/4 oz candied lemon peel,
  chopped
100 g/4 oz blanched almonds,
  halved
GLAZE AND DECORATION
2 tablespoons granulated sugar
4 tablespoons water
225 g/8 oz almond paste
2 tablespoons apricot jam
food colourings

Line a 23-cm/9-inch round cake tin with greased grease-proof paper. Preheat the oven to cool (150°C, 300°F, Gas Mark 2).

Beat the softened butter with the castor sugar, vanilla essence, salt and rum until pale and creamy. Stir in the eggs one at a time. If the eggs should curdle the mixture slightly, add a tablespoon of flour. Sift the remaining flour with the baking powder and mix with the sultanas, ground almonds and chopped peel. Fold this flour mixture gradually into the creamed mixture. Turn into the pre-pared tin, smooth the surface with the back of a wet spoon and arrange the almond halves in a circular pattern on top. Bake the cake for 3–3½ hours. Before removing from the oven test with a skewer; if the skewer comes out clean from the centre, then the cake is cooked through. Allow to stand in the tin for about 15 minutes then place on a wire cooling rack, leaving the greaseproof paper on the cake.

Heat the sugar and water, stirring continuously until the sugar is completely dissolved. Boil for 2–3 minutes. Cover the top of the cake with this glaze and leave to cool.

Spread the sides of the cake with the warmed jam. Roll out the almond paste thinly. Cut pieces to cover the sides of the cake, cutting into strips at the top, as illustrated. Colour the rest of the marzipan with the food colouring of your choice, cut out small Christmas tree shapes and attach to the cake with unbeaten egg white.

Cook's Tip

If you tie a double thickness of brown paper around the outside of the cake tin before baking, this will prevent the edges of the cake becoming brown and overcooked before the inside is cooked through.
The undecorated cake will keep well if wrapped in greaseproof paper and stored in an airtight tin.

Christmas Night Gâteau

SPONGE MIXTURE
4 eggs, separated
3 tablespoons water
180 g/6 oz castor sugar
1 tablespoon vanilla sugar
150 g/5½ oz plain flour
100 g/3½ oz cornflour
2 teaspoons baking powder
FILLING AND TOPPING
7 g/¼ oz powdered gelatine
600 ml/1 pint double cream
150 g/5 oz castor sugar
40 g/1½ oz cocoa powder
1 tablespoon boiling water
1 tablespoon rum
3 tablespoons cranberry jelly
DECORATION
100 g/4 oz plain chocolate
8 glacé cherries
1 teaspoon icing sugar
25 g/1 oz toasted flaked
   almonds

Grease the base of a 23-cm/9-inch cake tin with butter or margarine. Preheat the oven to moderately hot (190°C, 375°F, Gas Mark 5).

Beat the egg yolks with the water, half the sugar and the vanilla sugar until pale and creamy. Whisk the egg whites until stiff and fold in the remaining sugar, then carefully fold into the egg yolk mixture. Sift the flour with the cornflour and baking powder and carefully fold into the mixture. Turn into the prepared tin, smooth the surface and bake for 30–40 minutes. Cool on a wire rack. Leave the cake to stand overnight if possible then cut through twice to make three layers.

Dissolve the gelatine in 2 tablespoons water over a gentle heat. Whip the cream with the sugar until stiff. Cream the cocoa powder with the boiling water and rum, cool and mix a quarter of the cream with it. Spread this chocolate cream thickly on the first layer of cake and place the second layer on top. Warm the cranberry jelly, cool slightly and mix with the dissolved gelatine into a second quarter of the cream. Cover the second cake layer with this mixture and top with the last cake layer. Cover the cake all over with some of the remaining cream, place the rest in a piping bag fitted with a star nozzle and pipe 16 rosettes around the top of the cake.

Melt half the chocolate by standing in a basin over a pan of hot water and spread thinly on to greaseproof paper or foil. When the chocolate has set, dip a small star-shaped cutter into hot water and cut out 16 star shapes. Place a chocolate star and halved glacé cherry on each rosette. Coarsely grate the remaining chocolate. Sprinkle over the centre of the cake, sift lightly with icing sugar and decorate the sides of the cake with flaked almonds.

Cook's Tip

From the block of chocolate you can also make chocolate caraque, as illustrated. Spread the melted chocolate on to a clean flat surface. When the chocolate has just set, scrape off shavings with the blade of a knife. Leave the shavings to set hard then sprinkle on to the cake.

Chocolate Log

SPONGE MIXTURE
4 eggs, separated, plus 2 egg
  yolks
80 g/3 oz castor sugar
grated rind of ½ lemon
80 g/3 oz plain flour
FILLING AND TOPPING
350 g/12 oz plain chocolate
225 g/8 oz butter
125 g/4½ oz icing sugar
1 tablespoon rum
3 glacé cherries
1 teaspoon chopped pistachio
  nuts

Line a 33 × 23-cm/13 × 9-inch
Swiss roll tin with greased
greaseproof paper. Preheat the
oven to hot (220°C, 425°F,
Gas Mark 7).

Beat all the egg yolks with 1
tablespoon sugar and the lemon
rind until pale and creamy.
Whisk the egg whites until
stiff, fold in the remaining
sugar then fold into the egg
yolks. Carefully fold in the
sifted flour. Spread this
mixture evenly over the Swiss
roll tin and bake near the top
of the oven for 10–12 minutes.

Turn the cake out on to a
clean tea towel sprinkled with
sugar, remove the greaseproof
lining paper and trim off the
edges of the sponge. Cover
with a clean piece of greaseproof
paper and carefully roll up the
cake with the help of the tea
towel, keeping the clean
greaseproof inside. Cool.

Melt the chocolate in a
basin over hot water. Spread
approximately a quarter of the
chocolate thinly over greaseproof paper and leave to set.
Allow the melted chocolate to
cool. Beat the butter with the
sifted icing sugar until pale
and creamy; keep 2 table-
spoons to one side. Beat the
cooled melted chocolate and
rum into the rest of this butter
cream. Carefully unroll the
cooled cake and spread two-
thirds of the chocolate cream
over it. Roll up again and pipe
the rest of the cream in stripes
along the length of the cake.

From the thin sheet of
chocolate cut out small leaves,
using a warmed knife. Decorate
the log with the reserved butter
cream, the halved glacé
cherries, chocolate leaves and
pistachio nuts, as illustrated.
Cut off one slice and place
beside the cake.

Easter Bread

BASIC YEAST DOUGH
1 kg/2¼ lb plain flour
50 g/2 oz fresh yeast
550 ml/18 fl oz lukewarm milk
200 g/7 oz butter, melted
100 g/3½ oz castor sugar
2 eggs
pinch of salt
grated rind of 1 lemon
FRUIT LOAF
100 g/4 oz blanched almonds,
*   chopped*
200 g/7 oz candied lemon peel,
*   chopped*
300 g/11 oz sultanas
1 tablespoon rum
50 g/2 oz butter, melted
50 g/2 oz sugar
PLAITED WREATH
1 egg yolk, beaten to glaze
50 g/2 oz nibbed almonds
50 g/2 oz sugar
2 tablespoons rum

Sift the flour into a bowl and make a well in the centre. Cream the yeast with a little of the milk then stir in the remaining milk. Pour into the flour, sprinkle with a little of the flour and leave to stand in a warm place for 15 minutes, until frothy. Pour the melted butter into the yeast liquid and mix with the flour, sugar, eggs, salt and lemon rind, to form a dough. Knead for 5–10 minutes until the dough is smooth and elastic. Cover and leave to rise for 1 hour in a warm place.

Mix the almonds, candied peel, sultanas and rum together and leave to stand for 30 minutes.

Divide the dough in two and knead each half lightly. Mix one half with the fruit mixture and leave for 15 minutes. Pre-heat the oven to moderately hot (190°C, 375°F, Gas Mark 5).

Form the fruit dough into a loaf, place on a greased baking tray and leave to stand in a warm place for a further 30 minutes. Cut a cross on the top of the loaf and bake for 30–40 minutes. While still hot, brush the loaf with the melted butter and sprinkle with sugar.

Divide the remaining dough into three equal pieces and form into long strips. Plait these together, form into a wreath and brush with beaten egg yolk. Mix the almonds, sugar and rum and spread over the wreath. Bake as for the fruit loaf.

Coffee Cream Tart

PASTRY
100 g/4 oz butter
50 g/2 oz castor sugar
1 egg
1 tablespoon water
100 g/4 oz ground hazelnuts
150 g/6 oz plain flour
FILLING AND TOPPING
1 tablespoon instant coffee powder
250 ml/8 fl oz hot water
25 g/1 oz powdered gelatine
2 eggs, separated
125 g/4½ oz castor sugar
1 tablespoon vanilla sugar
2 tablespoons brandy
450 ml/¾ pint double cream
2 teaspoons chopped pistachio nuts
12 sugar Easter eggs

Knead together the butter, sugar, egg, water, hazelnuts and sifted flour to form a

dough. Wrap in foil or cling film and leave for 2 hours in the refrigerator.

Preheat the oven to moderately hot (200°C, 400°F, Gas Mark 6). Roll out the pastry and use to line the base and sides of a 23-cm/9-inch flan tin. Bake blind for 25–30 minutes. Leave the flan case to cool.

Dissolve the coffee in the hot water. Dissolve the gelatine in the hot coffee over a gentle heat. Beat the egg yolks with the sugar and vanilla sugar until pale and creamy. Stir in the cooled coffee and the brandy. Whisk the egg whites and separately whip the cream until stiff. Fold the egg whites and two-thirds of the cream into the coffee mixture. Fill the tart case with this coffee cream. When set, decorate with the rest of the cream, piped in rosettes, the pistachios and Easter eggs.

Polish Easter Ring

500 g/1 lb plain flour
30 g/1 oz fresh yeast
250 ml/8 fl oz lukewarm milk
120 g/4 oz castor sugar
375 g/12 oz butter
¼ teaspoon salt
grated rind of ½ orange
grated rind of ½ lemon
5 eggs
150 g/5 oz raisins
ICING
250 g/9 oz icing sugar
1 tablespoon lemon juice
3 tablespoons hot water
6 glacé cherries

Grease two 1·75-litre/3-pint savarin moulds and sprinkle with flour.

Sift the flour into a bowl and form a well in the centre. Cream the yeast with a little of the milk and a little sugar. Add the remaining milk and

pour into the flour. Sprinkle a little of the flour over the yeast liquid and leave in a warm place for 15 minutes.

Melt the butter, mix with the remaining sugar, the salt, grated fruit rinds and eggs, and beat into the yeast liquid and flour to obtain a smooth batter. Leave to stand in a warm place for 30 minutes. Beat the raisins into the batter. Divide the batter between the tins and leave to rise in a warm place until approximately 2·5 cm/1 inch from the top of the tins. Preheat the oven to moderately hot (200°C, 400°F, Gas Mark 6).

Bake the cakes for 50 minutes, covering with a little foil if they become too brown. Leave to cool in the tins for 20 minutes, then turn out to cool completely on a wire rack. Blend the sifted icing sugar with the lemon juice and water, pour over the cakes and decorate with halved cherries.

Lombardy Easter Loaf

500 g/1 lb plain flour
30 g/1 oz fresh yeast
250 ml/8 fl oz lukewarm milk
2 eggs
70 g/2¼ oz castor sugar
¼ teaspoon salt
generous pinch each of grated
  nutmeg and ground allspice
grated rind of ½ lemon
120 g/4 oz butter, melted
50 g/2 oz candied lemon peel,
  finely chopped
1 egg yolk, beaten to glaze

Grease a 23-cm/9-inch cake tin.

Sift the flour into a bowl and make a well in the centre.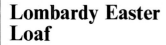
Cream the yeast with a little of the milk then add the remaining milk. Pour into the flour. Sprinkle a little of the flour over, cover and leave in a warm place for 15 minutes.

Beat the eggs with the sugar, salt, nutmeg, allspice and lemon rind. Add to the yeast liquid together with the butter and chopped peel. Mix to form a dough and knead until smooth and elastic. Leave to stand in a warm place for a further 30 minutes then knead lightly and divide into four equal portions. Roll each piece into a ball and place the balls in a ring in the prepared tin. Leave to stand in a warm place for a further 30 minutes. Preheat the oven to moderately hot (200°C, 400°F, Gas Mark 6).

Brush the loaf with beaten egg yolk and bake for 30–40 minutes. Leave to cool and serve with pats of butter.

Greek Easter Bread

60 g/2 oz fresh yeast
200 ml/7 fl oz lukewarm milk
50 g/2 oz castor sugar
1 kg/2 lb plain flour
pinch of salt
grated rind of 1 orange
250 ml/8 fl oz lukewarm water
50 g/2 oz sesame seeds
5 eggs, hard-boiled
red food colouring
1 egg yolk, beaten to glaze

Cream the yeast with a little of the milk and the sugar, add the remaining milk and leave to stand in a warm place for 15 minutes, until frothy. Stir in 125 g/4 oz flour, stir, cover and leave to stand overnight in a warm place.

Sift the rest of the flour into a bowl, form a well and add the prepared yeast liquid, salt and orange rind. Gradually stir in the water and mix to form a dough. Knead for at least 10 minutes, until the dough is smooth and elastic. Shape two-thirds of the dough into a long, smooth loaf, 5 cm/2 inches in height. Place on an oiled baking tray. From the rest of the dough make two thin rolls the length of the loaf, roll in the sesame seeds, twist and place round the loaf. Brush the eggs with red food colouring, leave to dry then press perpendicularly into the loaf. Brush the loaf with beaten egg yolk, sprinkle with sesame seeds, cover and leave to stand in a warm place for 1 hour. Preheat the oven to moderately hot (190°C, 375°F, Gas Mark 5).

Bake for 40–50 minutes then cool the loaf on a wire rack.

Easter Nests

500 g / 1 lb plain flour
30 g / 1 oz fresh yeast
250 ml / 8 fl oz lukewarm milk
50 g / 2 oz butter
1 egg
pinch of salt
50 g / 2 oz castor sugar
1 egg yolk, beaten to glaze
18 eggs (boiled for 5 minutes)

Sift the flour into a bowl and form a well in the centre. Cream the yeast with a little of the milk then add the rest of the milk. Pour into the well and sprinkle over a little of the flour. Cover and leave to stand in a warm place for 15 minutes, until frothy.

Melt the butter, beat with the egg, salt and sugar and work into the flour and yeast mixture to obtain a dry dough. Knead well then leave to rise for 1 hour. Divide the dough into 50-g/2-oz pieces and with

floured hands form into balls. Roll the balls into 50-cm/20-inch lengths, twist to form spirals, form into a circle and knot the ends (see illustration above). Place the nests on a greased baking tray, brush with beaten egg yolk and place one egg (still in its shell) in the centre of each. Leave to stand for 10 minutes.

Preheat the oven to moderately hot (200°C, 400°F, Gas Mark 6) and bake the Easter Nests for 15–20 minutes. After baking, decorate the eggs using water colours, coloured pencils, or felt-tip pens.

Easter Ducklings

500 g / 1 lb plain flour
30 g / 1 oz fresh yeast
60 g / 2 oz castor sugar
250 ml / 8 fl oz lukewarm milk
60 g / 2 oz butter, melted
1 egg
pinch of salt
1 egg yolk, beaten to glaze
225 g / 8 oz strawberry jam
DECORATION
2 tablespoons icing sugar
1 teaspoon lemon juice
currants
crystallised flowers (optional)

Sift the flour into a bowl and form a well in the centre. Cream the yeast with a little of the sugar and the milk. Pour into the well and sprinkle with a little of the flour. Leave to stand for 15 minutes. Add the rest of the sugar, the melted butter, egg and salt and mix to a dough. Knead well then leave to rise for 1 hour.

Roll out to 5 mm/¼ inch thick. From two-thirds of the dough cut out circles 7·5 cm/ 3 inches in diameter. Brush the edges of the circles with beaten egg yolk, spoon a little jam in the centre and place two circles together until all are used. From the rest of the dough cut out smaller rounds for the heads and ovals for the beaks. Attach the heads to the body and the beaks to the head with a little beaten egg yolk. Place on a greased baking tray and leave in a warm place for 15 minutes.

Preheat the oven to hot (220°C, 425°F, Gas Mark 7). Brush the ducklings with egg yolk and bake for 15 minutes. Blend the sifted icing sugar with the lemon juice. Stick the currants on to blobs of icing to form eyes and decorate the ducklings with crystallised flowers, if liked.

The Art of Baking

Baking is an art – but one which everyone can master with patience, a pride in working precisely and a certain amount of basic knowledge. By reading the following pages carefully, you will be able to acquire at least the beginning of this art.

Baking Hints

- Before you begin baking always remember to get out all the necessary equipment. Do not forget the small things such as spoons, knives, pastry brush, wooden spoon, pastry scraper, grater and absorbent paper, so that they are all easily available when you need them.
- Baking is an exact art! Therefore weigh or measure all necessary ingredients exactly. Unless specified otherwise, the recipes in this book have been tested using a size 3 egg: if you use smaller or larger eggs you may need to adjust the recipe accordingly.
- In our recipes we always use sifted flours. If you sift your flour you can be sure that no lumps will spoil the baking results.
- If the recipe indicates that the dough should be kneaded on a floured board, or rolled or worked in some other way, sprinkle the board with only a very little flour; dough absorbs flour readily and too much would alter the recipe proportions.
- Lemons or oranges whose rind is to be grated must be washed thoroughly beforehand.
- If the tin or baking tray is to be greased, sprinkled with breadcrumbs or flour, or lined with greaseproof paper, do this first. Then when the mixture is ready there will be no delay before baking. This is especially important with cake mixtures.
- Remember to always preheat the oven sufficient time in advance; an electric oven must be preheated 20 minutes in advance, a gas oven about 15 minutes. Place the oven shelves in the correct position before switching the oven on. As a general rule, yeast mixtures and pastry dishes should be cooked towards the top of the oven, cakes and biscuits should always be placed in the centre of the oven, while meringues should be cooked as low down in the oven as possible to prevent browning during the slow cooking time. This does not apply in fan-assisted ovens where there is constant all-round heat.
- Always place cake tins directly on to the oven shelf, never on to a baking tray, unless stipulated in the recipe.
- If the cakes are browning too quickly during baking, cover the tops with greaseproof paper or foil.
- Never open the oven door during the early cooking stage. You can look at small biscuits or cookies after 5 minutes, but generally the door should not be opened during the first 15–20 minutes.
- Test cakes with a skewer at the end of the given baking time, to see if cooked throughout. Insert a warmed metal skewer into

the centre: if it comes out with no uncooked mixture clinging to it the cake is ready.

Cook's Tips

- Apples, pears and bananas quickly turn brown when peeled and cut. Always use a stainless steel knife to cut and immediately sprinkle with lemon juice or lemon juice and water.
- If pastry dough is difficult to roll place between two floured sheets of greaseproof paper, or wrap in cling film and leave to chill in the refrigerator for 30 minutes before rolling.
- If you have made up pastry that you do not wish to bake immediately, wrap it firmly in foil or cling film and place in the refrigerator. It can remain there for up to a week and then be rolled, shaped and baked.
- Fruit cake with a high dried fruit content will stay fresh and moist after cutting if you keep it well wrapped in an airtight container.
- Ground spices will not keep their flavour for much longer than a year and then only if stored in airtight and light-proof containers. It is best to buy spices unground and to mark the purchase date on the container.
- Non-stick baking parchment saves time and effort. For all kinds of biscuits line the baking tray with this paper, then the baking tray need not be greased and will remain clean. When cool it is easy to remove the biscuits from the paper with a palette knife and they will be less likely to break. The paper can be used again several times.
- It is easier to turn a cake out of the tin on to a wire cooling rack if you place the rack on the tin, hold the tin and rack with a cloth and turn both together.
- Cheesecakes and cream cheese cakes should be left to cool in the oven after baking. Turn off the oven and leave the door open until the temperature inside the oven is the same as that outside. This will prevent the cheesecake from sinking.
- You can collect egg whites for meringues. When you need an egg yolk alone for a cake or glaze, lightly whisk the white and place it in a small screw-topped jar or freezing container and then freeze it. When thawed it can be used like fresh egg white.
- When cutting out shortcrust pastry or biscuit dough with small cutters, dip the cutter into flour to make it easier.
- When baking biscuits it is a good idea to bake one or two trial biscuits to see how much they spread during baking. You can then optimise the use of the space on the baking tray.
- If you notice too late that you have no icing sugar to sift over a cake, grind granulated sugar in a coffee grinder or blender and use this instead.
- Above all familiarise yourself with the basic recipes. There all the stages of work are clearly explained and much useful advice is given.

INDEX

almonds:
chicken with, 63
chocolate macaroons, 333
crumbly almond hearts, 382
date and almond stollen, 314
Italian biscotti, 335
leek salad with chicken and, 175
Linzertorte, 325
macaroon bars, 332
Mandorla almond cake, 325
orange almond cake, 350
orange almond cookies, 332
tartlets, 337
turkey schnitzel with, 64
alphabet biscuits, 360
Alsace apple tart, 340
anchovies:
anchovy and curd cheese, 112
Capri sauce, 242
Angelo's chicken salad, 278
aniseed:
biscuits, 333
marble bread, 307
scampi with aniseed cream, 275
apples:
Alsace apple tart, 340
apple and rice pudding, 145
apple lattice flan, 340
herby mackerel with apple sauce, 68
red beans with, 210
in red wine, 134
sausage with potato and apple mash, 56
apricots:
apricot plait, 316
apricot rings, 335
chicken with, 164
Dutch rice cake, 143
Arabian honey cake, 354
artichokes:
dips, 263
pizza, 26
stuffed, 102, 283
with tofu sauce, 191
vinaigrette, 121
asparagus:
omelette with prawns, 20
with two sauces, 179
aubergines:
Lyons-style, 101
moussaka, 59
Provençale, 91
scrambled egg on aubergine slices, 21
Austrian hazelnut cake, 324
avocado:
and ham salad, 278
avocado cream, 188

avocados with mussels, 277
chicken salad with, 125

bacon:
corn-on-the-cob with, 102
lamb's lettuce with, 117
olives and bacon, 236
pasties, 27
pâté and bacon open sandwich, 261
pizza, 230
plaice with, 70
quiche Lorraine, 228
trout with, 69
baked Alaska, 377
bananas:
curried rice with bananas in ham, 89
honey bananas with chocolate cream, 134
iced banana ring, 354
walnut and banana bread, 306
batch buns, 313
Bath buns, 330
bean salad, 118, 176
bean sprouts:
bean sprout pie, 208
rice salad with chicken and, 177
salad with prawns, 175
Béchamel potatoes, 109
beef:
beef mayonnaise open sandwich, 250
blintzes, 293
cabbage soup with, 15
classic steaks, 30
Cornish pasties, 227
couscous with stewed beef, 290
Creole fillet steak, 289
curried croquettes, 238
fusilli with Bolognese sauce, 84
meatballs, 260
minced steak pasties, 226
North German pepper pot, 32
pot-au-feu, 291
potato soup with mince dumplings, 13
roast beef and egg open sandwich, 261
rolled beef with ham, 33
rolled beef with mushrooms filling, 33
satay with peanut sauce, 294
smoked beef with kumquat sauce, 277
spicy beef salad, 129
steak tartare, buffet-style, 264
stew with sweetcorn, 52
stroganoff, 32
surprise tartlets, 225
sweet and sour beef with red

wine sauce, 31
beetroot, 97
Berlin-style calf's liver, 50
bilberries:
bilberry cream, 136
bilberry pudding, 216
birthday car cake, 361
biscuits:
alphabet, 360
aniseed, 333
apricot rings, 335
caraway, 221
cheese spirals, 220
cheese tricorns, 221
chocolate macaroons, 333
chocolate orange cookies, 382
crispy cheese biscuits, 222
crumbly almond hearts, 382
Dutch zebras, 336
Florentines, 337
French madeleines, 336
gingerbread family, 381
iced lemon bars, 334
Italian biscotti, 335
lemon ring biscuits, 329
macaroon bars, 332
Norwegian Christmas rings, 383
nutmeg, 334
orange almond cookies, 332
poppy seed and cheese biscuits, 220
shortbread Christmas tree, 381
shortbread fingers, 331
Shrewsbury biscuits, 330
Swedish yule biscuits, 383
black beans:
and sweetcorn, 211
Creole fillet steak, 289
blackberry meringue pie, 338
blintzes, 293
blue cheese and walnut open sandwich, 261
blue cheese dressing, 254
Bohemian plait, 315
Bohemian Schnitzel, 45
brandy snap ring, 349
bread:
aniseed marble bread, 307
baked Roquefort slices, 232
Bohemian plait, 315
brioches, 312
cheese bonnets, 234
croissants, 312
dinner rolls, 311
Easter ducklings, 391
Easter nests, 391
flat bread cakes, 188
flowerpot loaves, 309
French bread, 309
Greek Easter bread, 390
herb ring loaf, 308
luxury party loaf, 244
milk crescents, 310
mosaic loaf, 233
poppy seed plaits, 310

savoury butter slices, 234
spiced flat cakes, 308
strong ryebread, 304
stuffed French bread, 257
stuffed party rolls, 233
sugar buns, 313
Tuscan 'crostini', 232
wheatgerm loaf, 306
wholemeal bread, 305
wholemeal breakfast rolls, 305
bread pudding, cherry, 145
Bremer fruit loaf, 317
brioches, 312
broccoli:
with hazelnut butter, 96
individual flans, 25
and potatoes with cheese sauce, 187
brunch slices, 252
Brussels sprouts with smoked sausages, 58
buckwheat:
dumplings in gorgonzola cream, 194
pancake with scorzonera, 204
buns:
batch buns, 313
Bath buns, 330
sugar buns, 313
butter cream sandwich fingers, 319

cabbage:
chicken breasts in Savoy cabbage, 163
duck with red cabbage, 66
mince ring in cabbage, 47
Polish cabbage casserole, 57
soup with beef, 15
white cabbage au gratin, 92
cakes and gâteaux:
Arabian honey cake, 354
Australian hazelnut cake, 324
birthday car, 361
brandy snap ring, 349
butter cream sandwich fingers, 319
Caribbean coconut cake, 359
Chelsea cake, 322
cherry cream layer gâteau, 366
children's birthday cake, 361
chocolate cherry cake, 355
chocolate cream roll, 371
chocolate délice, 349
chocolate faces, 360
chocolate gâteau Alice, 347
chocolate log, 387
chocolate slice, 348
Christmas night gâteau, 386
classic sand cake, 355
classical petits fours, 362
coffee layer gâteau, 365
country butter cake, 319
cream cheese crumble cake, 320

crumble cake, 352
daisy cake, 351
date crumble cake, 345
Dresden slices, 321
festive chocolate gâteau, 364
festive light Christmas cake, 385
fresh cream pear gâteau, 369
fruit layer gâteau, 368
gingerbread house, 380
gooseberry meringue gâteau, 367
hazelnut ice cream cake, 376
hazelnut loaf cake, 352
honey cakes, 379
honey crunch cake, 356
iced banana ring, 354
iced lemon cake, 323
iced orange loaf cake, 357
iced rum cake, 356
Italian panettone, 379
marbled crumble cake, 321
marzipan cake, 357
nougat slice, 348
orange almond cake, 350
Polish Easter ring, 389
raspberry cream roll, 371
raspberry cream torte, 370
raspberry ice cream cake, 376
rum butter cake, 353
Sachertorte, 347
strawberry curd cake, 373
Swiss carrot cake, 358
traditional wedding cake, 363
Viennese cherry cake, 350
Viennese chocolate cake, 346
Camembert pâté, 258
canapés, smoked fish, 239
candied fruit, vanilla ice cream with, 130
cannelloni, 80
with tofu and spinach, 200
Capri sauce, 242
caramel, crème, 140
caraway biscuits, 221
Caribbean coconut cake, 359
carp, 72, 297
carrots:
carrot boats, 281
crispy corn with creamed carrots, 103
with nut vinaigrette, 173
salad with oranges, 115
Swiss carrot cake, 358
casseroles:
beef stew with sweetcorn, 52
cassoulet, 60
chicken and vegetable, 53
couscous with stewed beef, 290
fish and cucumber stew, 159
Genoese fish stew, 287
Hungarian pepper stew, 55
hunter's, 60
Italian mixed stew, 55

lamb and vegetable hotpot, 53
lamb ragoût with yogurt, 170
lamb stew with oranges, 171
lamb stew with quinces, 170
lentil with dumplings, 61
oxtail stew, 52
Polish cabbage, 57
Polish stew, 54
pot-au-feu, 291
potato stew, 56
rice and pork, 61
vegetable stew with chickpea balls, 195
cauliflower:
with cheese sauce, 91
in herb sauce, 90
salad, 118
celery:
au gratin, 99
Sardinian celery soup, 17
stuffed, 121
charlotte, strawberry, 138
cheese:
baked Roquefort slices, 232
blue cheese and walnut open sandwich, 261
broccoli and potatoes with cheese sauce, 187
buckwheat dumplings in gorgonzola cream, 194
Camembert pâté, 258
cauliflower with cheese sauce, 91
cheese and grape puffs, 225
cheese and peppers on tomato, 279
cheese and sausage salad, 125
cheese boats, 235
cheese bonnets, 234
cheese platter with Gorgonzola cream, 259
cheese puffs, 223
cheese salad open sandwich, 245
cheese sticks, 238
cheese tricorns, 221
chicory and cheese bake, 59
country cheese board, 259
crispy cheese biscuits, 222
Emmental spread, 268
fennel with blue cheese dressing, 283
fondue, 285
fried mozzarella, 191
fritters, 237
Gorgonzola dip, 263
ham and cheese horns, 224
individual cheese soufflés, 24
mooli salad with cheese dressing, 174
mushroom and cheese flan, 229
pastry pockets, 226
poppy seed and cheese biscuits, 220
potatoes with blue-vein cheese, 113

sauce, 242
spirals, 220
Stilton spread, 268
Swiss cheese salad open sandwich, 248
tomatoes stuffed with pecorino cheese, 100
Tuscan 'crostini', 232
wholemeal macaroni with cheese sauce, 82
wholemeal spaghetti with cheese and cream sauce, 198
cheese, soft:
and onion dip, 258
cream cheese crumble cake, 320
dates and cream cheese, 236
Dresden slices, 321
dumplings, 215
home-made curd cheese, 189
marbled crumble cake, 321
olive cheese, 188
quark and cherry strudel, 214
ravioli with herbs and ricotta, 201
savoury cream cheese layer, 269
soft fruit loaf, 316
spicy cream cheese slices, 235
strawberry curd cake, 373
cheesecakes:
baked vanilla, 374
rich cream, 375
rich lemon, 374
Chelsea cake, 322
cherries:
cherry bread pudding, 145
cherry cream layer gâteau, 366
chocolate cherry cake, 355
Morello cherry dessert, 133
Morello cherry pudding, 144
quark and cherry strudel, 214
stewed cherries with wine sauce, 133
vanilla cream with, 137
Viennese cherry cake, 350
chicken:
with almonds, 63
Angelo's chicken salad, 278
with apricots, 164
braised with vegetables, 162
breasts and kiwi fruit with orange sauce, 276
breasts in Savoy cabbage, 163
chicken and vegetable casserole, 53
chicken and vegetable mould, 270
chicken salad tomatoes, 279
Chinese-style, 165
curry, 300
exotic chicken, 165
gourmet's delight, 247

leek salad with almonds and, 175
paella, 54
pot-au-feu, 291
in red wine, 63
with rice 'hai nan', 299
rice salad with bean sprouts and, 177
rissoles, 163
with sage, 161
salad with avocado, 125
salad with grapes, 128
salad with green beans, 129
spicy rice salad, 256-7
spit-grilled herb chicken, 62
stuffed, 62, 160
Szechwan chicken, 298
wild rice with, 87
Windsor salad, 124
see also liver
chickpea balls, vegetable stew with, 195
chicory:
and cheese bake, 59
with ham, 98
salad with mandarins, 116
stuffed, 119
children's birthday cake, 361
children's lunch party, 256-7
Chinese gooseberry cream tart, 342
Chinese-style carp, 72
Chinese-style chicken, 165
Chinese-style scampi, 75
chocolate:
baked Alaska, 377
chocolate cherry cake, 355
chocolate cream roll, 371
chocolate délice, 349
chocolate faces, 360
chocolate log, 387
chocolate slice, 348
festive chocolate gâteau, 364
Florentines, 337
gâteau Alice, 347
honey bananas with chocolate cream, 134
Italian biscotti, 335
macaroons, 333
mousse, 141
orange cookies, 382
pears Hélène, 131
Sachertorte, 347
sponge with cream, 142
Viennese chocolate cake, 346
Christmas cake, 385
Christmas night gâteau, 386
Christmas stollen, 378
Christmas tree, shortbread, 381
club sandwich, 252
coconut:
Caribbean cake, 359
Fijian baked fish, 301
nut curry, 211
cod:
fish salad with peas, 128

foil-baked, 69
in scallop shells, 74
steamed cod on vegetables, 153

coffee:
coffee cream tart, 389
coffee layer gâteau, 365
corn-on-the-cob with bacon, 102
corned beef and egg sandwich, 251
Cornish pasties, 227

courgettes:
baked, and tomatoes, 196
gratin, 182

couscous:
salad, 176
with stewed beef, 290
cream cheese crumble cake, 320
cream dip, 263
cream horns, 326
cream slices, 329
cream strudel, 146
crème caramel, 140
crème russe, 141
Creole fillet steak, 289
cress soup with croûtons, 16
croissants, 312

croquettes:
curried, 238
game and mushroom, 236
prawn, 237
crudités, 115
crumble-based fruit tart, 345
crumble cake, 352

cucumber:
Danish salami and cucumber sandwich, 251
fish and cucumber stew, 159
potato and cucumber salad, 256
salad with yogurt dressing, 117
stuffed, 182, 182

curries:
chicken, 300
rice with bananas in ham, 89
lamb, 171
nut, 211
custard, plums with, 217

daisy cake, 351
dandelion salad, 116
Danish salami and cucumber sandwich, 251
Danish sandwiches, 247

dates:
date and almond stollen, 314
date crumble cake, 345
date and cream gâteau, 348
strawberries with, 216
Dauphinoise potatoes, 108
delicatessen meat salads, 253
dinner rolls, 311

dips:
à la Russe, 112

artichoke, 263
cheese and onion, 258
cream, 263
egg, 263
garlic, 263
Gorgonzola, 263
herb, 262
mayonnaise, 263.
orange, 262
sausage, 263
tomato, 262, 263
vegetable, 190, 262
Dresden slices, 321

dressings:
blue cheese, 254
egg and herb, 254
French, 254
sherry, 255
Thousand Island, 255
yogurt, 255

dried fruit:
Easter bread, 388
festive light Christmas cake, 385
pudding with nuts and sprouts, 213
see also teabreads

duck:
crisp-fried, 298
with pineapple sauce, 296
with red cabbage, 66
roast wild duck, 67

dumplings:
buckwheat, 194
cheese, 215
lentil casserole with, 61
liver dumpling soup, 18
mince, 13
plum, 143
Dutch fish soup, 19
Dutch rice cake, 143
Dutch rice speciality, 86
Dutch-style fried herrings, 73
Dutch zebras, 336

Easter bread, 388
Easter ducklings, 391
Easter nests, 391

eggs:
corned beef and egg sandwich, 251
dip, 263
egg and ham bake, 21
egg and herb dressing, 254
egg and pepper spread, 268
egg and tongue open sandwich, 261
egg tartlets with liver pâté, 243
ham and egg open sandwich, 245
ham sandwich with poached egg, 22
hard-boiled eggs with sauces, 242
mushroom with egg open sandwich, 246

party eggs, 240-1
piquant eggs with bean salad, 241
prawns with scrambled egg, 76
roast beef and egg open sandwich, 261
salad, 126
salami and egg salad open sandwich, 245
scrambled egg on aubergine slices, 21
scrambled egg and tomato sandwich, 22
tartlets with ham salad, 243
see also omelettes
Emmental spread, 268

fennel:
au gratin, 96
with blue cheese dressing, 283
salad, 115
with sesame dressing, 172
fig dessert, 137
Fijian baked fish, 301

fish:
Dutch soup, 19
Fijian baked fish, 301
fish and cucumber stew, 159
Genoese fish stew, 287
soup with vegetables and cress, 152
with vegetables, 156
flans, savoury **see** quiches
flans, sweet **see** tarts
Flemish-style pork chops, 43
Florentines, 337
flowerpot loaves, 309
fondue, cheese, 285

French and green beans:
chicken salad with, 129
creamed French beans, 90
piquant eggs with bean salad, 241
salad, 118
salad with tomato vinaigrette, 176
French bread, 309
stuffed, 257
French dressing, 254
French madeleines, 336
French orange flan, 342

fritters:
cheese, 237
prawn, 75

fruit:
crumble-based tart, 345
fruit flans, 323
fruit layer gâteau, 361
summer fruit dessert, 257
wholemeal savarin with stewed fruit, 212

fruit salads:
with cream, 132
exotic fruit salad, 132
fusilli with Bolognese sauce, 84

game:
game and mushroom croquettes, 236
hunter's casserole, 60

garlic:
dip, 263
Italian tomato and garlic sauce, 83
scampi in garlic oil, 287
spinach beet gratin with garlic bread, 184
spinach with garlic cream, 94
tomato rice with garlic, 87
Genoese fish stew, 287
gherkins and smoked ham, 236

ginger:
gingerbread family, 381
gingerbread house, 380
steamed fish with, 157
gnocchi in herb sauce, 203

gooseberries:
meringue gâteau, 367
meringue pie, 343
meringue tartlets, 344
Gorgonzola dip, 263
goulash soup, 12
gourmet fruit desserts, 133
gourmet's delight open sandwich, 247

grapes:
cheese and grape puffs, 225
chicken salad with, 128
grape cream flan, 341
Greek Easter bread, 390
green beans **see** French beans

haddock:
haddock mould, 272
with mushrooms, 71
oven-baked, 70
hake cutlets with mixed vegetables, 71

ham:
avocado and ham salad, 278
baked Roquefort slices, 232
chicory with, 98
curried rice with bananas in, 89
egg and ham bake, 21
egg tartlets with ham salad, 243
gherkins and smoked ham, 236
ham and cheese horns, 224
ham and egg open sandwich, 245
ham and pasta bake, 78
ham and salad platter, 266
ham and vegetable mould, 271
ham sandwich with poached egg, 22
Hawaiian ham rolls, 253
melon with Parma ham and piquant mayonnaise, 276
pepper and ham rolls, 58
quiches, 227

soufflés, 24
    vegetable rice with, 89
hamburgers, Spanish-style, 46
haricot beans:
    cassoulet, 60
    Hungarian bean soup, 14
    white beans Provençal, 210
Hawaiian ham rolls, 253
hazelnuts:
    Australian cake, 324
    broccoli with hazelnut
      butter, 96
    carrots with nut vinaigrette,
      173
    hazelnut loaf cake, 352
    ice cream cake, 376
    nutmeg biscuits, 334
    peaches with nut meringue,
      215
    stollen, 315
herb cream, 112
herb dip, 262
herb pancakes au gratin, 23
herb ring loaf, 308
herb spätzle, 202
herrings:
    Dutch-style fried, 73
    fillets with potatoes and
      quark sauce, 159
    green herring salad, 260
    herring platter, 260
    pickled, 73
    red herring salad, 260
    rollmop open sandwich, 261
honey:
    Arabian honey cake, 354
    honey bananas with
      chocolate cream, 134
    honey cakes, 379
    honey crunch cake, 356
    honey ice with orange salad,
      217
Hungarian bean soup, 14
Hungarian pepper stew, 55
hunter's casserole, 60

ice cream:
    baked Alaska, 377
    hazelnut ice cream cake, 376
    honey ice with orange salad,
      217
    raspberry ice cream cake,
      376
    vanilla ice cream with
      candied fruit, 130
iceberg salad, 118
Italian biscotti, 335
Italian mixed stew, 55
Italian panettone, 379
Italian salad, 122
Italian tomato and garlic
    sauce, 83

jelly:
    lemon wine jelly, 140
    plum mould, 142

kebabs:
    beef satay with peanut
      sauce, 294
    lamb, 41
    shashlik, 41
kidneys:
    flambéed, 51
    Normandy-style calf's
      kidney, 51
kiwi fruit and chicken breasts
    with orange sauce, 276
kohlrabi:
    in herb and cream sauce, 93
    stuffed, 98

lamb:
    barbecued saddle with
      coconut pears, 39
    chops with tomato and
      peppers, 40
    curry, 171
    cutlets, 40
    cutlets in thyme sauce, 168
    fried with tomatoes, 169
    herby steaks, 167
    kebabs, 41
    lamb and vegetable hotpot,
      53
    medallions with rosemary
      potatoes, 168
    moussaka, 59
    ragoût with yogurt, 170
    roast leg of, 38
    rolled shoulder of, 38
    shashlik, 41
    stew with oranges, 171
    stew with quinces, 170
    stuffed shoulder of, 166
lamb's lettuce with bacon, 117
lasagne, 80
leeks:
    au gratin, 99
    country leek flan, 229
    salad with chicken and
      almonds, 175
    stuffed, 281
lemon:
    iced lemon bars, 334
    iced lemon cake, 323
    lemon cream dessert, 139
    lemon ring biscuits, 329
    lemon wine jelly, 140
    rich lemon cheesecake, 374
lentil casserole with
    dumplings, 61
lettuce:
    iceberg salads, 114, 118
Linzertorte, 325
liver:
    Berlin-style calf's liver, 50
    liver dumpling soup, 18
    Milan-style calf's liver, 50
    spicy chicken liver open
      sandwich, 249
liver pâté, egg tartlets with, 243
lobster, grilled, 288
Lombardy Easter loaf, 390

luncheon meat, pasta salad,
    257
luxury party loaf, 244
lychee cocktail, 280
Lyons-style aubergines, 101

macaroni:
    with basil sauce, 83
    macaroni bake, 78
    pasta salad with salami, 122
    pastizio, 79
    wholemeal macaroni with
      cheese sauce, 82
    wholemeal macaroni with
      tomato sauce, 82
macaroon bars, 332
macaroons, chocolate, 333
mackerel:
    with apple sauce, 68
    smoked mackerel open
      sandwich, 249
Madeira sauce, pickled tongue
    in, 49
madeleines, French, 336
Mandorla almond cake, 325
mariner's breakfast (open
    sandwich), 261
marzipan cake, 357
mayonnaise:
    dip, 263
    melon with Parma ham and
      piquant mayonnaise, 276
    orange dip, 262
    spit roast pork with herb
      mayonnaise, 265
meat:
    delicatessen meat salads, 253
    giant meat platter, 267
    Italian mixed stew, 55
    lasagne, 80
    meat loaf with egg, 48
    meat loaf sandwiches, 256
    meat platter, 260
    mince ring in cabbage, 47
    pastizio, 79
    Polish stew, 54
    puff pastry mince roll, 48
    Spanish-style hamburgers, 46
    Viennese meat loaf, 47
    meatballs, 260
    melon with Parma ham and
      piquant mayonnaise, 276
meringue:
    blackberry pie, 338
    gooseberry gâteau, 367
    gooseberry pie, 343
    peaches with nut meringue,
      215
    raspberry meringue nest,
      343
    rhubarb tart, 339
Milan-style calf's liver, 50
milk crescents, 310
mince ring in cabbage, 47
minestrone, 19
mooli salad with cheese
    dressing, 174

Morello cherry dessert, 133
Morello cherry pudding, 144
mosaic loaf, 233
moussaka, 59
mousse, chocolate, 141
mozzarella, fried, 191
mushrooms:
    boiled potatoes with
      mushroom sauce, 186
    braised, 104
    with braised onions and
      tomatoes, 106
    cream of mushroom soup, 16
    deep-fried oyster
      mushrooms, 105
    game and mushroom
      croquettes, 236
    haddock with, 71
    mushroom and cheese flan,
      229
    mushroom and potato dish,
      106
    mushroom with egg open
      sandwich, 246
    mushroom rice, 88
    piroshki, 27
    risotto, 104
    rolled beef with mushroom
      filling, 33
    salad, 127
    sauce, 242
    tofu schnitzel with green rye
      and, 192
    wholemeal pizza with
      tomato and, 207
mussels:
    au gratin, 74
    avocados with, 277
    mussel and cress open
      sandwich, 248
    pork with, 286
    rice with seafood, 77
    with saffron sauce, 274

noodles:
    wholemeal with sesame, 202
Normandy rice salad, 124
Normandy-style calf's kidney,
    51
North German pepper pot, 32
Norwegian Christmas rings,
    383
nougat slice, 348
nut curry, 211
nutmeg biscuits, 334

olives:
    Capri sauce, 242
    olive cheese, 188
    olives and bacon, 236
omelettes:
    asparagus with prawns, 20
    potato, 28
    vegetable, 193
onions:
    cheese and onion dip, 258

flans, 26
mushrooms with braised onions and tomatoes, 106
pizza, 230
stuffed, 100
open sandwiches:
beef mayonnaise, 250
blue cheese and walnut, 261
cheese salad, 245
Danish, 247
egg and tongue, 261
gourmet's delight, 247
ham and egg, 245
mariner's breakfast, 261
mushroom with egg, 246
mussel and cress, 248
New Yorker, 250
pâté and bacon, 261
pinwheels, 246
prawn and mock caviare, 261
roast beef and egg, 261
rollmop herring, 261
salami and egg salad, 245
sausage and peppers, 245
smoked mackerel, 249
smoked trout, 248
spicy chicken liver, 249
Swiss cheese salad, 248
tomato and fish, 248
vegetarian special, 246
orange:
carrot salad with, 115
chicken breasts and kiwi fruit with orange sauce, 276
chicory salad with mandarins, 116
chocolate orange cookies, 382
dip, 262
French orange flan, 342
honey ice with orange salad, 217
iced orange loaf cake, 357
lamb stew with, 171
orange and wine cream, 139
orange almond cake, 350
orange almond cookies, 332
orange windmills, 327
radiccio salad with, 114
ossobuco, 34
oxtail stew, 52
oysters, classic, 274

paella, 54
palmiers, 327
pancakes:
blintzes, 293
buckwheat pancake with scorzonera, 204
herb pancakes au gratin, 22
pigeon pancake pie, 292
rum and raisin pancake pudding, 144
stuffed, 23
wholemeal pancake with vegetables, 205

partridge, stuffed, 67
party eggs, 240-1
party nests, 239
party rolls, stuffed, 233
passion fruit cream with raspberries, 136
pasta:
ham and pasta bake, 78
pasta bake with spinach, 81
salad, 257
salad with salami, 122
pasties:
bacon, 27
cheese and grape puffs, 225
cheese pastry pockets, 226
Cornish, 227
ham and cheese horns, 224
minced steak pasties, 226
mushroom piroshki, 27
spinach triangles, 85
vegetable, 209
pastizio, 79
pastries:
cream horns, 326
cream slices, 329
iced vanilla slices, 328
orange windmills, 327
palmiers, 327
strawberry ring, 373
Swiss choux rings, 328
pâtés:
Camembert, 258
pâté and bacon open sandwich, 261
peaches:
with nut meringue, 215
peach Melba, 131
in white wine, 133
peanut sauce, beef satay with, 294
pearl barley soup, 14
pears:
barbecued saddle of lamb with coconut pears, 39
fresh cream pear gâteau, 369
pears Hélène, 131
peas, fish salad with, 128
peppers:
cheese and peppers on tomato, 279
egg and pepper spread, 268
Hungarian pepper stew, 55
lamb chops with tomato and, 40
mixed peppers, 93
pepper and ham rolls, 58
ratatouille, 91
risotto, 88
Russian sauce, 242
sausage and peppers open sandwich, 245
stuffed, 183
persimmons, stuffed, 280
petits fours, 362
pheasant, roast, 65
pies:
bean sprout, 208
walnut cream, 324

pigeon pancake pie, 292
pike cooked in stock, 68
pilchards:
tomato and fish open sandwich, 248
pineapple sauce, duck with, 296
pinwheels, 246
pistachios:
pudding with nuts and sprouts, 213
spinach with, 94
pizzas:
artichoke, 26
bacon, 230
onion, 230
puff pastry, 231
wholemeal with tomato and mushrooms, 207
plaice:
with bacon, 70
fillets in herb sauce, 154
plums:
country plum strudel, 318
with custard, 217
fresh plum tart, 338
lattice tart, 341
plum dumpling, 143
plum mould, 142
in red wine, 133
polenta slices with tomato sauce, 199
Polish cabbage casserole, 57
Polish Easter ring, 389
Polish stew, 54
poppy seed and cheese biscuits, 220
poppy seed plaits, 310
pork:
Bohemian Schnitzel, 45
brunch slices, 252
chops aux fines herbes, 43
Dutch rice speciality, 86
fillet in yogurt sauce, 44
Flemish-style pork chops, 43
macaroni bake, 78
with mussels, 286
Polish cabbage casserole, 57
rice and pork casserole, 61
salmon and pork, 301
shoulder with prunes, 42
spit roast with herb mayonnaise, 265
stuffed fillets, 45
stuffed rolled, 42
sweet and sour, 44
pot-au-feu, 291
potatoes:
Béchamel, 109
with blue vein cheese, 113
boiled potatoes with mushroom sauce, 186
broccoli and potatoes with cheese sauce, 187
Dauphinoise, 108
foil-baked with sauces, 112
gnocchi in herb sauce, 203
Italian salad, 122

lamb medallions with rosemary potatoes, 168
mushroom and potato dish, 106
omelette, 28
potato and cucumber salad, 256
potato and tomato bake, 111
potato and tomato gratin, 184
potato bake, 110
potato cake, 108
potato cake with soured cream, 107
potato fingers with sage butter, 185
potato pan with sausagemeat balls, 29
potato pan with shrimps, 29
puffs, 28
sausage with potato and apple mash, 56
soup with mince dumplings, 13
soured potatoes, 109
stew, 56
stuffed jacket potatoes, 113
tortilla, 185
Viennese potatoes, 107
prawns:
asparagus omelette with, 20
bean sprout salad with, 175
croquettes, 237
fricassée, 77
fritters, 75
grilled, 158
in herb sauce, 158
marinated Dublin Bay prawns with sole fillets, 275
potato pan with shrimps, 29
prawn and mock caviare open sandwich, 261
with scrambled egg, 76
Provençal-style scampi, 76
Provençal-style tofu ragoût, 196
prunes, shoulder of pork with, 42
pudding with nuts and sprouts, 213
puff pastry mince roll, 48
puff pastry pizzas, 231

quark and cherry strudel, 214
quiches and savoury flans:
cheese boats, 235
country leek flan, 229
egg tartlets with ham salad, 243
egg tartlets with liver pâté, 243
ham, 227
individual broccoli flans, 25
mini quiches, 25
mushroom and cheese flan, 229
onion flan, 26
quiche Lorraine, 228